ꝤED AMERICAN

THE AVERAGED AMERICAN

Surveys, Citizens, and the Making of a Mass Public

SARAH E. IGO

Harvard University Press
Cambridge, Massachusetts
London, England
2007

Excerpt from "The Forgotten Woman" copyright 1952 by
Phyllis McGinley, from *The Love Letters of Phyllis McGinley*
by Phyllis McGinley. Used by permission of Viking Penguin, a
division of Penguin Group (USA) Inc.

Library of Congress Cataloging-in-Publication Data

Igo, Sarah Elizabeth, 1969–
The averaged American : surveys, citizens, and the making of
a mass public / Sarah E. Igo.
p.   cm.
Includes bibliographical references (p.   ) and index.
ISBN-13: 978-0-674-02321-5 (alk. paper)
ISBN-10: 0-674-02321-8 (alk. paper)
1. Social surveys—United States—History—20th century.
2. United States—Social conditions—20th century.
3. National characteristics, American. I. Title.
HN29.I44 2007
301.072'073—dc22   2006043659

for my parents, John and Mittie Igo,
and
for Ole
with love and thanks

Contents

List of Illustrations   *ix*

Introduction: America in Aggregate   *1*

1 Canvassing a "Typical" Community   *23*

2 Middletown Becomes Everytown   *68*

3 Polling the Average Populace   *103*

4 The Majority Talks Back   *150*

5 Surveying Normal Selves   *191*

6 The Private Lives of the Public   *234*

   Epilogue: Statistical Citizens   *281*

   Notes   *301*

   Acknowledgments   *379*

   Index   *386*

Illustrations

The Lynds' map of Middletown   57

Cartoon of Robert and Helen Lynd, 1937   77

American Institute of Public Opinion questionnaire   120

George Gallup on the cover of *Time* magazine, 1948   159

Alfred Kinsey conducting a mock interview   210

Chart from *Sexual Behavior in the Human Male*   257

America in Aggregate

The committee will study the American people, their jobs, the insides of their houses, what they do evenings and holidays, what they learn in school, what they think of their neighbors, what is wrong with their health, and so on. It may even track down that slippery spectre, the average American, so long pursued by novelists with kodaks and fountain pens.

—*Outlook and Independent,* on the Committee on Social Trends, 1930

This is the great age of confession . . . We tell Dr. Gallup how we are going to vote and Mr. Hooper what we propose to listen to on the radio. Our psychiatrist delves into our sex dreams and Dr. Kinsey into our actual performance along those lines.

—*New York Herald Tribune,* 1948

The 1947 James Stewart film *Magic Town* tells the story of Grandview, an American community so perfectly average that the views of its citizens mirror those of the national population. Stewart's character, Rip Smith, is a struggling opinion pollster who discovers this statistical shortcut and hopes to profit from it. Posing as an insurance agent, he arrives in Grandview determined to keep its typicality a secret, its ways just as they are. Naturally, however, the secret gets out, and the townspeople become too self-conscious about

1

their own opinions to make them representative. Further undermining Grandview's ordinariness is the fact that Americans from all over the country flock to the town, aspiring to live in this most normal of communities.

Appropriately enough for a Hollywood movie, *Magic Town* played upon two sorts of fantasies in the modern United States. One was the promise of empirical surveys to disclose the society to itself. The other was the possibility of locating a definitive midpoint in an infinitely heterogeneous nation, whether through a typical community like Grandview (almost certainly modeled on an actual social survey, *Middletown*) or through more elaborate techniques of scientific sampling. In the middle decades of the twentieth century, this core America was the elusive target of social scientists but also marketers, commentators, and politicians. As *Magic Town*'s fascination with statistical normality suggests, average America could be an alluring entity for ordinary moviegoers as well. But how could they know what the average was, or what typical Americans did or believed? New social scientific techniques of polling, sampling, and quantifying the nation developed in these same years would provide compelling answers. Bound up with citizenship in ways obvious and subtle, surveys demarcated lines of inclusion, exclusion, and affinity in a national public. As such, they sat in complicated relationship to both social reality and mass culture. In the pages that follow, I explore the ramifications of this knowledge about "ourselves" in the public sphere.

Americans today are accustomed to a seemingly endless stream of questions from survey researchers, political pollsters, marketers, and census takers. They are equally familiar with the battery of results flowing from social scientific investigation, of knowing that the majority of the nation supports the death penalty or that half of all marriages end in divorce. Public life is awash in statistics documenting phenomena as diverse as consumer confidence and religious faith. None of this will surprise twenty-first-century readers. *Of course* experts tabulate buying habits, political tendencies, and attitudes toward work and family. *Of course* we rely on statistics to gauge our economic status and follow polls to know whether we swim with or against the aggregate tide. Being studied, and being privy to the results, is an understood and unexceptional feature of modern life. It is perhaps the principal way that we know ourselves to be part of a national community.

Despite our daily immersion in social data, we generally do not inquire into how certain kinds of facts have achieved their prominence, their stability, and their seeming inevitability in public life. What is surprising about this intimacy between social scientific inquiry and U.S. culture is that it is so new. Only in the years after World War I did mass surveys telling Americans "who we are," "what we want," and "what we believe" enter the public domain. Over the next several decades, they would transform it. But this was a fitful, if relentless, transformation. It was not obvious in the 1920s that citizens would accept prying questions from market researchers or opinion surveyors, or that they would trust the assembled answers as either trustworthy or true. Even those who stood to benefit from such data gathering were not convinced of its value. It took considerable work, for example, to persuade business owners in the 1910s and 1920s that collecting information about their customers' buying habits was worthwhile. And as one historian has noted, in the 1930s "it was a commonplace that the United States had better statistics on its pigs than on its unemployed people."[1]

If it is nearly impossible for us to imagine a world without such facts—what a journalist called the "nuggets of knowledge that have replaced anecdote, hearsay, imagination and history as the fodder of so much modern discourse"—Americans in the middle decades of the twentieth century were clear-sighted about their novelty. For them, "surveys" were a catch-all category containing a multitude of modern information-gathering techniques: market research, academic surveys, opinion polls, community studies, and quantitative reporting. Social critics and commentators, but also ordinary individuals, were alert to the gradual infiltration of new kinds of questions and new kinds of data into everyday life. As a journalist remarked in 1948, "Our living—so poll-minded has it become—has reached such a state of public and private inquisitiveness that taboos of even a previous decade are rendered obsolete." Mused another just a few years later, "Today, unless you can say 'According to the Poop-A-Doop survey, Umpty-ump percent of the people chew gum while they read Hot Shot News!' you fail to make an impression." Such observers commented quizzically upon the modern mania for data and complained about being "statisticized." Whether they welcomed or decried it, they recognized a culture of surveying—and a surveyed culture—coming into being.[2]

Surely an awareness of these social facts altered citizens' views of the American public and their place within it. But how? In what ways is a society changed by the very tools employed to represent it? In the modern United States, such tools were increasingly those of empirical social science: graphs, percentages, and curves professing faithfully to reveal the nation to its members. There were, of course, many other ways to envision America, beginning with works of literature, photography, and history. But the modern survey, as one commentator has noted, is "an instrument of special power for viewing mass populations in industrial societies, especially in their character as social facts, political publics, and economic markets." Scientific surveyors—bolstered by newfound authority and armed with new knowledge-making techniques—would assert a unique ability to measure and express the nation. Crucially, the information their techniques yielded was not intended solely for experts. It was for the citizen as well. Surveys are a peculiar sort of social investigation in which the public is simultaneously object, participant, and audience. In the twentieth century, Americans would take part in, and depend upon, social scientific surveys as never before. Many learned to offer up information about themselves to strangers. And masses of new facts about national habits, practices, and attitudes found their way into public forums. Social data, freely divulged and widely broadcast, would come to bear profoundly on how Americans understood their society and themselves.[3]

Professional statisticians, government bureaucrats, academic social scientists, and all manner of planners claimed that survey methods, newly "scientific," were essential for understanding the changes sweeping the United States and for managing a complex industrial society. Carefully collected data could be used to assess economic conditions, tap efficiently into public opinion, guide national policies, and perceive social reality more clearly. In 1939 Henry D. Hubbard, a spokesman for the National Bureau of Standards, put it this way: "There is a magic in graphs . . . Wherever there are data to record, inferences to draw, or facts to tell, graphs furnish the unrivalled means whose power we are just beginning to realize and to apply." Scientific surveys were trumpeted as both a sign of, and a route toward, a modern culture that prized empirical investigation over faith, tradition, approximation, common sense, and guesswork.[4]

Many contemporary observers thus viewed surveyors' aggregating techniques as the inevitable product of a "mass society." But national polls and surveys, we shall see, were as much responsible for creating a mass public as they were reacting to its arrival. Social data were not, of course, the only force driving in this direction during the peculiarly cohesive era marked by the Great Depression, World War II, and the Cold War. A truly national public was bolstered in this period by the popular culture of radio and film, the joining together of different ethnic groups in the unions of the Congress of Industrial Organizations, the spike in citizenship rates after the curtailing of immigration in 1924, wartime bond drives, and anticommunist rhetoric. We know much about these forms of national glue. What, however, of the impact of knowledge about "ourselves"—all the more potent for its status, not as entertainment or propaganda, but as truth? Ways of knowing, although less visible than memberships in civic associations and labor unions, are equally critical resources for fashioning public identities and political communities, and for structuring people's encounters with the social world.[5]

Midcentury surveyors' depictions of the population were at once the essential means by which individuals could perceive a mass society *and* the incontrovertible evidence for its existence. That is, in the statistics, surveys, and spectra now available to them, citizens could see themselves as part of a new collective, one constituted by and reflected in data compiled from anonymous others. This book offers a history of Americans' encounter with modern surveys, and especially these surveys' bid for legitimacy, their popular diffusion, and their cultural power. It documents the emergence of novel ways of knowing society as well as the sharp controversies they provoked. Along the way, it charts the deeply entangled fates of mass surveys and the U.S. public. And it highlights a little-noticed transformation: one whereby statistical majorities, bell curves, and impersonal data points came to structure Americans' social imaginations.

Survey data did not arrive out of the blue in the twentieth-century United States. Social statistics themselves have a much longer career, emerging originally as a "science of state"—that is, the gathering of information useful for governing. Rulers have counted, administered, and made "legible" populations for military service and taxation stretching back at least as far as William the Conqueror's Domesday Book of 1086. Modern nation-states have depended on the systematic collection of demographic data to manage public health, assess economic progress, and craft social policies. In the

United States, the official census initiated in the 1780s was coincident with the nation itself. Too, already by the turn of the eighteenth century, a variety of nonstate enterprises were tabulating birth and death rates, or "vital records," in order to track epidemics and devise insurance tables. Western countries in the nineteenth century witnessed a wave of surveying by private citizens and philanthropists, producing a veritable "avalanche of numbers" in the service of industrial and social reform. This latter sort of information gathering about national bodies, whether to track fertility or poverty, is what Michel Foucault so provocatively called the "bio-politics of population," a distinctly modern mode of governance more attentive to regulating individual persons than territorial claims.[6]

Clearly, social information encased in numbers is not, in and of itself, a recent invention. But the purposes and effects of gathering such data shifted dramatically in the twentieth century, and nowhere as rapidly as in the United States, where, as Olivier Zunz points out, "new ideas about statistical distribution . . . were to flourish in ways unfathomable in Europe." Not only did efforts to collect social facts intensify in all corners of American society. Surveyors also probed more deeply into the character of the citizenry, tallying not just observable characteristics but less visible behaviors, attitudes, and beliefs. New individuals—notably, white middle-class Americans—were targeted for investigation as old strictures guiding whom and what could be asked were loosened and then discarded. These changes were related to the new status of social science in the early twentieth century. Shedding an older language of reform, social investigators proclaimed that their goal was to provide neutral descriptions of, rather than prescriptions for, society. Yet, again especially in the United States, they also billed their methods as democratically useful, instruments of national self-understanding rather than bureaucratic control. For this reason, the gatherers of facts and figures sought not to restrict their data to elite decision makers but to disseminate their findings widely. Indeed, they proclaimed the special relevance of aggregate data in a representative democracy. Modern surveys had an egalitarian ring to them, purporting to discern just who Americans were and what they wanted. Relying on voluntary rather than state-mandated cooperation, surveyors emphasized the participatory aspect of their work, as well as the virtues of contributing information for the good of the whole. All of this would permit social data to play a novel role in the public sphere as well as individual lives.[7]

How and why did these survey technologies arrive on the scene when they did? Several streams—scientific, institutional, commercial, and cultural—converged to permit survey data to take on a new prominence in the twentieth-century United States. These ranged from innovations in sampling techniques to the professionalization of social science, and from the waging of war to the expansion of the national media.

One stream was scientific: the invention of new or newly precise methods for calculating change and measuring variability across populations. Standardized questionnaires and formal interview schedules had been pioneered in the nineteenth century. Refinements of these techniques, but especially the development of scientific sampling, would be of central importance in extrapolating from small numbers to national publics in the twentieth. A related current was the advance of social scientists into the academy. Sociology, anthropology, economics, political science, and psychology—not yet truly separate disciplines—gained sharper definition after the Civil War, answering calls for a "science of society" from across the Atlantic by Auguste Comte and Herbert Spencer, and in the United States by William Graham Sumner and Lester Frank Ward. A loose tradition of social investigation crystallized at the turn of the century as universities carved up intellectual inquiry into discrete departments, and professional societies such as the American Economic Association and the American Sociological Society codified legitimate social scientific practice.[8]

Still other streams were bureaucratic. Statistical information answered the demand of an advanced industrial society for ways to order a diverse and swelling population. The federal government had sponsored the U.S. census as well as labor statistics bureaus and the ethnographic surveys of the Smithsonian in the nineteenth century. But it was during World War I that bureaucrats would discover a broader utility to social scientific knowledge, especially in the areas of motivation, morale, and persuasion. The war era itself saw new techniques of evaluation, such as army intelligence tests, employed on a national scale. Architects of the "technocratic" state of the 1920s, with its managerial charge and emphasis on planning, took a further step, seizing upon social statistics as objective, seemingly nonpolitical instruments for decision making. Government and foundation support for the social sciences was crucial to surveyors' growing cultural authority. In President Herbert Hoover's two ambitious information-collecting projects of the late 1920s and early 1930s, the Committee on Recent Economic Changes and the Committee on Social Trends, official statistics were elevated as ends in themselves, tools for expressing facts about the population and capable of giving shape to the nation. The Great Depression and World War II would bind surveyors and the state even more tightly, as federal agencies tapped academic social scientists to advise the government directly.[9]

Emerging alongside academic, foundation, and state investment in statistics was a corresponding private and commercially based commitment to social scientific practices. This much is evident in the sheer range of enterprises devoted to quantifying and sorting the stuff of American life in the early decades of the twentieth century. Modern market research arrived in 1911 with the establishment of the Harvard Bureau of Business Research. Intelligence measurement began in earnest in the years just before World War I, and standardized achievement assessments were launched by the Carnegie Corporation beginning in the late 1920s. In that decade, some four million schoolchildren submitted to mental tests annually. Management science and "human relations" came of age with efficiency and productivity experiments such as those at the Hawthorne Plant in Chicago between 1924 and 1932. Widespread personality testing was soon to follow, as would systematic newspaper and radio audience research. A broad array of corporate, educational, and media interests in these years created a market for ever-more-precise social indicators, embedding survey techniques in far-flung corners of American society.[10]

Scientific innovations, accredited experts, statecraft, and commerce were all critical to the circulation and use of new social scientific facts. But there was also a broad cultural demand, palpable by the early twentieth century and generated by a complex of worries about modern industrial society, for new ways of visualizing and making sense of the nation as a whole. As historian Robert Wiebe observed, "It seemed that the age could only be comprehended in bulk," and so "people everywhere weighed, counted, and measured it." Americans in this period confronted a new corporate order, rapid rates of urbanization, and at least early on, a heavy flow of immigration. It was an era whose commentators invented the phrase *mass society*, a capacious term used to denote the transition from local communities to a national one, and not usually for the better.[11]

Anxious public discussions about the ebbing of traditional social bonds raised urgent questions. How, with diverse peoples clashing in cities, would the nation summon unity and stability? How, given accelerating bureaucratic organization and economic consolidation, could it remain democratic? How, amidst a dazzling array of new commercial entertainments, might common mores be determined? Many commentators in the new century sensed a crisis in older notions of the American public, and particularly the breakdown of conventional religion, culture, or morality as regulating ideals. Social surveyors were among those who searched for a replacement, for new definitions of community, citizenship, and norms when the old moorings no longer seemed to hold. The alignment of national introspection and social scientific description across the first half of the century was thus not accidental. Surveyors' questionnaires and statistics were tightly intertwined with the distinct challenges facing the society in which they lived. Crucial to the intersection of pressing questions and new techniques that aimed (however imperfectly) to answer them were the actions of information gatherers themselves. Here it was not so much government agencies like the Census Bureau but entrepreneurial pollsters, marketers, and academics who aggressively expanded the terrain of social investigation. Surveyors thereby hoped to arrive at a more robust and trustworthy knowledge of the contemporary world. They aimed to explain the workings of mass culture, to discern more accurately public opinion, and to provide detailed accounts of actual rather than idealized social behavior. They did so, most significantly, by turning to empirical descriptions of the mainstream, designing instruments to measure everything from what citizens were buying, to what they believed, to what they did in the privacy of their homes.

Scientific characterizations of "average" or "typical" Americans were a striking phenomenon of the new century. This constituted a shift away from the almost exclusive study of "degenerates, delinquents, and defectives" that had marked nineteenth-century social investigation: "the numerical analysis of suicide, prostitution, drunkenness, vagrancy, madness, crime, *les miserables.*" To be sure, an understanding of the "normal" had informed earlier medical practice and social theory; otherwise pathologies and deviants could not have been classified as such. Too, statisticians across the nineteenth century plied their tools to establish demographic medians and outliers. But rigorous inquiry for its own sake into the typicality of everyday practices and opinions was a twentieth-century enterprise. Investigators would successfully colonize new realms, from routine habits to social and political attitudes to the most intimate areas of personal experience.[12]

Surveyors' turn from the margins to the presumed center of

American life engendered popular fascination. By bringing "normal" behaviors, beliefs, and personalities into their orbit, surveyors found new consumers for their facts. But their studies did not make their way to the lay population unmediated. The demand for social data was fueled by a revolution in mass communications, a dramatic expansion of the media that by the end of the 1920s "formed a new constellation of power . . . visible to a vast public, national in scope." Media establishments were themselves in need of the kind of information surveys supplied, their audiences invisible and too large to "know" otherwise. Surveyors were thus abetted by print and broadcasting networks that saw a profitable market in reports about "average" Americans and were ready to transform aggregate data into news. This merger between new facts and new outlets for them meant that ordinary people now had access to sorts of data once reserved for a few. It also meant, in a powerful fashion, that the public could now find out who "the public" *was*. As Diana Mutz writes, "What media, and national media in particular, do best is to supply us with information about those beyond our personal experiences and contacts, in other words, with impressions of the state of mass collectives."[13]

But media coverage alone cannot explain the rapt attention many paid to detailed surveys about mainstream America. There was a keen interest in surveyors' tabulations in segments of the public itself. Over the course of the century, this appetite for social facts would lead more and more individuals to participate, either as research subjects or as consumers of information, in a dense traffic of social scientific numbers, knowledge, and norms.

Surveyors' modes of representation were ubiquitous in the twentieth century, and crucial to the making of a self-consciously mass society. Yet this is a theme strangely absent from discussions of American nationalism, mass culture, and public life. Apart from those interested in public policy, scholars of the modern United States have barely registered the movement of social data into everyday life as a question or problem. This is true even as they regularly treat survey results as historical or sociological evidence. Those who have studied the rise of the modern social sciences, on the other hand, have focused first and foremost on professionalization and disciplinary consolidation. By foregrounding the producers rather than the consumers of new knowledge, they too have missed the key role that social facts played as they moved out of research institutions and into popular venues. Even those attentive to the uses of social scientific authority have generally asked how elites—whether states, corporations, or courts—mobilized empirical data for particular ends. Few have paid attention to what ordinary people, "the studied," did with the same kinds of information.[14]

At the turn of the twentieth century, surveys were the province of statisticians, social reformers, the federal Census Bureau, and scattered businessmen and entrepreneurs. By the century's end, social scientific methods, findings, and vocabularies were omnipresent. What had been quite unfamiliar several generations earlier had become as natural—and invisible—as the air Americans breathed. To understand how ordinary individuals grappled with the ascendance of social scientific ways of knowing, we need to look closely at several formative surveys of the first half of the century: Robert and Helen Lynd's Middletown studies of 1929 and 1937; George Gallup's and Elmo Roper's public opinion polls beginning in 1935; and Alfred Kinsey's sexual behavior reports of 1948 and 1953. The Middletown studies, the Gallup and Roper polls, and the Kinsey Reports were among the most successful purveyors of quantitative facts about "average" Americans, and the best-known and most talked about social scientific productions of their day. They attracted surprising amounts of publicity, cropped up in radio broadcasts and comedy sketches, and became household words.

Neither these surveys, nor the individuals who conducted them, were "representative" of their era. Their very prominence suggests the opposite. Yet they reflected a new strain in American social inquiry. Unlike earlier reform-oriented efforts and many contemporaneous studies, these were not aimed at specific social problems or "marginal" populations—whether racial or ethnic minorities, southerners, immigrants, gang members, or the poor. Nor were they engaged in sorting or grading the population for bureaucratic ends, as were parallel enterprises in intelligence, personality, and achievement testing. Each aimed instead to sketch the collective whole of society, to profile the mainstream. The Lynds made a midwestern town the archetype of a supposedly typical American community. Pollsters publicized the "average American's" viewpoint on subjects ranging from cereal brands to presidential nominees. Kinsey professed to investigate and portray for the first time "normal" citizens' sexual behavior. In fact, it was from such promises that these studies derived their popular appeal. Surveys of typical communities and majority opinions piqued national interest—and provoked intense protests—because of their claims to represent not just their research subjects but the entire U.S. population.[15]

"The behavioral and social sciences," write two observers, "have undoubtedly found a more receptive market in the United States than anywhere else in the world." Certainly, social scientific inquiries into the contents of the "average" were undertaken in industrial nations beyond the United States. The British Mass-Observation project, begun in 1937, was akin to *Middletown* in its attempt to capture ordinary people's lives and create an "anthropology of ourselves" on topics ranging from wartime rationing to pub sociability. After establishing his polling operation in Princeton, New Jersey, George Gallup swiftly set up affiliates to measure opinion in England, Australia, Canada, Sweden, and France. Similarly, a "little Kinsey" research effort was undertaken in Britain to replicate the scientist's work on sexual behavior in the United States. Readers around the world were transfixed by the *Sexual Behavior* studies, which were quickly translated into German, Swedish, and French and found admirers as far away as Japan. Each of these projects, however, arrived later and was received less enthusiastically than its American counterpart. Public opinion polls were especially resisted by other national governments, which perceived surveyors as infringing upon the prerogatives of traditional decision shapers, namely, political leaders and journalists. Polls would not become a crucial aspect of public life in Britain until after World War II, and in France until the 1960s. Surveys had a distinctive career in the United States, not simply because of Americans' often-remarked-upon fascination with data about themselves but because of the extensive, entrepreneurial, and unrestricted character of American-style social investigation.[16]

Close attention to surveys like *Middletown* and the Kinsey Reports allows us to trace just how social data entered twentieth-century Americans' lives. Investigators' private papers and the raw materials that underpinned their studies permit a view into the production of survey knowledge: how conclusions were fashioned out of empirical results and unarticulated assumptions, science and conventional wisdom. But it is also critical to examine how ordinary citizens encountered such knowledge. This part of the story can be gleaned from media reports on social scientific findings, interchanges between researchers and subjects, correspondence between surveyors and their audiences, and the passage of social scientific concepts into everyday language. The publicity surrounding the Middletown studies and the Gallup Poll, the adoption of their techniques in magazine articles, radio broadcasts, and self-help literature, and the very experience of being studied—an increasingly common fate—all helped usher social data, and statistical thinking, into the mainstream.

The new surveys were the subject of widespread fascination. But they also generated abundant conflicts, surprises, and suspicions.

Consumers of social data did not always readily accept the conclusions of survey research. On the contrary, competing claims of authoritative knowledge and personal experience regularly greeted surveyors' facts, especially investigators' claims to speak for "average" Americans. Behind collections of seemingly dry and neutral data lurk stories of criminal charges, religious outcries, and congressional investigations. Social information may have flowed fast and thick, but it was never accepted passively or wholesale.

It was not just survey data but survey methods that were controversial. Listening to the Americans who first answered the Lynds' questionnaires, found an opinion pollster on their doorstep, or submitted to one of Kinsey's interviews exposes how unsettling the new modes of investigation were, and how wide-ranging was the opposition to something we now take for granted. Particular techniques—from participant observation to statistical sampling—could seem strange, offensive, or even illegal to the people who were first subject to them. As the reaction to Robert and Helen Lynd's community study shows, some residents of Muncie, Indiana, in the mid-1920s protested furiously about being placed under a social scientific microscope. Decent people, local critics insisted, would not "permit this peeping into the deepest recesses of their lives." Many Americans similarly resented the intrusiveness of opinion polling and consumer surveys, not to mention the detailed personal interviews that Alfred Kinsey would conduct during the next three decades. If some were bothered by surveyors' invasions of privacy, others worried about the implications of quantifying the details of human existence, or the destruction of old values (and the creation of new ones) that might come simply from knowing what others did or thought. Fierce debates over everything from what questions citizens could be asked, to what dangers might lie in publicizing their answers, reveal how much was at stake in social scientific representations.[17]

Yet, despite challenges from all quarters, it is undeniable that a new relationship among social scientific facts, their creators, and their consumers was emerging as the century progressed. Even as statistics like Gallup's and Kinsey's were challenged, commonsense notions about "average Americans" based on their findings were legitimized. Moreover, surveyors' peculiar ways of collecting and displaying information were coming to define the social landscape. Individuals complained bitterly about the depersonalization that came along with the torrent of statistical information. They could not always resist its lures, however. Some gave new weight to aggregate data, willingly and even eagerly submitted to surveys, and found themselves in social scientific categories. By midcentury, it was clear that impersonal techniques and facts about strangers could penetrate the most private domains of individuals' lives. Americans were in effect speaking a new language, one they could not unlearn. But it is also true that the individuals who wrestled with and adapted social scientific ways of knowing were joint authors of the statistical public they had come to inhabit.

The word *survey*, Jean Converse has observed, carries at least three distinct meanings, one being to measure or count. Two other definitions point in opposite directions. On the one hand, surveying means to *oversee,* or examine closely. On the other, it refers to *seeing over* in order to gain a broad perspective. This book takes up all three meanings of the term. It inquires into the specific techniques surveyors used to characterize Americans. It explores the probing scrutiny of individuals that surveying entailed. Finally, it considers the new representations of the national public that surveys made available. It asks: What were the ramifications of surveyors' questioning presence, as they reached more deeply into people's lives for information? How did the influx of facts and figures purporting to describe "average Americans" shape understandings of the collective and of possible social identities within it? And what were the political and social effects of an aggregated America?[18]

Social data have a reputation for being dull and dry, the inconsequential means (or even the only means) by which we know things about populations, economies, and societies. But the figures marshaled to portray American beliefs and behaviors have been anything but inert pieces of information. Because they appeared not to interpret or opine—but instead to offer "just the facts"—questionnaire findings and poll results moved into public life with considerable authority. This characteristic of the factual, its seemingly unassailable neutrality, is what makes it so very powerful. Surveyors like the Lynds and Kinsey may have purported to depict social reality with unprecedented transparency. But always, they offered more than simple summaries of data: they encouraged new ways of seeing, perceiving, and imagining. In so doing, surveyors subtly transformed the entities under investigation. Ultimately, it would become nearly impossible to know the nation apart from their charts and curves.[19]

A self-consciously modern society was in this respect as much an outgrowth as an object of survey techniques. To begin with, aggregate data gave shape and substance to a "mass public." Midcentury social scientists were covert nation-builders, conjuring up a collective that could be visualized only because it was radically simplified. Investigators' task, after all, was to generalize broadly from a small number of data points so as to make sense of a messy social world. (After gathering "millions of social facts" over five years of fieldwork in one community, for example, anthropologist Lloyd Warner was able to distill 5,800 "symbolic activities" into 284 "forms" and nineteen "types," and to determine that there were a total of eighty-nine possible "behavioral situations" or "statuses" within its relational system.) But theirs was a patterned incompleteness. Proclamations about "Americans" could not be made without suppressing the voices and experiences of some, and here surveyors more often perpetuated than challenged the assumptions of their day. Their presuppositions about who constituted the public meant that some Americans—African Americans, immigrants, and poor

people, among others—were systematically excluded from their statistics, and that the nation surveyed was always a partial one. None
of this, however, prevented Gallup's and Kinsey's facts from exercising a forceful sway over perceptions of the social body.[20]
Surveyors' aggregating technologies, by their very nature, placed
new cultural emphasis on the center point, the scientifically derived
mean and median. They helped shift the ground under the concept of normality, so that its meaning increasingly lined up with
quantified averages—although not without a fight from those who
feared this would upend religious, ethical, or cultural values. This
was a tendency perhaps inherent to statistical techniques, evident as
early as the 1830s in the Belgian Adolphe Quetelet's famous search
for "the average man," that "fictitious being, for whom every thing
proceeds conformably to the medium results obtained for society in
general." The drive to determine the average was part empirical
quest, part cultural preoccupation. Its calculators did not always
take care, as did Quetelet, to highlight its fictional qualities. In
1947, for example, *Newsweek* could announce that there was a
"shadowy figure beginning to emerge" from the day's public opinion polls, which it promptly labeled the "American Majority Man."
Such composite types, placeholders for the nation itself, flowed easily from social scientific tables and graphs. And they took root in
places far afield from statisticians' counting machines. Especially
during decades of economic crisis and war, social scientific findings
about "typical Americans" and the search for a coherent Americanism in the culture at large were symbiotic. Even if it was never particularly accurate or representative, invoking a "mass subject" to
stand in for the whole could play a vital role in consolidating the
national public.[21]
    This figment of surveyors' imaginations could work to highlight
and regulate differences, permitting individuals not only to discern
an aggregate norm but also to measure themselves against it. As
such, the flood of data on majority beliefs, average communities,

and mainstream Americans afforded individuals a new means of relating to the collective. The rhetorical turn from studying "others" to studying "ourselves" in this era's social scientific practice carried with it both a confessional mode and a voyeuristic stance. What did it mean, for example, for a woman to respond to a thirty-four-page family survey that asked for intimate details of financial, marital, and social adjustment to the Depression? Her personal information, once disclosed, was made the property of experts, merged with others', and then returned to the public, transformed, as data. Transmitted far beyond the initial exchange, such statistics enabled Americans to peer into their neighbors' lives, and, sometimes, to look at their own differently. Access to information about others enabled individuals to filter their experiences through tables and percentages, to fit themselves into social scientific categories, and to identify with strangers. To borrow a phrase from philosopher Ian Hacking, surveyors' facts could in this way remake "the space of possibilities for personhood." Indeed, many sought out and were changed by such knowledge.[22]

As did an earlier generation of social scientists, contemporary historians have vigorously debated whether a mass society existed in the twentieth-century United States. Those who have argued for the emergence of a modern national culture, however defined, have linked it to one of several developments: the triumph of a corporate-industrial order, the growth of national politics and labor unions under the New Deal, the effects of standardized advertising and consumption, or the emergence of the mass media itself. Others have underscored instead the resilience of local, ethnic, religious, and familial affiliations in the face of homogenizing trends. Emphasizing either the tangible institutions of mass society or the particular social bonds that endured despite it, what most of this scholarship neglects is the *consciousness* that many individuals in the midcentury decades had of living in a new kind of public. To a great extent, this consciousness was the product of newfound, widely available, scientific data about "average" Americans. By proclaiming the necessity of their impersonal techniques, by presenting collections of facts as more authoritative than individuals' perceptions, by publicizing cumulative data about strangers, and by fostering communion with abstract others, surveyors helped to manufacture the idea and perhaps even the experience of "the mass."[23]

Americans' engagements with the scientific facts meant to represent them reveal a process at work that we have not yet fully grasped: a broad shift in consciousness linked to the technologies of social surveying. Immersion in a mass-information economy necessarily conditioned citizens' thinking about their ties to other people and to the nation. Some twenty years ago, historian Benedict Anderson described the nation-state as an "imagined community." Taking seriously the possibility of not just imagined, but *statistical,* communities will help us uncover the knowledge regimes and intellectual frameworks that allowed Americans to relate in new ways to "the public." That many believed they lived in a mass society does not mean that this was so. However, if we are to understand how this new society operated—at the level of perception, if not of fact—we will need to put aside questions of reality for more ephemeral, although hardly less important, ones of thought and belief. The answers are extremely important if we are to know anything about the kind of public that evolved in tandem with opinion polls and sex surveys. We will also, against at least a half century of scholarship and commentary, have to rethink "the mass" itself: as a social experience distinguished as much by connection as conformity, and composed of actors better described as self-conscious than submissive.[24]

Why care about the sort of public that social statistics projected, or the arguments triggered by composite data? To realize that our poll-saturated culture is of recent vintage is of course a reminder that our present is an historical artifact. More significantly, a history of surveyors' instruments helps us appreciate how influential they have been in bounding and enforcing perceptions of social reality across the last century. We need to understand social scientific representations—of "typical communities," "majority opinion," and "normal Americans"—not as reflections of the body politic but as an index to political and epistemological power. We also need to reckon with popular modes of knowing in the twentieth century, the social thought not of masses but of ordinary people using the tools at hand to make sense of the world. Only then will we begin to see that a particular form of modern consciousness is anchored in the practices of social surveyors.

1

Canvassing a "Typical" Community

How is one to set about the investigation of anything as multifarious as the gross-total thing that is Schenectady, Akron, Dallas, or Keokuk?

—Robert S. Lynd and Helen Merrell Lynd, *Middletown,* 1929

What impresses me . . . is the readiness and sympathy with which the good people of Middletown entered into this unusual survey . . . They answered queries about getting a living, making a home, training the young, the use of leisure, and the nature of their religious and community activities, without resentment or reserve.

—*New York Herald Tribune,* 1929

"No one who wishes a full understanding of American life today can afford to neglect this impartial, sincerely scientific effort to place it under the microscope slide," announced a writer for the *New York World.* A reviewer for the *New Republic* agreed, calling it "a fascinating and valuable book, one that will give the reader more insight into the social processes of this country than any other I know." Even the characteristically cynical H. L. Mencken proclaimed: "I commend [it] to all persons who have any genuine interest in the life of the American people . . . It reveals, in cold-blooded, scientific terms, the sort of lives millions of Americans are leading." And Stuart Chase raved in the *Nation:* "Nothing like it has ever before been attempted; no such knowledge of how the average American community works and plays has ever been packed between the covers of one book . . . Who touches the book touches the heart of America."[1]

Such words were extravagant praise for a survey that began its career as an investigation of the religious institutions and impulses of a small midwestern community. That *Middletown,* Robert S. and Helen Merrell Lynd's 1929 "study in contemporary American culture," was a major popular success was deeply surprising, perhaps especially to the agency that sponsored it. One of the survey's overseers at John D. Rockefeller Jr.'s Institute for Social and Religious Research (ISRR) called the manuscript "different from anything that I imagined in connection with this study when it was first proposed" and found "its range of ideas and subjects . . . positively bewildering." The resulting volume, tracing the changes that had come to an American community between 1890 and 1924, was not the usual best-seller fare. On the contrary, it was a lengthy compendium of facts and figures about the daily lives of ordinary individuals—their work, their homes, their schooling, their modes of worship and of leisure.[2]

The fact that *Middletown* captured the national limelight was still more remarkable because social surveys had become common currency by 1929. Empirical investigations into the workings of U.S. society had been fixtures of the American scene since the late nineteenth century. Part of a culture obsessed with facts and increasingly alarmed by the social effects of rapid industrialization and urbanization, the Lynds joined a crowded field of players who sought through the gathering of data to capture and explain the modern age. By one count, some 2,775 such surveys had been carried out by the time *Middletown* appeared. Yet no other study was instantly pronounced a revelatory account of American culture, a "mirror held up before us." And none would have the impact—or the reach—of the Lynds' investigation. *Middletown* would be judged uniquely illuminating of the modern United States only through the peculiar alchemy of surveys, surveyors, and surveyed in the 1920s.[3]

A New Type of Survey

Hannah Arendt famously argued that the very idea of "the social" developed only in the nineteenth century. In this understanding, social conduct, social problems, and social harmony all became part of an expanded political terrain with the invention of "society as a whole" by reformers and social workers. Others have noted the "merger between the desire to quantify and the desire to see" in the traditions of late-nineteenth-century realism and naturalism, the sense that the knower of society required "numbers, counting, and calculation." Vexing problems of the industrial age, from poverty and labor unrest to commercial leisure and urban vice, were the proximate cause for both the emerging notion of the "social" and the invention of tools to observe it. Social surveys were born of this complex. Not only did empirical studies help formulate modern ills; social scientific techniques also promised a modern method for rationalizing and, ideally, remedying them. Social surveys, whether conducted by private individuals or philanthropic institutes, flourished in the latter part of the nineteenth century throughout the industrialized world. Frederic LePlay, a French reformer and economist, compiled thousands of European working-class family budgets for his 1855 study *Les Ouvriers Européens*. Across the Channel, Charles Booth undertook a monumental study of poverty, issued as the seventeen-volume *Life and Labour of the People in London* between 1889 and 1903. Booth's work served as a model for many American community studies, from Jane Addams and Florence Kelley's *Hull-House Maps and Papers* of 1895 to W. E. B. Du Bois's *The Philadelphia Negro* of 1899. These ventures—concerned at once to comprehend and contain the turmoil of advanced capitalism—tabulated urban crime, mapped African American and immigrant neighborhoods, tracked transformations in rural life, and exposed industrial working conditions.[4]

Turn-of-the-century American surveys, propelled by the Social Gospel movement's "practical Christianity" and Progressive Era moral and scientific campaigns, had as their aim not simply the description, but the amelioration, of social conditions. The survey impulse, by turns altruistic and anxious, was by nature interventionist. It drew upon a particular understanding of the relationship between facts and progress. As Thomas Haskell has observed of the mid-nineteenth century, "Merely to gather the most elementary statistical data about society was so difficult . . . that it was easy to believe that adequate information would, in itself, lead almost automatically to vast social improvement." Belief that the patient accumulation of data would lead ineluctably to social harmony was everywhere in evidence in the decades to follow. Some social scientists of the day, individuals like Herbert Spencer and Lester Frank Ward, sought generalizations and lawlike regularities in social life. But there were other trends afoot. Settlement houses, statistical societies, muckraking journalists, and benevolent associations as well as many state and professional organizations increasingly placed their faith in "social intelligence," grounded in fact gathering, to solve the problems they spied all around them. Carroll Wright's Massachusetts Labor Statistics bureau, beginning in 1869, collected statistics on the hours, recreation, "moral and mental" culture, housing, and drinking habits of workers in order to recommend improvements in factory conditions. Members of the American Social Science Association, an early professional society, mounted an extensive canvass of state agencies in the service of prison reform and public health. Others launched systematic investigations into the lives of the poor in the name of "scientific charity." Perhaps the most comprehensive marshaling of data in the service of reform was Paul Kellogg's Pittsburgh Survey of 1909–1914. Kellogg, editor of *Charities and the Commons* magazine—soon to change its name, tellingly enough, to the *Survey*—assembled more than seventy researchers to investigate work, household, political, and environmental conditions in the industrial city. The Pittsburgh researchers publicized their findings in speeches, a traveling exhibition, and six exhaustive volumes proposing specific remedies for modern hazards, from workers' compensation to pollution control.[5]

What would eventually be termed "amateur" social surveys depended for their existence upon civic support, philanthropic funding from organizations such as the Russell Sage Foundation (the backer of the Pittsburgh research), and volunteer workers. Many of the latter were educated middle-class women who were able to leverage settlement house surveys and welfare investigations into public policy roles at a time when few women were admitted to graduate school or professional programs. Such information-gathering projects, however, were completed on the outskirts of American academic social science as it was forming in the latter half of the nineteenth century. When this kind of inquiry moved into professional settings such as the university, private philanthropies, still the most important source of funding for the social sciences, reallocated their priorities. After World War I, the preference of the Carnegie Corporation and the Rockefeller Foundation was for disinterested research—not on the symptoms, but on the underlying causes, of social problems. This was even more true of powerful entities of the 1920s such as the National Bureau of Economic Research and the Social Science Research Council. These organizations channeled support to credentialed social scientists and away from the volunteer-based and reform-oriented local survey. Women and other "nonexpert" investigators were thus written out of the social scientific enterprise.[6]

Although the boundaries between social work and social science were rather permeable into the early twentieth century, the post–World War I era marks the emergence of the modern social sciences.

As Dorothy Ross has argued, "scientism" became the brass ring for social researchers in these years. There were two aspects of this shift: first, a strictly empirical approach to the contemporary world, evident across the consolidating fields of psychology, economics, political science, and sociology; and second, an ethos that envisioned research as a theory-building enterprise that aimed to understand general societal processes. Social science would always be intertwined with social problems. But casting off their roots in Victorian and Progressive Era social reform and distancing themselves from a feminized social work tradition, "scientific" surveyors elevated scholarly neutrality as a badge of honor, marginalizing the kind of knowledge that could be gained through "value-laden" social activism. University of Chicago sociologists Robert Park and W. I. Thomas in the 1920s were standard-bearers for this approach. Compared to new methods that permitted "unpartisan . . . discoveries of scientific caliber," as one of their students put it, the old social surveys were a "stagnant backwater." This putatively definitive split between amateur social investigation and scientific research performed by professionals served as the modern social sciences' legitimating myth. What united the diverse practices given the imprimatur "social science" was not a resolve to alleviate social problems but an embrace of certain techniques: objective observation, intensive fact-collecting, and quantification. This perspective on social life, and the kind of knowledge that flowed from it, were considered uniquely modern scientific achievements.[7]

Helen and Robert Lynd, then, embarked upon their research at a crucial moment of transition in the social scientific field. As investigators, they straddled the old and the new, relying upon the varied methods and critical zeal of earlier social surveyors but with the aim of producing an objective description of American culture. On this latter count, the Lynds would be singled out for praise. One reviewer, placing the Pittsburgh Survey and *Middletown* side by side, wrote approvingly, "They differ so widely in form and manner of treatment that they seem to have little in common." In contrast to the usual authors of social surveys, he asserted, the Lynds "desired to discover facts not about evils that should be remedied but about situations and interrelationships that would throw light on the process of social change."[8]

In one key respect, however, *Middletown* differed from both "amateur" and "scientific" studies. Nineteenth-century surveyors had taken populations deemed social problems as their subject: the immigrants, working girls, and black migrants who appeared to be both bearers and products of a rootless modern economy. The topical classification in a 1930 bibliography of surveys is revealing, encompassing accident prevention, child welfare, truancy, and venereal disease as well as Czechs, Greeks, Finns, and widows. The Chicago School also homed in on specific urban denizens and places, churning out ethnographic reports like *The Hobo: The Sociology of the Homeless Man* (1923), *The Gang* (1927), *The Gold Coast and the Slum* (1929), and *The Taxi Dance Hall* (1932). Their studies inspected fragments of industrial society in order to understand processes such as assimilation and neighborhood transition; and they refrained from making claims about American life writ large.[9]

The explicit object of the Lynds' investigation, on the other hand, was a "representative" community meant to stand in for the nation. Unlike surveyors who had gone before them, wrote the author of *Middletown*'s foreword, the Lynds' attention was trained not on worrisome subgroups—"coal miners, teamsters, working girls, etc."—nor indeed on any particular fraction of the population. Many others recognized *Middletown*'s bold departure from "special studies . . . made of the notorious trio, 'dependent, defective and delinquent.'" The Lynds' quarry was not the problematic or the particular but the *normal* and the *whole,* and the scope of their conclusions was much more sweeping than that of any other contemporary survey.[10]

There was another crucial difference. A few prior studies, notably the Pittsburgh Survey, staged educational programs and attempted some community outreach. But most such projects were aimed first and foremost at policymakers or a small coterie of philanthropists. Well known as they were by communities of reformers, pre–World War I studies like *The Philadelphia Negro* were not meant for general consumption. Similarly, none of the Chicago School projects, from William I. Thomas and Florian Znaniecki's 1918 *The Polish Peasant in Europe and America* to F. A. Ross's *School Attendance in 1920,* attracted broad public notice. *Middletown,* on the other hand, was the very first social scientific bestseller. Its wide audience would give it a platform that few surveys could have hoped for.

The Small City Study, as it was initially called, was sponsored by the Institute for Social and Religious Research and funded by the Laura Spelman Rockefeller Memorial. The ISRR was formed out of the shards of John D. Rockefeller Jr.'s failed Interchurch World Movement, an ambitious information-gathering program in the service of Protestant domestic and foreign outreach. Rockefeller Jr.'s philanthropy was rooted in a deep Baptist faith. But like many other foundation leaders, he also viewed a modernized Protestantism as a foundation for social stability and civil order—and science as a solvent for industrial conflict. In this sense, the Small City Study was of a piece with other religious surveys of the period. Originally conceived as "a Basic Religious Study of the people in a small industrial community containing a high percentage of foreign residents," the survey was to "drop a plumb line into American Christendom via the Small City," to illuminate the challenges for religious organizations under contemporary conditions, and to suggest ways in which Protestant churches in particular could respond.[11]

The survey that eventually became *Middletown* would wind up taking a very different course, however. In 1929, just after publication, Robert Lynd admitted, "I know the study has been a troublesome one for the Institute because I was attempting to bend a new technique to compass a difficult array of material." This was something of an understatement. Struggles over the study's mission, methods, and interpretations plagued the project from the moment of its genesis in the fall of 1922. As one historian summed up *Middletown*'s strange history, "The community was chosen largely by accident and studied by a person unqualified to do so, with results that did not represent what the sponsoring organization had wanted." In continuous contention with their funders, the Lynds feared at many points during their years of fieldwork and writing that the Institute would abandon the project.[12]

The trouble began on October 1, 1923, when the Institute placed the study in Robert Lynd's hands, with Helen Merrell Lynd joining the project soon thereafter. The pair were social scientific amateurs. In fact, the ISRR's executive secretary, referring to Robert Lynd, feared that the Institute "was giving too great liberty to a man who was confessedly new at such work." Illustrating the not yet fully professionalized state of social science, it was only after *Middletown* was published to wide acclaim that the researchers became accredited experts. Robert Lynd was awarded a professorship in sociology at Columbia University as well as a key position with the Social Science Research Council on the strength of the manuscript, and Helen Merrell Lynd took a position as a professor of philosophy at Sarah Lawrence College. In 1923, however, when they took the reins of what would become the Middletown study, Robert was a graduate of Princeton and Union Theological Seminary and contemplating entering the ministry. He had worked briefly in publishing and advertising in New York City and enrolled in a few social science courses at Columbia. Helen had taught for two years in secondary schools after graduating from Wellesley, and had completed her master's degree in philosophy at Columbia. In what constitutes almost too perfect a social scientific story, the couple first met, and discovered a common interest in economist Thorstein Veblen's *Theory of the Leisure Class*, while hiking in New Hampshire's White Mountains in 1919. Two years later they married.[13]

As this meeting of the minds suggests, both Lynds were critics of what they called the "pecuniary civilization" that they saw developing around them. Robert harbored strong opinions about the impoverishment of modern life and the inequities of contemporary social organization. His goal, he later claimed, was "working on my own *human* terms with the problem of helping people to think out their values in a so-heavily business-centered culture." Both Lynds were deeply interested in how individuals came to their spiritual and ethical foundations. But neither of the would-be directors of a "Basic Religious Survey" had a conventional approach to the subject. Despite his divinity degree, Robert's outlook on the world was moving swiftly away from institutionalized religion. By 1921 he had concluded that preaching was outmoded and the wrong approach for effecting social progress. His major influences were not the faculty at Union Theological, but his teachers at Columbia: philosopher John Dewey and economist Wesley Mitchell, whose essay "The Backward Art of Spending Money," along with Veblen's writings, inspired Lynd's critique of consumption practices. Helen Lynd's intellectual orientation too was as social and philosophical as it was religious. Once in their charge, the Small City Study began to shift slowly but surely toward broader, and less overtly religious, ends. Robert Lynd's initial outline of the study, projected at that time to center on South Bend, Indiana, explained its purpose as uncovering "the origin and nature of [the site's] spiritual energies." But these were spiritual matters loosely construed. Adamant that the study would not be "an efficiency survey of the churches . . . but rather a new type of survey," the Lynds would focus their social scientific attention on individuals' adjustment to what they saw as the defining elements of modern life: industrial work and the consumer economy. While seeming to toe the Institute's line, the researchers explicitly rejected its emphasis on religion in favor of broader social and cultural developments.[14]

This shift in focus did not sit well with the ISRR. As the Lynds sent bulletins from the field and the manuscript edged closer to completion, the study's overseers generated longer and longer lists of complaints. This was true even once the Institute had lost the battle over its religious emphasis. One stumbling block was the Lynds' rather critical perspective on the contemporary industrial order. This was in part because the bankroller for the study—Standard Oil magnate John D. Rockefeller Jr.—was a key component of that order. Funded as part of a concerted attempt to smooth social unrest, the ISRR had been conceived in the crucible of industrial violence and followed from Rockefeller Jr.'s unwelcome entanglement in capital–labor standoffs, most dramatically the 1914 Ludlow Massacre of strikers and their families at the Colorado Fuel and Iron Company. The great puzzle of *Middletown*'s history is that just a year before he was hired to direct the study, Robert Lynd had been a severe—and public—critic of Rockefeller. Serving at the time as a student preacher in the oil fields of Elk Basin, Wyoming, Lynd stated that he was trying to "'kill or cure' [the] prob[lem] of whether I wanted to go into [the] ministry." Appalled at the conditions in the Standard Oil–controlled camp, Lynd published his findings in good muckraking fashion in both *Harper's* magazine and the *Survey*—but not before being called in by Rockefeller's associates and promised a marble community library in Elk Basin in exchange for his silence. The ISRR's decision to hire Rockefeller's critic to supervise the Middletown project may have surprised Robert Lynd, but it was certainly a clever means of demonstrating the organization's commitment to disinterested research.[15]

Equally important to the ISRR's appraisal of the Lynds' work was precisely this growing valorization of objectivity—and its presumed correlate, quantification—in social inquiry. The scientific merits of the Small City Study were the subject of numerous debates within the Institute. At a 1926 conference on the manuscript, for example, one reviewer praised the study for its "quantitative approach to such elusive variables as public opinion, social attitudes, and the like," while another argued that "the material represents an admixture of fact and opinion such that it cannot be classified as a thoroughly scientific study." Again and again, the ISRR's most vigorous criticisms of Robert Lynd (whom it regularly, if erroneously, treated as the sole author of the study) were for failing to excise his own opinions from the write-up. Noting that the section on "Religious Observance" was "based apparently more upon the author's theories than upon specific data," for example, the Institute staff urged that Lynd "not for a moment lose sight of . . . presentation of the facts." The ISRR's first condition for revising the manuscript by the spring of 1927 remained the elimination of "gratuitous subjective appraisals reflecting personal bias": the researchers' "natural sympathy with the bossed as opposed to the bosses," for example, and signs of their "general disgust" with Middletown's "pathetic standards of art." Such reproaches indicate that the Institute had fully absorbed the tenets of modern academic social science, whereby valid knowledge was produced only at a remove from social commitments.[16]

In the end, being chosen as the director of a religious survey sealed Robert Lynd's conversion from preacher to social scientist. But for him the two callings had the same objective: they enabled individuals to question the status quo, and thereby build a meaningful culture. Just beneath the surface of debates between the researchers and the ISRR, the most important conflict of all may have been a fundamental divide between the Lynds' faith in social science as a consciousness-raising tool and Rockefeller Jr.'s wager on social science as a guarantor of industrial order. Disagreements between the study's backer and its authors did not subside with the manuscript's completion. In 1927, with all the revisions made, the Lynds moved on to new endeavors. But the ISRR judged the study uninteresting, "irreligious," and ultimately unpublishable. With the study "locked . . . away in their safe as dead for a year," Robert Lynd managed, only with outside intervention, to persuade the Institute to release the study to its authors—which it did, he suspected, solely because ISRR staff were convinced the manuscript would not find a publisher. Alfred Harcourt of Harcourt, Brace surprised them, however, by jumping at the chance. In a development crucial to *Middletown*'s eventual reach and influence, Harcourt would publicize the study in ways more familiar to the best-selling novelist than to the social surveyor.[17]

The Lynds' transformation of a "Study of the Socio-Religious Influences and Agencies of a Small City and the Attitudes of the People toward Them" of 1923 into the much broader "Study in Contemporary American Culture" of 1929 amounted to the hijacking of a religious survey. The Lynds made not the Protestant church but the entirety of modern American life the object of their inquiry. The resulting book would have a major influence on the social science of the day. Less noted but at least as dramatic was the study's impact on Muncie, Indiana, the ultimate site of the Lynds' investigations—and on the culture for which it stood.[18]

Anthropologists at Home

In January 1924, the two young investigators and their staff of three research assistants arrived in Muncie, Indiana, or "Middletown." Planting their operation in the city for a good part of two years, the Lynds and their staff attended community meetings and religious services, examined census data and court records, surveyed schoolchildren, interviewed wives, distributed questionnaires, collected family budgets, read local newspapers, compiled statistics, observed townspeople's activities, and lived among their subjects. Determined to reveal not only Muncie's present but its recent past, they read anything they could find from the town's "frontier" days of the 1890s, including diaries, yearbooks, scrapbooks, school examination questions, and minutes of organizations such as the Ministerial Association and the Woman's Club.[19]

Acknowledging that when he embarked upon the Middletown research, he was a rank amateur—he had never taken a course in statistics or sociology—Robert Lynd later confessed that he "began to get an [education] on that job." He would credit his professional career to the happy accident of being chosen by the Institute for the survey. The Lynds more or less invented their method for investigating American culture as they went along. Noting, for instance, that they had not originally intended to interview "ordinary people"— this was a suggestion of a research assistant—Helen Lynd wrote that it "was one of the best things we did." As she recalled in her memoirs, "After eight or nine months [of fieldwork], the people at the Institute were discontented because they didn't know where the study was going. And neither did we. Something would come up, and that would lead to something else, which wasn't on any chart . . . what we were doing didn't fit into any category."[20]

The Middletown survey was indeed difficult to categorize. The Lynds' eclectic mix of interviews, tabulations, anecdotes, questionnaires, observations, and historical research resulted in a voluminous and chaotic set of findings. The investigators clearly struggled with how to present the material they gathered, caught between their own impulse for critique and new admonitions to neutrality. Highly aware that their research needed to appear impartial, they professed allegiance to the Institute's standards of detached observation. As Robert Lynd wrote to his sponsors in 1924, the presentation of the Middletown findings would be an "objective statement" of conditions, and "no effort would be made to make the study eventuate either in a program or in a thoro[gh]-going criticism of any institution." The memorandum, drawn up after just a few months in the field, is revealing. His method, Lynd assured, would be "quantitative," despite the fact that his files were "bristling with suggestive qualitative material." Two years later, he was still trying to persuade the ISRR. "In view of my great professional stake in the study," he explained in a letter to a member of the Institute, "no one can be more concerned than I that the manuscript be made as nearly as is possible in this difficult field an objective, scientific piece of work."[21]

Wrestling with the problem of how to "look at the life of a city objectively," Lynd later recalled in his characteristic shorthand notation, "I hit on idea of trying to do what an anthropologist w'd do if he studied an Amer. community." Professional anthropology in the mid-1920s consisted of at least two schools, a British social functionalist approach and an American culturalist one. But with no training in the field, what Lynd really meant by this was a loose collection of tools and a framework, "some kind of scheme for throwing familiar things into less immediate, more universal categories." He was especially fascinated by the stance of the "naïve observer" who was a participant in, but also a stranger to, the culture being investigated. For Helen and Robert Lynd, although both were originally midwesterners—from Illinois and Indiana, respectively—the sensibility of a New Yorker was enough to qualify them for outsider status. Robert acknowledged that the "ideal person for this job w'd have been a Chinese anthropologist." On the other hand, he reasoned, the Lynds' insider-outsider position afforded an advantage in penetrating Middletown's culture. After all, a foreigner "w'd have had a devil of a time in M'n getting into homes, being a reg'r fellow at Rotary [and] Ch[amber] of Com[merce], [and] generally hob-nobbing." Lynd was proud to be considered enough of an insider to be asked to serve as a pallbearer for one of Muncie's leading citizens.[22]

Stumbling upon an anthropological perspective, the researchers turned its gaze upon a new object: a modern industrial community.

To structure their data gathering, the Lynds borrowed the notion of "fundamental human activities" from British functionalist anthropologists W. H. R. Rivers and A. R. Radcliffe-Brown. "Whether in an Arunta village in Central Australia or in our own seemingly intricate institutional life of corporations, dividends, coming-out parties, prayer meetings, freshmen, and Congress," wrote the Lynds, "human behavior appears to consist in variations upon a few major lines of activity." Below the surface gloss of social complexity, they suggested, American villagers were just like their Aruntan counterparts. They could be studied through the same categories, their societies judged by the same rules. Robert Lynd asked in 1926, "Are not the 'basic processes of society' these few large Main-trunk life activities that we observe men doing everywhere—whether in Muncie, Timbuctoo, or New York?" Middletown's way of life was thus distilled into six distinct tasks: getting a living, making a home, training the young, using leisure, engaging in religious practices, and engaging in community activities.[23]

The Lynds, importing the naïve observer to native soil, hoped to glean the same kind of insights into 1920s American culture that anthropologists had gained about "primitive" ones. As they put it: "To many of us who might be quite willing to discuss dispassionately the quaintly patterned ways of behaving that make up the customs of uncivilized peoples, it is distinctly distasteful to turn with equal candor to the life of which we are a local ornament. Yet nothing can be more enlightening than to gain precisely that degree of objectivity and perspective with which we view 'savage' peoples." Many of the Institute's referees saw the anthropological tack as a gimmick and a distraction from the straightforward empirical data to be contained in the study. But the Lynds' choice of this stance toward their subjects was no gimmick in the sense that the Institute meant it. Rather, the Lynds hoped their approach would open to scrutiny—and adjustment—many taken-for-granted aspects of contemporary life. This much was clear in the question posed by a member of the Muncie research staff regarding figures they had compiled on adultery. She asked: "Can't an observer from 'another civilization' comment on the absurdity of this?" The "impartial observer" attempting to understand a culture from the outside gained much from the comparison of American ways to the mysterious rituals and bizarre practices of "primitive peoples." Anthropology was for the researchers an indispensable tool, both for criticism and for enlightenment.[24]

Middletown, the Lynds asserted, had no thesis to prove, no point of view to further. Instead, the study attempted to record lifeways that had undergone rapid change since 1890, a benchmark they chose because it marked a divide between Muncie's "pioneer experience" and its "industrial phase." Trained on the problem of modernization, the Lynds hoped to illuminate "the whole range of 'growing pains' of our contemporary . . . urban industrial civilization." No fact or observation seemed too trivial to include in their purview, from the contents of seventh-grade school curricula to that of popular movies, from the number of hours spent on household washing to the size of Middletowners' backyards, from attitudes toward labor unions to opinions on whether "the United States is unquestionably the best country in the world."[25]

The study, however, was more than a collection of telling details. As the Lynds tabulated their findings on Muncie's practices and beliefs, they also reached damning conclusions about how life was lived there—and by extension, in the modern United States. The surveyors found much to bewail in Middletown. First and foremost was the "outstanding cleavage" of social class; the accident of membership in either the "working" or the "business" group, they argued, was the most important determinant of any particular Middletowner's existence. But looking back three decades, they also recorded a general loss of personal autonomy, craftsmanship, and free thinking; the triumph of an artificial consumer society; and a worrisome standardization of work and family life. As the Lynds saw it, the hardy frontier individualism and vigorous culture of the 1890s—symbolized for the authors by Middletown's once-flourishing but now defunct Ethical Society—were on their way to extinction in the mid-1920s. Much like contemporary ethnographers busily documenting the "vanishing" American Indian, the Lynds captured in their study's pages the demise of an earlier, seemingly more authentic, American community.[26]

Comparing present-day Muncie to a romantic picture of its past, the Lynds claimed, first, that Middletown had become a "pecuniary society," using a phrase that recurs throughout the study. "More and more of the activities of living are coming to be strained through the bars of the dollar sign," they wrote, betraying Veblen's influence. If the community was a primitive tribe, money was its ruling totem—the center of its rituals and the guiding force in its life. Routinized work was made bearable only because it was converted into compensatory consumer goods. The getting of money dominated all else in Middletown, the "long arm of the job" coloring personal contact, family relations, leisure pursuits, youth training, and patterns of "neighborliness." Even those aspects of the community seemingly most resistant to the philosophy of "getting ahead" were infected. Religious organizations, unsure whether their ministrations could compete with the preachings of commerce, approximated the dominant business ideology of accumulation. For a project sponsored by an institute for religious research, *Middletown* offered a particularly harsh analysis of spiritual matters. Churches, the Lynds stated, no longer had any inherent value for Middletowners; rather, they served the instrumental function of furthering social status.[27]

And yet, despite the swiftly changing conditions of modern life, Middletowners did not know how to respond adequately to the industrial-commercial society they inhabited—or even recognize its existence. A second conclusion pointed to what the Lynds called "cultural lag," a concept they borrowed from sociologist William Ogburn, and by which they meant a lack of synchronized responses to modernization. Although work and leisure had been transformed by industrialization, for instance, these developments had made little impact on the avowed goals of family or religious life. That is, although society was becoming ever more complex, specialized, and technical, Middletown's inhabitants held fast to old platitudes. Cultural lag, as the Lynds understood it, was encapsulated in the fact that, in Muncie, "a man may get his living by operating a twentieth-century machine and at the same time hunt for a job under a laissez-faire individualism which dates back more than a century." A kind of "social illiteracy" spoke to the resistance of Middletown's institutions to recognize and adapt to change. The community's essential conservatism in this and other matters was apparent in its age-worn economic maxims, its "patterned avoidance of unusual living," its quiescent political culture, and the bland slogans of its civic clubs. Ultimately, the Lynds found in Middletown an unwillingness to face up to the challenges of modern times.[28]

A third finding, then, concerned Middletowners' lack of self-knowledge, marking their profound similarity to "primitive peoples," anthropologists' usual objects of study. This conclusion was in fact predetermined by the Lynds, who had positioned themselves as all-knowing outsiders uniquely able to penetrate the culture's irrationalities. Carefully exposing the schisms between Middletowners' beliefs and practices, the Lynds noted that many things were "more valued in Middletown as a symbol for things hoped for than for [their] specific content"—for example, "the relative disregard of most people in Middletown for teachers and for the content of books" and yet their "large faith in going to school." Likewise, Middletowners seemed "to regard romance in marriage as something which, like their religion, must be believed in to hold society together." Clinging to outmoded symbols and myths, the towns-people operated by a set of rules that they could not articulate and never bothered to investigate. When one of the community's central values—be it individualism, laissez-faire, or upward mobility—seemed, to the outsiders, to have failed, the Lynds noted that townspeople typically did not question its premises. Instead, there would be "a redoubling of emphasis upon the questioned ritual and a cry for more loyalty to it." The Lynds' study brimmed with evidence of a profoundly self-deceptive culture, or as they put it, "the twisted habits that are living for the 38,000 people of Middletown."[29]

Scrutinizing shibboleths about love, education, religion, and work, the Lynds made it their project to strip away the layers of mystification that obscured the true nature of modern industrial conditions. In so doing, the researchers were able to launch a powerful indictment of American class relations, consumerism, and social conformity—all the while masking their criticisms with scientific detachment.

Muncie under the Microscope

In their preface to the published study, the Lynds expressed their gratitude to "the patient subject of this picture, the people of Middletown, without whose generous friendship the marrow of the study would be lacking." Upon their initial arrival in town, the Lynds were invited to dinners by Muncie's "social leaders," and they quickly made themselves members of the community, Robert Lynd meeting weekly with a local doctor, banker, and real estate agent for dinner and even regularly singing solos in a local church. His talk before the Rotary Club upon his return to Muncie ten years later emphasized his indebtedness to the townspeople not only for their participation in the study but for the "friendships formed that have lasted." A local paper stated in 1935 that "anyone who has been intimately connected with Dr. Lynd during his stay here, is convinced of his genuine affection for Muncie," and indeed both researchers seemed to enjoy their work in the community. As Robert recalled in 1954, "When, by luck, Helen and I were doing the Muncie ('Middletown') job, I remember exclaiming to her at the end of hard days of work: 'Just think of being paid money for doing a job like this!'" Late in her life, Helen Lynd noted that the first telegram she had received after her husband's obituary appeared in the *New York Times* came from a Muncie acquaintance.[30]

The people of Muncie of course shaped the Lynds' many months of data collection and observation. Not just research subjects but companions, antagonists, and informants, Middletowners at times praised the Lynds' work and at others set them straight. Some, such as schoolteacher Rosa Burmaster, were asked to comment directly on the manuscript-in-progress. She actively collaborated with the surveyors, reviewing the questionnaires that they distributed in Muncie's classrooms and correcting wordings she thought the locals might not understand. Others assisted in the collecting of "Munciana." Laborers as well as bank vice presidents corresponded with the Lynds once they left Muncie to do the writing up. Some stayed in touch through and beyond the completion of the couple's restudy of the town, *Middletown in Transition,* in 1937—whether to congratulate the researchers on the birth of their children, to bring the Lynds up to date on their own news, or to impart information about developments in Muncie. One such correspondent was Leslie Kitselman of the upper-class "Y family," as she typically signed her letters. Highly critical of Muncie's hypocrisy and "the low mental plane" of its people, she saw allies in the Lynds and endorsed their conclusions; she also warned them about bad press and mailed them clippings from the local papers. George Dale, mayor and later editor of the *Muncie Post-Democrat,* was a fan of the researchers and a friend. He offered the advice: "Writing about Muncie is a hell of a job, and about all I can say is 'your blood be on your own head.'"[31]

Most townspeople were not on such intimate terms with the Lynds. But they certainly felt the effects of the study. Hundreds of club members and high school students filled out detailed questionnaires, for example, and 164 families submitted to lengthy interview sessions with the researchers. The Lynds noted that the latter occasionally required "breaking through an apparently impenetrable wall of reserve or of embarrassed fear" but that the staff was "able to carry through the interviews in something over four out of each five families" that met their requirements. Describing how she gained access to working-class people's living rooms, Helen Lynd recalled how their initial distrust faded away: "I'd sit and they would talk, perhaps while they were doing the ironing. Often just as I left they'd say, 'Oh, I'm so glad you came, it gets so lonesome with nobody to talk to.'"[32]

Not everyone, however, was as pleased to be scientifically investigated. Some believed quite emphatically that their lives should be off-limits to the surveyors. Mused one subject of the Lynds' investigation some years later: "A sophomore in the Central high school, I was, with many others merely irritated by the questionnaires we were expected accurately to reply to. It seemed to be nobody's business how many times a week I took a bath or whether or not I 'necked.'" To some, the most novel—and troublesome—aspect of the Lynds' research was that such questions could be asked at all. A local writer lamented the invasion of privacy the Lynds' study had occasioned, charging that "even the Average Citizen may have his temples that are not to be profaned." A cartoon depicting a survey taker in the *Saturday Evening Post* in 1929 played off this anxiety, even as it poked fun at inquisitive social scientists. The caption read: "Does your husband drink? What is the pathological history of your family? Do you believe in behaviorism? Let me see your bedrooms."[33]

Townspeople, the raw material of the Middletown study, squirmed under the researchers' scrutiny, but they also challenged the Lynds' interpretations, strenuously questioning whether social science could provide an adequate picture of the place they believed *they* knew best. The very first mention of the Middletown study in local papers was a report on an October 1924 talk by "Robert Lynde" to the Kiwanis club, with such findings as the number of automobile owners in town. The article stated that Lynd "presented many other figures to show the great change that has come over living conditions in the last thirty years" and was in the process of conducting a social survey of the city. The neutrality of this early news story would soon give way to a vigorous debate about the surveyors' fact-finding mission. The *Muncie Morning Star*'s announcement of *Middletown*'s publication hit the mark in predicting that it would be the "most widely criticised" book of 1929, "for the reason that Middletown is Muncie." Locals would argue with just about every aspect of the Middletown survey—from the accuracy of specific descriptions, to the overall portrait of the town, to the usefulness of the social scientific method itself. Their engagement with the Lynds and the national media over their own representation laid bare the tensions between local understandings and those of an emerging mass-mediated society, where individuals knew modern culture as much by reading about it as experiencing it.[34]

Many in Muncie (although perhaps not as many as claimed to) read the Lynds' study. Early in 1929 it was noted that three copies of *Middletown* had arrived in town and that residents "have been awaiting its release with no little curiosity." The public library's eight copies were loaned for only a week at a time due to "special demand"; by June 1929 it reported that the library "has taken 101 reservations for one week each, has already loaned the copies 79 times, and has 22 on the waiting list." Bookstores sold approximately a hundred copies. There were also organized discussions of the Lynds' findings in town. A local religion course listed one of its sessions for 1930 as "Community Study," with *Middletown* as its text. Topics for discussion were: "Our community portrait. What do we see? How did it get that way? Things good? Things otherwise? What may we do?" Upon the study's publication, one of Muncie's women's clubs proclaimed: "Be it resolved, That we urge our citizens to become acquainted with the contents of this book and strengthen our weak places and improve our good points so that we may be a truly ideal city which will attract strangers to come and dwell in our midst." A copy of *Middletown* was placed in a corner of the High Street Methodist Church along with the Bible, photographs of church leaders, and copies of the local newspapers—suggesting the survey's importance to Muncie's civic identity.[35]

In the years after the volume's appearance, the Lynds were distressed by accounts that made Muncie residents out to be "cheap" or "dumb," or that charged the studiers with being cynical, cold-blooded or, worse, keyhole-peepers. They worried about the "emotional scar tissue" the survey had produced in town. Robert Lynd apologized for any resentment toward the researchers' procedures, and addressed Muncie's criticisms of *Middletown* directly in the follow-up study he would conduct in the mid-1930s, making a point to ask: "What statements in the study of ten years ago do you Middletown people feel to have been distorted or inaccurate?" He believed the more thoughtful locals agreed that the findings were largely on target or, as he put it, "right about everyone else but about me."[36]

There were indeed those in Muncie who believed that the survey "describes us as we really are." Some wrote to the Lynds to relate their surprise at how effectively outsiders had understood the community. Clarendon Ross sent a glowing tribute: "To one who has been in and out of Muncie for forty years, your book came more as a joy than a revelation . . . You got everything—from old Doc Kemper to Shedtown." He continued, "I wish I could corner you two some time and have you talk about Muncie all night long." Other readers were fascinated by an anthropological perspective on their lives. As Ray N. Towers wrote to Robert Lynd in 1929, "It is very interesting to have such an outside view point as you are presenting." The Lynds' research was also occasionally touted as a route to self-knowledge. Even though he found plenty of particulars to challenge in the survey, *Muncie Evening Press* editor Wilbur E. Sutton urged his readers to familiarize themselves with it, arguing, "If you have not read 'Middletown,' . . . you have not taken proper stock of yourself." Despite the fact that he had lived in Muncie his whole life, whereas the Lynds had visited for a mere eighteen months, Sutton was astounded to discover that *Middletown*'s conclusions matched his own. His analysis, that the outside expert was more capable of "facing the facts" than were the community's own citizens, indicated that, for some in town at least, social scientists could know Middletowners better than they knew themselves.[37]

Perhaps predictably, a greater number of Muncie residents found fault with the Middletown surveys, in both specific and general terms. The Rotary Club complained about their characterization as "'a congenial band of back-slappers,' who meet weekly, eat heartily and then go back to [their] respective jobs for another week." Educators, although admitting that some of the Lynds' criticisms were accurate, explained with some defensiveness, "The situation in our schools has vastly changed since the study was made in 1924." A reporter for the *Muncie Evening Star* wondered: "Isn't there a possibility that the authors interviewed too many of the hip-hip-hooray men and failed entirely to reach a certain class?"[38]

Furthermore, a chorus of local critics, much like those at the Institute for Social and Religious Research, believed the study was not the objective science it purported to be. Calling Robert Lynd a "sociological swimming teacher of the conventional type that has never been in the water," one Muncie columnist contended, "Those who have lived in Middletown all their lives know that the author [*sic*] found about what he was looking for," namely, a confirmation of "certain preconceived social and economic theories." This was the case even for one man, Elbert Scoggins, who wrote to Robert Lynd applauding "the truth and fairness" of the study and the authors' "admirable objectivity." Despite all this, Scoggins went on to say, "I am aware that it was your intent to make the survey quite impersonal; if you didn't quite succeed in hiding your own point of view, it is because you and your assistants were all human." As he put it, "Your dauntless young point of view was always interesting to me—and don't try to tell me you haven't got one! Mrs. Lynd, of course, was too tactful ever quite to expose hers." To another Muncie resident, Robert Lynd was "as objective and as unbiased" as he could have been, under the circumstances. The surveyor "surely did not mean to have the big city [man's] attitude toward a comparative small provincial town." Such critics took the researchers to task for bringing to Muncie their personal predilections, political agendas, and scorn for the hinterlands. And each insisted that the researchers could not fully trade subjectivity for detachment, no matter what social scientific rules decreed.[39]

Some went so far as to accuse the investigators of inventing a fictional community. The Lynds' manner of selecting facts, it was charged, made the "real" Muncie unrecognizable. One editorialist in 1929 resented the "melancholy impression of the mental level of the Middletowner" found in the study, and complained that quoting "extracts from his unguarded utterances" was a "trick" rather than solid research. Similarly, reporter E. C. White wondered, "Is Muncie Really 'Middletown'?" She asked: "While masquerading in the guise of truth—as a serious study in anthropology, if you please—how do the authors of Middletown achieve their purpose of making an entire community appear as having stone age ideas and living without ambition or worthy ideals?" White answered her own question by criticizing the research strategy that the Lynds pursued, whereby they recorded "only such facts as suit their purpose" and excised "anything that might reflect some degree of credit on Middletown . . . or its inhabitants." She noted "the singular faculty of the authors for selecting a chance remark or a ridiculous situation and investing it with the appearance of universal truth."[40]

This writer's closing words, responding to a piece in *McCall's* magazine where Robert Lynd discussed the Middletown research, cleverly lampooned the researchers' theories and personal habits—much as she believed the Lynds had done to Muncie's. Robert Lynd, she wrote:

> is sufficiently magnanimous to let the world know that Middletown is modern in one respect at least—the inhabitants use tooth-brushes! But they have not entirely arrived, for he proceeds to recount the fact that they sing church hymns that are a hundred years old . . . Mr. Lynd says nothing at all of the incongruity of riding a bicycle (Mr. Lynd did ride a bicycle, believe it or not), of the vintage of the gay '90's while using an up-to-the-minute tooth brush at odd times. It is amazing that he should lend himself to such a maladjusted manner of living! Now that Mr. Lynd has diagnosed the trouble he should in all fairness tell the people of Middletown how to set about the task of adjusting themselves to normal living. Shall the tooth brushes be thrown away or the ancient hymns be discarded? Let the oracle speak!

Thus were "cultural lag" and the authority of the social scientist summarily dismissed.[41]

Whether the charge was selective reporting, ideological bias, or simply errors born of interviewing the wrong people, the citizens of Muncie approached the Middletown surveys with a generous dose of skepticism. Not all locals, however, were content to quarrel with mere details. Buried among Muncie's complaints, large and small, was a strain of critique concerning social science itself, and especially its distant mode of knowing. In what was easily the most dominant theme in townspeople's criticism, many contended that mere counting and observing could not capture the fullness of life in Muncie. This sentiment was well expressed in a 1931 editorial in the *Muncie Evening Press*. Its author, George Lockwood, mused: "Those who had long lived in Muncie, and had a comprehension of its human side which no scientific survey could develop, realized that while the facts collected were no doubt correctly stated, there was much in 'Middletown' to which the eyes of strangers would necessarily be blind." Lockwood proposed that it was only by becoming "intimately acquainted" with a place that one could know anything of value about it. "There are many truths . . . that may be discovered in a physical laboratory," he reasoned, "but a human laboratory cannot produce such definite and unquestionable results."[42]

The argument that social scientific facts could not tell the whole story found many adherents in Muncie. One local, for example, dubbed *Middletown* "a microscopic study which caught everything a microscope would catch." Although in many cases impressed by the extent of the Lynds' data collection, these critics drew a contrast between issues of core importance and superficial statistics—and claimed that amidst all the facts, the Lynds had "failed to find the heart of Muncie." Commented schoolteacher Rosa Burmaster after reading their unpublished manuscript, "The chapters on Ed-[ucation] were better than I [thought] they would be. You know I felt you hadn't come enough into contact with actual teaching. I know you had the statistics." Again and again, Middletown's subjects counterposed "human" understandings to "scientific" ones, with a clear preference for the former. Some even implied that social scientists' detached techniques were inversely related to their humanity. In this vein, *Muncie Evening Press* editor Wilbur Sutton called Robert Lynd "a calculating machine," saying, "If there is anything that could warm the cockles of his heart it must have gone out when prohibition came in."[43]

Local critics, condemning the thinness of social scientific descriptions, thus seized upon the limitations rather than the potential insights of the outside observer. In direct contention with the Lynds, who had written of the inability of Middletowners to comprehend their own community, residents claimed a privileged place for their readings of the study and town. As Lola Goelet Yoakem would write in response to the Lynds' follow-up study, having been born in Muncie "on the *right* side of the tracks, but still ON the tracks, my attitude toward the town, its residents, and your treatise on it and them, is probably one of the most realistic you'll find." Similarly, Clarence Millspaugh, who reported that he had "lived in 'Middletown'" all his life, wrote to Robert Lynd claiming that he could "speak with some authority" on the "effect" of Lynd's work. Self-styled experts on their community, townspeople made clear that they, and not outside observers, were the best judges of the survey.[44]

At the same time, Muncie residents were quite conscious that their "representative community," as presented in the Lynds' studies, was becoming a touchstone for America. "How could the inoffensive people of Middletown know," one writer demanded, "that their idiosyncrasies were to be spread in sensational form before a credulous public, for the sole purpose of giving the authors a bestseller?" Other detractors were equally infuriated by the study's profiting from Middletowners' reputations. The fact that the Lynds had "gained considerable fame—and we trust, dollars—by making Muncie a sociological laboratory," in the words of one reporter, was enough to arouse suspicion about the study's legitimacy. But most galling were the supposedly "scientific" impressions that the nation was gaining of Muncie's practices and values. Noting Middletown's status as a typical American community "in many of the colleges of the country," a columnist in 1931 lamented the fact that "many of the heavy thinkers have emitted weighty generalizations as the result of the publication of this work." Those who were critical of the enterprise were especially irked that outsiders took the researchers at their word. In some locals' view, it was the prestige of social scientific explanation, rather than its truth, that explained the study's broad circulation.[45]

Years after *Middletown*'s publication, and stoked by the appearance of *Middletown in Transition* in 1937, the local debate over the Lynds' portrayal of Muncie raged on. Hillyer H. Straton, pastor of Muncie's First Baptist Church, would make it a personal crusade to expose the Lynds' inadequate understandings of Middletown. Particularly upset by characterizations of the ministry as poorly trained, highly paid, and "lazy," he charged the books with being "nothing more than a cross-section of the minds of Mr. and Mrs. Lynd." Bothered by what he assumed were the prejudices of East Coast intellectuals, the minister branded the studies as "misleading and untrue" despite their acclaim in "certain sociological circles." Straton took special pleasure in correcting the cosmopolitan reviewers who praised the survey. Singling out one who had called *Middletown* "careful" and "fair," he retorted: "How he knows is a puzzle for he has never been here." The minister's campaign, like many of his fellow townspeople's criticisms, was a challenge to surveyors and commentators who claimed knowledge from a distance. Even as he refuted the survey, however, Straton employed social scientific techniques to persuade. In an irony he did not note, some of his best evidence that the Lynds were wrong came not from his decade of living in Muncie, but from a competing questionnaire that the minister prepared and sent out in order to disprove *Middletown*'s conclusions.[46]

Written, in the *New York Sun*'s words, as if its subjects, "instead of being American citizens, were merely anthropological specimens—Todas, Aruntas or blond Eskimos," the Middletown studies made for uneasy reading in the community they were meant to represent. Muncie's argument with the Lynds was in part a battle over new kinds of expertise, and over whose characterization counted as "the truth." But it was also an argument about the value of the close-hand view and the shortcomings of strangers' understandings. Posing an "intimate acquaintance" against social scientists' techniques, many of *Middletown*'s subjects contended that outsiders could not "know" a community objectively, that survey data distorted as much as it clarified, and that certain aspects of life were unquantifiable.[47]

Middletowners' insistence on the humanity and fallibility of the researchers made them dubious about the viability of scientifically measuring people's beliefs, habits, and values. In this, small-town experts, relying on their own knowledge of place and people, were cannier than the social scientific interlopers had given them credit for. Yet, as Straton's recourse to a questionnaire for proof of this revealed, even these critics were cognizant of the growing power of social surveys to define that which they investigated. Local commentators were not persuaded that the Lynds had found the real Muncie, but even they could not discount the effects of social scientific representations.

Representative Citizens

As investigators of modern social life, the Lynds eagerly adopted anthropological language and tools. Such an approach toward a "representative" American city enabled the researchers to penetrate Middletown's boosterism. It also allowed them to deliver a devastating social scientific critique of America's myths—myths, they suggested, that it took an outsider to expose. But in portraying American villagers of the 1920s and 1930s as irrationally clinging to static rituals, the Lynds themselves fashioned myths with great staying power about United States culture.

Part of anthropology's allure for the Lynds was its ability to make the usual routines of contemporary life appear strange. The other was its foregrounding of the concept of culture itself. By the 1920s, leading American anthropologists—especially Columbia University's Franz Boas and his students—were reworking older meanings of that term, as either "high culture" or a descriptor of evolutionary progress, into a more democratic formulation. Culture was becoming not just the province of elite sectors of "civilized" societies but the property of all human groups. The Lynds' depiction of Middletown's lifeways as the integrated system of a particular society was indebted to this understanding. Robert Lynd referred to culture in 1939 as "all the things that a group of people inhabiting a common geographical area do, the ways they do things and the ways they think and feel about things." He argued that "explicit use of the concept 'culture' compels overt recognition of the fact that all the jumbled details of living in these United States—automotive assembly lines, Wall Street, share-croppers, Supreme Court, Hollywood, and the Holy Rollers—are interacting parts in a single whole."[48]

Relying upon this unitary understanding of culture, *Middletown*'s authors hoped to shed light not merely on a local community, but on the entirety of modern America: its economic relations, its social practices, its reactions to change, its core values. The Lynds were not alone in this excavation of the typical or in their desire to find a capsule of the whole. As one of their contemporaries, the anthropologist Lloyd Warner, explained some years later in the preface to his own community study, "To study Jonesville is to study America; it is a laboratory, a clinic, a field study for finding out what we are as a people." Part and parcel of surveyors' faith was the view that close attention to the diverse cogs of American communities would yield a functioning, organic unit every bit as comprehensible as other studies had rendered, for example, Australian aboriginal societies. Such research was driven by a scientific, but also a deeply felt cultural, quest for an account of the nation in its totality. Embedded in that search, however, was a consequential assumption: that people who lived together shared ways of thinking and feeling, common attitudes and symbols.[49]

What was most important for American culture about the Lynds' investigation—and their substitution of Muncie for the whole— was what it left out. Like many surveys of the day, *Middletown* had been brought into being by unruly social and economic changes, not the least of which was the growing presence of immigrants and black migrants in urban centers. The original plans for the Small City Study thus placed the demographic complexity of America's cities at center stage. The ISRR set several criteria for the prospective field site: it had to be of relatively small size (in order to permit comprehensive study), to be growing quickly, to have a history stretching back a generation, to be undergoing rapid and varied industrialization, and to be "near the centre of life of the U.S." Importantly, it was also to be home to "all the chief denominations" as well as "varied foreign elements (especially Continental) and Negro." This call for racial, religious, and ethnic heterogeneity at the site prompted the ISRR to recommend that the research staff include an African American.[50]

Robert Lynd dropped these latter conditions. In *Middletown*'s transformation from a traditional survey of social problems into a sketch of a "representative" American community, the composition of the population under investigation itself shifted. No longer were "foreign elements" or "Negroes" deemed crucial to the study. Rather, they became hindrances to locating the typical, and the surveyors instead aimed their questions at Muncie's white native-born residents. "Civilizing" anthropology's traditional subjects by turning from "exotics" to "ourselves" would have the effect of almost completely excising nonwhite, non-native, non-Protestant Americans from the study's pages. Given the fact that the site the Lynds selected would earn a cultural status as America's most typical of communities, this decision would have far-reaching consequences.

Middletown's focus on native whites was not an oversight, but a carefully considered aspect of the research design—and one that broke dramatically with the emphasis of prior social surveys. Robert Lynd abandoned South Bend, Indiana, as a field site precisely because of its "cultural and religious heterogeneity." He eventually chose Muncie, indeed sought it out, for its atypicality in one key respect: what he believed to be its insignificant African American and foreign-born population. Explained Lynd in 1923 to the Institute regarding his decision to limit the study to native white American stock: "The reason for this is obvious: since we are attempting a difficult new technique in a highly complicated field, it is desirable to simplify our situation as far as possible. The interaction of the material and cultural trends in the city with our native psychology is problem enough without introducing into this initial study the complicating factor of a psychology molded by a foreign environment." Certainly this decision stemmed from the Lynds' preeminent interest in social class. But the researchers reasoned that there were scientific advantages to dealing with "a homogeneous, native-born population." Namely, instead of "being forced to handle two major variables, racial change and cultural change," the field staff could concentrate solely on the latter. Cultural developments and the demographic makeup of the city were thus divorced, and race and ethnicity were converted into "variables" of little account to the sweeping changes under investigation.[51]

What was supremely incongruous, given Middletown's received status as a representative American community, was that a population as ethnically homogeneous as Muncie's was, as the Lynds themselves pointed out, "unusual." Subsequent scholars have echoed this assessment, pointing out that Muncie in the 1920s "was strikingly different" from the majority of American industrial cities because its ethnic diversity was so limited. Populated largely by farm-born factory workers, it was a "demographic curiosity," more "old stock"—88 percent of the population—than any other city in the Midwest of its size, apart from New Albany, Indiana, where coincidentally enough Robert Lynd himself had been born. On the other hand, the overall percentage of African Americans in the city more closely matched national patterns. In fact, in contrast to the Lynds' belief, Muncie's black population was growing faster than the native white population and was larger, proportionally, than that of cities like Chicago, Detroit, and New York. To "simplify

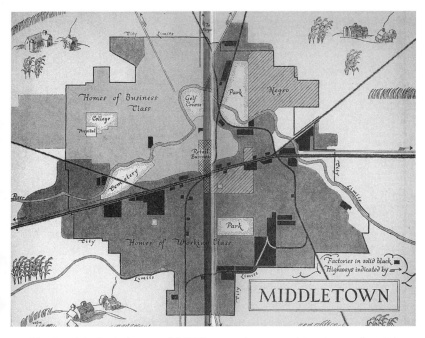

The Lynds' physical map of Middletown demarcated its class and racial divisions even more sharply than their survey did. (Reprinted by permission of Staughton Lynd.)

[the] situation," therefore, Robert Lynd stipulated "the elimination in so far as possible of consideration of the negro element," which he noted made up 5.6 percent of the community. In flat social scientific language, *Middletown*'s "Note on Method"—itself an innovation praised by many scholars—announced, "No answers from negroes were included in the tabulations."[52]

For the Lynds, Muncie's African Americans and immigrants were, in social scientific terms, "complicating factors," not constitutive components of the community. So too were most of the pressing—and even typical—problems of American cities in the 1920s. "The very middle-of-the-road quality about Middletown would have made it unsuitable for a different kind of investigation," declared the Lynds in the opening pages of their 1929 volume. Here they reinforced the novelty of their survey, its turn to the purportedly normal and average: "Had this study sought simply to observe the institution of the home under extreme urban conditions, the recreational life of industrial workers, or any one of dozens of other special 'social problems,' a far more spectacular city than Middletown might readily have been found." By labeling the everyday forces reshaping U.S. cities "spectacular" and "special," the Lynds implied that such forces were aberrant, and therefore not truly representative of American life. Muncie, on the other hand, was sought out because it was sheltered from "extreme," if common, urban conditions. This was a very peculiar vision of the normal. In fact, the more deeply the Lynds' field site is probed for signs of typicality, the more the claim unravels. Of all American cities of Muncie's size in 1930, for example, 90 percent had a greater proportion of women in paid employment.[53]

The exclusion of black and immigrant Muncie from their "total-situation study" suggests that the Lynds' representative community was less an empirical than a normative proposition. Their social scientific account resembled contemporary fictional works such as Sinclair Lewis's *Main Street* (1920) and *Babbitt* (1922), in its equation of white natives and American culture. Robert Lynd's choice of Muncie, Richard Wightman Fox argues, was "the product of his belief that the hope for social progress lay uniquely in the spirit and vision of the 'substantial type' of American, the native-born Protestant of the Middle West," rather than the foreign-born industrial workers he would have found elsewhere. Even in selecting a small and midwestern city for their site, the Lynds and the ISRR betrayed their presuppositions regarding what parts of American culture, and which Americans, could stand in for the whole. The romance of the small town, still linked to its pioneer origins, during a period of mass urbanization structured the *Middletown* project from the beginning. Despite their professed interest in contemporary trends, the Lynds looked backward to find the modern United States.[54]

That the Lynds began their investigation with a concern for "urban industrial civilization" and wound up in Muncie, with its homogeneous and not at all typical population, is telling. Middletown in 1924 was a representative community more wished-for than real, its studiers steeped in nostalgia for a purer, simpler, even preindustrial, America. This meant that although the Lynds promised an anthropological distance from their object of investigation, their study would promote a vision of the typical that their readers would find quite familiar.

And so, for all that the Lynds did see, they passed over the experiences of those who did not fit within their broader scheme, especially Muncie's nonwhite, non-Protestant populations. This is not because the Lynds held a monolithic view of the community. *Middletown* was remarkably attentive to the divergent ways in which men and women participated in the community, and it placed the heaviest significance on the division of the population into a business and working class. Yet gender and status divisions seemed to fit the Lynds' intellectual preconceptions, and their sense of who was truly American, better than did racial, ethnic, or religious ones. Thus, although *Middletown* recorded the fact that Jews were barred from membership in the Rotary Club and the "rigorous taboo upon the mingling of Negroes and whites in religious observances," the lines of race and religion were peripheral to their analysis. The Lynds looked briefly at the Ku Klux Klan's role in heightening "potential factors of disintegration" in town. But it did not lead them to an understanding of "contemporary American culture" as built upon certain groups' systematic exclusion from it. This was despite the common knowledge that the Klan controlled Muncie's city government and led boycotts against Catholic and Jewish businesses.[55]

Fixed on group solidarity rather than strife, the Lynds did not consider in their first study the methods by which Middletown's values were enforced or what explained the dominance of its seemingly uniform ideologies. In their analysis, all Middletowners were equally subject to myths that no one actively propagated, and all parts of the community functioned together to create a mostly frictionless unit. Finding two classes but not two sets of class consciousness, the Lynds presented a culture that was bound tightly together regardless of differential amounts of power and status. An anthropological predisposition toward holism led them to emphasize certain features of the town, such as Middletown's obsession with the high school basketball team, the "Bearcats," and neglect others, such as the attempts by the business class to steer town policies on a course to their liking. The Lynds wrote of the former as a "widespread agency of group cohesion . . . No distinctions divide the crowds which pack the school gymnasium . . . North Side and South Side, Catholic and Kluxer, banker and machinist—their one shout is 'Eat 'em, beat 'em, Bearcats!'" A basketball team is a precarious foundation for community to rest upon. However, an assumption of cohesion allowed the Lynds to avoid the awkward question of whether Middletown in fact constituted a "community"—even when their evidence might have spurred them to ask it.[56]

The starting point of "culture," almost always imagined as a singular, if complex, entity, thus limited the Lynds' vision. This weakness was evident in their selection of Muncie as a proper field site to begin with and in their sidelining of problematic "variables." Neglect of the latter may have prevented them from coming much earlier to an unstated but almost perceptible conclusion of their follow-up study: that class and racial consciousness might in themselves demand separate investigation, that middle-of-the-road Americanism might not fit all members of the community equally.

A popular and critical success, *Middletown* was followed by a 1935 "restudy" of the town, *Middletown in Transition* (1937). Harcourt, Brace again published the study, which was co-authored by the

Lynds although only Robert returned to Muncie; the Institute for Social and Religious Research had closed its doors in 1934. The second survey again used the device of a "representative community" to trace America's fate during the Depression years. But much had changed in the interim. In the decade between 1925 and 1935, Robert Lynd became a professor of sociology, served on President Hoover's Research Committee on Social Trends, launched a major study on consumer affairs, took positions at the Commonwealth Fund and the Social Science Research Council, and worked as a member of the New Deal Consumer's Advisory Board. Lynd's penchant for "planning," with experts taking the lead in solving social problems, was buttressed by the examples of New Deal programs he witnessed in the Roosevelt administration. Lynd's immersion in consumer issues also heightened his sense of an uneven contest between workers on the one side and capitalists and advertisers on the other. In the years between the two Middletown surveys, social scientific rules had changed too, becoming more explicit and rigorous. Academic sociologists, economists, and anthropologists would all weigh in more critically regarding the Lynds' grab bag of techniques by 1937. In the introduction to *Middletown in Transition*, Robert Lynd found it necessary, as he had not in 1929, to indicate his upbringing, his economic views, his scholarly biases (against laissez-faire solutions, for example), and his professional perspective—his "unfamiliar ways of looking at familiar things."[57]

If Robert Lynd's return to Muncie highlighted major shifts in his own life and in the scholarly playing field, it exposed many continuities in Middletown. The town, the Lynds asserted, blundered on in its "uneven, waddling gait of cultural change," remained "bound into service to moneymaking," and still preferred not to interrogate its beliefs too closely. Taught in school the "community values of group solidarity and patriotism," townspeople could not conceive of their economy and culture as artificial developments. But not even Middletown could ignore the Depression, and this was what the Lynds hoped to investigate. The economic crisis provided them a unique opportunity, an experimental laboratory of sorts for their study of culture. Using their previous work as a control condition, the Lynds asked new questions. To what extent had the economic crisis affected the townspeople and their beliefs? Had cultural lags been closed, and had Muncie's citizens been shaken out of their economic and social equanimity?[58]

Devastated by the Depression, both Middletown and its buoyant boomtown mentality were subject to stress, and the Lynds did find "benchmarks of change"—although they feared such changes would not last if the renewed economic stirrings of 1935 bore fruit. In particular, the researchers claimed that some of Middletown's workers had begun to question the dominant business ideology of the 1920s. Hit first and hardest by the economic crisis, workers departed from owners in their attitudes toward the federal government and, at least temporarily, the benefits of unionization. Reactions to Roosevelt and the New Deal, the Lynds noted, were "uneven and sharply marked by class differences." In the 1936 election, both the working class and the less affluent sector of the business class had thrown their support behind Roosevelt despite a massive propaganda campaign by the industrialists.[59]

At the same time, the Lynds found that the power exercised by the town's elite had become more manipulative and subtle. The most striking aspect of their second survey was its discovery of the "X family," whom the Lynds placed at the center of their new analysis of "business-class control." The prominent Ball (or "X") family, gas-boom industrialists, had long been established in Middletown. But only in *Middletown in Transition* was an entire chapter devoted to an exposé of the family's vast influence in matters ranging from banking and industry to education policy, news reportage, and local politics. For this, the Lynds were indebted to Muncie residents, a number of whom criticized the first study for understating the X family's sway. As one put it, "I do feel the authors either purposely or otherwise missed one big point about this town, namely that the Balls dominate the whole town, are the town in fact." Such a critique indicated that Middletowners were more aware of economic inequities than the Lynds had given them credit for, and perhaps more attuned to class conflict than were the social scientists themselves. As one man explained matter-of-factly, "For five years, 1931–1936, I taught in X State Teachers College, lived in an apartment owned by the X family, bought my clothes at the X department store and banked my cash in the X bank." As their vague understanding of power relations gave way to a more trenchant analysis—in part through an acquaintance with Marx and Engel's writings in the 1930s—the Lynds converted such evidence into ideological terms. If Muncie had not undergone a revolution in the decade between 1925 and 1935, its researchers had, replacing their benign understanding of shared middle-of-the-road beliefs with one pointing to the hegemony of a particular class.[60]

In rather contradictory fashion, however, the Lynds managed ultimately to reaffirm Middletown's unity. Despite their advances in understanding Muncie's power structure, many of their interpretations nonetheless were couched "in terms of general formulations for Middletown without specific class differentiation." Most importantly, even though by 1937 the Lynds were convinced that Muncie's platitudes about free enterprise and upward mobility were the work of a dominant class, they painted a picture of a homogeneous community knitted together by common values. The Lynds did caution that "one cannot talk about 'what Middletown thinks' or 'feels' or 'is' without a large amount of distortion," but went on to say that "Middletown can be lived in and described only because of the presence of large elements of repetition and coherence." Indeed, the Lynds' second investigation largely confirmed their first. The hold of simplistic laissez-faire assumptions on Middletowners of all backgrounds persisted. Potential changes wrought by the Depression were too weak to withstand prevailing ways of thinking, and sources of challenge to social conformity, such as new educational philosophies, were sure to be squashed.[61]

That the normal had not been sufficiently revised even by a major crisis brought the Lynds to a kind of despair. Comparing the community of the mid-1930s to its earlier incarnation, they asserted in the closing pages of *Middletown in Transition* that "the texture of Middletown's culture has not changed." Ideologically speaking, Middletown was not "in transition" at all. The problem was to be found in the community's "thick blubber of custom," the elements of which the authors catalogued in a chapter entitled "The Middletown Spirit." Its long list of seemingly unshakeable beliefs—in being "loyal," "average," "like other people" and in doctrines such as "the natural law of progress," "American civilization," "fundamental institutions," "the small businessman," "the middle course," "hard work," "success," "the land of opportunity," "the two-party system," "churchgoing," and "fending for oneself"—perhaps convinced the researchers that their dream of "a culture seeing itself," notwithstanding the aid of social scientific expertise, was futile.[62]

Middletown's stake in the typical placed it within twentieth-century developments in the social and human sciences less interested in investigating the pathological than the "normal state." Robert Lynd had an unwavering concern with the normal as an object of study. As executive secretary of the Social Science Research Council in the early 1930s, he rejected funding for a research proposal on "divided immigrant families," not because he thought the project unworthy, but because "we know so little about the great modal group of 'normal' families." In a letter to a potential SSRC donor describing the scope of the projects the Council was hoping to undertake, Lynd again homed in on the normal. Noting the "bewildering host of deep-seated social problems that beset all of us,"

Lynd stated his preference for funding inquiries into "normal marriage in its various functions, as over against the earlier preoccupation with the 'broken home.'" Later in the decade, writing as only a social scientist could of the research subjects newly available as a result of the Depression crisis, he would return to this theme. Lynd observed that "ordinarily . . . an important section of the population—the normal-enough-to-get-by—is difficult of access by family researchers." He was pleased to note, however that it "is actually notably easier now to get intimate family data from 'normal' families than it was prior to the depression."[63]

If Robert Lynd was aligned with modern social science in this regard, his emphasis on social problems that "beset all of us," even the "normal," signaled his allegiance to an older model of the social investigator as critic. Lynd's emphasis on the typical was always in the interest of challenging it. One of his and Helen's hopes for *Middletown* had been that in focusing upon the normal, social science could provide a corrective for national trends: corrosive consumerism as well as widening economic inequality.

This had been a key motivation behind their anthropological approach. Explaining the social scientific ethos in a 1938 lecture, Robert Lynd argued that learning to view culture objectively allowed individuals to free themselves from a "habituated past." The social scientist, he noted, necessarily approached American life from a different vantage point than did the average Middletowner. Muncie, he said, was "busily living along, trying to hold [the] boat steady, avoiding all possible troublesome questions." The "outside analyst," on the other hand, made it a point to evaluate people's habits and rationalizations. Acknowledging Muncie's criticisms of *Middletown,* he noted that this could make the social scientist appear "cold, critical [and] cynical." But what social scientists did as their stock in trade, suggested Lynd, so too might ordinary individuals. In fact, this was an approach to the world that Americans needed to cultivate in modern times. All citizens, he believed, should be anthropologists of their own culture.[64]

Certain that the key to social change was consciousness, the Lynds anticipated that their surveys would trigger a more reflective society, one that might become aware of and judge its own values. In a sense, heightened self-consciousness had been a goal of the Middletown project all along. The Small City Study had aspired "to develop a method by which smaller cities may be helped to appraise their own life" and "to realise by methods that are at once Christian and American a proper norm of life for this type of community." More concretely, its findings were supposed to "point the way to the working out of a method for perennial self-study and readjustment by the socio-religious agencies of the city studied and of other cities." Similarly, Middletown's surveyors in 1937 announced that researchers as well as ordinary citizens could stand outside their culture and understand "its symbols . . . *as symbols,* its rationalizations *as rationalizations.*" American society, from its most mundane activities to its most symbolically complex ones, could be made into a social scientific object.[65]

In the end, it was this objective portrait of "typical" Middletown that would derail the Lynds' aim to transform American culture through self-knowledge. Strong exhortations to neutrality by the Institute for Social and Religious Research, and in the social scientific field more generally, ensured that there were no explicit calls for reform in the Middletown studies as there had been in earlier social surveys. Products of modern social science, they plied descriptive rather than prescriptive norms. The Lynds quite deliberately presented American culture as it *was,* not as it should or could be. And their conclusions on this score would be persuasive—if not in Muncie, then in the rest of the nation—because they seemed to contain no moral message, none of the old language of exposure and correction. The Lynds mounted a critique of American life in the hope of changing it. But they would also put into circulation an authoritative social scientific and "objective" portrait of that culture, one that could easily become fixed as truth. As such, their surveys would not enlighten readers in ways the authors had expected.[66]

The Lynds' decision to place "contemporary culture"—rather than a particular social problem demanding a solution—at the center of their inquiry thus had important consequences. Their impulse toward cultural wholeness allowed African Americans, immigrants, Catholics, and Jews to be written out of their "representative" community, and permitted a quite atypical city to serve as the norm. Even the social fractures that the researchers took pains to highlight were submerged in a holistic framework of culture. Despite the Lynds' insistence that a glaring class divide was the crucial fact about Muncie in the 1920s and 1930s, this analysis could easily be lost when they or others made recourse to the "average." Bracketing all they considered deviant, special, and abnormal, the researchers made Middletown a distorted but resonant icon of American modernity.

With its focus on the mainstream United States, its claim to document rather than moralize, its rhetoric of empiricism, and perhaps most importantly, its unexpected arrival on the best-sellers charts, *Middletown* was emblematic of a new strain in American social investigation. It was also indicative of a new relationship emerging between social surveys and those they surveyed. The Lynds' joining of objective science to the "typical" had powerful effects as the Middletown research left Muncie and made its way into the mass-mediated public sphere. National reactions to the studies over the course of the 1930s document as nothing else a culture coming to know itself through social science.

2

Middletown Becomes Everytown

Muncie, Ind. is the most interesting small town in the U.S. For 12 years it has been surveyed, studied and talked about more than any other city its size in the world. Sociologists use it as a specimen, advertisers as a test tube.

—*Life* magazine, 1937

We think we are a typical city of typical Americans. We do not mind being in the nation's spotlight.

—Muncie Mayor Rollin H. Bunch, 1937

To some in 1929, the most striking aspect of *Middletown* was neither its anthropological approach nor its empirical portrait of United States culture. Rather, it was how many non–social scientists—and how many readers far from Muncie—were talking about it. Helen Lynd recalled, "Nobody was as surprised as we when it came out with front page reviews in the *Times* and *Herald Tribune*." A reviewer noted with astonishment that *Middletown* could "be found in the show window of nearly every city bookstore." He reflected, "Not many years ago it would have seemed incredible that any social survey could achieve the distinction of a big seller in the book trade. This, however, *Middletown* has accomplished." Publisher Alfred Harcourt told Robert Lynd that, initially, popular book sellers "wouldn't believe it was the sort of book which might have a sale," but that they were coming around to the idea. He was reinvesting all of *Middletown*'s profits because there was "an excellent chance for a considerable sale."[1]

In fact, bookstores and libraries could hardly keep the book on their shelves. The first Middletown study went through six printings in its first year of publication alone. Part of the demand was scholarly: in the 1929–1930 academic year, at least thirty-eight colleges and universities were using *Middletown* in their courses. Commentators, however, were more impressed by the book's generalist appeal. One reported that *Middletown* "might be expected to win the acclaim which it has received from professional students. But it has broken into the field of popular reading. At club meetings and dinner conversations it is discussed by mounting thousands of lay citizens, and small-town libraries keep waiting-lists of patrons eager for their turn." A *New York Times* editorial concurred, noting that *Middletown* "is meeting with such an eager reception that circulating libraries have had to order extra copies, and at the Public Library there is no end in sight to the long list of requests to have the volume reserved."[2]

Sales and readership figures are only the most conservative measures of public fluency with *Middletown*. There were many other ways to encounter the Lynds' "new type of survey." To begin with, *Middletown* was discussed on the front pages of a remarkable range of publications, from Florida's *Fort Myers Church News* to Ohio's *Dayton Herald,* and from *American Teacher* to *New York Medical Week*. It was also invoked in classrooms, community centers, and churches across the nation. Something of the stir the study created was evident in a letter from an instructor at Indiana University to Robert Lynd: "'Middletown' is going to have quite an influence," he wrote. "I hear a great deal about it around Indianapolis. One of my students is preparing a paper on it for my seminar. I have been asked to make two addresses on it to the Men's Class at the

Unitarian Church the last of March, and I think it is possible that the Torch Club will stage a debate on it." Ministers devoted sermons to *Middletown,* social workers familiarized themselves with it, and speakers based their commencement addresses on it. It was even reported that "one of the largest New York advertising agencies is requiring that this book be read by all its staff." Already by 1930, the style of the book was so familiar that other social scientific studies in the public eye were dubbed "Middletowns"—from Charles S. Johnson's *The American Negro* (a "Negro Middletown"), to Robert Redfield's study of Tepoztlán ("Mexico's Middletown"), to President Hoover's Committee on Social Trends (a "larger 'Middletown'").[3]

Clearly, "Middletown" was coming to stand for much more than a research project. Culturally, it served as shorthand for contemporary America and a summation of "who we are." Extensive interest in Robert and Helen Lynd's report on life in a "representative community" signaled a growing curiosity about what ordinary Americans did and believed. But it also expressed a fascination with the very social scientific mode that permitted such discoveries. To cultural critics and general readers alike, *Middletown* presented modern life in an arresting new format: empirical, detached, and most of all, objective. As such, the Lynds' survey was a crucial step in the social scientific production of typical America, one that permitted the nation and its inhabitants to be understood in new ways. Its publisher was perhaps justified in its advertisements trumpeting *Middletown* as "the latest and most indispensable word in the new American vocabulary."[4]

Seeing Ourselves

What accounted for the astounding success of this more-than-five-hundred-page survey of an anonymous town in the Midwest? If the Institute for Social and Religious Research had been baffled by the "indefiniteness and breadth of the Study," general readers were not. Instead, they seemed spellbound by the ocean of details that *Middletown* presented and the sweep of the Lynds' findings about an American community, circa 1924: that workers rose earlier in the morning than their employers; that schoolgirls desired silk rather than cotton stockings; that movies were a site of family togetherness as well as disruption; that the newest homes in town lacked spare rooms and parlors; that public speeches were getting shorter; that business associations were growing but trade unions declining; that belief in hell was weakening. What its sponsor had not counted on was an immense appetite for facts about national habits, behaviors, and lifestyles that the study tapped into. Evidently, social scientists were not the only Americans interested in the accumulation of facts about contemporary culture in 1929.[5]

In this sense, the survey impulse was shared, and propelled, by ordinary citizens. *Middletown* spoke to a widespread curiosity about modern life that was acute in the United States after World War I. According to one commentator, "That complex of hopes and fears, aspirations and fatigues, which so drives the Middletowners, is so vital a part of this young, new life of ours that any people as self-conscious as we would wish to read it." Or as *Good Housekeeping* put it, "Nothing is so interesting as ourselves, and this was like looking at yourself in a mirror." The desire for summations of society, and for expert techniques to analyze it, stemmed from a heightened sense of living in "modern times," times in which, it seemed, individuals could barely keep up with the pace of social, industrial, and technological change. The 1920s were not in any simple way the beginning of a modern era. But the decade was "distinguished by Americans' growing consciousness of change, a perception that a yawning gulf separated them from the world of only a decade before." Writing in 1931, historian Frederick Lewis Allen believed that the culture around him—its mores, styles, entertainments, obsessions—would have been entirely foreign to an American in 1919.[6]

Such diagnoses of modern culture were the hallmark of an age

riddled with anxieties over standardization and conformity, industrial modes of work and leisure, and shifting gender roles and moral
codes. But national self-consciousness also flowed from new understandings of "culture" itself, helping to explain *Middletown*'s resonance. Anthropologists' concept of cultural relativism was popularized in the interwar years for a middlebrow reading public through
Margaret Mead's articles and books as well as Ruth Benedict's best-
selling 1934 *Patterns of Culture*. Historian Warren Susman pinpointed the 1930s as a time when many in the United States "began
thinking in terms of patterns of behavior and belief, values and lifestyles, symbols and meanings" and made "the effort to find, characterize, and adapt to an American Way of Life." Contemporary observers from abroad viewed this as a recent, and peculiarly American, quest. Noted a British reviewer of *Middletown*, "Not the least
remarkable of the many changes that have taken place of recent
years in the United States has been the development of the habit
of national introspection." Marveling at the publication of a book
in which the "habits, tastes, desires, houses, clothing, automobiles and ideals of every citizen of a town in the Middle West were
tabulated," another reader from across the Atlantic concluded,
"This is the sort of looking-within-themselves that Americans so often do."[7]

What many have missed in noting this tendency toward "national introspection" is the role social scientific studies played in its
expression. A work like *Middletown* offered Americans a trustworthy account of what their culture was, a catalogue of national values distilled from fieldwork in a "representative" community. Like
Herbert Hoover's ambitious data-collecting projects, *Recent Economic Changes and Recent Social Trends,* and the social documentary impulse that would engage so many artists and writers across
the next decade, *Middletown* was at once a symptom of cultural
change and an agent in crystallizing the terms of the discussion. In
one reader's words, "The portrait of a community, representative of

millions of our population, barely groping for a national culture still to be born, jumps out of [the Lynds'] careful paragraphs." In this light, *Middletown* was less a social scientific revelation than a vital installment in the making of modern America.[8]

To be sure, there were many others—writers, reporters, and artists—seeking to elaborate an American "way of life" in the 1920s and 1930s. Documentary photographers, social critics, fiction writers, and radio broadcasters all participated in the production of a distinctly national culture. As many saw it, however, the value of the Lynds' study was precisely that it was *not* impressionistic, anecdotal, or journalistic. Regularly contrasted to the novels of Sinclair Lewis and other depictions of small-town America, *Middletown* garnered praise for its impartial and statistical description of social life. One reviewer proclaimed the end of "a literary monopoly on Main Street" now that "the sociologists have found Main Street worthy of a 'survey.'" A writer for the *New York World*, explaining that "looking through the keyholes of prairie cities is rapidly becoming one of the leading sports of our intelligentsia," pronounced: "Now, however, we have a survey built scientifically and out of carefully gathered facts." Public discussions of *Middletown* centered on its systematic character and stringent empiricism, its careful separation of observer and observed. To many, the scientific survey was a definite improvement over competing accounts of modern culture.[9]

It was telling that many chose metaphors drawn from the biological and physical sciences—the microscope, the laboratory, and the experiment—to describe the Lynds' achievement. "The authors of this volume have treated the American for the first time to a laboratory examination," explained one journalist, "and we are now enabled to know scientifically just what manner of man we are." Pointing out *Middletown*'s superiority to previous attempts to understand contemporary society, she continued, "This, ladies and gentlemen, is . . . not the idea of any muckraker or any dispenser of sweetness and light. These are the cold, objective facts, as impersonal as the fluid in a laboratory test tube." Placing the Middletown study squarely at the end of a trajectory of the scientific method that began with astronomy, another lauded "the capacity of man to observe *himself* objectively," a feat that had come only at "a late stage in a long process of experimentation." As such commentary reveals, it was not just social scientists who put a premium on empirical studies of modern trends. General readers also were willing to trust the Lynds' conclusions in a way they would not trust the seeming advocate's or amateur's.[10]

Critical to the persuasiveness of this way of knowing modern culture was the view that *Middletown*'s researchers were in the simple business of collecting and recording facts. As neutral parties observing their subjects, one commentator reported, the Lynds "simply turn[ed] the lens of social science upon the flow of community life and let its folkways disclose themselves." The researchers, of course, did quite a bit more than this. They were hardly passive receptacles for data, as their selection of the site, their calculated use of the naïve observer, and their sharp critique of "pecuniary culture" made clear. Those in Middletown, like those at the ISRR, had doubted the Lynds' claims to neutrality, judging the researchers to be critics as well as observers of Muncie's habits. In terms of *Middletown*'s national reception, however, it did not matter that the Lynds were untrained social scientists when they set off for Muncie, nor that they brought definite points of view with them. The technical apparatus of social science and its particular style of reportage could make it seem otherwise.[11]

Middletown was a primarily narrative account interspersed with tables, tabulations, and direct excerpts from interviews—far from the modern sample survey of the later twentieth century, and in one historian's words, "almost novelistic." Yet contemporary readers enthused over its scientific look and tone. Explained a journalist, "Our authors do not tell us [their conclusions] in so many words.

They are too unbiased and too scientific to do so." The Book-of-the-Month Club declared *Middletown* to be "the result of a survey in which every device known to sociologists was used to find out the facts." Yet another commentator praised the survey's "case reports, impressively fortified by statistical tables and the computation of percentages." As such commentary indicates, the presentation of the Lynds' findings endowed their conclusions with considerable authority. The form that their knowledge took, in other words, could trump the conditions of its creation. In contrast to the study's own subjects, awed national reviewers deemed *Middletown* "an amazingly painstaking study," "an extraordinarily objective piece of work," "a gold mine of social data," "scientific and sociological to the last degree," and governed by "the austere principles of modern anthropology."[12]

It was not just any science, of course, but anthropology that provided the framework for the Lynds' survey. In his foreword to *Middletown,* anthropologist Clark Wissler of the American Museum of Natural History anticipated the shock it would create, since "to most people, anthropology is a mass of curious information about savages"—that is, not a tool that had been applied to "civilized" white Americans. The study's publisher played up the comparison, touting the "party of scientists [who] burrowed their way into the heart of America with less difficulty but with quite as much detachment as if it were the heart of Africa." Journalists followed suit, the *Boston Herald* reporting that the Lynds had "made an anthropological study of the genus Americanus just as their fellow-scientists frequently study the habits of primitive man in Africa or of the Indian tribes in Central America." Another wrote in wonderment that the researchers "sought to study [Middletown's] citizens as impersonally as though they had been brown-skinned, fuzzy-haired inhabitants of some atoll in the far Pacific." If the ISRR had questioned the researchers' anthropological tack, it was this same feature of the survey that heightened its appeal for many readers.[13]

The Lynds' participant-observer approach to Muncie stamped their study as scientific. But as the language of "primitives" and "savages" suggests, it also lent a certain exoticism to American life. By the time *Middletown* appeared, anthropologists were moving away from crude characterizations of "backward" peoples and reevaluating the complexity of purportedly simple cultures. However, in most popular venues their endeavor remained steeped in the mysterious—and even when turned upon white midwesterners, retained its voyeuristic appeal.

Themes of invasion and detection run through dozens of reviews of *Middletown,* suggesting the immense novelty readers found in gaining access to their compatriots' private lives. The *Literary Digest* compared *Middletown* to "a peep through the keyhole at American life," while the *Chicago Daily News* called it "a revelation of the people next door." H. L. Mencken went further, pronouncing the study "as exhilarating as even the dirtiest of the new novels." Some observers were surprised that Middletowners would stand for such an invasion of their privacy. But this was almost always overshadowed by commentators' fascination with the prospect—perhaps because, unlike Muncie residents, they weren't the ones directly under scrutiny. "Scientists, armed with questionnaires and statistical charts, have . . . penetrated the inmost privacies of the town with patience and cunning," reported one reviewer in this vein. Making reference to anthropologist Bronislaw Malinowski's research, another proclaimed, "Never were the Trobriand Islanders more helpless, more completely open to the scrutiny of some curious alien who had come to stare at their ancestral dances and their potlatches" than were Middletowners.[14]

Such commentaries made it clear that one of the chief sources of the survey's allure was its object of investigation: "typical" white Americans. Hundreds of studies of gangs, immigrants, and paupers

"Look, Herman, those Lynds are in town again."

To many, Robert and Helen Lynd—here wielding calipers and a notebook—signaled the new inquisitiveness of social surveyors. (Reprinted with the permission of Scribner, an imprint of Simon & Schuster Adult Publishing Group, from *Scribner's Magazine,* vol. 102, July 1937. Copyright © 1937 by Charles Scribner's Sons; copyright renewed © 1965.)

predated *Middletown,* but so-called respectable citizens had not before been subjected to such rude prying. The Lynds, simplifying their study of cultural change by excising African Americans and "ethnics" thus altered an older, more hierarchical relationship between surveyor and surveyed. The repeated contrasts between Middletown's people and "brown-skinned, fuzzy-haired inhabitants" of other lands and "primitive men of Africa" made this clear enough. That white midwesterners both could be and were willing to be examined like the usual objects of anthropology or the targets of scientific charity bespoke a new role for social surveys. This shift in subject matter, in who was being looked at, also helps explain the great interest with which the Lynds' experiment was received. The rhetorical turn from "others" to "ourselves" was a key factor propelling *Middletown* to best-seller status.

Such intense curiosity about Middletowners, which was at the same time curiosity about U.S. culture, indicated that the Lynds had succeeded in objectifying American manners and beliefs in the same way anthropologists had objectified those of far-off lands. The popular press made much of this new way of looking at the United States. But professional social scientists also extolled the Lynds' approach, asserting that ethnographic methods could reveal American culture anew. In their rush to catalogue and analyze other peoples, they suggested, anthropologists had left domestic norms woefully neglected. As Chicago School sociologist Harvey Zorbaugh put it, "Ethnologists and sociologists have been examining the cultures of other peoples in such fashion for a half century, but have only begun to give us an equally objective interpretation of our own culture." *Middletown,* he stated, "cannot fail to increase our objectivity in considering the social life of which we are a part."[15]

Indeed, the discipline that until so recently had focused on "savages" seemed to carry unique explanatory clout for the predominantly white middle-class readers of the Lynds' study. Intrigued by the notion of an anthropology of "ourselves," a journalist mused, "We are supposed to know what civilized people do and what they believe [but] . . . there is no sufficient accumulation of facts from which anything can safely be induced about the habits and the tendencies of modern peoples." Twentieth-century Westerners, this writer implied, were unable to know their culture with the same confidence that anthropologists knew "primitive" ones. This analysis was furthered by those who judged it no longer possible for ordinary citizens to glean direct knowledge of contemporary society, so complicated and heterogeneous had it become. A Congregationalist church bulletin lamented that the "man who would know his community depends upon a wide range of expert investigation that he cannot make himself and upon a mass of facts and statistics that he cannot himself acquire." Persuaded that they lived in a uniquely complex time, and increasingly reliant on specialists, such observers were coming to believe that laypeople had lost the ability to apprehend the world around them.[16]

This, of course, was where *Middletown* came in. Readers of all kinds heaped praise on the study's ability to clarify modern conditions. "Obviously, a great change is coming over American life," declared a reporter from Walla Walla, Washington, "[and] it is through such surveys as this that we can recognize it and estimate its nature." Wrote the *American Economic Review* of *Middletown:* "It stiffens the edges of our knowledge and hardens the surface, it gives a peculiar and satisfying sense of reality, of body, to what has been in the past rather fuzzy and remote." An Iowa journalist put it this way: "Here is the chance to look at yourself from the outside, to see what you and your neighbors are up to in the year 1929 in this great country." The apparent faculty of survey techniques to describe and detail—and render knowable—the modern United States was evident in such commentary. The expert elaboration of American culture, it seemed, permitted citizens to see their society objectively for the first time. It also promised, in a time of marked social turmoil, to reveal what bound them together.[17]

The "Genus Americanus"

The fact that *Middletown* seemed to offer definitive scientific knowledge about the mainstream United States certainly allowed it to resonate differently than had prior surveys. But its appeal was also rooted in its reassuringly familiar picture of the "genus Americanus," in the words of a *Boston Herald* reporter, amidst un-settling social, demographic, and economic developments. *Middle-town* made "the typical" visible, and empirically real, at a moment when any sense of American commonality was difficult to discern and national culture seemed deeply fragmented and unstable.[18]

Noting the intense class, racial, ethnic, and political conflicts of the early 1920s, one historian writes that, to many, urban industrial society had come to appear "a monstrous perversion of American ideals and ways of life." This analysis was in fact undergirded by survey data—specifically, statistical evidence from the 1920 census—which indicated that the rural–urban balance of the country was tilting decisively toward the latter and that the foreign-born were overtaking old-stock Americans. Rather than viewing these trends as harbingers of inevitable social change, alarmed citizens sought to reverse the current. It was, of course, a coincidence that the Lynds embarked on their Muncie fieldwork in 1924, the same year that the Johnson-Reed Act, "crudely discriminatory" in its effort to curtail immigration from all countries save those of Western Europe, became law. But in the context of renewed nativism, eugenic designs, and postwar patriotism—indeed, the height of "racial nationalism" in the twentieth century—a scientific description of the United States, trained not on urban problems but on a white midwestern town, could serve as a compelling cultural arbiter. Like national origins quotas, facts about life in an average community might stabilize and consolidate America.[19]

Over the course of the 1930s, debate swirled in Muncie over the Lynds' portrayal of the town. But elsewhere the notion that Middletown typified America was crystallizing. For those prepared to accept the community as a capsule of the whole, what mattered was not that the Lynds had determined that "Muncie had 500 clubs of all kinds" or tabulated "representative" rates of unemployment and divorce; indeed, most readers would not have been able to evaluate such claims. Instead, it was the claim that anthropologists had penetrated the very heart of the nation's culture: its guiding habits, political and economic beliefs, and modes of living. Reviewers in publications ranging from the middlebrow to the academic easily slipped between "Middletown" and "America" or "Middletowners" and "ourselves," rarely challenging—instead more often creating—an understanding of the study as a scientific explication of mainstream American values. Collapsing any distinctions between Middletowners and himself, for example, a writer for the *Saturday Review of Literature* stated, "38,000 of us were recently observed to work, learn, love, and play in a typical though anonymous Middlewestern city." Comparing the study to an unforgiving mirror, he continued: "If you believe it would do your soul good to look at such a reflection of yourself—yourself and all the rest of us—then look into this book's pages—and if you can, keep from unhappy pondering as to what manner of man—and woman—you and all the rest of us are apparently becoming!" "Surely these people cannot be our fellow citizens," lamented a scholarly commentator, "they cannot be us. But they are."[20]

Embracing Middletowners as "us," this sort of reportage reinforced Muncie's status as an authentically representative place. Indeed, one of the most striking aspects of public discussion about *Middletown* was the speedy acceptance of the notion that the Lynds had uncovered a community reflecting the entirety of the United States. Just as a group of villagers could illuminate a whole society in Margaret Mead's Samoa or Robert Redfield's Tepoztlán, Middletown could stand for America. So much is apparent in the constant use of the words *average, normal,* and *typical* to describe the Lynds' findings. Remarking on their portrait of Muncie, a writer for the *New York Evening Post* asserted, "These are normal activities, and 'Middletown' is a normal city." One reporter claimed that in Middletown, the Lynds had found Aristotle's "mean man . . . the average man." Another discerned in the community "the spiritual lineaments of Hometown." For John Dewey as well, Middletown was "Anytown."[21]

There were deep ironies in such endorsements of Middletown's typicality. One British commentator stated that the Lynds were "determined to get at the *normal* in American life." This was certainly true. However, the Lynds explicitly eschewed any endorsement of their site's typicality in the introduction to the first study. They wrote: "Although it was its characteristic rather than its exceptional features which led to the selection of Middletown, no claim is made that it is a 'typical' city, and the findings of this study can, naturally, only with caution be applied to other cities or to American life in general." Of course, by titling the study "Middletown" and characterizing it as an account of "contemporary culture," the Lynds did suggest that Middletown was representative of something larger than itself. As a shrewd reporter for the *New York Evening Post* observed, "To have called the book by the actual name of the city . . . would have made it only another social survey. But to call it *Middletown* stirs connotations of the average American city . . . The term becomes generic and symbolic. Middletown is—or at least is meant to be—America."[22]

Many would follow this pronounced tendency in the Lynds' work rather than their social-scientifically framed cautions about Muncie's representativeness. In a 1929 sermon delivered in Louisville, Kentucky, for example, Reverend Lon Ray Call described *Middletown* as "an intensely interesting study of the normal life of a real city at the heart of America." He went on to tell his congregation what was so unusual and revelatory about the Lynds' study: "For once we have had the searchlight of social science turned upon a typical American town . . . We've had so many studies of the abnormal. We've heard so much about the defective, delinquent and dependent . . . Now we are glad to see 'Main Street' brought under the searchlight and the folk-ways and mores of modern American living placed fully and clearly in sight." As Lon Ray Call saw it, Middletown was a proxy for the nation because it was "almost entirely native born," had a "natural" and "characteristic" history, and was experiencing "all the problems of modern living." In one broad stroke, the minister was able to relegate "unnatural" aspects of the United States—the urban areas, nonwhite people, and immigrant neighborhoods that had populated prior surveys—to the margins. Thus did *Middletown* encourage readers to associate the real America, the imagined national community, with white native midwesterners.[23]

What *Middletown*'s "normality" really registered—that is, its omission of blacks and marginalization of "ethnics"—was seldom noted by either general or academic readers. The few observers who were skeptical about the Lynds' rendering of typical America were social scientists wary of making claims outside a strictly defined scope. A member of Indiana University's Department of Economics and Sociology, for instance, contacted Robert Lynd regarding the "rather live controversy over the relative merits and limitations" of the "case study" versus the "statistical study," and decreed *Middletown* an example of the former since it did not permit "generalization beyond the cases studied." Those who challenged the survey's other obvious source of ungeneralizability were rare indeed. Perhaps not surprisingly, such recognition came mainly from a handful of readers closely linked to surveyors' old terrain of "social problems": religious and social workers. In an otherwise laudatory review of the Lynds' work, the *Christian Century* noted, "There is no way of proving that the community which they have studied is typical. In some respects it is not entirely so, chiefly because it is too homogeneous racially, has too few foreigners and Negroes. The typical American city is not so strictly 'American.'" Similarly, the *Social Service Review*'s write-up of *Middletown* stated: "One of the unwarranted claims of this investigation is that it is a 'total situation study of a contemporary civilization.' . . . The student of race relations would look in vain for adequate material dealing with this perplexing problem." If this oversight escaped most readers, many, including this last writer, critiqued other omissions in the Lynds' coverage of modern conditions, such as their neglect of any analysis of Prohibition.[24]

Commentators, believing the surveyors had found something "as close to the average as could be attained," did not reflect upon what was missing from the Lynds' picture of a "representative" community. Even when they did, they were more likely to applaud than to condemn the researchers' method, as did one reviewer who praised the Lynds for choosing to study a city that "remained 'American'" because it contained "comparatively few foreigners and fewer Negroes." That astute observer, H. L. Mencken, caught a key distinction, commenting that the authors, in selecting a site for the study, "did not seek the one that was most completely typical, but simply the one that was as thoroughly American as possible." His words neatly capture the analytic confusion in the term *typical*. The same confusion can be glimpsed in a report that listed Muncie's defining feature as the "absence of peculiarities—lack of contact with big cities, absence of large foreign or negro elements, and non-domination of one industry." Following the logic of the Lynds' research design, readers not surprisingly concluded that it was Middletown's lack of "peculiarities," no matter how common those peculiarities were, that made it typical.[25]

It is worth noting that other regions or populations of the United States could not make this same leap from the local or specific to the national. Consider the anonymous community "Southerntown" (Indianola, Mississippi), the field site for John Dollard's 1937 study, *Caste and Class in a Southern Town*. Southerntown was "much less a 'typical' American community than Middletown," in the words of one reviewer, "typical only of the average small Southern town in a rural county devoted to a staple crop and traditionalized by a black belt history and psychology." Such an economically, historically, and of course racially distinctive community, it seemed clear, could not represent America. Middletown, on the other hand—small, isolated, midwestern, industrial, white, native-born—required no similar list of qualifiers. Although as racially distinctive as Southerntown, it could stand in for the nation because of its already-imagined averageness, a quality that bore little relation to empirical foundations. In a strange transmutation, that which made Muncie particular at the same time made it typical. Especially during a time of demographic upheaval, native white subjects could embody America, while black and immigrant Americans could only represent themselves. A general public fascination with social science thus coexisted seamlessly with a decidedly unscientific notion of representativeness.[26]

Uses of the Typical

Middletown's dubious claim to representativeness did not prevent the wide circulation of its image as an icon of the typical. National commentators, as we have seen, rushed to affirm Muncie as "average America." A conjunction of interests—economic and cultural, tangible and intangible—would conspire to maintain Middletown's typicality far beyond the purposes of the original survey.

This was nowhere more evident than in the enthusiastic embrace of *Middletown* by those who stood to profit from a scientifically derived capsule of the nation. One of the ironies of the study's career, given the ideological bent of its authors and their critique of "pecuniary civilization," was its fervent embrace by business strategists. Advertisers were keenly interested in this most typical of towns, and quick to see in the survey a valuable resource for the burgeoning field of market research. From this angle, disinterested social scientific knowledge was a prized commodity, and averageness a powerful claim. *Middletown*'s savvy publisher encouraged this interpretation, describing the study as a tremendous boon to salesmen for the clues it provided as to consumer behavior: "This is a book by Robert S. and Helen M. Lynd. It was not made by a newspaper that wants to sell you space. It was made by a group of research workers who actually *lived* in a carefully chosen representative small American city. For 18 months they were *citizens* of this community,—joined its clubs, read its papers, *knew* its people socially." In another instance, Harcourt, Brace publicists proclaimed: "Here is the scientific low-down on how the Average American Citizen lives—what he buys, eats, reads, thinks, does in his spare time—and *why* . . . it would cost you $50,000 to get this information!" *Middletown* was vaunted as "just the book that every advertising man has always said he'd go out and make for himself if he only had time."[27]

Those in the marketing business happily agreed, one expert pronouncing that the Lynds' book "automatically created a definite place for research study." He continued, "Cities like Muncie are undoubtedly the fundamental heart of America and, as such, they are the places where national marketers of products seek to place their goods." Muncie had of course become the "fundamental heart of America" only through the accident of being chosen for the Lynds' survey. For commercial interests seeking to expand their sales of consumer goods nationwide, however, new data about the habits of typical Americans in a typical community could only be good news. *Business Week* echoed this assessment in 1934, calling *Middletown* a godsend to marketers and noting that companies "preparing campaigns for refrigerators and automobiles found it helpful in charting the course of prospective buyers' expenditures, habits and desires."[28]

The equation of Middletowners with the general American consumer market only intensified in the years to follow. Economic statistics were still in their infancy in the 1930s, and policy makers eyed the second Middletown survey for its insights into consumer behavior and attitudes in the wake of the 1929 crash. As one analysis had it, "People almost gave up jewelry, built hardly any houses, bought few automobiles, went without candy, used their old furniture, and dined at home." More important, the Lynds' findings documented how credit buying and sales appeals worked to fuel nonnecessary consumption even during the depths of the Depression. Harcourt, Brace eagerly advertised that *Middletown in Tran-*

sition revealed "what boom and depression has [*sic*] done" not merely to individuals in Muncie, but "to the average American individual, his home, his city, his ideas, and his future." Even if the volume couldn't enlighten marketers as to superficial matters such as toothpaste preferences, noted a piece in *Advertising and Selling,* it had much more to offer on a deeper level about average America's "human wants." For this reason, *Tide* magazine noted, "admen and marketers will read it as a matter of course."[29]

By the time *Middletown in Transition* appeared in 1937, a sales journal could proclaim: "The only two books that are absolutely necessary for an advertising man are the Bible and MIDDLETOWN!" Scores of marketers were not content to stop there, but made pilgrimages to the site itself, a steady stream flocking to Muncie to find out what kinds of products "Mr. and Mrs. John Citizen of Middletown, U.S.A." were willing to buy. Trade journals as specialized as *Electrical Merchandising* made trips to Middletown to monitor sales figures and buying patterns. Marketers of school products seized upon Muncie—"as nearly the typical U.S. city as any in the country," with a school system "as typical as could be found" ("the administrator has typical problems, handles them typically" and "the Board of education, while smaller than U.S. average, is made up of typical members," it was noted)—as the ideal place for targeting their buyers. When the journal *Sales Management* commissioned a public relations survey on ordinary citizens' view of large corporations, this too entailed a visit to Muncie, indeed every twentieth residence thereof, to tap into the townspeople's ostensibly representative opinions. Middletown, the same journal commented approvingly, was the perfect "testing laboratory." The Lynds' field site, it seemed, had become not simply a social scientific object but a marketer's dream. *McCall's* magazine, which visited every Muncie subscriber's home to document "the re-enactment of typical examples" of residents using their products, certainly thought so. "Representative" communities like Middletown, noted the writer, "in the aggregate constitute by far the most important group of people sociologically and market-wise in America."[30]

To the marketers and advertisers who plumbed the Lynds' survey to discover the mind of the typical consumer, Middletown had become a synecdoche for America. Many others similarly relied on the cultural summation that the Lynds had provided, if for different purposes. A certain investment in Middletown as an icon for the nation, for example, was evident in Margaret Bourke-White's 1937 assignment to photograph Muncie for the brand-new *Life* magazine. The resulting photo essay was published to coincide with the début of *Middletown in Transition*. It cashed in on the city's status as the "typical community" and helped to establish the magazine's reputation as a chronicler of mainstream America in the process. Bourke-White's images—the vice president of a local union giving a member of the prominent Ball family a shave, the orderly rows of middle-class housing plots—were meant to encapsulate characteristic patterns of small-town life, work, and family. "Since Muncie, Ind. is today accepted as the typical U.S. city," the caption under one photograph read, "this picture is a vital document of U.S. life." The magazine announced, "Here, set down for all time, you may look at the average 1937 American as he really is." Readers' letters to *Life* included several from admirers of the "set of factual scenes" the photographer had produced, one raving that "in years to come it will be a priceless picture portfolio of the average 1937 town and its people." Bourke-White, added a complimentary reporter for the *Chicago Daily Tribune,* had "photographed some of the statistics, human, architectural, and natural of 'Middletown.'"[31]

Marketers, journalists, photographers, and social surveyors all joined the quest to determine and reaffirm the typical in the 1930s. This desire to locate average America, its contours and its contents, was especially pronounced in the years of economic hardship and domestic instability that followed the release of the first Middletown study. The Depression-era search for national unity, historians have argued, surfaced in celebrations of the "common man" and the "American Way of Life." This imperative helps explain how a social scientific study quite critical of tendencies in modern United States culture—its allegiance to habit, its lack of self-consciousness, its unexamined ideologies—could begin to mutate into something else entirely: an affirmation of the unchanging, essential, and even laudable core of American life.[32]

In 1929 many commentators had viewed *Middletown* as a "warts and all" description of a representative community. Reviewers credited the study, for example, with making evident not only "the material progress of the past thirty-five years" but also the "moral and spiritual decline." Many readers decried the ill effects of standardized work and leisure on Middletowners' existence, or used the Lynds' findings to decry the narrow-mindedness of American culture. The survey, for example, confirmed H. L. Mencken's suspicions about "the almost unbelieveable stupidities" of small-town Americans. Some cosmopolitan reviewers' disdain for Muncie as being representative, not of their own sensibilities, but of a middling, and mediocre, subset of the whole, was evident in his statement. However, even those who considered Middletown "Anytown" found something troubling in its portrait. They hoped, as did the Lynds, that the study would provoke a reconsideration of cultural habits. But as the 1930s progressed and the Depression took its course, the purportedly average American lifestyle that the Lynds described in their survey was slowly revalued, taking on a different, more generous cast. This was most apparent in national coverage of *Middletown in Transition,* which subtly shifted the meaning of the "typical" even as the Lynds' critique of it—notably Muncie's laissez-faire ideology and social inequities—intensified.[33]

The Lynds' second study, another best seller, won the same kind of plaudits for its objective approach to culture in the national media as had its predecessor, even if social scientific criticism was more abundant this time around. Many would echo the *Boston Herald*'s judgment that the study offered "countless trustworthy facts about the changes which have come in 10 years, through a time about which most people have only impressions." For a *Toledo Blade* writer, the scientific aspects of the volume—"the numerous graphs and statistical analyses, lengthy footnotes and appendices, five-syllable words and complicated tables"—still dazzled. And once again, there was glowing praise for the researchers' ability to distill modern America from the lifeways of a typical town. *Scribner's Magazine* asserted that the Lynds had chosen Muncie not for its small number of African Americans and immigrants, as the researchers had indicated in the introduction to the first study, but because of its "complete lack of distinction, its omnipresent and pervasive averageness": "Pick a man up from Springfield, Mass., or from Fresno, Calif., and set him in Middletown—and, despite all differences between New England hills, San Joaquin orchards, and Midwest flatlands, he will feel instantly at home."[34]

The tone of such reports had changed, however, between the first study and the second. Although a handful of commentators used *Middletown in Transition* as a platform for bewailing the entrenched laissez-faire beliefs of the populace, reviewers harbored few criticisms for its objects of study. Rather, by 1937 many were praising the modal American found in the Lynds' pages, some wondering if there was anything wrong with Muncie as the Lynds pictured it. The *Christian Century* reported on the Lynds' cataloguing of "the median American mind" without irony or distaste. Another commentator remarked that *Middletown in Transition* was "packed with the very stuff of American life," not at all intending this as a derogatory statement. One reporter could not remember another book that had "thrown such a clear light upon the American way of life." He admired "The Middletown Spirit"—the Lynds' 1937 summation of what Muncie believed—as the "most brilliant synthesis of the American credo of life and living that has been made in our generation." A writer for the *Chicago Herald-Exam-*

iner went further, offering a ringing endorsement of the Lynds' research site. "More cities like Middletown are needed here—good, sane, substantial, hard-working communities that breed the best citizens," he proclaimed. Reversing the surveyors' negative assessment of Muncie as an ostrich with its head in the sand, the commentator was reassured by their judgment that "Middletown remains singularly the same."[35]

In a period rife with international tensions, the commonality of the American people and their beliefs, as uncovered by the Lynds, could also be marshaled politically. Noting that Hitler's propaganda minister had referenced the Lynds' survey to argue that FDR did not speak for average Americans on the question of refugees from Nazism, the *New York Times* in 1938 stated, "Herr Goebbels no doubt considers himself a very well-informed man on America because he knows about one of our fine books, 'Middletown.'" But "what Herr Goebbels does not know about America," editorialized the paper as war loomed, "is that when it comes down to a test of American fundamentals, Mr. Roosevelt of Washington, and Mr. Smith of Middletown . . . think alike." Indeed, if one followed the Lynds, the two were united by their faith in the "land of opportunity," free enterprise, Christianity, progress, and in being loyal as well as "average." Patriotic Americans could coalesce around a set of values the investigators had identified. The social surveyors' microcosm had achieved symbolic purchase in the culture at large: there was clearly something comforting about a Middletown *not* in transition. Moreover, in some quarters the Lynds' account was being treated not simply as a descriptive account of American life, but as a prescriptive one—even in the typical community itself.[36]

Middletowners' status as typical Americans put them in a unique position to criticize that designation, not to mention the Lynds' broader understanding of American culture and how best to know it. After all, the objects of *Middletown*'s anthropological gaze had launched multiple challenges to the study's validity in 1929 and after. But although many in Muncie disputed their own characterization, they too would come to believe that "average America" was an objective reality and that Middletowners could serve as its spokespeople.

Like the first study, *Middletown in Transition* was a focus of curiosity and debate in "the town that represented typical American life," as a local bookstore offering special discounts for residents put it. Labor organizer Max Mathews wrote to Robert Lynd, "I have had time only to sketch and compare your new & old book, but believe me it has been town talk." Another Muncie resident corroborated this. "Every one is discussing the book, pro and con. Mostly con," she noted. A Catholic priest charged that the role of the church in Muncie had been drastically underplayed, while the publisher of a local newspaper was "mad as hell" about the researchers' claims of "financial influence" upon its content. One man in town wryly explained to Robert Lynd: "There was much howling over the city when your book first came out. Everybody read about himself first and was pretty sore. Then the folk read the other chapters and decided they got right down to the truth." The headline of the *Muncie Evening Star*'s report provided a rather concise summary: "Muncie Unlikely to Agree with Findings of Dr. Lynd."[37]

Admirers and detractors could agree that the Middletown surveys loomed large in Muncie. Sometimes the point was brought home humorously: a brief story in one of the local papers in 1937 detailing the hapless scheme of a local businessman was entitled "Don't Tell Lynd." Similarly, a local man joked, "Every time the average Middletowner sees pad and pencil in the hands of earnest-eyed persons of schoolteacherish demeanor he shies and makes for the nearest exit. Housewives divide their guesses as to the nature of the man at the door between 'it's another peddler,' and 'it's another

Lynd.'" The *Muncie Star* reported in the summer of 1935, at the conclusion of the follow-up study, that "Muncie will be able to draw its first easy breath in several weeks with the departure of Dr. Robert S. Lynd and associates." Loathed as it was by some, the Lynds' survey was what put Muncie on the map. In 1941, part of Muncie finally became "Middletown" via the Delaware County Housing Authority's Middletown Gardens housing project. Inviting Helen and Robert Lynd to the grand opening, a county official wrote: "We have been complimented many times for naming the principal street, Lynd Avenue."[38]

But for all their uneasiness with the Middletown surveys, and for all their rejection of some of the Lynds' findings, something of the allure of the typical would seep into the very terms of townspeople's arguments. Local reaction to the *Life* photo-shoot is instructive on this score. Other readers of the magazine had judged Bourke-White's images as faithfully documenting and memorializing American life as it was being lived. Those in Muncie begged once again to disagree. Initially many in town had been flattered by the attentions of a famous photographer. But *Life*'s supposedly definitive portrait would stir up plenty of controversy in the city it was meant to represent. As one of the Lynds' correspondents related after the Middletown issue hit the newsstands, the magazine had "the town mad as anything." He speculated that *Middletown in Transition* was meeting a better reception from locals than he had expected, but only "because they have a new villain, Margaret Bourke-White." Another would report that "the LIFE pictures were vigorously resented here, by practically everybody."[39]

What about the photographs had riled people? In eleven pages of images, two in particular—which pictured four Middletown living rooms of families ranging across the social spectrum—drew local fire. The Lynds' studies had classified 70 percent of Muncie's population as working class and only 30 percent as business class. Yet Muncie residents strongly objected to this visual depiction of class differences, the stark presentation of the shabby one-room shack in "Shedtown" alongside the opulent parlor of the Ball family. "Margaret White certainly did not lean toward Muncie's best features," observed one local woman. Penned a local partisan to *Life,* "Muncie is a town of interesting houses, beautiful churches and modern city buildings. Why did Margaret Bourke-White pass all these up?" Still another complained that although "there were many beautiful things Margurite Burk White [*sic*] could have taken," the photographer chose to focus on the town's negative qualities. This woman was glad she had denied the photographer access to her house and, referring to both Bourke-White and Robert Lynd, declared, "It will not be healthy for either one of them to visit Muncie again."[40]

It was not simply the fact that *Life* had depicted some of Middletown's less attractive aspects that ruffled its residents. It was that, in exposing the town's contrasts, the magazine had failed to capture what some believed to be the truly representative members of the community. One man described Bourke-White's approach this way: "She 'shot' the upper crust and the lower (soaked) crust, but left out the middle filling, which is the most important part of any community-pie." Similarly, a reporter for the *Muncie Press* wondered where the pictures were of the "good, substantial middle class." In a letter to *Life,* he echoed the Lynds' distinction between the "spectacular" and the "middle-of-the-road," protesting that, "The most common adverse criticism (and most of it was adverse) of your series on Muncie . . . was: 'They didn't show the average Muncie family—only extremes.'" Attempting to regain local control over the town's representation, he went so far as to append to the letter his own competing photographs of a truly typical Muncie family.[41]

This repeated emphasis on the middle, whether the "middle filling," the middle class, the "middle-of-the-road," or the largely implicit Middle West, illuminates what the typical was coming to mean in Middletown, as in the nation. In this understanding, a panoramic view of the diversity of Muncie's people and houses was not representative. Instead, "important," "good," and "substantial" middling people could best stand in for the whole. Bourke-White's accounting of class differences could thus be seen as showcasing "extremes." Growing economic disparities had of course been one of the Lynds' major findings in their survey, but the researchers' critical account of Middletown's ever-widening gap between working and business people had been lost in the rush to uphold average America. In this respect, *Life*'s images made unavoidable what much of the press coverage of the Lynds' studies had skirted—and this was precisely what angered so many in the "typical" community.

Sensitive about their portrayal in the Middletown surveys, many townspeople saw in the *Life* photographs yet another distortion of themselves and their community. To many in Muncie, the power to define their habits and values seemed to be in the hands of outsiders, whether social scientific experts or the national media. Middletowners' criticisms of the Lynds' surveys and Bourke-White's photographs revealed not just the community's boosterism but a deep suspicion of the impersonal representations that seemed so easily to trump local knowledge. But if the furor over *Life* magazine and the studies was, on the surface, about accuracy, bias, and the awkwardness of being under the investigator's microscope, it was more deeply rooted in a strange slippage between the typical and the good, the average and the ideal. The concepts had merged in much of the national coverage of *Middletown in Transition*. Likewise, a 1937 editorial in the *Muncie Morning Star* anticipated that Bourke-White's photo-shoot would reveal that Muncie was not only the most typical, but also the "best city of any its size" in terms of "its schools, its churches, its industries, its stores and its cultural life." Once the typical had been so thoroughly idealized, it was not surprising that it could not countenance the hard facts of class and poverty in Muncie.[42]

In fact, the convergence of norms and ideals in the "representative community" had begun early in the study's career, blurring scientific and commonsense understandings of the average. The very first mention of the Middletown survey in local papers in 1924 announced that the researchers had chosen Muncie for their investigation "because of its being a typical American city, devoid of a large foreign population and having diversified industries and interests." This was already a misreading of the Lynds' project, but it was not an uncommon one. The claim, usually with a touch of pride, to Middletown's typicality—often conflated with its being predominantly native-born—was a recurring theme in local reportage of the studies. Muncie's Chamber of Commerce, for instance, declared itself honored to represent "the most typical American City." It then went on to proclaim in its promotional materials that the community had been "selected as the ideal American City" (pointing to the statistic that 97.8 percent of Muncie's citizens were American-born as one of the reasons people came to live there), and even mounted a sign on Main Street reading "Muncie: The Ideal American City." This fusing of the typical and the ideal involved more than a booster's sleight of hand. It demonstrated the ease by which a particular kind of "middleness" was becoming a worthy aspiration, and how social surveyors could, even if inadvertently, create new cultural ideals.[43]

Although their experiences had taught them to be wary of scientific surveys, many in Middletown began to subscribe, if rather selectively, to their claims. As early as 1930 a local newspaper challenged the Lynds' portrayal of Muncie based on the remarks of a "statistician and research worker of New York City," who was "well qualified" to launch a critique based on his background doing "research study for many national advertisers." Years later, the *Muncie Star*'s editorial page declared itself proud that "business men down East use Muncie as one of their yard sticks." The editorialist, somewhat defensively, claimed that market researchers "consider Muncie an average American city and their opinion is not based on the book that was written by the bicycle author who visited Muncie some years ago." He noted that the editorial director of *Collier's* magazine "'made' Muncie regularly and he learned that the city was made up of average American citizens. [His] opinion is that what is read in Muncie will be read the country over. And he's right."[44]

Middletowners, it is evident, could simultaneously be dismayed by their social scientific portrait and eager to be called average. In this light, perhaps the strangest offshoot of the Lynds' work was a contest run by the *Muncie Evening Press* in 1937 to locate the town's most "typical American family." The designation was based solely on the Lynds' statistics and had as its prize a trip to Chicago and New York—the latter sponsored by the National Institute for Straight Thinking. One of the Lynds' local correspondents noted that although it was "too early yet to announce definitely whether the typical Muncie family wishes to be known as such," quite a few contestants had filled out questionnaires. The eventual winners, above and beyond fitting the statistical profile, professed to "believe in every opinion cited by Dr. Lynd as held by the typical Muncie resident." The national press had fastened upon Middletowners as typical Americans, paving the way for marketers and Muncie residents alike to employ the claim for their own purposes. Unusually homogeneous, native-born, middle-of-the-road Middletown had become an icon of "average" American life. And this, it seemed, was a title worth competing for.[45]

As their enraged reaction to *Life* magazine's unflattering photographs demonstrated, Muncie folk as well as national audiences had a strong investment in the typical. Told again and again over the course of the 1930s that they exemplified the best qualities of average America, Middletowners began to believe it. "We think we are a typical city of typical Americans. We do not mind being in the nation's spotlight," announced Muncie's mayor in 1937. A Muncie-born bishop reflected that because of where he grew up, he had often been characterized as an "average American." His response to such remarks was, "Yes, I am just an average American from an average American city where civilization is at its best." Local businessmen also understood the label's worth. One of Robert Lynd's correspondents let him know that although local newspapers had at first been angered by their characterization in *Middletown in Transition,* their advertising departments were mollified by the fact that the book was attracting "some of those profitable 'test tube' national accounts." Muncie businesses, staggering through the Depression, were not averse to depictions of their community as average. Several years after the second study, a local writer observed that national advertisers had taken to using the town as "a testing ground for their products, thinking that if these would 'go' in this city they should sell everywhere." Happy to claim the label *typical,* so long as it was confirmed by others than the Lynds, some in town literally gained from the designation.[46]

Despite Middletowners' protestations, the widespread circulation of the Lynds' facts—coupled with an urgent desire for information about "ourselves" at a moment of uncertainty about the national community—had allowed a survey of a single midwestern town to constitute the U.S. mainstream. As stand-ins for the average American and as an icon for the nation, it appeared that Middletowners and Middletown were more palatable to the Lynds' multiple audiences than the country's vast and challenging diversity.

The Road from Middletown

This valorization of the average could not have been what *Middletown*'s authors expected. Robert and Helen Lynd had shied away from labeling Muncie as "typical," but saw Middletown quickly enshrined as the epitome of American life. Robert Lynd would later disavow the label more explicitly. "I was always careful to avoid calling Muncie 'typical,'" he wrote to a reporter for the

Muncie Star in 1960. "The Chamber of Commerce gave it that name, & since then the advertisers, et al., have carried it on." His comment underscores a second irony: the Lynds sought to reverse the corroding effects of a commercial culture, but saw their "representative" research site used as a basis for extensive test-marketing and scientific selling. Perhaps most significantly, the amateur anthropologists attempted through the device of the naïve observer to heighten awareness of disturbing tendencies in modern America, only to watch their critical portrait reified as "how things are." In the end, the Lynds' concerns with economic irrationalities and class divides were overshadowed by the all-too-compelling portrait they painted of typical America. This, more than any sort of social critique, would be *Middletown*'s legacy.[47]

In yet another twist, the researchers had despaired at Middletown's lack of self-knowledge, finding its people unable to see their culture for what it was. Yet what they unleashed was a virtual industry of studying Muncie and, through it, "average" American life. Middletown would achieve the status of being the "most studied community" in all of American social science, meaning that the afterlife of the Lynds' studies would be as significant as their original appearance. Muncie, chosen in part for its atypicality, became a scientific "everytown" after 1929, subject to one survey or poll after another, whether by marketers, political analysts, or sociologists. As a local reporter explained half a century later, Middletown was "the place to analyze, to look at, to probe for the 'typical' American reaction to almost anything, from Jimmy Carter's presidency to the impact of divorce on school children to the marketability of a new dog food." One Muncie resident mused in 1982: "The rest of the world perhaps will pardon us if we express the wish that the Lynds had climbed off the train in some other town."[48]

Nearly all of these successors to the Lynds took it on faith that a town chosen for its purportedly small percentages of ethnic and racial minorities could represent the nation. Even in times more politically attuned to a differentiated America, social scientific rules of longitudinal comparison kept a truly representative Muncie from view. As Theodore Caplow, Middletown's most prolific scholar apart from the Lynds, has acknowledged, later studies of the town were straitjacketed by the lack of early data on African Americans as well as Catholics, Jews, and immigrants. A form of social scientific collusion thus kept Middletown whiter, more native-born, and more homogeneous than it actually was. Replications of the Lynds' original questionnaires and survey schedules in the 1970s and 1980s, perhaps not surprisingly, uncovered the centrality of traditional family and religious values to Middletown's—and by inference, the United States'—population. In the end, the Lynds had indeed chosen a "representative community." But what it represented was less an empirically typical place than an ideologically loaded argument about which Americans properly stood for the nation.[49]

Yet in 1929 it was Middletown's *unusualness* as a social scientific specimen that stood out. As an anthropological entity, it was unique because it was not "primitive" or foreign. As a sociological one, it was remarkable because its people were not deemed deviant or abnormal. Part of what made Muncie fascinating to contemporary observers was the fact that it had been studied at all. That a community could enthrall simply because it had been surveyed speaks to the powerful hold social scientific techniques were coming to have on the public imagination. The fact that it *did* enthrall meant that it would soon seem not peculiar, but obvious, that one could know America by surveying Middletown.

In a lecture at Princeton University in 1938, Robert Lynd reflected upon the role his surveys had played in the culture at large. A decade after *Middletown* was published, he admitted that the overwhelming praise for and staying power of the study gave him pause.

He noted that he became "uneasy" when people would "over-play" the Middletown research or treat him as an authority on American life. Pointing out weaknesses in the studies, Lynd called them "a good try, but not that good!" Continuing in this vein, Lynd announced that his and Helen Lynd's analysis of what Middletown "seems to think or feel" was "simply our best jud[gmen]t based on what evidence we managed to get. Now that's baby science!" Were they to do it over again, he asserted, the researchers would have collected life histories, designed better instruments for measuring attitudes and opinions, and focused more intently on a specific research problem, whether the class system or the power structure. Lynd ultimately belittled the empirical quality and scientific authority of the research, comparing his technique in the Middletown studies to a "sensitive news reporter's" and cautioning readers against "false awe."[50]

The social scientist's reflections might have offered a useful counterweight to the way the Middletown studies operated in the public sphere. But it was too late for that. Breaking away from older, reform-oriented survey conventions and acting as anthropologists of contemporary culture, the Lynds—in a particularly authoritative way, and at a critical juncture in national life—had created a new social scientific object: "average America." Given its wide circulation, the study's vision of who and what was typical, and equally, who and what was marginal, would be broadly influential.

It was not just the Lynds who, in looking back at *Middletown,* found their research method rudimentary. By the late 1930s a growing number of sociologists and statisticians would claim that the Lynds' understanding of Muncie as America was flawed. Indeed, there were critics who charged that the Middletown studies were not social science at all. One scholarly reviewer contrasted the Lynds' methods with "the task of scientific sociological research." The researchers' attitude toward the culture they studied, and especially their apparent adherence to a "social creed," was "appropriate to the theological seminary" but not the academy, he maintained. The *Journal of the American Statistical Association* judged the technique of the Middletown studies to be "far beyond that of the sociological novel" but not yet "concerned with the problem of generalizing illuminating incidents, anecdotes, and case studies into a system of principles or laws." Others were unpersuaded by the conceit of studying the United States through the lifeways of a single community. The reviewer for the *American Journal of Sociology* charged that the anthropological approach—the idea that "Middletown and its people can be studied in the total situation in much the same fashion as an isolated primitive tribe"—was itself "questionable" since Middletown's "total situation" was not Muncie but the whole of the United States.[51]

These scientific cautions about how properly to represent America were signs of change. And yet other surveying ventures would be similarly influential in shaping the nation they purported only to describe—not only by publicizing facts about the "mainstream," but also by subjecting more and more citizens to their scrutiny. This was especially true of two intertwined fields of social inquiry that were just maturing as the Lynds wrote up their second study of Muncie. Market research, a bundle of techniques for probing consumer desires, was the first. Public opinion polling, a newly systematic method for discerning the "people's voice," was the second. Both would become ubiquitous, if contentious, methods of surveying the nation in the decades to come.

3

Polling the Average Populace

The polls are charting virtually unexplored sectors of the public mind, discovering where the contours are sharp and jagged, and where they are covered in mist and fog.

—George Gallup and Saul Forbes Rae, 1940

I saw [opinion polling] as a veritable gold mine if we could learn fast enough how to use it in all of its ramifications. And also I saw this as a potentially great tool for democracy.

—Elmo Roper, 1968

"What is the common man thinking?" asked George Gallup, along with his collaborator Saul Forbes Rae, in 1940. Offering "a modern answer," they announced the birth of "a new instrument—the public opinion poll," which could "provide a continuous chart of the opinions of the man in the street." Gallup and fellow "scientific pollsters" Archibald Crossley and Elmo Roper made a dramatic entrance onto the national stage in 1936. Each publicly challenged the famous *Literary Digest* straw poll, an established survey of ten million Americans, which had correctly projected the outcome of the past five presidential elections. All three surveyors supplemented the *Digest*'s mail-in ballot method with one-on-one interviews. More astonishingly, employing scientific sampling, they relied upon a fraction of the magazine's respondents to arrive at their forecasts of how Americans would vote. And, unlike the *Literary Digest*, each predicted—correctly, it turned out—that Democrat Franklin D. Roosevelt would prevail over Republican Alfred Landon.[1]

Pinning the legitimacy of their novel technique to the very public test of an election was risky, and a decision the pollsters may well have regretted later. But the bet paid off, enabling surveyors like Gallup and Roper to make strong claims for their new science and its ability to reflect the views of the American public. Soon enough, pollsters were weighing in on not just electoral races but citizens' opinions on topics ranging from war plans to tax policy, working women to venereal disease, radio programs to dental care. By 1940, just four years after the pollsters' crucial election-day victory, an estimated eight million people encountered George Gallup's triweekly report, *America Speaks!*, in the form of a syndicated newspaper column. A decade later, more than a million people were interviewed annually by the likes of Gallup or Roper.[2]

Pollsters and their close allies in the field of market research claimed to uncover what the American public wanted. They located that public in a different way than had the Lynds, whose mix of quantitative and anecdotal reportage was already coming to seem outmoded by the mid-1930s. Whereas *Middletown*'s authors had tapped into the contemporary United States via a "representative" community, pollsters devised more ambitious tools for tracking the nation. As part of a movement away from the community survey and toward modern sampling methods, George Gallup, Elmo Roper, and their colleagues developed statistical techniques that permitted a tiny cross-section of citizens of different regions, classes, and races to stand in for the whole. Their scope was national rather than local, their subjects no longer rooted in a specific, if generalizable, geographic place. Pollsters' respondents were quite deliberately *not* a collection of neighbors, identifiable by particular quirks or characteristics. Rather, they were a scattered collection of individuals, strangers to each other, linked only by percentages marking majorities and minorities. Muncie was an actual community that became a placeholder for the nation. Pollsters worked in the opposite direction, gathering atomized bits of opinion and then grafting them together so that they might speak for "America."

The public that opinion researchers fashioned was not a fixed entity but a constantly evolving one, taking shape through thousands of separate surveys conducted over the middle decades of the century. Like market researchers who fashioned a composite consumer out of discrete, privately expressed preferences, the questions pollsters put to anonymous respondents created, in the words of George Gallup, a "week-by-week picture of what Americans are thinking." As the Lynds had, pollsters and marketers designed their America-in-capsule informed by certain assumptions, chief among them the notion that there was something such as a national public, more or less united, to be discovered; that there was value in knowing it; and that theirs were the best tools for revealing it. Another of their suppositions was that the marketplace of goods and the marketplace of social and political expression were analogous, and could be measured through the selfsame techniques.[3]

There was a significant difference, however. Market researchers deposited their data behind closed doors, defining the consuming public for a private corporate audience. Opinion polls, by contrast, were placed in plain view of the public they measured. Like the Lynds' typical community, Gallup and Roper's "man in the street" simultaneously simplified social life and complicated the usual ways people had come to know it. More distant from the individuals upon whom they depended for data than were the Middletown surveys, public opinion polls would play a key role in mediating between "the people" and the nation in the decades after 1936.

In Search of Average Opinion

In his manifesto for the scientific public opinion poll, Gallup did not pause to explain why Americans might be interested in knowing the thoughts of the "common man." Perhaps this was because, to both pollsters and their audiences, the answer was self-evident. "Public opinion," a vaguely defined but powerful entity, had been a force to reckon with in republican regimes since at least the French Revolution. In the United States, where majority rule and political legitimacy, in principle anyway, hinged upon knowing the people's will, assessing the national mood was a time-honored pastime for journalists, politicians, and social critics. In this sense, the scientific poll was simply the latest claimant to a long tradition—even if it was, as Gallup suggested, a distinctly precise and systematic variant.[4]

Certainly, before Gallup and Roper arrived on the scene there were manifold ways to gauge public sentiment, including speeches, petitions, rallies, riots, strikes, elections, and letters to the editor. There were also attempts to canvass political opinions, notably in the straw polls that many U.S. newspapers ran during election seasons beginning in the 1820s. Designed for readers' entertainment and partisan jockeying, these "straws" were conducted by reporters as well as interested citizens. Political scientist Susan Herbst cites the example of a man who in his abundant train travels in the summer of 1856 took it upon himself to question 2,886 people for a total of twenty-three separate polls on the upcoming presidential contest. Still more intriguing, the *New York Times* published them all. Supplementing the straw polls were what Herbst calls "people's polls": surveys that workers, students, farmers, fraternities, clubs, and neighbors took of their own communities and then submitted to newspapers as evidence of popular support for electoral candidates. Especially when they aligned with the editor's political affiliations, these too were printed and circulated. Several national magazines joined the straw poll field after the turn of the century, the first entrants being the *Farm Journal* in 1912 and the *Literary Digest* in 1916, followed by the Hearst newspapers, *Pathfinder,* the *Nation, College Humor,* and the *Woman's Home Companion.*[5]

Measurable opinions—in the service not of entertainment but of management and control—were simultaneously becoming an object of keen interest within universities, industry, and the federal government. In their 1918 study of immigrant families' adaptation to American cities, University of Chicago sociologists W. I. Thomas and Florian Znaniecki were among the first to quantify subjective attitudes. Following their lead, social scientists developed questionnaires, interviews, and attitude scales to test the intensity and malleability of individual perceptions on subjects ranging from voting behavior to race relations. A new corps of industrial psychologists, responding to problems of productivity in the workplace (as well as corporations' consuming interest in the topic), designed tools to measure worker morale, most famously in Elton Mayo's experiments at the Hawthorne Works of the Western Electric Company from 1927 to 1932. Awakening to the benefits of opinion assessment, the Roosevelt administration formed a Division of Rural Attitudes and Opinion within the Department of Agriculture at precisely the same moment that Gallup and Roper were preparing to take on the *Literary Digest*. The federal government became directly involved with ongoing attitude surveys through the establishment of the National Opinion Research Center in 1941. As these developments suggest, scientific pollsters were just one party to a broad twentieth-century search for what James Beniger terms "mass feedback technologies." Such feedback was becoming increasingly vital to advertisers, state agencies, and politicians who desired knowledge about the national public in order to "attract and hold its attention," "stimulate and control its consumption behavior," and "influence its opinions and its vote."[6]

The very notion that something like a "mass public" existed lent a palpable urgency to discussions of American opinion in the years following World War I. Worries over mass production, mass entertainment, and "the masses" themselves—the tension between conformity and individualism, the tendency toward mediocrity, echoes of Tocqueville's tyranny of the majority—had preoccupied cultural critics since the latter half of the nineteenth century. Concerns about large-scale bureaucracy, the complexity of modern affairs, and the new suasion of advertisers and propagandists mingled in the first decades of the new century to make "the public" one of the core problems of modern democratic politics. The war itself, its mobilization of minds as well as bodies, raised these issues directly. The head of the U.S. Committee on Public Information, George Creel, observed that the war was not fought solely on the battlefields of France. "It was [a] fight for the minds of men, for the 'conquest of their convictions,' and the battle-line ran through every home in every country." He boasted that it was in the "recognition of Public Opinion as a major force that the Great War differed most essentially from all previous conflicts" and that his committee had stepped up to the task, launching a "plain publicity proposition, a vast enterprise in salesmanship, the world's greatest adventure in advertising."[7]

Creel, alongside new "public relations" proponents such as Edward Bernays, applauded such efforts to filter information—whether about the enemy or consumer goods—through expert channels. Propaganda, in this view, was simply the most efficient method for communicating ideas to the populace. Most, however, cast a jaundiced eye on the techniques by which populations could be persuaded. Journalist Walter Lippmann and philosopher John Dewey were only the most prominent thinkers to worry about citizens' capacity for meaningful and informed decision making in an age of mass organization. Lippmann (himself the editor of a propaganda unit during the war) fell on the skeptical side of this debate, and Dewey on the hopeful, but their argument stands in for a whole host of misgivings about the size, scale, and competence of the modern U.S. public. Developments abroad in the 1930s only sharpened the apprehension, as Americans watched Hitler and Mussolini harness the mass media to appeal to populations that seemed only too willing to cede their individuality and rationality. From the 1930s to the 1950s, discussions of "the masses" and their susceptibility to persuasion flowed from many quarters, not just journals of social criticism but communications research outfits and psychology laboratories. In these years, Solomon Asch's and Kurt Lewin's psychological theories of suggestibility and Elihu Katz and Paul Lazarsfeld's sociological findings on the personal influence of "opinion leaders" posed Lippmann's and Dewey's questions anew. Proffering a democratic, scientific, and "modern" answer to this dilemma, pollsters would secure a sturdy niche for their profession.[8]

In the early decades of the century, however, the most vigorous seekers of a science of opinion were not state agencies, university social scientists, propagandists, or even pollsters, but commercial researchers. Marketers' and advertisers' rapt interest in *Middletown* hinted at the close association emerging between social research and sales. The Lynds' studies dovetailed with the avid search for business facts, their critique of commodity culture with a concerted drive to promote demand for consumer goods nationwide. When pollsters Elmo Roper and Archibald Crossley merged their expertise in gathering social data with their search for commercially useful knowledge—establishing a "'laboratory' for fundamental research in marketing problems" in a series of "test-tube" cities— they were not doing anything unusual. This venture (Middletowns, Inc.) they even described as a "Middletown of advertising."[9]

The marketing profession had its roots in the economics of abundance, specifically the problem of excess production in the last decades of the nineteenth century and again in the early 1920s. Forced to concoct new ways to stimulate spending, many businesses shifted their attention from manufacturing to marketing, from needs to desires, and from products to consumers. Modern advertisers cut their teeth on convincing Americans to forsake out-of-date economic motives, to labor for a higher standard of living, and to purchase items they had not known they needed from window displays and mail-order catalogues. By the early twentieth century, "ad men had entered into a new social relation with the public, one in which, with ever-growing resources, they bent their efforts to the creation of wants." Herbert Hoover's Committee on Recent Economic Changes—itself formed in 1929 to gather accurate data about the national economy—testified to marketers' success in this regard. The committee found that even as Americans met their primary needs for food, clothing, and shelter, their "wants are almost insatiable; that one want satisfied makes way for another." It named advertising and "scientific fact finding" as key components of the demand equation.[10]

Scientific approaches to selling lagged behind Frederick Winslow Taylor's innovations in scientific management in the 1910s, but they were often billed as the necessary correlate to more efficient production. Already by the turn of the century and long before the U.S. Department of Commerce began supplying systematic economic data in 1929, some businesses were estimating their markets by mining available city and census statistics, running crude tests of advertising effectiveness, and surveying storekeepers. Still, it was only in 1911, after overcoming "considerable resistance from business men," that commercial research came into its own as a field with the establishment of the Bureau of Business Research at Harvard's Graduate School of Business.[11]

Business historian Richard Tedlow has made the case that the distinctive U.S. contribution to selling was the concept of "profit through volume." This strategy required not just the assembly lines of mass production, but new methods of mass marketing. Companies sought to stretch regional markets into national ones, to increase recognition for branded products, and to create constant demand for items that once had been seasonal, such as soda fountain drinks and pancake syrup. With mass consumption the goal, corporations were particularly determined to find the national "average," the widest possible market for their homogeneous goods. J. George

Frederick, editor of the journal *Advertising and Selling,* waxed eloquent on the subject. "The law of averages," he wrote in 1920, was a "delicate and wonderfully useful tool." Frederick explained that whereas "an individual man is easy enough to study as to his age, sex, color, height, weight, etc., . . . most facts which concern large groups are hidden." This was where the magic of the statistical average came in: the concept could apply to anything from the "composition of soil to the emotional reaction of a woman bargain hunter." As Frederick saw it, the average was something to be sought, calculated, and led by. For without it, many commercial products were "planned and shaped for a minority rather than a majority of users . . . not for the average man, but the exceptional or rare prospect."[12]

Locating that average man was more difficult than it sounded, especially in a nation as ethnically and regionally various as the United States. C. S. Duncan, professor of commercial organization at the University of Chicago, noted that in their quest for this consumer, businessmen could look to already-existing data. He pointed to a military study revealing that in World War I men wore a larger shoe size than they had in previous wars as one such useful nugget of information. But rather than discovering such crucial facts by chance, he implored, merchants needed to conduct their own research. "The day of shrewd guesses in business is fast drawing to a close," he warned in 1919; "the urgent demand now is for facts which have been carefully collected and scientifically analyzed." Other advocates of market research in the early 1920s preached social scientific methods vigorously to the not yet converted. J. George Frederick, for one, pummeled his readers with the indispensability of "facts" to business success. The savvy businessman, he wrote in *Business Research and Statistics,* "will elongate his ears and extend his eyesight by making use of modern investigative and research science." Reliable sales required neither intuition, genius, native business ability, nor direct knowledge of the customer but "fact-getting, fact-weighing and fact-compari-son." Slowly but surely, Frederick's advice would be heeded. By the 1930s, businesses were depending upon experts, rather than their own sense of things, to determine how best to move products.[13]

Research into consumer desires—measuring not what individuals actually purchased but what they said they *wanted* to buy—developed haphazardly. Advertising agencies, notably J. Walter Thompson's, began gathering some such data on consumers for their clients as early as 1915. Discussions of questionnaires and mail surveys at this stage usually assumed that these methods were aimed not at "the man in the street" but at those with secondary knowledge of consumer preferences. The questions Duncan proposed for the novice market researcher—"Does the customer demand a certain brand?" and "Is the purchaser insistent on getting the brand asked for?"—were directed to the storekeeper or distributor, one or even two steps away from the consumer him- or herself. Increasingly, however, experts trained in opinion gathering went straight to the source. The Psychological Corporation, established in 1921 as a survey outfit offering the expertise of psychological consultants, began running continuous polls of consumers in 1932. Its first "Brand Barometer" study was based upon personal interviews with 1,578 housewives. Consumer panels or "juries," popular with big corporations such as General Foods, the *Woman's Home Companion,* and General Motors, similarly relied upon a set of regular interviewees who agreed to evaluate food products, listen to radio programs, or react to magazine advertisements.[14]

Stimulating demand was becoming the chief province of commercial research. This in turn meant questioning consumers thoroughly, whether through panels, questionnaires, or door-to-door surveys. Such research could be quite invasive. Radio audience studies, an early and intensive area of market research, often entailed entering consumers' living rooms to track program preferences as well as the demographic groups turning the dial. The Nielsen Company, for example, sent a representative once a month to every home in which one of its "audimeters" was installed in order to exchange the used recording tape for a new one. But that was not all. While inside, the representative would also take "an inventory of radio-advertised commodities (found in the pantry, bathroom, etc.)" to determine the impact of particular broadcasts, hoping to trace systematically the steps between advertisement and purchase. Through such methods, the power of expert opinion surveyors and the power of "the people" as consumers were becoming symbiotically connected. The creation of an ever bigger and more standardized mass market in the early decades of the century was in this way tightly linked to survey techniques. These same tools, some perceived, were capable of bringing another entity, the "American public," into sharper focus.[15]

Commercial researchers may have been precocious in devising ways to glean the preferences of the American public, but they would soon have plenty of company. Inspired by innovations in marketing, George Gallup, Elmo Roper, Archibald Crossley, and a host of other "pollers" transferred the techniques honed for selling soap and cereal from the buying to the voting public. The rise of social and political issue polling was inextricably tied to commercial research, and the boundary between the two fields was porous. In a 1940 speech to a business audience, Roper granted chronological preeminence to the marketers, asserting that it was "the advertising men" who deserved credit for "the early development of the technique which has been evolved for sampling public opinion." The "big three" pollsters each got their start not in academic attitude research or in journalistic straw polling, but in the world of business. They were first and foremost market researchers, devoted to the science of improving corporate profitability through carefully crafted advertising campaigns and public relations stratagems.[16]

This commingling of marketing and other kinds of survey research was by no means an unusual path for social scientists of the time. Robert Lynd, too, had spent a short stint as an advertising man early in his career. Already wary of business tactics by the time he traveled to Muncie, however, he became an increasingly vocal critic of the profession. By the time *Knowledge for What?* came out in 1939, Lynd was an avowed foe of corporate advertisers and what he considered to be their manipulation of unwitting consumers. Not so the victorious triumvirate of 1936. Gallup, Roper, and Crossley, alongside fellow opinion surveyors like Hadley Cantril and Henry Link, made no bones about their involvement in market research, their dogged search for "Mr. and Mrs. Consumer." Gallup, who won the first of many awards for his "distinguished contribution to advertising research" in 1935, emphasized the similarities in "how people think . . . from politics to tooth paste." Roper announced in 1940 that he would rather be known as a "Marketing Consultant" than a "Poll-Taker."[17]

Archibald Crossley was the earliest to enter the polling field. Just graduated from Princeton in 1918, he was looking for a copywriting job at an advertising agency when, to his surprise, he was asked to create from scratch the J. H. Cross Company's research department. Apart from census data, he had little to go on in his quest for facts, but Crossley took the job and managed to build a research division for the firm. He moved on to four years of advertising research at the *Literary Digest,* coincidentally enough, establishing his own market research company in 1926. Crossley, Inc., completed a study of the national appetite for shredded wheat, its first project, only after borrowing a staff of part-time interviewers from the Philadelphia Federal Reserve. Crossley made his real mark in radio research, however. He founded the Cooperative Analysis of Broadcasting for the Association of National Advertisers and the monthly Crossley Radio Survey in 1930, early ventures into the burgeoning field of audience ratings, soon to be joined by C. E. Hooper and A. C. Nielsen. This in turn led the Hearst newspapers to engage Crossley's services as an election forecaster in 1936. Despite his successful prediction for FDR, however, the surveyor—who was perhaps in a unique position to know—"did not think the market would bear a third poll of public opinion outside of the presidential campaign season," and he decided to stay in market research almost exclusively. Elmo Roper and George Gallup, equally bound to the world of marketing, were thus positioned to become opinion polling's household names.[18]

The Nebraska-born Elmo Roper was first exposed to the power of surveys when crisscrossing the country in 1933 for a jewelry company, asking stores which engagement and wedding rings were selling and why. Richardson Wood at the J. Walter Thompson advertising agency got wind of the survey and was intrigued. As Roper later recalled, "That was the first time in my life that I had ever heard the words 'marketing research.'" He was soon introduced to Paul Cherington, a professor at Harvard's School of Business, and the two joined up with Wood to form a market research consulting practice in New York City. In 1937, Roper, like Crossley, created his own firm, signing up corporate clients such as the American Meat Institute, Standard Oil, the Tea Bureau, Ford Motor Company, Time, Inc., the National Broadcasting Company, RCA-Victor, and Spiegel, Inc.[19]

Two years beforehand, Roper's other career—public opinion polling—was launched when he became the director of *Fortune* magazine's new Quarterly Survey. Aimed at a "business oriented audience," the poll experimented with sampling and personal interviews to deduce national trends in opinion. Roper, who drew upon contacts developed while a traveling salesman to recruit a corps of interviewers, later called this the "first-ever scientifically conducted poll." It was so novel that even the publisher of *Fortune* was skeptical, as were many readers, who although interested in the survey did not put much stock in its findings. By 1938, however, Roper's survey was coming out monthly, and he had embarked upon another project for *Fortune*, the "Consumer Outlook," which charted subjective attitudes toward the economy. Through these national surveys, Roper quickly became known as an authority on public opinion. Sought out like many others for his expertise during World War II, Roper took a post as deputy director of the Office of Strategic Services responsible for public opinion research, and as a special consultant to the War Production Board and the Office of War Information. More central to his national reputation, Roper authored a weekly column, "What People Are Thinking," for the *New York Herald Tribune* and syndicated papers beginning in 1944, hosted a weekly radio program for CBS called *Where the People Stand* beginning in 1948, and then for NBC beginning in 1952, and served regularly as a television commentator.[20]

Just a few months after the debut of the Fortune Survey in 1935, George Gallup's first syndicated national poll, *America Speaks!* appeared. But the man who would become the most famous of the pollsters had been interested in tapping into public opinion long before that. Perhaps thinking of *Middletown,* a writer for the *New Yorker* quipped that it might have been Gallup's childhood in "utterly normal" Jefferson, Iowa, that made it seem natural to him that the views of a small group might reflect those of all Americans. More directly, it was Gallup's early work in audience research that drew him into his future career as a pollster. Gallup pinned his interest in public opinion to a summer job he had taken while an undergraduate at the State University of Iowa in 1922, canvassing readers' views about the *St. Louis Post-Dispatch.* This eventually led to his Ph.D. dissertation of 1928 in applied psychology at Iowa, entitled "An Objective Method for Determining Reader Interest in the Content of a Newspaper." Financed by Gardner Cowles Jr., the newspaper publisher who would later create *Look* magazine with the assistance of the pollster's insights, Gallup's dissertation—and the readership studies he conducted during his short tenure as a journalism professor at Iowa, Drake, and Northwestern universities—attracted more than mere scholarly attention. Poring through newspaper issues page-by-page to find out precisely what respondents had read (comic strips, obituaries, and features much more than international news and editorials, it turned out) became known in the marketing world as the "Gallup Method." Lever Brothers was the first to take advantage of the technique, contacting Gallup the day after learning about his readership studies and hiring him as an advertising consultant in 1931. The Hearst Sunday papers and General Foods were not far behind. Young & Rubicam hired Gallup the next year as its director of research. "I had only one assignment and that was to find out all I could about how advertising works and how to make it more effective," the pollster later remarked.[21]

Gallup remained in Young & Rubicam's employ for fifteen years. During this time, on weekends and lunch breaks, he created what became known as the Gallup Poll. The *Literary Digest* had conducted some issue polling once a year, notably on attitudes toward Prohibition. Gallup, however, had the brainstorm of "polling on every major issue—a continuing poll on issues of the day." It was an idea that easily gained the support of the Publishers Syndicate. As it was for Roper, opinion polling was the work Gallup would become known for, but it was not the work that made him a living. Lucrative ventures like Audience Research Inc.—which Gallup cofounded in 1937 as a consulting firm to moviemakers such as Walt Disney, Paramount, and David O. Selznick—and the Opinion Research Corporation, which he established a year later, would take care of that. Gallup nevertheless created a polling empire with his 1935 founding of the American Institute of Public Opinion (AIPO) in New York and Princeton, New Jersey, adding international affiliates in subsequent years. Its reports, first issued weekly but soon two and then three and four times a week, were published in major metropolitan newspapers across the country: 60 of them in 1935, and 106 by 1940. Upon its first release, *America Speaks!* was called by *News-Week* the "most ambitious newspaper feature ever devised." Gallup's name was on its way to becoming virtually synonymous with opinion polling.[22]

Market research proponent J. George Frederick had written triumphantly in 1920, "It is no longer necessary to regard the states of mind of consumers . . . as matters to be guessed at in business, since they can be reduced to the forms of reliable statistics." Two decades later, Gallup must have sensed his achievement when he proclaimed, "The polls are charting virtually unexplored sectors of the public mind." For Gallup and Roper, market research and public opinion polling had fundamentally the same promise: each held out the possibility, as Roper put it, of knowing the "mass mind."[23]

A "Tool for Democracy"

The founder of the Gallup Poll had preached the virtues of a science of opinion beginning with his readership studies in graduate school. As early as 1930 he was arguing that the common methods of gauging opinion—"protest letters and fan letters, conversations of editors' friends, contests, questionnaires, interviews"—were "inaccurate and untrustworthy." Once the 1936 election was behind him, he would portray the break between the "Straw Vote Era" and the "Modern Polling Era" as stark and decisive, the latter substituting "candid-camera studies" for "impressionistic and florid descriptions," systematically culled data for erratic local knowledge. Aware that maintaining a united front enhanced their image as a group of seekers after scientific truth, Gallup and his colleagues swiftly built a modern profession. They forged links with academic social scientists, contributed to scholarly journals such as *Public Opinion Quarterly*, formed their own credentialing organization (the American Association of Public Opinion Research), banded together with their competitors when necessary, and most of all, made tenacious and oft-repeated claims to the objectivity and precision of their particular kind of knowledge.[24]

Pollsters labored to present themselves as scientists rather than political beings. Indeed, Gallup regularly publicized the fact that he did not vote. Furthermore, he asserted: "We have not the slightest interest in who wins an election. All we want to do is be right." Gallup, who always placed "Doctor" in front of his name, said that he was drawn to public opinion work first as a researcher and scientist. Measuring public opinion, in his view, required a "'laboratory' attitude of mind" and researchers "trained in the scientific method," who excised bias through "constant vigilance, self-questioning, and experiment." His polling organization was not content to rest there. The AIPO announced that it was gradually "building up a neutral vocabulary—a public-opinion glossary—within the comprehension of the mass of people" to ensure absolutely accurate results from its questioning. Roper, active in liberal causes and an advisor to and supporter of Democratic candidates for office, was much more likely to reveal his political views. Yet he maintained a neutral stance when it came to the production of his research. The job of the public opinion analyst, Roper explained in a broadcast for CBS, entailed "divesting himself of all emotional bias" and "approach[ing] the problem detachedly." Despite differences in outlook, the two major pollsters agreed that public opinion polls could be an objective and scientifically accurate gauge.[25]

Gallup and Roper, in their telling of it, were special kinds of authorities: experienced in discerning the "people's voice" but with no interest in swaying it, able to tabulate public preferences but with no investment in policy making. Quintessentially modern experts, they were pledged to exact measurement with no regard to the content of what they were measuring. At the same time, they hitched their scientific vocabulary to a civic one. Distinguishing themselves from other pretenders to knowledge of the public mind—newspaper editors, political commentators, and "so-called 'thought leaders'"—pollsters aligned themselves with "the people." They would serve as the instrument by which ordinary Americans' voices could become audible to those in the corridors of power. Pollsters made

--THE GALLUP POLL-- SET 176-B 11-8-39
THE AMERICAN INSTITUTE OF PUBLIC OPINION
Wants YOUR Opinion

1. What do you think is the most important problem before the American people today?

2. a. Do you believe in government old-age pensions? ☐ Yes ☐ No ☐ No Opinion
   b. Do you think pensions should be given only to old people who are in need, or to all old people?
   ☐ Needy only ☐ All old people ☐ No Opinion
   COMMENT
   c. How much per month should be paid to a single person? $
   d. How much per month to a husband and wife? $
   e. Do you think the government could afford to pay such pensions at the present time without increasing taxes? ☐ Yes ☐ No ☐ No Opinion
   f. Have you heard of the Townsend Plan for Old Age Pensions? ☐ Yes ☐ No
   g. Do you recall how much per month each person is supposed to receive under the Townsend Plan?
   ☐ Yes Amount $ ☐ No

3. Do you think Congress was right or wrong when it changed the Neutrality Law so that England and France or any other nations can buy war materials, including arms and airplanes, in the United States? ☐ Right ☐ Wrong ☐ Undecided ☐ No Opinion
   COMMENT

4. Do you think England and France have made clear what they are fighting for?
   ☐ Yes ☐ No ☐ No Opinion
   COMMENT

5. If Germany is defeated by England and France, should the peace treaty be more severe on Germany or less severe than the treaty at the end of the last war?
   ☐ More severe ☐ Less severe ☐ Same ☐ No Opinion
   WHY?
   How strongly convinced are you of this? ☐ Strongly ☐ Mildly
   (SHOW CARD TO RESPONDENT.)

6. Which of these statements best describes your opinion about the Communist party in the United States?—
   ☐ The Communist party in this country takes orders directly from Russia.
   ☐ The policies of the Communist party in the United States are decided on by Communists in this country in consultation with Russia.
   ☐ The policies of the American Communist party are decided entirely by Communists in the United States.
   ☐ Know nothing about the Communist party.
   COMMENT

7. a. About how many members would you guess there are in the Communist party in the United States?
   b. Do you think members of the Communist party should be allowed to hold public office in the United States? ☐ Yes ☐ No ☐ No Opinion
   WHY?

8. Considering your income and cost of living, do you feel you are better off today than you were a year ago? ☐ Yes ☐ No ☐ No Opinion

9. Would you prefer to see the Democrats, or the Republicans, win the Presidential election next year?
   ☐ Democrats ☐ Republicans ☐ Other ☐ No Opinion

Beginning in the mid-1930s, organizations like the American Institute of Public Opinion probed individuals' views on an eclectic mix of topics, ranging from old-age pensions to war in Europe to the American Communist Party. (Gallup Poll questionnaire, 1939, reprinted by permission of The Gallup Organization.)

extravagant promises on behalf of their science. Regular public opinion surveys would cure many of the ills of the modern polity by combating the deleterious effects of unresponsive legislatures, political machines, and pressure groups, all of which Gallup described as "minorities representing themselves as the majority." "As vital issues emerge from the fast-flowing stream of modern life," pledged the surveyor, public opinion polls "enable the American people to speak for themselves." Pollsters' new technology, they boasted, was even more representative and inclusive than elections, the bedrock of American political life. Polls, after all, ascertained the views of those who never made it to the voting booth. Roper declared that polling techniques were the "greatest contribution to democracy since the introduction of the secret ballot."[26]

Pollsters' public statements were nearly always leavened with this sort of stirring civic rhetoric. Writing against the backdrop of fascism and dictatorship abroad in 1940, Gallup painted polling as a democratic and particularly American instrument, its invention a product of free institutions and characteristic U.S. ingenuity. Totalitarian regimes ruled through secret police and manufactured public opinion—the "artificial creation of an apparent majority"—so that the dictator was incapable of knowing "the real mind of his people." Americans instead faced up to the challenge of their 130-million-strong democracy, embracing "new techniques to meet the impact of this strange new decade."[27]

Gallup and Roper went so far as to equate voicing opinions—directly to surveyors and indirectly to political leaders and corporations—with democracy itself. The explanation for individuals' willingness to answer pollsters' queries, in Gallup's words, was "the average American's belief that what he thinks is important; that expressing himself is part of his birthright." Submitting to surveys thus constituted active participation in national affairs, and even helped to construct rational citizens. A psychologist writing in *Public Opinion Quarterly* agreed, proposing that merely taking part in opinion surveys had "socially beneficial" effects, including intellectual stimulation and clarification of views. As one of Gallup's interviewers put it, "For many," being polled was "a first lesson in being articulate." Pollsters thus worked to make their technology not a cause of passive spectatorship, as some might have feared, but a tool for fostering democratic values and improving citizenship. It was in these terms that they invited individuals' trust and participation in the surveying project.[28]

Not surprisingly, then, a populist message infused surveyors' public statements about the polls. Here they departed from the Lynds, who had judged Middletowners ill-equipped to navigate modern society. In speech after speech, article after article, Gallup cited his faith in the people to make good decisions. Debates of theorists and statesmen stretching back to the country's founding regarding "the political wisdom of the common people," he asserted, "can now be settled on the basis of a mountain of factual data." The people were almost always ahead of their leaders, Gallup argued, and he was able to prove it scientifically. His most repeated pieces of evidence for this belief were that the public was readier than Congress had been to build up the military before World War II; was in favor of conscription before any leader had suggested it; and was in favor of lower and more "equitable" tax rates on all income brackets. (Gallup was careful to add, however, that as "mere reporters of public opinion . . . it makes no difference to us whether Congress follows poll results or not.") Roper echoed this belief in the fundamental "intelligence of public opinion." As he mused in a wartime broadcast: "If we were to believe much of what we hear these days from certain quarters about the average American citizen, we would have to feel hopeless about the ability of our American democracy to prosecute this war successfully." In conscious counterpoint, Roper spent his time on the airwaves affirming the sagacity of the "average" American. At the same time, pollsters characterized opinion surveys as public instruments, megaphones for the people's voice, right or wrong. Placing power with the polled rather than the polling profession, Roper and Gallup made their statistics "democratic" and thus more difficult to dispute without simultaneously challenging the will of the citizenry or the presumption of the majority's fundamental claim to rightness.[29]

Gallup and his colleagues thus placed themselves in the camp of science and democracy, presenting their craft as the technical answer to the problem of the modern public. Gallup expressed a fair amount of nostalgia for "old face-to-face relationships" and the small-town meeting: the Middletown of 1890 rather than 1920. But the pollster made it clear that he was a realist, ready to accommodate contemporary circumstances. Instead of lamenting the loss of an older community, as did the Lynds, he believed he might remake that community with the aid of scientific sampling. Gallup never tired of quoting James Bryce, author of *The American Commonwealth* (1888), who in his hopes for the active role of public opinion in governing national affairs looked forward to a day when "the will of the majority of citizens [would] become ascertainable at all times." Finally in the twentieth century, the pollster proclaimed, there were the means at hand to make Bryce's vision come alive. Drawing on the past while forecasting the future, Gallup placed a potentially unsettling technology within the framework of an older America.[30]

But the new polls did not simply apply scientific methods to old problems. They were also the leading edge of progress, satisfying a need for accurate and up-to-date information in a complex and bureaucratic world. Practitioners characterized the polling process as a swift and effective nationwide operation for tapping into the public mind. Unlike the situation in 1914, "an instrument was in readiness to test America's attitudes and reactions" when war broke out in 1939, pronounced Gallup, and research was under way in the "never-ending job of improving the machinery of opinion measurement." The very speed of their information gathering—their near simultaneity with the events they registered—aligned the polls with other modern technologies such as radio. The crowning proof of scientific polling's ascendance, in Gallup's eyes, was the fact that it was "difficult for many oldsters to adjust their thinking to this new instrument." He added proudly, however, that "few persons under the age of forty (mentally or chronologically) fail to see the value of polls."[31]

Alluding to the same dilemmas of the twentieth-century public that Walter Lippmann and John Dewey had underscored, Gallup and Roper reassured their readers and listeners that scientific surveys could resolve them. Opinion polls would allow "the inarticulate majority" to speak and to be heard in an age of mass democracy. A parallel argument applied to consumer surveys. Corporations had grown so large that modern management was "pretty well insulated from the ultimate consumer," observed Roper in a 1942 speech. Market research could reestablish the older "direct contacts" between businesses and their customers— the days when the heads of manufacturing plants were "close to the public" and had a "good knowledge of what the consumer wanted." The democratic promise of such surveying was well expressed in the pollster's statement that it was "the public's turn to say to the manufacturer, 'You'll make what we want, in the shape we want, in the color we want, and sell it at the price we want to pay or else we will exercise our inalienable right to refuse to buy your goods.'" By this logic, opinion surveys were a necessary counterweight to a large, bureaucratic, impersonal mass society. Collecting information about the public was a means to civic empowerment, the aggregated voice of representative Americans a force for good.[32]

Yet pollsters treaded lightly in a treacherous cultural field. Gallup and Roper always had to make sure they tuned their social scientific instrument to democratic rather than propagandistic purposes in an era of heightened fears of manipulation from above. The concern that poll results might sway the opinions of independent Americans was breezily written off by Gallup, who strenuously denied the existence of such influence throughout his career. He argued that although it was often assumed that "the American people behave like sheep," there was "not one bit of scientific evidence" to support the notion. Roper wavered on this question, occasionally wondering if his well-publicized numbers were shaping election results. Some contemporary studies suggested that the "bandwagon effect" might indeed exist. But pollsters' democratic rhetoric relied on a notion of individuals able to know and speak their own minds, free of the kinds of pressures that sociologists and psychologists were discovering to operate in most realms of social life.[33]

The polls' chief defenders also tended to disregard the uses to which social data, once collected, could be put. In the same 1942 speech promoting the value of market research, Roper claimed it was "indisputable" that "those things . . . which the public have a really deep-seated desire to change *are* going to be changed, somewhat, sometime" via the information they communicated to surveyors. But the only instances of gathering information about "the people" he went on to describe—individuals' attitudes toward meat eating, the telltale signs of the tardy bill-payer—were designed to help companies sustain higher profits or avoid risks. These victories had little to do with the consumer speaking to power. In the political arena, pollsters likewise ignored the possibility that politicians would rely on opinion research to fashion targeted messages for public consumption as much as to guide policy making. Franklin Roosevelt, an early and avid convert to the polls, studied them not to discover the people's views, for instance, but to shape them and gain support for actions he had already determined to carry out. As one historian has described it, for FDR, "reports on public opinion were seen as 'intelligence'—that is, information on the goings on in that unknown territory, the American mind. They were the starting point of informational campaigns designed to furnish that mind." Furthermore, the administration's own pollsters, Hadley Cantril and Gerard Lambert (the man famous for the overwhelmingly successful Listerine advertising campaign), included in all their public opinion reports advice "on how the attitude reported might be corrected." This relationship between fact-finding and the exercise of governmental power was a far cry from Gallup's rosy vision of opinion polls as the "pulse of democracy."[34]

Finding the People

When explicating their craft in radio broadcasts and newspaper columns, Gallup and Roper presented the "people's voice" as transparent and wholly unmediated by their method of calling it into being. Pollsters discovered Americans' views, they said, by asking about them. Of course, opinion researchers did more than that. They carefully selected representative samples, formulated questions, tested them for reliability and clarity, and analyzed interviewers' reports that arrived in the mail. The techniques for creating the modern science of polling emerged, piecemeal, over the first few decades of the century, most notably in 1935 with the development of statistical methods for estimating standard errors based on sample size. But finding the public—or rather, the right cross-section of it—was a project laced with difficulties. And it brought Gallup and Roper face-to-face with the challenge of reconciling their democratic and scientific aims on the one hand, and more practical pressures on the other.[35]

Opinion surveyors in the decades following 1935 devised ever more elaborate procedures for reaching and then measuring the public. For example, knowing that the *Literary Digest*'s failure to correctly predict the outcome of the 1936 election had stemmed from the class bias introduced by mailing ballots to lists of automobile and telephone owners, Gallup and Roper gained access to the lower economic echelons, particularly "reliefers," by supplementing mail-in questionnaires with personal interviews. Finding interviews a more controlled method for getting at the right sample and eliciting accurate answers, they abandoned mail ballots of any kind soon after 1936. Over the course of the 1940s and early 1950s the profession moved toward more precise techniques of quota (or "purposive"), area, "pin-point," and ultimately, probability sampling. The art of questioning itself went through several modifications. A reporter who accompanied Gallup interviewers as they worked in three different cities in 1940 noted that "phrasing the ballots is a nightmare in semantics" and that the individual interviewers' measurements of strength of opinion were highly erratic. Methods for calibrating biases in question wording (the "split-ballot technique") and testing respondents' intensity of opinion and depth of knowledge (the "quintamensional plan of question design") were refined and given impressive scientific monikers by pollsters in subsequent years.[36]

In one way or another, however, surveyors' most intractable problems in locating public opinion had to do with their staffs in the field, those individuals who conducted doorstep interviews and reaped the raw material for the polls. National surveys were beholden to this cast of thousands spread across the country ready to be tapped for timely answers to questions on current affairs. Citing such matters as "tact, reliability, [and] personal approach," one supervisor of field interviewers stated: "Every element in research can be reduced to scientific, absolute mathematical accuracy—everything excepting the field work, upon whose findings the entire structure depends." If she exaggerated the simplicity of other aspects of pollsters' science, this writer did not underestimate the challenges facing those who hoped to standardize interviewing. Furthermore, regulating a far-flung group of part-time staffers was not a task that pollsters were always interested in taking on. Gallup, for example, trained most of his staff by mail and had no supervising structure for his corps of interviewers, the ranks of which numbered approximately eleven hundred by 1940. Instead he relied on their status as white-collar, well-educated men and women, recommended by the "leading persons" in their communities, to establish their competence in carrying out his poll. Roper employed a smaller and better-trained staff, but would be party to many of the same problems as was his competitor.[37]

Interviewers, despite their middle-class background, were low-paid, nonprofessional workers, and, increasingly over the years, women. Theirs was a new and crucial kind of work. It was the sum total of thousands of their interactions with strangers that made pollsters' and marketers' facts legitimate. Interviewers were expected to approach a wide range of potential respondents, to overcome suspicion and reluctance, and to elicit truthful answers. Essential links in the polling chain, they could not themselves always be trusted to be reliable. Questioners could improperly reveal their own biases, guide the respondents too much, or simply bungle the job. When a respondent showed no understanding of the word *atheist,* for example, a Gallup Poll interviewer was reported to have rephrased the question as: "Would you vote for a sinner for President?"[38]

Less obvious problems, such as "cheating" interviewers, also plagued the polls. Cheaters were those who, under time pressure to fill their quotas, filled in answers themselves or otherwise falsified data. As one field director put it, "In a desperate attempt to keep up with assignments and please the supervisor, a person of limited ability will be forced to manufacture interviews." A market researcher noted the tendency of some interviewers to make several legitimate visits to respondents and then "do the 'mind reading act' on subsequent calls; they believe they know what the replies will be and record them without asking the questions." This particular form of mind reading—unlike Gallup's or Roper's—was strictly forbidden, of course. The number of articles in professional forums on building "check-ups" and "cheater traps" into polling procedures testifies to the significance of this concern. As Roper wrote to a marketing colleague in 1942, "We have been aware of the problem for eight years and have spent a very considerable amount of money in trying to lick it."[39]

Despite all this worry about cheaters, acts of deliberate deception were the least of the pollsters' problems. Guesswork and subjectivity were part of the day-to-day work of collecting opinions. Especially in the early days of "quota" polling, interviewers had broad leeway in selecting respondents. As Gallup explained it, "The interviewer is not given the names of any persons to poll; he is merely given the types"—some predetermined number of women and men, old and young, upper- and lower-class—and "it is up to him to find the individuals in his local community to fit the types." One Gallup interviewer recalled that in 1937, his task was simple: "The way I would fill my relief quotas was to walk around town until I saw a WPA [Works Progress Administration] construction gang and I would get them on their lunch hour, three or four men sitting around . . . I'd pull out my questionnaire and say, 'Do you approve or disapprove of a treaty with Germany?' or whatever it was, and then I'd say, 'How about you, and you, and you?' I got four interviews very quickly that way." This was not the method for finding "A-level," or upper-class, respondents, he noted, and so "you'd have to screw up your courage and go through a fancy part of town and try to figure out which house looked the most approachable."[40]

Tracking down individuals to fit even Gallup's relatively loose categories presented considerable challenges. Social class was a case in point. As direct questions about income were considered too sensitive, interviewers were asked to make estimates based on criteria such as the respondent's neighborhood, house, dress, and material possessions. For this reason both Roper and Gallup preferred interviews to take place in the home rather than on the street, because a glance around the domestic interior allowed a better assessment of the interviewee's financial status. (Pollsters later modified this approach, directing respondents to look at a card listing income brackets and then indicate their category.) Interviewers would also often eschew asking the respondent's precise age, assuming that women in particular might be offended by the question and, in any event, were likely to dissemble. On the other hand, pollsters believed that "sex and color are attributes which can be readily determined by the interviewers."[41]

Poll taking was a human transaction, shot through with all the unease and awkwardness of social interactions in other realms of American life. Estimating the economic status and age of interviewees was only the clearest manifestation of this fact. The question of rapport constituted an even more fundamental problem, going as it did to the heart of Gallup and Roper's project to make "the people's voice" audible. Some members of the public, it turned out, were difficult to find, resisted social scientific questioning, or made middle-class interviewers uncomfortable. Multiple studies of opinion surveying as early as the 1940s documented the tendency of the interviewer's social class to influence not just the selection of those to be interviewed but the responses he or she received. Polls' consistent slant toward the white-collar and Republican was known to result "in large part from the reluctance of middle-class interviewers to approach the lowest income groups, who are most likely to be inarticulate and suspicious." Further evidence indicated that "the greater the difference between the status of the interviewer and the respondent, the more likely is [the respondent] not to report his true opinions." Social psychologist Daniel Katz found in 1942 that white-collar and working-class interviewers operating under the same instructions received markedly different answers from working people on issues related to both labor and the war. Working-class questioners extracted opinions "consistently more radical than those reported by the middle-class interviewers."[42]

Pollsters made some efforts to reckon with the problem of rapport across social divides. In the early 1940s, for example,

Archibald Crossley had African Americans on his staff interview southern blacks. But in the North and in general, all opinion surveyors had whites do the majority of their interviewing, regardless of the race of their respondents. Pollsters admitted to having even greater class imbalances in the composition of their staffs, reasoning that less-educated individuals were unable "to understand and do the difficult work" they required. Despite recommendations from fellow social scientists to hire "special supplementary interviewers" as well as "regular" white middle-class ones so as not to introduce biases into their results, pollsters knowingly risked such distortion. This would, of course, have implications for what mainstream public opinion looked like in their polls.[43]

All these challenges were brought into sharp relief in the late 1940s as the pollsters moved away from quota and toward probability sampling, that is, the random selection of respondents. The goal was to make opinion polling one notch more scientific, excising subjectivity and chance from the interviewer's job. Although taking the decision of whom to question out of the interviewer's hands was more "objective," it presented new and formidable problems. This Roper knew from early experiments in probability sampling in New York City. Interviewers were instructed, simply enough, to sample every so many residents in designated city blocks and housing units. Their difficulty fulfilling this basic requirement was telling of the host of obstacles they faced in reaching "the public."[44]

One of Roper's field interviewers, Elizabeth Wagner, began her report of her "statistical adventures" in probability sampling by explaining, "I started out with an open mind, sincerely interested in this new method of selecting a cross section." Soon enough, however, she encountered barriers. In many cases, no one was at home in the specified buildings. Some apartments had no mailboxes or doorbells by which to count off and select units; others were in buildings with a locked front door, or were multiple-occupancy dwellings crowded with several heads of household. Then there was the problem of doormen in upper-income (or, in pollster lingo, "A and B") buildings who ejected the hopeful interviewer "like a Third Avenue drunk." However, "much worse was to follow" once Wagner made her way to Harlem, where the housing stock was in such disarray that the counting system Roper had devised was impossible to follow. "Needless to say, there were no lists of tenants or individual doorbells," she wrote, so that "one side of a block occupied me for most of a very frustrating afternoon." Wryly noting the "non-conformance of New York landlords and building operators with our survey requirements," Wagner summarized: "So the interviewer clutching her well-thumbed book of rules . . . climbs up and down stairs, arrives at the lucky (?) number to be greeted never or hardly ever by the duly elected respondent. To the left, the mister or missus is loudly at home, to the right, likewise . . . who is to judge her and point a finger if she relaxes a bit at this point and says 'what the hell, I'll turn to the left! I've got to fill this quota in time for my Christmas check!'"

More worrisome to Wagner was the distrust and resistance she encountered from neighborhood people she did manage to track down. She enclosed with her write-up a "notice of a protest meeting in Harlem which may or may not explain the suspicion with which I was received, the unwillingness of the tenants to give me information as to neighbors' hours or habits, in some cases even the refusal to answer my questions." Wagner surmised that she was seen by landlords and tenants alike as a "checker-upper" or bill collector, if not a social worker. She reported that one "colored woman" in particular was terrified by her visit. "Convinced that the F.B.I. was after her," this woman informed Wagner "that her concern over the inquiries I had made was responsible for a nervous condition that had kept her from her job that day." This same respondent was, not surprisingly, hostile during the interview. "Frankly," Wagner stated, "this kind of an experience is one I should not care to repeat."[45]

Another member of Roper's field staff, Mary Crawford, corroborated these tales. Having set out to find respondents in a "Negro section," she pointed to "the question of it being safe or wise to work" in certain areas; some interviewers, she noted, "might have run into serious trouble if they weren't able to cope with a situation quickly and tactfully." Crawford confirmed the problem of rapport, believing it was "particularly bad for a white interviewer to work on this part of the job." In low-income areas especially, she noted, "you are automatically looked upon with suspicion," and she further speculated that "even when you do finally get your interview you are not getting the most honest answers possible." Recounting her experiences interviewing residents of a Puerto Rican neighborhood in English, Crawford reported: "While I did manage to take most of the respondents through a complete interview—by hook or by crook—I most certainly had the feeling that they didn't know what I was talking about most of the time." The problems of accurate polling were compounded by the dilemma of a presumably middle-class woman assessing the economic status of respondents so different from herself. The grim living conditions Crawford encountered, she acknowledged, led her to designate a person "who might normally be classified as C in any other area" as a "D," or lower status.[46]

The interviewer closed by arguing that attempting to locate respondents according to probability sampling was a wasteful and tiresome task, full of "unpleasantness and difficulties." Roper agreed. After receiving these dispatches, the pollster asked his staff: "*Can* the kind of interviewers we or anyone else has available to us do a probability sample—particularly in the slum areas of big cities—if they want to?" and "Even assuming they can—will they?" The profession, he believed, could not count on such intrepid dedication from its interviewers, most of whom Roper suspected would descend into cheating if forced to undergo such travails. This constituted a recognition of the trade-off between a more representative sample and a more easily reached one. It was also an acknowledgment that certain kinds of respondents—poor, black, and non-English-speaking—were straightforwardly avoided in the old quota sampling system. In a case of wishful thinking, the pollster cavalierly dismissed probability sampling as something that "seems to have momentary acceptance on the part of theoreticians."[47]

In attempting to obtain a more accurate accounting of a "representative public," surveyors had only become more aware of its elusiveness. This is something they had long known, evident even in the difficulty their interviewers had in establishing a rapport with those they hoped to question. Yet scientific attempts to find the public went only so far. Although particular techniques may have brought Gallup and Roper closer to the people, they did not always consider that goal worth their trouble or expense. Instead, they preferred to work with a less inclusive but infinitely more practical public. In fact, the polls undersampled certain portions of the population by design.

There were other obstacles to locating the public beyond missing the designated doorbell. Chief among them were surveyors' own presuppositions about which members of the public truly counted. Despite pollsters' talk of a tool for democracy, their claims to representativeness in their cross-sections were questionable on a number of levels.

A key source of unrepresentativeness was pollsters' founding decision to align their new instrument with electoral contests. Roper and Gallup both believed the social benefits of the election poll to be insignificant—largely because that "poll" was already destined to take place in the voting booth. Gallup stated that "the only useful purpose served by election forecasting is to provide a check on polling methods and techniques," and Roper regularly wondered if pollsters should quit the business altogether. But they well understood its economic value. Accurate election results seemingly proved the validity of opinion polling more generally, and surveyors could profit financially from a correct forecast, since new clients viewed elections as a litmus test for sampling methods. Publicity from Gallup's electoral polls, for example, "enhanced his reputation in Hollywood" because "executives using film research believed it gave them a similar ability to predict public opinion." Wanting to be sure that they were paying for reliable information about the consumer market, but having no solid measures of that information's truth, corporations took electoral projections as a proxy for their other investments. Knowing this, Roper would feel it necessary to send out a letter explaining two misconceptions in the media about his preelection statistics in 1952 to a handful of social scientists but also a long list of clients—Ford Motor Company, Hormel & Co., Dole Hawaiian Pineapple Company, and Marshall Field, among others.[48]

Surveyors had deposited their own hopes for a democratic science not in verifying voting outcomes but in conducting social issue polls, believing their surveys might encourage more deliberative and informed public debate. Not surprisingly, however, given the incentive structure in place, researchers diverted the bulk of their funds and attention into presidential and congressional contests. Electoral polls were based on much larger samples and subject to more careful cross-checking than were the hundreds of surveys on topics from foreign policy to family life. Those polls that could not be disproved, that is, were considerably less rigorous in construction.[49]

An intense focus on elections—the gold standard for corporate clients—introduced distortions into the polls more generally, since the cross-sample for what George Gallup termed the "miniature electorate" was composed solely of those who, in surveyors' assessment, were most likely to vote. In practice, this often meant measuring a United States that was more male, white, and affluent than the actual population in social-issue polls as well. As Daniel Robinson has found, the polity Gallup sampled was a peculiar version of the adult "general public," underrepresenting women, African Americans, and individuals at the bottom of the economic ladder. In twenty-one Gallup surveys conducted in 1936 and 1937, for example, men constituted 66 percent of the sample. African Americans, although approximately 10 percent of the population in the 1930 and 1940 censuses, made up a slim 1.9 percent of respondents. Robinson's comparisons of census data and the AIPO sample further reveal that professionals and semiprofessionals were interviewed far out of proportion to their numbers in the population.[50]

Just as had the Lynds, pollsters advanced what they considered to be a good social scientific reason for this pattern of under- and overrepresentation: namely, the need to eliminate nonvoters. Because the general public and the predicted electorate were not one and the same, Gallup in particular did not attempt to draw up demographically accurate samples of the population. Instead, he keyed his sampling design to likely voters. This intersected neatly with prevailing ideas about who the informed and reflective citizen was. New restrictions on voting at the end of the nineteenth century and the breaking up of urban political machines in the Progressive Era had reworked the franchise by the time Gallup set up shop, dampening the voting rates of workers, women, nonwhites, and "ethnics." Furthermore, the laborers and immigrants who had taken a robust role in nineteenth-century politics were increasingly described as problematic or irrational voters, "lacking the qualities of 'publicness' and disinterest that the discourse of dominant groups enjoyed." On the other hand, middle-class and elite whites "appeared in the public sphere as representative, normative, and able to speak for the whole."[51]

Gallup, and to a lesser degree Roper, similarly permitted middle-class whites to speak for the whole. Pollsters carried into their craft a good deal of conventional wisdom about the kind of individual who voted. First among these precepts was that "people in the lower income levels are usually not as much interested in issues as people in the upper levels." Nearly as important was the orthodoxy that "women on the whole are less well-informed than men," and that housewives in particular voted infrequently. As Roper put it in one of his broadcasts, it was not that women did not express their opinions; they were simply "more interested in such practical matters as how to bring up their children . . . or perhaps at times, what Mrs. Jones wore last Friday to tea." Men, by contrast, were "inclined to take upon themselves the solution of the weightier affairs of state."[52]

In an explanation of how to predict elections, Roper revealed some of the other judgment calls he and his colleagues made regarding which segments of the public were unlikely to vote. Some of the groups in this category were too "obvious" to merit discussion: those under twenty-one years of age, those in mental hospitals, and significantly, southern blacks. Trying to replicate the voting public in miniature and aware that most blacks were barred from the polls, surveyors deliberately undersampled African Americans in the South—Gallup not assigning a "Negro quota" at all. Likewise, pollsters often excluded the non-English-speaking, assuming they would not go to the voting booth. Daniel Robinson has noted the irony: in order to obtain an accurate reading of what "the people" wanted, it was necessary to downplay some of those people's numbers. The "average American" of the polls was therefore in some ways as skewed as was the Lynds' "typical" community. But while Middletown's surveyors acknowledged that they were excluding some groups to simplify their analysis, pollsters were convinced that only by silencing some voices could they reach the most representative ones.[53]

Segments of the public did not always behave in the ways surveyors predicted. Indeed, this would contribute to the pollsters' greatest public embarrassment: their projection of the Republican

Thomas Dewey rather than Democrat Harry Truman as the winner of the 1948 presidential election. Gallup's and Roper's surprise at working-class voting levels, boosting the Democratic percentages, was a leading explanation for their inaccurate forecast. Surveyors made this out to be less their mistake about laborers than a dramatic and unexpected shift in workers' exercise of their political rights. Roper implied that the pollsters could hardly be faulted for their miscalculation, since "there was no pat formula which anybody had to precisely measure the impact of this new-found awareness of citizenship responsibilities on the part of working people." African Americans also came out to vote in larger than usual numbers in 1948, motivated in part by Truman's civil rights plank. This defiance of expected patterns unsettled the pollsters, who had in the past worked with assumptions about different social groups' stable and predictable levels of interest in politics. Gallup further noted that he and his colleagues had been taken aback by the relatively high voting rates of "women in the low income and education groups." These were individuals, he observed, who "normally show the least interest in elections." His explanation, hardly squaring with his populist rhetoric elsewhere, was that "if pressure is put on them on Election Day by labor unions, the Church, and party machines . . . they do vote."[54]

It is not surprising that there were links between pollsters' political prejudices and their predictions, their imagined public and the one they projected back statistically. What *is* remarkable, given the potential consequences—not only professional but financial—is that pollsters found it so difficult to overcome certain rather unscientific notions about the public they surveyed. Much like the Lynds' use of native-born Muncie to reflect the nation, Gallup and Roper fell back upon the template of a white, educated, male populace when they set out in search of "the public." American political life and the pollsters' new science were supposed to converge around the principle of representation. But instead of functioning as a tool for democracy, opinion polls were deliberately modeled upon, and compounded, democracy's flaws. Following the imperatives of the accurate election poll rather than their own civic talk, surveyors deliberately made their new science *less* representative.

Producing the Public

That Gallup and Roper underrepresented women, African Americans, laborers, and the poor in their samples was significant. Equally consequential were pollsters' invocations of "the public" itself. Notwithstanding the well-known distortions caused by "cheaters," interviewer bias, faulty estimation, and failed rapport, mid-century surveyors made confident claims about what Americans felt and thought. Such claims already reflected the exclusion of certain sectors of the population. But the form they took—in newsprint and on the air—often concealed the reality of segmentation even in the public that the pollsters did reach.

Gallup's American Institute of Public Opinion, beginning in 1935, nearly always showcased poll results by region (New England, East Central, Middle Atlantic, South, West Central, Mountain, and Pacific) and political affiliation (usually Republican and Democrat), with an occasional nod to the "views of special groups," such as "persons on relief," farmers, young people, women, city voters, lawyers, Irish Americans, and very occasionally "Negroes." These categories were meant to capture "every shade of political preference" on questions from universal military training to the United Nations as well as opinions on social matters such as family size, Bible reading, and the common cold. Roper's Fortune Survey included especially rich narrative descriptions and explanations of polling results. The pollster tabulated Americans' views in 1940 on the question of entering the European war, for example, by sex, age, race, economic level, and region, noting that although there was no marked difference in the opinions of the "poor and prosperous," those in the Southwest were much more eager to join the fight than were those in New England or the Midwest. In other early polls, Roper tracked middle-class, upper-class and "Negro" opinion on FDR, the effect of city size on viewpoints, and preferences for cigarette brands based on consumers' age and sex.[55] Surveyors were, on a daily basis, engaged in classifying and dividing the U.S. population by education, class, gender, and age, among other axes. This was because they understood those categories to have something to do with how people arrived at their views. In some instances, as they had in 1936, surveyors pointed out social fissures in the electorate. In every case, pollsters documented at the very least a minority and a majority position. But the form of the syndicated polls subordinated those disagreements that were unrelated to ephemeral opinions on the "issues," meaning that deeper divisions within the public were much more evident to pollsters than they were to their audiences. Gallup's and Roper's data therefore did not easily lend themselves to a broad understanding of enduring patterns—attitudes linked to sex, race, or religion, for example—in the breakdown of "public opinion." Social factors and social structures were usually invisible in surveyors' presentation of their results, if not in the making of the polls.

Roper and Gallup did make regular statements about the vast diversity of American society, as well as their polls' ability to capture it. Gallup, referencing the Lynds' study, wrote in a 1941 piece for the *New York Times* that "the American people are as various as their land. A cross-section of them includes cotton workers in Louisiana, storekeepers in Vermont, farmers and field hands in the Dakotas, bustling business men in Chicago, Detroit, Los Angeles, and Middletown." This vision of the public was pared down significantly in his article's title, however: "We, the People, Are Like This—A Report on How and What We Think." The "we" in the headline was the averaged-out entity surveyors labeled "public opinion," a coherent, distilled viewpoint. As Gallup's shift from the plural to the unitary suggests, the very format of the polls made it easy to slide into singular thinking about "the public"—even though the viewpoint in question often expressed a bare majority of respondents. In newspaper and radio presentations of their survey results, the numerically dominant view was almost always the overwhelming fact, 51 percent support for any given issue endowing that position with the weight of "what America thinks." In the same 1941 article, Gallup ten times invoked, not percentages of the population or even majority and minority views, but the "average American" or "average man." Roper similarly proclaimed that the subject of his broadcasts was to discover "what makes the average American tick." He played up this character in his CBS radio show, allowing listeners to determine how they stacked up against an aggregate archetype. As the pollster announced on one occasion, "Next week, I'll be talking about a problem many of you must be thinking about . . . are you more or less worried about [the communists] than the average American?"[56]

For all their skill at disaggregating the public in order to create the miniature electorate, then, pollsters could bestow the people with a unitary voice, describing survey findings not as how citizens articulated their diverse views, but as how "America speaks," the catch-phrase of the Gallup Poll. Their language was revealing. Gallup could ask: "Where is the American public headed in 1939? What will it be saying and thinking?" *Where the People Stand,* Roper's radio program, was billed as making clear "the people's viewpoint" on issues from presidential popularity to sporting competitions. Statements such as "The public is rapidly developing a frame of mind which will tolerate no interference with the defense production program," and "The average American takes the attitude that conscription is . . . necessary" were commonplace in surveyors' explanations of their results. Pollsters in this way made of multiple, conflicting social groups a national "we," or a "mass subject." The resulting portrait was far more harmonious and coherent than their own cross-sections told them it could be.[57]

Even the use of majorities and minorities, pollsters' primary categories, stabilized the citizenry into two internally undifferentiated masses. This form could impede interesting facts from coming forth. A colleague of Roper's at CBS, a news editor, expressed doubts about the simplistic fashion in which poll data were relayed. Responding to a broadcast on attitudes toward religious intermarriage, he noted that "no attempt was made to relate the statistics of answers to the statistics of population." This meant that a fraction of Americans were said to favor intermarriage but that there was no way of telling which religious groups these people came from, not to mention which groups they favored or opposed intermarrying with. "I wonder whether there is much significance to overall figures that are unrelated to the particular group to which the person answering the question belongs," the editor wrote, adding, "It would almost appear, when listening to your broadcast, as if you only polled Protestant Americans." Roper's colleague pressed the surveyor for more rather than less segmenting of public opinion, believing this would present a more realistic accounting of the issue.[58]

Too many trends in the profession worked against such analyses, however. Polls were built for a mass-mediated age, and it was their locating of the *majority*, that fixed data point amidst all the chaos of viewpoints and variability in the population, that made them so appealing to politicians and media outlets alike. Indeed, a 1948 investigation of the most prominent pollsters by the Social Science Research Council criticized them for precisely this reason: Gallup, Roper, and others were overly influenced by commercial concerns, obeying "journalistic rather than scientific demands." These were not demands that pollsters could easily ignore, however. All of its practitioners acknowledged that opinion polling as a profession depended fundamentally on corporate support. Gallup's polls could run only because client newspapers subscribed to them. Similarly, corporations "paid the rent" for Roper's Fortune Survey, which otherwise would have been an unthinkable proposition for the pub-

lisher. Polls like Gallup's were the most expensive syndicated features newspapers had ever run. In 1940 the AIPO was employing a
thousand part-time field interviewers, who ran up bills of $1,600 a
week in conducting Gallup's surveys, and this represented only the
pretabulation expenditures. The steep production cost meant that
opinion polling was an entrepreneurial science that answered not
simply to "the public" but to the polls' buyers: newspaper publishers, broadcasting companies, and other corporations. It also meant
that private market research from the beginning subsidized the public polls.[59]

Publishers and studios set the standards for how poll data were
displayed, and required surveyors to encapsulate complicated findings in an easily summarized chart or a fifteen-minute broadcast.
The stated goal of the Fortune Survey was "not [to] confront the
random citizen with the frequently perplexing choice of saying yes
or no to a simple question" or to separate "all men into black and
white" but instead "attentively to notice their uncertainties and to
seek to remain the barometer of the *nature* of opinion rather than
the referee between a positive and a negative." Roper was also careful to point out the large difference between "the answers that the
majority of the people *with an opinion on each subject* give" and
"Public Opinion . . . a thing of many shades and subtleties." These
cautions, however, were swept aside by his editors' proclamations
that, despite the fact that the Survey was still in the "experimental
stages . . . [the] answers presented here represent Public Opinion—
the opinion of all the people." Moreover, as early as 1936 the pollster was condensing the results of his nuanced surveys in a simple
ten-point table, provided for "the impatient reader." There, poll
findings were once again exhibited as if the public spoke in one
voice. Americans believed, for example, that "salaries paid by large
corporations to their officials are too high"; and "the public—mo-
torist as well as pedestrian—is in favor of mechanical limitation
of the speed of automobiles." This homogenizing move was even

clearer in Roper's overall summary for another set of findings that year. He stated, "Public Opinion expresses itself strongly on war and foreign policy, divides into four attitudes toward the Roosevelt Administration, speaks on four other public questions and three industries, and proves to be favorable to the Jews." Roper himself railed against this tendency toward simplification, bewailing the fact that his editors at the *Herald Tribune* had "gradually deleted the little 'how to read these tables' hints" he had initially included with his published polls. He complained to a fellow surveyor on another occasion about *Fortune*'s inclusion of data he had asked to be deleted that made his figures less accurate, but perhaps more interesting: "I lost my argument and the figures were published." Pollsters were wary of the media's ability to streamline opinion even more radically than did their own techniques, exaggerating a single finding or distorting the meaning of their statistics. Roper lodged a complaint with *Fortune* for this reason in 1946; he noted that, to his surprise, one of his key findings in a survey about anti-Semitism had been "buried in a footnote."[60]

In a sense, those in the polling business were victims of their own success. Advertisers and audiences—themselves increasingly defined by market research—were crucial factors in determining the kind of knowledge opinion researchers could convey. Newspapers could claim, via the "Gallup Method," that readers wanted more definitive findings than public opinion surveys had actually turned up. The manager of the National Newspaper Syndicate, for example, indicated to Roper one of the member paper's desires for clear answers and "more 'facts.'" He explained that the newspaper in question wanted "specific data the readers can cite in conversations" to compete with "opposition papers" that ran columns by Gallup and the popular Samuel Lubbell. This was true despite the recognition that the simpler displays of his competitors provided "nowhere near the complete picture offered by Roper."[61]

Roper had to heed the financial ramifications of his clients' unhappiness, given that Gallup's column competed with and outpaced his, at times by a ten-to-one ratio. The pollster periodically worried about his radio show's Hooper ratings as well as cancellations of his weekly column—the latter by newspapers citing readership studies that registered declining interest. Showing a distinct lack of trust in surveying techniques when it suited him, Roper wrote upon hearing that his radio program rating had fallen: "I have a great respect for Hooper . . . but I doubt if he measures closer than four-tenths of 1 per cent, and my guess is that the actual rating was around 2 and still is. But for those who credit the instrument with more delicacy, we are faced with a drop from 2.7 to 1.6." Pollsters could not always thumb their nose at the technology they in other venues so vigorously defended. In a letter to a newspaper that had canceled his column, Roper wrote, "So long as your decision was taken solely on the grounds of probable reader interest, I can find little to argue over." Scientific surveys could be a double-edged sword for their inventors.[62]

Pollsters' sponsors delimited not just the form but the content of public opinion. Responding to a 1946 inquiry about participating in a radio show devoted to current affairs, for example, Roper noted that he could not be involved if the program were to be sponsored by a competitor of any of his commercial clients. Syndicated pollsters' links to corporations and advertisers also colored their reportage. Regularly sought out as speakers by business audiences, surveyors constantly reassured those they worked for that "the public" believed in free enterprise and was loyal to corporate America. Perhaps not surprisingly, given the polls' commercial underpinning, pro-business attitudes crept into the construction of the surveys themselves. Industrial psychologist Arthur Kornhauser, scrutinizing seven pollsters' questions over six years, documented a consistent anti-labor bias. He announced that "the simple outstanding fact is that the poll questions concentrate heavily on negative and vulnerable aspects of organized labor" rather than their accomplishments for working people. Robert Lynd, a regular critic of the polls, lambasted them instead for what he saw as their suppression of class conflict altogether. In a 1941 letter to Elmo Roper, he wrote, "The bald fact is that class lines are hardening in American life, whether we Americans like it or not." But the Fortune Survey, Lynd protested, "screams aloud to its readers over and over again that class is a myth in American life."[63]

The long reach of corporate sponsors shaped what questions pollsters asked in weekly surveys; it also meant that some issues were off the table altogether. The fact that Gallup's polls depended on client newspapers, many of them based in the South, is the likely reason that race relations were rarely addressed in his early opinion research. Roper was more eager than Gallup was to take on fractious issues, especially his pet cause, antiminority sentiment in the United States. In multiple polls and broadcasts in the 1940s, he brought this topic to public notice. When pondering whether to run them, however, Roper wondered "whether or not I'm getting into too much dynamite." The pollster was right to worry. An executive at the *Louisville Times* objected to Roper's series on antiminority sentiment for just this reason, writing, "The newspaper reader is habituated to spot news and frothy features. He doesn't expect to get, outside the editorial page, any serious discussion of the type which you've been giving him. He doesn't quite know what to do about it when he does." This was not an isolated incident. Roper had to assure the companies he worked for that his shows and columns were generally nondivisive, and that he dealt in "hot" topics only occasionally.[64]

In the mid-1940s Roper noted that his heaviest mail—"50 to 100 letters of controversy, some favorable, some unfavorable"—came in response to polls on anti-Semitism and civil rights. Given that these were the issues that got "the public" engaged, it may have been the case that directly tackling contentious topics would have been profitable for publishing and radio corporations. Media establishments, it seems, did not contemplate this possibility. NBC's internal code for radio programming in the 1930s and 1940s, for example, prohibited explicit mention of "labor and/or labor controversies." The same station's promotion of Roper's radio show to advertisers assured potential clients that the pollster's "non-partisan, factual" research methods guaranteed that his program would "avoid the partisanship that all too often means disgruntled customers." It added, "Whether you're of the Hard Sell or institutional school of advertising, you'll find that the Elmo Roper Program is right for your messages." The audience's exposure to polls on thorny social issues might have made for a more active public, aware of the nation's internal divides and disagreements. But this would not come to pass.[65]

Not all of the pollsters' clients, however, were invested in an undifferentiated majority. As Roper noted in 1942, the classification of economic levels he used in the Fortune Survey "often does not meet the requirements of other market research studies." Commercial clients demanded much finer gradations of the population than did the subscribers to public opinion polls. Unlike his social issues research, Gallup's market surveys homed in on class and gender differences, such as the fact that men paid more attention to weather reports and political cartoons; women to birth notices, health columns, and continuing serials; and wealthy women to advertising. Market researchers in the field of radio also aggressively sought out programs and commercials that attracted different demographic slices. These categories—"men, women, workers, immigrants, Southerners, migrants, housewives"—were exactly the ones pollsters routinely ignored in their aggregate depictions of public opinion. Poll numbers almost magically revealed otherwise obscure trends, summarized changeable views, and summoned up quantitative support for those who had something to gain from such information. Pollsters' careful segmenting of the U.S. population made perfect sense for the private uses of corporate clients. Yet when it came to the public consumption of their statistics, surveyors all but dissolved that same bundle of conflicting preferences and desires into a collective "we."[66]

As public opinion experts, George Gallup and Elmo Roper spent their careers in pursuit of what Americans wanted. Making "the people" or "the public" their object, they brushed over competing or opposed interests. By 1955 even Roper had come to the conclusion that too much attention had been devoted to majority opinion: "I have become convinced that one of the things which is going to place the researcher at a considerable advantage in the years to come is an ability to recognize what I call 'the significant minorities.'" Here again, it was less scientific accuracy or democratic pluralism that led the way than the desire on the part of many corporations—and politicians—to target new market niches. Segment marketing and fine-grained polls that took racial, class, gender, sexual, and other identities into account would be the wave of the not-so-distant future.[67]

Yet surveyors in the early scientific polling era imagined a mass subject that could be identified, heard, and made effective through their techniques. Authorized by no governmental entity and responsible chiefly to their own commercial enterprise, pollsters like Gallup and Roper made strong claims on behalf of a statistically derived "public." That public was measured by staffs ill-equipped to tap into the views of the "miniature electorate," not to mention the actual population of the nation. Pollsters' charts and percentages likewise dampened the voices of many groups in the society at large, including those who might have benefited most from a representative science of opinion. The weekly survey results that Americans encountered thus distorted what the actual public likely wanted and thought. Although the shortcomings of polling techniques had shown the people's voice to be unstable and elusive, the polls reified settled public opinion *and* the soundness of the majority view. Yet Gallup and Roper infused their commentary on survey data with promises about the democratic choices both market research and political polls permitted. As such, pollsters were in the business not simply of querying but of creating and constantly remaking "the people."

The early history of the polls illuminates how a new social scientific instrument defined the boundaries not simply of public opinion but of the public itself. Pollsters' conjuring of a singular public, a mass voice, made it possible to fix some citizens in the center and consign others to the outliers of American opinion—and, by implication, the nation. The version of "public opinion" that Gallup and Roper brought into view would therefore have serious ramifications for the people they surveyed. Anonymous poll respondents had more trouble, and less authority, in challenging their social scientific portrait than did those in Muncie, who could call upon local knowledge and a close-hand view of their community. Citizens could not always find a place from which to debunk the public polls, much less the private commercial surveys commissioned by corporations. And yet consumers of the polls had ways of inserting themselves into the surveys and scrutinizing the surveyors, as the overflowing mailboxes of the Fortune Survey and the American Institute of Public Opinion testified.

4

The Majority Talks Back

Perhaps it is a symbol of our lost individualism that one can to-day look at a crowd of people at a ball park and feel sure not only that most of them carry in their pockets cigarettes of three leading brands, but that 62 per cent of them think that government regulation of the stock market has helped investors and 76 per cent are against Philippine independence. The "man in the street" may wear a poker face, but we have learned to feel that he can't fool us. We know what he is thinking to the third decimal place.

—"These Public-Opinion Polls," *Harper's*, 1938

Day after day across this mighty land,
While thunderous presses roll,
Young men with hat and briefcases in hand
(Or so I understand)
Wander from poll to poll,
Asking odd men in some peculiar street
Which candidate is theirs, which breakfast food
They least dislike to eat,
Which heresy offends their current mood.
But, left or right though thick the issues fall,
Nobody asks me anything at all . . .

—Phyllis McGinley, "The Forgotten Woman," 1952

Unlike the Middletown studies, the Gallup Poll and Fortune Survey were not discrete social scientific events. Opinion polling was instead a continuous technique for monitoring shifts in Americans' attitudes and beliefs—an ongoing constitution of "the public" through anonymously expressed views. The sheer frequency of opinion polls made their methods more visible than their specific incarnations, their content ephemeral except in the case of a few well-publicized election forecasts. More significant as a practice than as a solid body of fact, polling techniques would become part of the social landscape, an increasingly familiar way of knowing the public in the decades following 1936.

As useful as pollsters' technical claims were in knitting together the growing community of opinion researchers, these claims alone were insufficient to establish the wider cultural authority of their craft. Scientific polling presented a particularly tricky problem for its practitioners for a simple reason: its chief audience was the very public it surveyed. Gallup and Roper were fundamentally dependent upon Americans' acquiescence to their questions. They pressed individuals for private data, their personal opinions about a broad range of social and political issues. But they also required a certain faith in their techniques, a willingness among general readers to accept descriptions of themselves in surveyors' percentages. This made polling a solicitous science: the public needed to be courted and cultivated as much as it needed to be surveyed.

Americans had ample opportunities to see the polls at work, to notice their flaws, and to track their record. Even more so than the Lynds and Middletowners, the pollsters were locked in an argument with their audience and subjects. And to a greater extent, they saw their project as one of persuasion. Because they claimed to speak for the mainstream, pollsters had, at least in part, to speak *to* the mainstream. Elmo Roper and George Gallup, both of whom were well versed in sales tactics, attempted throughout their careers to convince the public of the validity and value of their surveys—mobilizing arguments about the polls' scientific rigor, the modern exigencies that made them necessary, and the democratic participation they fostered. Gallup was especially unremitting in pleading polling's cause. The "public," he would find, was equally tenacious in arguing back.

Citizens energetically debated the polls throughout the early decades of scientific polling. Well-publicized misfires in surveyors' practice—notably their unanimous forecast for Thomas Dewey rather than Harry Truman in the presidential election of 1948— eroded their legitimacy in many Americans' eyes. Perhaps more important, many believed opinion polling to be unrepresentative in its methods and undemocratic in its effects. These conflicts between the pollsters and the populace would leave an ambiguous legacy. Although opinion surveys were widely employed in the post-1936 years, many Americans' distrust of them did not ebb. Citizens continued to supplement declarative poll numbers with their own impressions of commonly held attitudes. But it is also clear that the official-looking numbers produced by Gallup and Roper entered everyday discussions, disturbing the unscientific but fervently believed statistics that many individuals carried in their heads. As such, opinion polls subtly reshaped Americans' understanding of the national polity and their place within it. Reading between the lines of their protests, one discovers a gradual resignation to national polls as the main way majorities would be measured—but also a desire to influence the numbers however they could.

"Gallup Never Asked Me"

Public doubts about Gallup and Roper's new technology were thrown into sharp relief upon the pollsters' symbolic defeat by Harry Truman in 1948. Just a year or so before the electoral debacle, Roper had pinpointed the largest problem with the polls as the citizenry's "blind faith" in their accuracy. This was a danger, he felt, "not only to this infant science but to public opinion itself." Roper had no more cause for concern after Truman's upset of Dewey. Weighing in on the matter, one social scientist worried about the polls losing the support of scholars and commentators. But he made an even stronger case for shoring up the general population's confidence in the polls, urging the entire profession to assure the public of surveyors' "willingness to consider and give due weight to the opinions of all." Observers of all kinds worried about the implications of 1948. In a 1949 article in the *Public Opinion Quarterly,* two sociologists referred obliquely to the "traumatic November episode" casting a pall over their field. Their essay went on to discuss the crucial importance of polling's public image. Their "widespread, relatively prolonged, and intense" adverse reaction to the inaccurate forecasts, the authors feared, would not only undermine popular acceptance of opinion research but might also "radiate" out to "the more remote field of social science" as a whole. This was especially true if the lesson the public had learned was "the intrinsic unpredictability of human behavior." Such commentaries speak to practitioners' belief that social scientific ways of knowing had not yet found a secure place in American culture. As one opinion surveyor put it, the 1948 election had thrown "a bright light on what might be called the public relations of social science at the present time."[1]

Research organizations responded promptly. The Social Science Research Council (SSRC) Committee on Analysis of Pre-election Polls and Forecasts was appointed just eight days after the election, with funds from the Carnegie and Rockefeller foundations. It immediately stepped in to perform a thorough investigation of the national polls—Gallup's, Roper's, and Crossley's, in particular—reasoning that "quick action" was necessary because "extended controversy regarding the pre-election polls among lay and professional groups might have extensive and unjustified repercussions upon all types of opinion and attitude studies and perhaps upon social science research generally." At stake were two rather weighty matters: first, the credibility of social science with the public, and second, the very reliance, by 1948, of modern politics, and other domains of American society, on polling techniques. Opinion surveys were "one of the fundamental research tools" of social science, and the SSRC could not simply dismiss Gallup's poor showing or decide to do without polls. Barely concealing its anxiety, the Committee urged: "The public should draw no inferences from pre-election forecasts that would disparage the accuracy or usefulness of properly conducted sampling surveys in fields in which the response does not involve expression of opinion or intention to act."[2]

Critics of all sorts were able to invoke 1948 to cast doubt on polling techniques, whether related to other political forecasts or social issue surveys. To many, this one spectacular miscall had the power to bring the entire enterprise into question. "You were wrong in the election and you are wrong now to tell the Congress we want any part of war," penned a woman protesting Roper's assessment that Americans supported intervention in Korea in 1950. One letter arrived at Gallup's AIPO office in 1952, rebuking Gallup's preelection polls of that year. It was addressed simply to "Wrong Again," Princeton, New Jersey. Another writer requested that Roper never use the word *accuracy* in connection with any of his findings. As he put it, "Your reputation and past record is too greatly fresh in our minds." Yet another critic, an NBC listener, wrote to Roper to critique his performance in the two previous elections and thus his expert status: "It amazes me—just how any human can stake a claim to 'public opinion analyst' and a 'reporter' on the state of mind of the American people with a record reavealing [sic] a fantastic fiasco in 1948 and a hesitant fence-straddling in the Republican 1952 landslide."[3]

For *this* public anyway, the pollsters' infamous error was an invaluable plank in the discrediting of their surveys more generally. Having set up election results as a litmus test, Gallup and Roper had incited such distrust, creating the possibility that their carefully built professional apparatus would collapse around them. Challenges to the polls by ordinary citizens were not simply a product of

1948, however. Opinion polls from the beginning stood in uneasy relation to the American public. Indeed, distrust and dependence went hand in hand with new survey technologies.

But the pollsters depended on the people too. Ordinary citizens' opinions were surveyors' lifeblood and a sought-after commodity. Gallup claimed that "nine people in every ten" were willing to talk to pollsters and, moreover, were eager to furnish their opinions. When the interviewer arrived at the door, "there oftentimes goes up a shout summoning the whole family to see 'the man who's come to get our vote,'" he wrote in 1941, noting that the pollster's problem was sometimes just the opposite of silence. Occasionally, the poll worker had to prevent the interview from becoming a forum where everyone in the household chimed in. According to Gallup, once the early days of scientific polling had passed, instances of suspicion or refusal to answer were infrequent. Instead, "the anonymity of the surveys, their fact-finding objectives, and the natural though often shy curiosity which most people feel in their own and in their neighbor's opinions—all these factors dispose the public to co-operate with the surveys." It was only in rather un-American places such as Louisiana under Huey Long that citizens "were guarded in their replies for fear of reprisals and coercion." (In 1939, Gallup reported, AIPO interviewers there were warded off with shotguns and arrests, running into "almost as much 'resistance' as they might face in a dictatorship.")[4]

The pollster's optimistic view of people's desire to talk to his corps of interviewers was certainly inaccurate in the case of some poor and nonwhite respondents, as Roper's experiments with probability sampling in Harlem had made plain. Refusal, a contemporary researcher reported, was "most frequent among poor people, women, and in large cities." The problem was familiar enough that pollsters invented new categories of citizens in order to discuss it: the nonrespondent and the "hard to reach individual." Gallup's characterization of willing volunteers was further undercut by some of his own interviewer reports as well as scholarly articles that plumbed the topic of breaking down respondents' resistance. An entire literature was spawned by the problem of "refusal," dwelling on coercing respondents to talk, and to talk truthfully. A corresponding literature explored which interviewers could do this most skillfully (women, it turned out). The "interesting research problem," observed market surveyor Alfred Politz, was obtaining honest answers: "Why should a respondent tell the truth to a stranger?" What was needed was methodical investigation into "how to treat a respondent, how to question him in order to make him tell the truth." The element of force implied here was not uncommon. As the 1948 report of the SSRC explained, "Evidence suggests that undecided responses are evasions which can be broken through by persistent questioning."[5]

As these discussions suggest, familiarizing citizens with the stranger seeking personal information was not a challenge pollsters alone faced. Many enterprises, social scientific, commercial, and bureaucratic, were coming to depend upon ordinary people's feedback for their functioning. Resistance to official information-gathering sparked new techniques for eliciting data. The U.S. Census Bureau, for example, felt it necessary to establish a Public Relations Division in 1940. Its attempts to persuade citizens to take part in its work included compelling slogans: "To know America, tell America" and "You can know your country only if your country knows you." Pamphlets urging "This is *your* 1940 census" showcased the effort's democratic function, one that afforded "an opportunity for almost everyone to participate in a national enterprise." Pollsters devised their own strategies. One Gallup interviewer explained that individual "resistance can be overcome, usually, by understanding the reason for it." Those who were apathetic could be engaged. Those who were afraid—which accounted for most cases, she noted—could be reassured by the skillful questioner who promised anonymity, explained why the opinion was requested, and "removed" from the respondent "any feeling he may have that what he is going to say may be the wrong thing. He must be made to think that what he is saying is important." Cajoling wary respondents to consent to being questioned was thus as much a part of the interviewer's task as was marking down answers.[6]

Most individuals who were polled in the street or on their doorstep, it seems, did cooperate. But responses to standardized questionnaires constituted only a small fraction of the opinions that pollsters would be privy to over the years. Having set up shop as gatherers of the people's viewpoints, surveyors would be buffeted by them—mostly of the unsolicited variety and from every possible direction. This was in part because pollsters were eager popularizers. Experts in public relations, Gallup and Roper made plugs for the polls in a broad range of middlebrow venues, from *Good Housekeeping* to *Scribner's Magazine,* not to mention their regular radio broadcasts and newspaper articles. Roper, chronicling his "killing schedule" to a correspondent in 1952, noted his annual obligation to "fifty-two radio shows, fifty-two newspaper columns, [and] thirteen television shows," not to mention "a very large backlog of industrial business which is needed to pay the freight!" These commitments gave him a visible and audible public platform, his column appearing in three million homes in 1948 and his radio show airing in nearly one hundred affiliate stations across the United States in 1953. Although his polls were syndicated, they nevertheless sparked an intimate back-and-forth with readers and listeners. Roper reported receiving several dozen letters in response to some of his columns, and fifty to one hundred after certain radio broadcasts. Gallup was an even more prominent national figure, a target of both fan and hate mail.[7]

Pollsters were, on the one hand, compilers of anonymous opinions; on the other, they were highly familiar weighers-in on contemporary events. "I enjoyed your recent appearance on [CBS's] PERSON to PERSON television show," wrote one Patricia Filbert to

George Gallup and his wife, Olivia, in 1956. Given that the Gallups were "expert measurers of American political trends," she wanted to know their opinion on recent legal developments in her hometown of Orlando, Florida. Another fan of Gallup's from Carlisle, Pennsylvania, sent him a missive on topics ranging from divorce law and murder rates to commercial medicine and women in politics. At the end of the letter she paused to explain her reason for writing. "You [sic] a man of wisdom and may have a Poll of some of the things I have mentioned." Similarly, Mrs. W. G. Rouse from Montana wrote to Elmo Roper, "I have listened very attentively [sic] to your broadcasts and as you appear to me to have more common sense and intelligence than some I know of in Washington I just thought I would like to ask you a few questions pertaining to some things our foolish government is doing." She proceeded to grill him about several different federal policies. Assuming that Gallup and Roper had special acumen in the arena of public affairs, some citizens took up their pens to inquire about the pollsters' opinions, reversing the usual direction of questioning.[8]

Others who wrote to the pollsters hoped instead to extend a conversation that had already begun on their doorstep. They often chose not to remain anonymous. Elizabeth Stein, who identified herself as a retired New York City teacher, began a letter to Roper by mentioning the poll she had just taken part in the day before, the topic of which had been radio and television programming. "She was a fine woman," she wrote of her interviewer, "and I welcomed the opportunity." Stein's letter indicates that she attempted to engage her questioner on a much broader range of topics than the latter had intended: "When I criticized the average music she was not sure if you were interested tho she agreed that in the main it was 'noise.'" Stein went on to elaborate upon this opinion, and many others for the pollster, including "youth's taste for music," American cultural influence abroad, the violence of children's toys, and the quality of commercial advertisements. Such correspondents per-

After 1936, George Gallup became a household name, virtually synonymous with public opinion. (*Time* magazine cover, ©1948 Time Inc. Reprinted by permission.)

haps assumed that because surveyors had been curious about their views on one aspect of a social issue, they might well be interested in others.[9]

Many more poll watchers were moved to tell Roper and Gallup how they would have spoken on the issues had they been asked—in one woman's words, to add her "penny's worth to the discussion." Large numbers of the unpolled wrote in unsolicited, as did "A Contented Ford Employee" in 1947 to say to Roper: "I did not happen to be one of those selected to answer questions on your recent [poll], but I would like to express my views." Gallup and Roper had taken pains to present their new technology as a democratic instrument, and it seems that some of their readers and listeners treated it that way. Charles Moore mused in a letter to Gallup in May 1956, "I do not know where you get your figures." But he wanted the pollster to record "all four votes from my family" in opposition to a visit by Soviet premier Nikita Khrushchev to the United States. Moore employed the terminology of elections to express his wish that his opinions be weighed. This equation between votes and poll responses was adopted by many others as well. A man by the name of R. F. Holmes who saw a Gallup Poll in the *Los Angeles Times* in the mid-1950s fired off a missive to the pollster the same day, explaining, "I want to get my vote in against the U.N. and all foreign entanglements." Still another reader, this one anonymous, sent a curt note to Gallup regarding a survey on daylight saving time: "Sir, you may add 3 more *no*." Much as citizens had responded to straw polls, these writers evinced a desire to opine and to be heard, whether as part of a scientific sample or not. Their letters also reveal a faith that their voices would make a difference to the pollsters and their tallies.[10]

Far from slamming the door on inquisitive surveyors, many individuals believed that they counted in the eyes of the statisticians. One Pennsylvania man's rather personal relationship to the national polls illustrates this well. In a letter to Roper just after the miscall of the 1948 presidential election, he reported: "Perhaps I had one small part in causing that error." Taking some of the blame upon himself for the failure of the polls, he explained that he had indicated to a field interviewer that he would vote for Dewey, but in the end had voted for Truman. The man apologized, stating, "I didn't deliberately try to deceive. I changed my mind in the last week of the campaign," and noted that a couple of his friends had done the same. Roper told a similar story about a woman from Pittsburgh who also changed her mind in 1948. She wrote to him: "I have been feeling badly about that [ever] since I read that the polls had failed." Some of the surveyed believed they were individually responsible for the results, and that one opinion could be determinate.[11]

Other citizens made their voices heard in a different way. They wrote not to respond to already-formulated questions but to offer their own singular views about which way public opinion was going to swing next. Not ready to cede judgment to the pollsters, they evaluated the public's pulse themselves and shared their insights with the experts. "I wonder if the [R]epublicans really know what a beating they are going to take in the next election," wondered one writer. Revealing the multiple channels of opinion open to the polls' consumers, she told Gallup that her conversations with like-minded women in the grocery store were proof of great discontent with prices, the national budget, and taxes. Others proffered friendly advice. Hoping to help Roper sort out the polls' mistake in 1948, for instance, Reverend Joseph D. Mitchell from Signal Mountain, Tennessee sent the surveyor a three-page letter outlining his hypothesis regarding the effects of last-minute campaigning in changing voters' minds. Claiming to be "no 'expert,'" this man acknowledged, "It may seem audacious on my part to offer any thoughts or suggestions . . . [but] you said in November you would welcome any suggestions. This one really comes from one who admires you very much." A final category of poll watchers contacted Gallup and

Roper to find out how the questions were phrased or how large the sample was for particular surveys so that they could assess for themselves whether they were willing to trust the conclusions. Pollsters, it seems clear, had summoned a certain closeness to their audiences by presenting themselves less as distant authorities than as approachable readers of the public mind.[12]

The ocean of opinions that Gallup and Roper triggered suggests something of the polls' civic potential. Exchanges with the pollsters may have encouraged some Americans to engage in political debates, an effect for which surveyors claimed credit in their arguments about making the unheard "articulate." E. Dayton, a reader who encountered a Gallup Poll on juvenile delinquency in 1954, was prompted to write to its creator: "I have never before written to any paper or persons expressing my views but I feel this time I must get it off my chest." This writer's opinion—that working mothers and married women were at the root of the problem—led to a four-page letter analyzing the reasons. Once made aware of others' views, however impersonally, citizens may also have gained a new sense of belonging to a broader civic discussion.[13]

But this constituted a critical difference from earlier workings of public opinion. Interactions between the public and the pollsters did not actually occur in public. Nor, in expressing their opinions to field interviewers, did the polled aspire to alter fellow voters' or citizens' views. In fact, revising one's views might undercut the polls' accuracy, as the last-minute vote switchers in 1948 who wrote to Roper recognized. Their apologetic tone suggested that changing one's mind after being surveyed was somehow irresponsible. Furthermore, individual opinions, whether asked for or not, were increasingly directed to national experts, and one suspects that the dialogue ended there. A Gallup interviewer observed in 1940 that respondents frequently had queries of their own while being questioned, wondering who would be elected, how polls worked, or simply "what other men and women are thinking." Regarding the last of these she commented, "Eight out of ten, after answering a question, will either ask directly what most people said about it or will remark indirectly, 'I suppose nobody else said that.' They are delighted if told that everybody said it. It makes them feel that they were right." Respondents and consumers of the polls alike were discovering a new community of opinion. They were also, more and more frequently, going through social scientific intermediaries in order to talk in public.[14]

For every poll watcher seeking to be heard, scores more believed they were being silenced. The vast majority of Americans who wrote to Roper and Gallup did so not to tender their views but because they were troubled that a science claiming to speak for them had never bothered to ask their opinion in the first place. To put it mildly, polling's key methodology aroused public distrust. The logic of scientific sampling—that the nation's spectrum of beliefs could be divined from doorstep interviews with as few as a thousand people—was never intuitive to many citizens, who saw the practice as fundamentally unrepresentative, if not magical.

To begin with, opinion sampling did not square with popular conceptions of what was scientific, leading to countless charges of "guess-work," hocus-pocus, and hucksterism from pollsters' presumptive subjects and audiences. Upon seeing a Gallup Poll favoring Dwight Eisenhower's nomination for the Republican ticket in 1952, for example, the chairman of the opposing Robert Taft committee charged, "Dr. Gallup's findings are [of] the Ouija board variety. Gallup freely admits his poll is based on what he calls 'cross-section sampling' of somewhere between 1,500 and 3,000 people . . . so even at the maximum Gallup polls on the average less than one voter in each county." This method's fundamental dubiousness, it was implied, was so obvious as to require no further rebuttal.[15]

Rejection of the statistical basis of pollsters' facts was commonplace. This much is evident in George Gallup's and Elmo Roper's correspondence with those who read their poll results or listened to their radio broadcasts. Elinor Nevins from Nashville, Tennessee, summed up the general bewilderment in her missive to Gallup: "I notice you always say 'The Public' in the headline, but further down in very small print you say the question was put to a carefully selected sample of 1,536 persons. Now, how in the world, by any stretch of the imagination can 1,536 people be termed '*the public*'?" A New Yorker made the same point even more succinctly, suggesting that Roper's weekly column, *Where the People Stand,* ought properly be titled "Where the People Questioned Stand." Another writer's words, this time aimed at Gallup, borrowed the language of the U.S. Constitution to make the case: "Obviously, you haven't asked the majority of 'We The People.'" As the frequency of this complaint demonstrates, many critics of the polls did not buy the conceit that a handful of respondents could stand in for them, much less "the people."[16]

Some who contacted Gallup and Roper regarding scientific sampling were genuinely curious as to how the pollsters selected their respondents from a nation of millions. But most who had not been surveyed believed that their omission from the polls alone belied the polls' validity. Given surveyors' frequent statements about representing the public, many Americans found it surprising or even reprehensible that they had never been polled. "I am 48 years old— Have lived in Calif., N.Y., Colo., and Massachusetts and *never* in my long life have I ever known anyone who was quizzed by you or even approached! *Who* do you quizz [*sic*] and where and when??" inquired a woman of Gallup. Similarly, Robert Robusto of Baltimore informed the pollster: "As I have skeptically been following your recent Polls, I have been conducting one of my own. The first question is: 'Do you know of anyone that has ever been polled by Gallup'.??? Upon failure to find ANYONE yet to answer in the affir[m]ative my next question is then asked: 'Do you know of anyone that knows anyone that has ever been polled by Gallup'.??? Well, needles to say, I again fail to find ANYONE to say yes . . . So, WHERE do you find these people that you poll, I'd really like to know."[17]

This writer may have borrowed surveyors' techniques in his makeshift poll, but he did so, as he noted, with a good deal of skepticism. So did D. J. Stoner, who contacted Roper after hearing one of his radio shows, demanding: "Where do you get your information? I am 44 yrs old and have never been interviewed by a poll taker." This man said he ran a cigar stand in Pittsburgh and talked with hundreds of people every day, none of whom had been interviewed either. He went on to challenge Roper's figures indicating that a significant fraction of the public supported raising revenues. "I haven't met a person yet, that thinks the taxes should be higher," he charged. In his doubt that scientifically selected "representatives" could express his or his community's views, Stoner was not alone. Gallup confirmed the regularity of this vein of criticism, remarking that the most common query he received from individuals was "Why haven't I been interviewed?" and that this continued to be the case all the way through the late 1950s.[18]

Even complimentary consumers of the polls were hesitant to grant that they represented legitimate public opinion. A salesman for Squibb Pharmaceutical Company, R. D. Keim—who described himself as a regular reader of Roper's *Herald Tribune* column and Fortune Survey—confessed that he "sometimes wonder[ed] what persons are interviewed and give the replies to the questions that are asked." Although he claimed to have no interest in being interviewed himself, Keim was prompted to inquire because "among the 500 Squibb sales representatives throughout the United States" he had been unable to locate a single one who had been interviewed for any of Roper's surveys. (Keim, alas, did not indicate what sort of survey he had conducted to determine this fact.) The salesman deemed this a major oversight since his co-workers held worthwhile opinions and made for excellent polling material. He urged the pollster not to overlook his colleagues in the future, writing, "I think that you will agree with me that sales representatives of a highly respected firm like the House of Squibb are very likely to hear opinions expressed by many persons throughout the United States on subjects that are of vital interest to the American people." Keim assumed that thoughtful and judicious respondents would be of interest to the pollsters. He also implied that his fellow salesmen were useful less for their individual views than for their ability— through conversations and experience—to arrive at a considered perspective on the issues of the day. In effect, he drew upon an older understanding of how public opinion was formed and could be known.[19]

Gallup and Roper responded to these sorts of queries by emphasizing how rare it was, statistically, to be selected for one of their surveys. A typical reply from Roper's office emphasized "how small are any one individual's chances of being interviewed." To the Squibb sales representative, for instance, the pollster wrote, "The question you raise is one that often comes up in connection with surveys." He estimated that the chance of a particular person currently twenty-one years of age being interviewed by either the Fortune Survey or the Gallup Poll was something close to one in twenty-seven by the time that individual turned seventy-seven years old. Roper admitted that he himself had gone years without having been polled until a Crossley radio surveyor reached him on the telephone one day. He went on to assure Keim that "if no Squibb salesman has been interviewed, his counterpart has been." If he had not questioned Keim or any of his colleagues, that is, the pollster had questioned someone equivalent. In such replies, surveryors emphasized the interchangeability of their respondents and the well-oiled statistical process that chose them. This explanation was not very satisfying, of course, to those who felt their particular opinions deserved careful weight and respect. A technology of representation could appear to its critics much like an instrument of voicelessness.[20]

Pollsters, partly through their mailboxes, were well aware of their problems with the public. And they fretted regularly about the widespread distrust of sampling. "It is exceedingly difficult to convince the public that a sample or a cross-section of the general population can be selected in such a way as to represent with a high degree of accuracy the entire population," Gallup wrote with some frustration as early as 1936. "In most fields of research, particularly those in which the public is relatively untutored, findings are readily accepted," he complained. On the other hand, "the average man is quite vocal when political opinions are involved. Tell him that it is possible to select a few hundred or a few thousand persons in his state who represent the divergencies in point of view of the entire voting population of that state, and he will laugh, if he does not swear." This was a rather precise summation of pollsters' interactions with a disbelieving public.[21]

Attacks on the plausibility of sampling procedures came in some cases from those who had a hand in their circulation. Susan Herbst's study of the uses of public opinion surveys by journalists and legislators in the 1930s and 1940s reveals that both groups remained wary of Gallup and Roper's new science, trusting instead their own unaided power to evaluate public sentiment. Reporters continued to travel door-to-door or to public places with their questions and relied on surrogates—cabdrivers and train conductors, labor leaders and lobbyists—to get a bead on opinion trends. Machine bosses were in one journalist's view "more reliable than the polls" since surveys could assess only the current state of opinion and not the deep patterns in constituents' relationships with the political parties. Polls, of course, impinged on reporters' domain, their claim to authoritative characterizations of public affairs; Elmo Roper accused both *Time* and *Life* magazines of prejudice against surveys in favor of their old-fashioned political reporting. On their part, politicians continued to count letters, telephone calls, editorials, and even shows of hands. When legislators commissioned polls, they did so as much for public relations purposes as for garnering useful information—and then went ahead and relied upon their instincts and best judgment. This ambivalence was only heightened by the events of 1948. One newspaper editor reported in the aftermath that he had "lost faith in election polls and will decline to be guided by them in [the] future unless they coincide with [my] own observations." Deciding to return to prescientific assessments of the lay of the land, he was doubtful that surveys could "give reliable answers on any type of problems, unless the poll gets opinions from an extremely large fraction of the population." Of course, it was exactly this article of faith—that accurate results could be achieved only through massive numbers of respondents—that pollsters believed they had challenged so successfully in 1936.[22]

Strength in Numbers

Pollsters advertised themselves as the voice of the public, and they corresponded regularly with that segment of the public who hoped to modify, amplify, or otherwise correct that voice. Roper proclaimed in his final broadcast for CBS in 1952 that the variety and volume of popular commentary on his polls "amazed" him: "Some of it took me to task for not really knowing what the facts were, some for stating the facts in a way that created the wrong impression; some charged me with having a note of sadness in my voice when I announced the opinions of a majority as though I felt sure the majority was *always wrong*—others assumed I always *agreed* with the majority and assailed *me* when *they disagreed* with that majority." The pollster's sketch of the range of criticisms directed his way suggests the trouble midcentury surveyors faced in winning over the people they aimed to describe. Having carved out a niche in 1936 as readers of the public's mind, Gallup and Roper struggled to maintain it. Many Americans—from members of Congress to the fabled "man in the street"—were suspicious of pollsters' methods as well as their potential sway over elections, administrations, and individual voters. Opinion polls were routinely accused of creating a "bandwagon" effect and of muting or corrupting public discourse. Charges of personal bias and illegitimate power were part and parcel of pollsters' trade.[23] On the political front, the U.S. Congress and state governments made numerous attempts to rein in the new technology. Gallup noted that "bills to prohibit polls or to regulate them out of existence" had been proposed since scientific polling's inception. Congressman Walter M. Pierce of Oregon introduced legislation in every Congress beginning in 1932 to investigate the political influence of opinion surveys. Gallup himself came under congressional scrutiny in 1944 for his underestimation of Democratic wins—partly because FDR suspected that the pollster was on his opponent's payroll. Similarly, charges circulated in 1948 that pollsters systematically inflated the Republican vote, manipulating results to suit the editorial preferences of the newspapers that hired them. "Public election polls have become so integrated in the American political scene that they are substantially analogous to public offices in that they are public trusts," editorialized an Indiana newspaper that year. "If they cannot or will not be conducted accordingly they should be outlawed."[24]

Gallup and Roper were oftentimes seen to have different slants, the former tilting more Republican and the latter more Democratic, but each was regularly attacked by individuals from all points of the political spectrum. Much of his mail, Roper lamented, came "from people who are quite sure that we have sold out to either big business or organized labor, the Republican or the Democratic Party, or Joe Stalin." A single poll could trigger diverse and contradictory accusations of bias. Responding to a survey reporting on the popularity of various American leaders in 1948, a Los Angeles man wrote to Roper, "I can tell you loaded that poll so that you could give your New Deal, Communist pal Roosevelt another plug." Another, writing from New York City, charged of the same survey, "Your faked poll results are part of the campaign . . . to vilify the good name and candidacy of a great American," in this case Henry Wallace, the standard-bearer of the Progressive Party. Yet another, a southerner, accused Roper of helping the Republicans rig the poll in favor of their own Harold Stassen.[25]

Disregarding pollsters' repeated avowals of neutrality, many readers and listeners thought they detected in purportedly impartial percentages partisan agendas. The charge of political tampering was often straightforward. "Your polls usually make good propaganda for the *administration's* program," charged one woman of Gallup; another correspondent noted sarcastically, "The Communist[s] know they can rely on *you* to take a Poll in their favor." It was difficult for some readers to believe that surveyors were neutral to the outcomes of their polls and, given the opportunity, would not be motivated to manipulate public opinion. The fact that newspapers until recently had been partisan affairs and that media objectivity was a relatively new imperative may have underwritten such concerns. Whatever the cause, new experts who derived their authority from channeling "the public" needed to be watched carefully, these critics implied, because they held a uniquely influential tool in their hands.[26]

Some of the pollsters' most astute watchdogs criticized not particular findings but an overall pattern of distortion they saw in the statistics. One of them was Harry Baruchin, a laborer from New York City, who had determined, following one of Roper's 1950 CBS broadcasts, that the pollster had it out for the unions. Here, he echoed leading labor unions, such as the Congress of Industrial Organizations (CIO), which—in one of the few concerted attacks on public opinion research—had critiqued the polls "for their lack of objectivity so far as labor was concerned." Baruchin had his own suspicions as to the reason. "Since your bread and butter depends on your slanting your stuff in favor of management instead of actual facts in reference to labor—one cannot expect you to do less. Otherwise you would be out of a job." Baruchin's worry was not simply Roper's supposed bias, but his ability to attract adherents to his cause, and he criticized the pollster for "the harm that you do to help create public opinion which does not present the true facts of labor." Baruchin well understood the force of amassed numbers speaking for the popular will. He also perceived how easily such surveys might exclude certain groups from the mainstream public. To that end, he wanted to know why the surveyor had posed questions about organized labor's responsibility to the nation in a 1950 poll but had not asked the same about corporations.[27]

Baruchin was a formidable critic. Well versed in the literally hundreds of variables that might affect the results of any given opinion poll, he put Roper through the paces as to the survey's construction. Baruchin wanted to know not just how many people were questioned but where they resided; if the questions probed attitudes toward labor, he reasoned, it ought to be clear whether interviewees came from an industrial state or a union town. He also wanted to know what percentage of those critical of organized labor were bosses or bosses' wives: "You did not expect the boss to be in favor of the CIO or any other union did you?" he demanded incredulously. In favor of further segmenting the respondents along income and occupational lines, he quarreled with the pollster's categories— asking, for instance, if the farmers in the sample were large, small, or absentee proprietors, and how many belonged to a cooperative. Furthermore, he inquired as to how many interviewees still assumed John Lewis was head of the CIO, which would perhaps explain their negative opinion, and about the poll's particular timing. "Since the CIO is still in the process of purging the communist or claimed to be communist-led unions this is ce[r]tainly a poor time to ask people about the CIO," he charged. In closing, Baruchin invited Roper to visit "a half-dozen coal mines [in] both company and non-company towns" and "speak to the miners and their families" to get a fuller and presumably unmediated understanding of "the facts of labor." Insisting that political views were attached to people's life circumstances, Baruchin argued for a socially embedded understanding of how people came to their opinions in contrast to the polls' presentation of atomized individual attitudes.[28]

Baruchin's discerning critique of Roper's poll revealed his familiarity with social scientific methods. It also demonstrated how important it was for some groups, fearful of marginalization, to scrutinize public opinion surveys because of the influence they assumed those same surveys to exert. Many critics worried about the compelling nature of poll results, the authority numbers almost automatically wielded; others about the potentially manipulative uses of survey data. Letters from readers and listeners provide ample evidence that Gallup and Roper did not manage to convince all or most of the public of the validity of their statistics. Those same letters nevertheless indicate that, whether skeptical or credulous about surveyors' facts, citizens recognized the ability of polling data to persuade. Indeed, they were learning that majority and minority percentages were useful weapons in political combat.

Some expressed faith in the literal representations of the majority that the polls supplied, or at least adopted that stance for their own purposes. An exclamatory, full-page advertisement in the *Chicago Daily News* taken out by Eisenhower supporters in 1952 read: "In every accredited poll, Eisenhower has led Taft by substantial majorities! Not just one poll, but polls conducted by Elmo Roper, George Gallup, Archibald Crossley, by independent newspapers and by The Wage Earner's Forum, *all* point to one unmistakable fact! . . . Eisenhower is the majority candidate!" Quoting three separate polls by the American Institute of Public Opinion, the advertisement continued: "For a Republican victory in November *we must* LISTEN TO THE PEOPLE!" Others were willing to employ "the people," as defined by the polls, in similar fashion. By the early 1950s the necessity of tracking scientific opinion surveys was evident to many organizations, from the Women's National Republican Club to the Department of State to the Democratic National Committee. Individual politicians sought out pollsters on issues large and small, hoping these experts could help them tap into the public mind and "appeal to millions of middle-of-the-road people." This was Connecticut Congressman Chester Bowles's hope in sounding out Roper in 1946 as to whether he should write an article for *Life* magazine on the progressive Democratic program—and whether the pollster had any suggestions for how to write it. Aggregate opinion was useful in strategizing on any number of issues. Even Roper's survey of what the "typical American" ate attracted the attention of the Farm Security Administration's nutrition office, which believed the pollster's hard facts would help it better plan and persuade. Opinion entrepreneurs were becoming crucial middlemen in deciphering popular views and determining what public policy stances candidates and organizations should take.[29]

Plenty of individuals outside of politics or state agencies found specific poll results—if the statistics supported their mission—just as desirable, invoking majority percentages to marshal support for causes ranging from traffic safety to lower postal rates. Stewart Ogilvy of World Government News, Inc., not surprisingly applauded Roper's broadcast announcing an uptick in public approval of "world government." He went on to offer suggestions "we federalists might make concerning the wording of questions." Some made bids for surveys they believed would demonstrate the popularity of their own views, such as one man who wrote to Gallup asking him to "take a poll to determine what percent of voters think that [Tennessee senator Estes] Kefauver is drawing his salary under false pretense." Another writer, disturbed by the negative slant on Joseph McCarthy in the news and convinced his admiring view toward the senator was in the majority, prodded the pollster to draw up some questions: "You can do a true service for the USA by a *true survey, Gallup style, at this time!*" These special pleaders hoped surveyors would put their techniques to work in the service of partisan views and serve as a gateway to public and political influence.[30]

Some feared that the frequent broadcasting of mass opinion had more pernicious effects, creating the allure of universality and the desire to join the majority. Douglas Ward of Fontana, California, charged Gallup with "a slick and nasty method of campaigning by using your figures to prove your man is a winner." This he judged especially pernicious since "everybody wants to be on the Winning Side." Another angry writer sent a letter to Gallup care of the "American Institute for Measuring or Formulating of Public Opinion." To these critics, measuring *meant* formulating. The kind of influence surveys exercised could prompt parallel anxieties in the marketing business. The president of CBS, getting wind of results in 1946 indicating that black-and-white television was "acceptable" to a majority of consumers, demanded an investigation into the offending survey by Gallup, Roper, Crossley, or another "recognized research authority" to certify its fairness, "the extent to which those interviewed had viewed CBS color television," and so forth. To Roper he confided, "This type of research should be challenged at every turn."[31]

The potency of statistics claiming to represent the thinking of the American public was always most evident to those who fell in the minority. This was true even before Gallup and Roper came upon the scene. Prohibitionists earlier in the century, aware of the danger unfavorable numbers posed to their cause, had opposed or even boycotted straw polls on the topic. Pollsters' scientifically derived and "democratic" percentages raised the stakes. Lobbying groups like the National Rifle Association (NRA), wary of public opinion polls for the same reason prohibitionists had been, attempted to derail adverse statistics after the fact. In response to a poll displaying support for firearm legislation in the late 1950s, Gallup was besieged by angry letters from NRA members accusing him of doing damage to "the law-abiding gun owners and gun sportsmen of this country." To their challengers, pollsters' figures were not just numbers. They were the embodiment of the majority's will and therefore able to harm or help any number of agendas.[32]

Yet the strongest undercurrent in Americans' initial response to the polls was not the purported bandwagon effect, but just the opposite: the enormous consequence citizens invested in their own readings of aggregate opinion, even when unrelated to concrete outcomes such as social policies or financial gain. Myriad letters poured into the Fortune Survey and the AIPO testifying to people's anger at and disbelief in statistics that contradicted their own sense of the political mainstream. Ina Hazen from Youngstown, Ohio, was a case in point. She began by condemning one of Gallup's surveys showing support for Alaskan statehood. A vigilant poll follower, she went on to say, "I have yet to see a poll result published that agreed with my opinion or that of anyone I knew." Hazen declared: "I always disagree with you. I dare you to send a representative to interview me. I am a college woman with a broad education by the way, and quite well read, with a lively interest in politics. So again I repeat that I suspect your 'cross sections' are *very* carefully selected."[33]

Many who took up their pens to write to Gallup and Roper had an unwavering conviction in their grasp of national attitudes, and used their own numbers to buttress challenges to the polls. One such critic was Eleanor Holmes, of Ansonia, Connecticut, who complained in 1951 that Elmo Roper was "98 per cent wrong" regarding American support for universal military training. He might speak for "a certain group" (she suspected New Yorkers), but certainly not "the American people." That same year, W. C. Hollingsworth heard and promptly dismissed Roper's finding that a majority supported President Truman's recall of General MacArthur from Korea. "In Los Angeles county," he asserted, "it is 10 to 1 against the administration," and Hollingsworth did not require any sophisticated polling techniques to figure this out. "You will learn that the public is still for him [MacArthur] . . . Your statement tonight about the *People* being of majority opinion on Adm[inistration] policy is your opinion and you should say so," he argued, adding, "keep your figures straight."[34]

Citizens repeatedly expressed their sentiments in the same numerical language that Roper and Gallup had made popular. "You are certainly in error as far as the Great State of Texas is concerned as to only 6% of the voters being for Senator Jo[seph] McCarthy," announced Joseph Glenn, a reader of Gallup's column in the *Houston Post*. Another put the figure in the positive, but otherwise agreed, writing, "if you took a true poll of the American people . . . you would find them over 95% for Senator McCarthy." Similarly, J. M. Mottey, responding to a poll in Florida's *St. Petersburg Times* that ranked Eleanor Roosevelt as America's most admired woman, fumed to Gallup, "In regard to Mrs. Roosevelt you are crazy as a bed bug. She is made fun of and despised by 95% of the people. Your Polls are the biggest fakes I know of." Such challengers adopted the pollsters' quantitative argot. But their exaggerated numbers—95 or 98 percent of the nation was nearly always purported to agree with them—and their faith that "true" polls would bear them out expressed a stubborn confidence in their own judgments about where the majority stood. Such was certainly true of a worker who accused Gallup in 1956 of throwing his polls for the Republicans. He urged the pollster to "clamp your eyes on something true right from our plant. This straw vote was taken yesterday: Ike 3—Democrat 24 . . . Ike *can not get elected*." That same year, Alfred Petrash of Houston wrote to Gallup: "Dear Sir, Every time I open a paper and see your predictions and polls favoring Eisenhower, I cannot understand, [sic] where in the hell you get them. I travel around the country and find the people are sick and tired of hearing his useless doings." Part of Petrash's assurance was derived from "knowing" how his own communities would vote. "I am a catholic and know the catholic vote is against him," he explained, and "could write many pages to tell you why he [won't] be elected."[35]

There was no end to such arguments between the pollsters and the people over their relative abilities to know the public. Another Texan, a woman who claimed to know the "pulse" of the South, wrote to contest Roper's account of public support for integration in Little Rock, Arkansas in 1957. Contrasting her basis for judgment with his, she charged that the pollster wrote not only with "the North's superior attitude" but also "from the level of public opinion and apparencies [sic]." Margaret Jamison's competence in reading public opinion instead came from real experience. Quoting Roper back at himself, she wondered if he was "personally acquainted with the 'better elements' in L[ittle] R[ock]? Did you talk with them, and did they tell you they 'greeted the Federal troops with a wave of relief'[?] Did anyone of the 'better elements' tell you personally that they felt that the Federal troops were 'needed?'" Whether relying on old-fashioned straw polls or personal experience, some readers kept faith with their own assessments of the majority.[36]

Much like Middletowners had, these writers stressed their local credentials and on-the-ground perspective to discredit the polls. Offering proof of their broad social contacts or special insights, they believed the experts were too far from grocery store gossip or the factory floor to get a real bead on public opinion. Whether writers "knew" Catholics, the labor union local, or the "pulse" of the South, they contested pollsters' authority to speak for the nation. Evidently—given the volume of Gallup's and Roper's correspondence—many also believed that the old-fashioned technique of writing letters remained an effective channel for expressing public opinion. But the depth of many writers' antagonism toward the polls revealed misgivings that their ability to challenge scientific surveys might not last for long, and that old ways of assessing opinion were giving way to a new top-down regime of expert measurement.

Indeed, Elmo Roper wrote off individuals who disputed poll results as "crackpots" so sure of their opinions that "they cannot even conceive of a large group of their neighbors disagreeing with them." As he put it to the readers of his *Herald Tribune* column, "When anybody dares to say that such-and-such a percentage of Americans are inclined to think one way, and that happens to be contrary to what the man who reads about it thinks, then it follows, as night follows day, that it is the pollster and never the individual who must be wrong." But what prompted so many to write to the pollsters to urge them they were mistaken? And what explains their hostility toward surveys they disagreed with? Citizens' sense of the national mood, it seems clear, gave them their bearings, situating them in their own imagined public. This may account for the passion with which they protested findings that threatened to undermine their personal certainties. For those who had been accustomed to gleaning opinion from their local communities and networks, it could be alienating to discover that their specific public opinion community appeared to be so out of step with the larger, national one.[37]

A portion of the general public was always fascinated by the kind of knowledge pollsters supplied. New Yorker Byron Gloor, declaring himself a regular reader of Roper's *Herald Tribune* column, praised the pollster for "performing a[n] extremely useful function in the society of modern America." Across the country in Laguna Beach, California, Theodore Baer assured Roper, "There are many people most eager to get the facts your poll brings out." Through Gallup's AIPO surveys, proclaimed a commentator for *Forum and Century* in 1941, "America has had a firsthand opportunity to become acquainted with its own mind." Critics and fans alike understood opinion polling as a novel form of reportage "which has given the reading public data which it did not previously possess."[38] This newfound acquaintance with "the public," however, came as a shock to many Americans theretofore certain of their own aptitude in knowing the nation. The impersonal knowledge of the polls appeared to outmode local familiarity in favor of aggregate statistics, and individuals' understandings of political attitudes bumped up hard against pollsters' quantitative majorities and minorities. Citizens' firsthand perceptions about the world, and their assessment of the array of attitudes with which they came into contact, some were coming to sense, were no match for the experts' political and social facts. The public might be wise, as Gallup and Roper claimed, but amateur interpreters of national opinion had little standing in the scientific polling era.

Roper and Gallup seemed unaware that it was the very novelty of polling technology that prompted so much of the public's disaffection. Challenges to pollsters' facts and figures did not stem simply from an ignorance of sampling methods but from citizens' newfound—and often discomfiting—ability to measure their beliefs against a republic of strangers. When presented with scientifically determined majority opinions that contradicted their own sense of the mainstream, some rejected the data out of hand. Others strenuously resisted the implication that they might belong to a minority. In so doing, they betrayed a growing stake in the statistical majority, that entity so ardently praised for its aggregate intelligence by the likes of Gallup and Roper. Much as Middletowners desired to belong to a "typical" community, individuals clamored for a place in pollsters' particular version of the middle-of-the-road.

Given the fact that pollsters did undersample certain groups and skew their questioning in subtle ways, critics may have been right about specific surveys' inability to capture true public sentiment. Yet even if the surveyors had worked harder to uncover a representative America, it is likely that their means of measuring and displaying national opinion would still have been cause for agitation. Without granting the allure of aggregate support for individual attitudes, it is difficult to explain the vigor with which citizens challenged the pollsters or searched for evidence to counter their results. Many, it seems, had internalized the numerical notion of the people's will—that singular majoritarian strand pollsters distilled from the bewildering chaos of citizens' voices—and wanted to make sure, somehow, that they belonged to it.

Mediators of the Mass

Despite unceasing challenges from their readers, listeners, and respondents, Gallup and Roper claimed to speak for "the public" against elites: the editors of major newspapers and middlebrow magazines as well as national politicians. "It is fairly easy when you have to meet the daily deadlines of a newspaper or radio to grow to look upon the great unseen audience as an amorphous, faceless, nameless mass of humanity," intoned Roper, drawing the implicit comparison. But pollsters could themselves be seen as distant experts, as a 1942 cartoon in the *Chicago Tribune* suggested. It depicted Gallup dashing off a cliff labeled "oblivion" as a ballot box labeled "the people's poll" hit him on the head. This image portrayed the "people" as distinct from the polls, and the pollsters as remote from the public they purported to represent.[39]

Lodged in such reactions to opinion surveys was a persistent vein of humanistic thinking that countered pollsters' technological credo. CBS radio commentator Edward R. Murrow, reporting on the pollsters' underestimation of Eisenhower's win in 1952, encapsulated it:

Yesterday the people surprised the pollsters, the prophets, and many politicians. They demonstrated, as they did in 1948, that they are mysterious and their motives are not to be measured by mechanical means . . . It restored to the individual, I suspect, some sense of his own sovereignty. Those who believe that we are predictable . . . who believe that sampling depth, interviewing, allocating the undecided vote, and then reducing the whole thing to a simple graph or chart, have been undone again . . . And we are in a measure released from the petty tyranny of those who assert that they can tell us what we think, what we believe, what we will do, what we hope and what we fear, without consulting us—all of us.[40]

In this view, sampling techniques violated not just common sense. They also violated essential beliefs about individuality.

Counterposing the mysterious and the mechanical, individual unpredictability and reductionist social scientific methods, the sovereignty belonging to "all of us" and "sampling," Murrow played to real anxieties about the standardization that public opinion polling seemed to foster. The polls' failure, in other words, could be a resounding victory for "the people." Even Henry Luce, the publisher of the Fortune Survey, had his doubts about the desirability of an omniscient public opinion poll. "Thank God for free-will and for the heart which has its reasons which reason does not know," he wrote in 1949 in response to a charge of inaccuracies in the survey. Roper confided to a correspondent that the biggest problem following 1948 was "the so-called intellectuals who adopted a posture of 'Thank God, now that the polls have failed, maybe people will quit trying to figure out what makes mankind tick.'" Some ordinary readers were equally pleased that despite the advance of the polls, individuals still seemed to have minds of their own. "Just remember how impossible it seemed that Truman could triumph over Dewey as far as the press was concerned, but we voted for Truman," crowed Mrs. Frances Rasmussen of Alameda, California, in a letter to Roper. "They can't influence people that much, the pen isn't mightier than the truth!"[41]

Pollsters may have ridiculed such thinking in private, but they could ally themselves with this kind of critique when necessary, arguing against their own power when it appeared too threatening. "Contrary to popular supposition," *Today* magazine reported after talking with Gallup in 1936, "his tests showed that polls don't have nearly the influence credited to them." Roper proclaimed in a radio broadcast after 1948: "Any ideas that the people of this country are always ready to jump on a popular bandwagon, any ideas that the people are willing to have someone else make up their minds for them . . . can now be put to rest." The pollster closed by pointing to the "reassuring and inspiring picture of the kind of people Americans are" that issued from their rebuke to his poll. Gallup and Roper needed to keep their scientific claims afloat. In these instances, however, they took pains to downplay the polls' predictive ability. This disavowal of their own expertise represented a sensitive reading of the public mood. If surveyors could not always call elections, they were quite adept at picking up on the concerns their surveys engendered.[42]

Gallup and Roper's problem was similar to that of Helen and Robert Lynd, whose subjects had charged them with a cold and detached perspective on Middletown's people. Recognizing this, pollsters attempted to counteract widespread uneasiness about the impersonal, mechanical nature of the modern sample survey. In his very first radio broadcast, an analysis of Americans' views on food aid to Europe, Roper described in reassuring terms the elements of his craft: "Perhaps you're asking yourself on what basis we can make such claims." He explained that tracking public opinion entailed asking "representative cross-sections of the American people how they feel about this or that question." In another broadcast, he noted that although election sampling "sounds like a very technical subject," he believed it could "be made clear to the layman." Surveyors employed the simplest images possible to convey their polling operations, drawing analogies to everyday experience. A housewife tasting a spoonful of soup, a doctor drawing a sample of blood, and a boy eating the meringue, filling, and crust of a lemon meringue pie in one bite were all illustrations Gallup used to show why sampling "worked." Roper pointed to wheat and ore samples to express the relation between a small segment of a mass and the whole. In this way, surveyors aimed to translate abstract processes into familiar ways of thinking.[43]

Pollsters also worked to humanize their statistics, precisely reversing the process by which their knowledge had been made. In their explanations of survey methods, Roper and Gallup spoke in a folksy tenor that repersonalized the quantitative techniques behind the polls. The "man in the street" was only the most obvious instance. The working man and the farmer were prominent in their examples of the individuals pollsters queried in their search for "representative Americans." Roper regularly presented majority opinions in his weekly radio broadcasts using "a doctor who lives in the corn belt" or "a prosperous businessman in Detroit" to articulate those views. In a television program for CBS he made this technique explicit. "We have a lot of facts and figures and we could give you percentages on all sorts of odd aspects of life in America," Roper began. He immediately qualified this statement by saying, "But percentages have to come alive in terms of men and women like yourself and your neighbors before they mean anything. Percentages have to become what they actually are—different opinions and points of view."[44]

Believing feature stories and "the human element" were what audiences desired, newspapers and networks in fact consistently pushed pollsters in this direction. In its pitch to advertisers, the NBC radio network billed Roper's personal touch as his most marketable asset. Not only did the pollster put "warmth, life and showmanship" into his programs, but he also covered questions of human interest, "the questions that give listeners a chance to measure their reactions against the scientific findings of the Roper organization." Appealing to the audience directly and inviting involvement, the pollster's broadcasts helped to make aggregates seem less menacing. As Roper explained in a program on the economy in 1948, he was going to be talking about "the hopes and fears of the American consumer," adding, "the American consumer, is YOU." Gallup's descriptions of the public he sampled similarly evoked real individuals. "Both the stockbroker and the farmer," on "State Street in downtown Boston . . . [and] a backwoods road in Arkansas," he wrote, agreed about keeping the United States out of the war in 1940. But both figures in the next breath became "chance cogs in an endlessly functioning machine that samples public opinion." Gallup's use of these dual images—specific people and units in a mass—was indicative of a delicate balancing act: an attempt to convince Americans that opinion polling was a systematic science, and at the same time to win them over to it as a benign, comprehensible force.[45]

Gallup took care to depict the entire surveying operation as an essentially human interaction. As he told it, interviewers were heroic individuals who embraced the vast expanse of the country, traversing regional and class lines in order to deliver the voice of the people. They knew "what it is to drive through a Maine snowstorm to make a farm interview; to trudge across Kansas wheat fields on a blistering day to interview a thresher on the job; to travel through the red-clay mud of Georgia in a drenching rainstorm . . . They talk to the prominent industrialist . . . just as they talk to the old lady who silently mops his office." Gallup reported that members of his field staff were not infrequently asked to stay for dinner after asking their questions, "hunger for talk and politics" being "characteristic of small towns and homesteads." It was his interviewers, Gallup implied, not the cold numbers of his polls, who knitted national public opinion together. "On the unmapped back-country roads," he proposed, "the 'stranger with the questions' may be as welcome as the circuit-rider was a hundred years ago."[46]

Showing the real people on both sides of the doorstep interview,

surveyors sought to neutralize the unsettling aspects of the polls—
the stranger seeking personal information, the possibility of manipulation from above—and deftly made them part of an archetypical
American scene. Gallup returned frequently to this theme, in one
instance writing of his interviewers: "They provide the human case
material against which the 'people's own story,' as told in their own
words, can be more fully understood." Of course, the people's
"own words" were actually echoes of expert surveyors' questions,
translated into statistics that made their speakers indistinguishable
from each other, and unyoked from particular identities.[47]

As such, pollsters' attempts to stretch old metaphors of community to large-scale, impersonal survey technologies expressed the
cultural tensions of their time. Many Americans challenged surveyors' claims to locate public opinion. They also questioned how
much sway those who spoke for the majority ought to have. In response, pollsters downplayed their cultural clout, sidestepping critiques of influence and manipulation. But what pollsters could not
overcome in their campaigns of persuasion was a deep suspicion
that the kind of knowledge they produced was not, as they claimed,
a remedy for the bigness, complexity, and bureaucracy of modern
life but instead a contributing cause. The argument between the
pollsters and the public, then, did not turn merely on the legitimacy
of a particular form of social knowledge. It in many cases centered
instead on the new strains of living in a surveyed society: the dis-
placement of local beliefs by amassed national ones, the possibility
of incorrectly registering collective trends, the startling discovery
that one was attached to a minority cause. Apart from relatively infrequent election returns, there had been no easy or straightforward
way to measure one's place in the public before 1936. In the rift
between what people believed American opinion to be and what
was reported in authoritative percentages, there was some of
Middletown's dilemma writ large. But even more so with Gallup's
and Roper's polls, the scattered voices of respondents could not

effectively critique their aggregate self-portrait—nor even find each other in the mass.

The Lessons of 1948

Pollsters' dramatic miscall of 1948 illustrated the danger of one of their public relations strategies: using elections to prove the legitimacy of their science. But their quick recovery demonstrated rather forcefully that polling, culturally persuasive or not, had made itself indispensable to many areas of U.S. society. In the aftermath of 1948, while the Social Science Research Council took on the task of damage control, pollsters sounded out the harm done by Truman's defeat of Dewey in the way they knew best: by taking polls. In their surveys of the polls, researchers found that clients of polling agencies were divided over whether to continue their patronage. Members of Congress had become more hostile to the profession. Some editors claimed that they could not foresee running polls in their pages for years to come, believing the failed forecasts had made not merely opinion surveys but the newspapers that printed them the target of derision. After the 1948 election, the argument went, readers simply would not accept polls and were likely even to be insulted by their publication. One editor indicated that he would shy away from running poll results of any kind "until the public has had time to forget their bad showing," which he expected might be "four years, maybe eight, maybe twelve." He asserted, "I can say with virtual certainty that I wouldn't publish an opinion poll two years hence."[48]

And yet, in almost no time polling's crisis passed as if it had never happened. "Within six months," noted one observer, "market research agencies as well as public opinion polls were functioning at their 1948 levels." Roper wrote with great relief to a correspondent: "I'm finding that apparently [the 1948 miscalculation] didn't do any really substantial harm except the harm that comes to anybody who slips on a banana peel in public! Our interviewers are finding no trouble interviewing, the last employee attitude survey went off as well as they ever had before the election, and we've lost no clients." Indeed, he later reported to another acquaintance that marketing research had doubled between 1948 and 1956. Those newspaper editors who had sworn not to carry the polls for years did a quick about-face.[49]

How had this occurred? One factor was the polls' distinct blend of scientific and democratic rhetoric, promoted tirelessly by Gallup and Roper since 1936. The second, and related, factor was that polling techniques were firmly embedded in American society by 1948, after more than a decade of constant use. Writing in 1944, pollster Hadley Cantril spun a narrative of the rise of modern opinion research. As he told it, opinion surveys, first greeted with skepticism and ignorance, gradually earned their way to legitimacy. He asserted that "both social scientists and informed laymen have become familiar in a general way with the theory of stratified sampling" and that "public opinion research has become public property." The second of these claims, at least, was true. The durability of survey practices at a moment of crisis can be explained by polling's deep roots in the broader society: as an academic pursuit, a well-funded means of data collection by corporations and the government, and a popularly recognized form of social knowledge. Despite pollsters' difficulties in locating the people, and despite the distorted and unrepresentative public they projected, mass opinion surveys would become more and more foundational to the operations of American life over the course of the midcentury decades. Opinion polls, although privately owned, had indeed in some sense become "public property."[50]

Critiques of the polls from experts as well as ordinary individuals clearly did not cease after 1948. But the idea that this particular mode of gathering and displaying social data could be banished from American life was becoming increasingly implausible. In 1953 one scholar found that even four to five years after the election disaster of 1948, "the question of public opinion polling still strikes an intensely sensitive nerve among news executives of United States daily newspapers." Significantly, though, he noted that "whether a particular newspaper currently subscribes to or does not subscribe to a public opinion poll makes little difference in responses to the subject"—suggesting that use of the polls and faith in them was not at all the same thing. And even those newspaper editors who objected to the use of opinion polls after 1948 did not think of relinquishing their own use of market research, underpinned though it was by nearly identical sampling techniques.[51]

"The polling idea has been accepted in many fields," Gallup claimed just one year after the Truman-Dewey fiasco. Ever the businessman, he measured his field's success in financial terms. "According to present indications, more money will be spent for polling research in the present year than in any previous year in history. And I believe it is a safe bet that ten years from now the volume of this work will be double what it is today." By the late 1940s, he noted, universities offered courses in the measurement of public opinion, the government used surveys to understand such phenomena as "family income, unemployment, purchasing of government bonds, farm problems, and countless other things," and Americans were becoming acclimated to polls in daily life. "Young people in our high schools and colleges are growing up with polls," he noted with satisfaction. Soon enough, Gallup was certain, every foreign country and every major city would rely on poll data for its governance.[52]

There was never a definitive moment at which opinion surveyors' techniques gained acceptance, when a general consensus confirmed the polls' validity and worth. In this sense, 1948 was just an extreme case of what was in fact a persistent epistemological instability. Many citizens would continue to find polling techniques suspect and their implications for public discourse distressing. To Robert

Baker of San Francisco, polls were a sign of the downfall of modern culture, catering to "our almost universal demand for predigested thought and ready-made opinions." But such critics did not call for an end to opinion surveys. The same man wrote to Elmo Roper in 1952, "I do not believe that you should—or that you can—withdraw from the field of published political research. The demand would still exist, and the gap you would leave would be filled by someone else." Opinion surveys were a genie out of the bottle. Having helped create the demand for instantaneous knowledge about majorities, polls had become the only means to satisfy it.[53]

The Social Science Research Council's report on the public opinion polls of 1948 devoted 391 pages of analysis and charts to the myriad scientific and human problems built into the survey technology. From errors in punching and tabulating, to the subtle influences of interviewers' class status and political opinions upon the answers they received, to the limitations of quota versus probability sampling, the reliability of the polls as a window onto public opinion was challenged at every turn. The SSRC concluded that there were eight major steps pollsters took in making predictions, "at any of which error may enter," and that "there is no reason to believe that errors in magnitude such as those occurring in 1948 are unlikely to occur in future elections." It further recognized that electoral polls, for all their flaws, were the most rigorous kind of opinion surveys, far more carefully designed and implemented than those on social issues. Yet, despite all its ambivalence, the organization did not advocate disbanding the polls; they were far too important a tool for the social sciences.[54]

The same was true for society at large, where a broad array of corporations and state agencies depended and acted upon pollsters' dubious knowledge. George Gallup may have been correct when he hypothesized that even the volume of criticism leveled at the polls was "a testimony to their importance." Ordinary Americans' robust disagreements with particular findings and the techniques used to reach them revealed their investment in the polls—or at least, as *Time* magazine put it in 1948, their recognition that they were "here to stay." In fact, the polls' consumers, even the critical ones, solidified their standing.[55]

Some Middletowners in 1929 had argued that the Lynds had no right to invade their privacy or to turn ordinary people into anthropological objects. By contrast, it is striking how rarely Americans challenged the polling operation at its foundations. Gallup's and Roper's detractors almost never argued that opinion surveys should be banned or even restricted in scope. In disputing results that did not match up with their sense of social reality, few rejected the survey enterprise per se. Instead, they insisted that particular polls were biased, unrepresentative, or poorly conducted. Most seemed to take it as a given that what was needed from the pollsters was *more* respondents, *more* representation, *more* analysis to correct their instrument's most visible flaws. Polls in this way became a matter-of-fact technology, unremarkable and uncontroversial in its basic premises.

Responses to Gallup's and Roper's facts thus hint at the increasing hold of social scientific modes of knowing, if not always the specific conclusions that flowed from it. In this light, one man's objection to an opinion survey that Gallup carried out on the "most favorable climate" in the United States stands out in sharp relief. He wrote quizzically, "I'm not in the poll business, but if I were to make a report on cities with best climates I would not ask people. I would gather data from Weather Bureaus." Once the disaster of 1948 was behind the pollsters and poll watchers, polls would displace other, earlier ways of gathering political and social information, becoming the most legitimate—even if never fully persuasive—technology for telling "the public" what it collectively believed.[56]

5

Surveying Normal Selves

Scientists have been uncertain whether any large portion of the population was willing that a thoroughly objective, fact-finding investigation of sex should be made . . . Even the scientist seems to have underestimated the faith of the man of the street in the scientific method.

—Alfred Kinsey et al., *Sexual Behavior in the Human Male*, 1948

These studies . . . have demanded from Dr. Kinsey and his colleagues very unusual tenacity of purpose, tolerance, analytical competence, social skills, and real courage. I hope that the reader will match the authors with an equal and appropriate measure of cool attention, courageous judgment, and scientific equanimity.

—Alan Gregg, preface to *Sexual Behavior in the Human Male,* 1948

"The recent spectacular failure of polls to reflect truth has taught thoughtful people to take even long established and accredited poll-methods with a grain of salt," editorialized the magazine *Life Today,* pointedly referring to George Gallup's and Elmo Roper's electoral debacle of 1948. "How much salt, then, must be taken with a poll which judges and condemns 60,000,000 white males on the basis of only 5,300 interviews?" The "poll" the writer hoped thus to undermine was another social scientific production of 1948—Alfred C. Kinsey, Wardell Pomeroy, and Clyde Martin's *Sexual Behav-*

ior in the Human Male. Many others wondered along with the reporter for the Bloomington, Indiana, *Daily Herald* who asked, "If Gallup was wrong about the election—was Dr. Kinsey's report on sex and the American male still valid?" The *Boston Globe* quipped, "Dr. Gallup, subject to correction by election returns, has only envy for Dr. Kinsey." But most who made the comparison joined the archbishop of Chicago, who hoped that "now that other polls have proved wrong, maybe someone else will prove the Kinsey report to be incorrect."[1]

Plenty of Americans in the postwar years wished to discount Kinsey's research, revealing as it did startling findings about the high rates of homosexual, premarital, and extramarital sex among "ordinary" Americans. Debates over *Sexual Behavior in the Human Male* and its companion volume of 1953, *Sexual Behavior in the Human Female*—quickly dubbed the "Kinsey Reports"—represented the high-water mark of controversy over social scientific techniques and findings in the twentieth century. Heralded as the first truly scientific accounting of average Americans' sex lives, these studies were just the first two installments in a projected nine-volume, twenty-eight-year, massive data-collecting project. Kinsey's ambitious plan was to survey and quantify "normal" sexual behavior to arrive at a comprehensive account of "what people do." The knowledge he produced by conducting and then aggregating thousands of individual interviews would be a feat of industry and imagination, of science and subjectivity. Submerging individual eccentricity in favor of mean frequencies, the Reports displayed personal experience in a stark scientific mode best captured by their use of the orgasm as the primary unit of measurement.[2]

As contemporaries' comparisons between the Gallup Poll and the Kinsey Reports suggest, the *Sexual Behavior* research was seen as being of a piece with other trends in social investigation at mid-century. And yet the Reports also advanced survey practices into foreign territory. If the tabulation of political attitudes and consumer preferences had become a matter of course, Alfred Kinsey's inquiries into Americans' sexual habits overstepped familiar bounds and seemed to many observers a final social scientific frontier. Market research and public opinion polls had, of course, paved the way. As one commentator stated with resignation, "In an age when opinion polls are taken on nearly every conceivable subject it was probably inevitable that a mass study would some day be made on the most intimate of all aspects of human behavior." By claiming private acts and "normal" sexuality as social scientific property—as something measurable, comparable, and appropriate for public consumption—the Kinsey Reports sparked a new struggle over the role of social knowledge in American culture. This time it would be fought on more deeply cherished ground and intrude upon those areas of life seemingly most resistant to surveyors' probing.[3]

Sex and the Surveyor

With the *Sexual Behavior* volumes, Kinsey and his team of collaborators proudly announced their scientific colonization of novel terrain. They were not, however, the first to invite sex into the scholarly domain, nor the first to make their findings public. Turn-of-the-century European sexologists, from Richard von Krafft-Ebing to Magnus Hirschfeld to Havelock Ellis, had conducted medical studies of homosexual "inversions" and other sexual "variations," and Ellis at least had attracted some notice in the United States. Although probably unknown to most Americans, Yamamoto Senji was directing empirical surveys of sexuality in Japan in the 1920s, suggesting the growing interest of modern states and bureaucracies in tracking citizens' personal as well as civic behavior. In the same years, anthropologist Margaret Mead was actively engaged in studying and publicizing cross-cultural sexual mores, and Sigmund Freud's psychoanalytic theories were coming to suffuse Americans' understandings of sexuality in popular as well as social scientific discussions. Kinsey's study had even more direct predecessors in the field of sexual surveys, among them Katherine B. Davis's *Factors in the Sex Life of Twenty-Two Hundred Women,* Robert Latou Dickinson and Lura Beam's *A Thousand Marriages,* and Lewis Terman's *Psychological Factors in Marital Happiness.*[4] Clearly, sex had not been neglected by researchers. Nevertheless, Kinsey presented the *Sexual Behavior* research as the first of its kind. He distinguished his project by dismissing most prior sex studies as either moralistic or unscientific, to his mind equally damning terms. Singling out nineteen existing scientific surveys for review in his first Report, Kinsey charged each with serious flaws: their small and skewed samples, their reliance on questionnaire rather than interview data, and their sexual delicacy or squeamishness. His research, by contrast, relied on a vast sample of frank, detailed, one-on-one interviews with individuals drawn from the wide net of American society. "The day seems overdue," wrote Kinsey, "when scientists studying human material will forsake barbershop techniques and attempt to secure some taxonomic understanding of the human population."[5]

In interview after interview with curious reporters, Kinsey offered up a consistent, if selective, narrative explaining his introduction to the study of human sexual behavior. An entomologist by training, he had earned his Ph.D. at Harvard with a detailed study of variations in the gall wasp. This taxonomic research had occupied him for his first twenty years as a professor of zoology at Indiana University. Known for his dedication to his insect research and his biology courses, the story went, Kinsey was persuaded in 1938 to teach a course on "Marriage and the Family" that had been proposed by Indiana University's Association of Women Students. In this guise, Kinsey began counseling students on personal matters. Frustrated by the lack of definitive answers to their questions about human sexual "adjustments," and his scientific curiosity piqued,

Kinsey began taking confidential sexual histories from his students in an attempt to gather information about this understudied area.[6] This accident launched Kinsey's career as a sex researcher. Soon after agreeing to teach the marriage course, he began collecting histories in earnest, developing a standardized interview and coding method for the abundant facts he was accumulating about how early and how frequently his subjects were engaging in a wide variety of sexual activities. This practice would quickly develop into full-time research, taking Kinsey to Chicago to examine the sexual underworld there and then all over the rest of the country to survey the range of behaviors he would eventually reveal in his Reports. By 1947, Kinsey's project had expanded so prodigiously that he hired a full-time staff and established the Institute for Sex Research as an affiliate of Indiana University. There Kinsey maintained his interview data as well as his burgeoning collection of sexual materials and erotica from all over the world. This version of events, oft repeated in press coverage of Kinsey, was instrumental in establishing the legitimacy of his methods and findings. Its depiction of Kinsey as a man of science, drawn reluctantly into a new field of research by his students and his (merely) scholarly curiosity, helped the entomologist secure authority with the survey's audiences, not to mention the funding that made his research possible.[7]

Financial backing for the *Sexual Behavior* research initially came from Indiana University and Kinsey's own pocket. But the bulk of the expenses for staffing, travel, and data analysis eventually flowed from Rockefeller Foundation funds channeled through the National Research Council (NRC) Committee for Research in Problems of Sex. From the 1920s through the 1940s, the Committee "was both umbrella and impetus for much of the scientific sex research conducted in the United States." Established in 1921, the Committee was the product of turn-of-the-century crusades against prostitution, illegitimacy, venereal disease, and divorce. The direct trigger for its formation was New York's 1910 white-slave investi-

gation, for which John D. Rockefeller Jr. served as grand jury foreman. The philanthropist was inspired to organize the Bureau of Social Hygiene soon afterward, and it was his funds—first through
the Bureau, and then later through the Rockefeller Foundation—
that would support the Committee's work in the same years that
other Rockefeller dollars were sending Robert and Helen Lynd to
Muncie. Following the pattern of many such ventures, as the century progressed the Committee remade itself from a reformist organization that sought to abolish sexual evils into an impartial scientific body. The Committee's early funding for biological research
was aimed at hormones and animal behavior—safe and obviously
"scientific" scholarship. Investigation into human sex behavior,
however, had always been one of its central objectives.[8]

Aware that it was entering a risky field of investigation, the National Research Council since the early 1920s had been in search of
a scholar whose personal and academic record could legitimize its
program. Well-established as a scientist, highly regarded, and, crucially, a married man with a family, the Indiana University professor fit the bill perfectly. In some sense, his prestigious backers
needed Kinsey as much as he needed them. The zoologist answered
the NRC's demand for empiricism. And, fascinated by gall wasps
but seemingly not all that interested in sex, he promised a neutral
approach to a highly sensitive topic. Kinsey first applied to the
NRC for funding to support his growing collection of sexual histories, and received it, in 1941. But before allocating more substantial
funds to Kinsey's project, the Committee for Research in Problems of Sex engaged Kinsey in what amounted to a scholarly mat-
ing dance. Committee members George Corner and Robert Yerkes
traveled to Bloomington, Indiana, to check up on Kinsey's research
operation. There, they submitted to sexual history interviews. Extremely impressed by Kinsey's techniques, which seemed magically to unlock personal secrets for the researcher's perusal, Corner
sought in turn to impress Kinsey "by casually reporting to him that

he had read a recent book about homosexuality" and thus demonstrating that he wasn't "sex shy." Apparently Kinsey and the Committee were able to convince each other that they were committed to looking at sex scientifically. The next year the Committee quadrupled Kinsey's original grant; it then tripled *that* grant the following year. By 1947, Kinsey was receiving half of the Committee's total funds and had become the NRC's star researcher, validating its mission through his staunchly objective study of sex.[9]

In reciprocal fashion, the Rockefeller Foundation's and National Research Council's support shielded Kinsey so far as possible from public attack. Referring to the NRC, one reviewer wrote of the first Report, "Don't toss off Kinsey and his associates as a bunch of screwballs or snoops. The Kinsey project has the most impressive financial backing and scientific sponsorship [of the] most august scientific authority in the land." Noted another, perhaps more perceptive, observer, the Report's "formidable sponsorship seems to have intimidated the reviewers of the book." Moreover, when it came time to release the findings, Kinsey and his funders both understood the importance of securing a respected medical publisher, despite abundant interest from popular presses.[10]

Despite all this careful maneuvering, the *Sexual Behavior* study was regularly under siege. Challengers hounded Kinsey at every step of his research—from securing subjects, to interviewing them, to publishing his results. Sex research, it has been argued, almost automatically "makes its practitioners . . . 'morally suspect.'" This explains why the NRC had so thoroughly vetted the lead investigator. Likewise, Kinsey chose his co-researchers with care, emphasizing that they must have advanced training in the social or biological sciences as well as happy marriages. Although Kinsey would rely heavily on the expertise of many homosexual men in drafting the first Report—inviting some of them to act as "unofficial" consultants and collaborators—he well knew that his findings would be undermined by acknowledgment of such assistance. The men

Kinsey hired were required to lead private lives that would not attract any negative publicity to the Institute for Sex Research or otherwise imperil the *Sexual Behavior* project. The scientist's concerns about his staff's comportment extended even to their political affiliations. Clyde Martin recalled that Kinsey was initially "disturbed" when Martin joined the National Association for the Advancement of Colored People and the American Civil Liberties Union, the lead researcher's argument being "that we were in a controversial enough area without getting into new controversy." Kinsey's selection of these men for their personal as much as their professional characteristics demonstrated his keen understanding of the risks inherent in his research. Ironically, given the impact the study would have on social mores, Kinsey required its producers to "abide by the traditional standards of the community . . . the middle-of-the-road standards that any banker or minister was expected to adhere to."[11]

The makeup of his research team Kinsey could control. But there were less containable challenges to the *Sexual Behavior* project that stemmed from his decision to place the research, not before a specialized audience, but before the public at large. Sexual behavior—popularly viewed as the province of either moralizing or pornography—was not easily transformed into a topic for serious inquiry. It was indicative that some reviewers of the first Report could compare it to *Forever Amber, Gone with the Wind,* and *The Origin of Species* in the same breath.[12]

Public uneasiness with the *Sexual Behavior* research centered first on the means by which intimate knowledge could be gathered. Kinsey reported facing "organized opposition" from medical groups, a lawsuit for practicing medicine without a license, "police interference" in several cities, political and other investigations, a hotel manager who refused to let anyone "have his mind undressed in my hotel," and numerous attempts to censor the study or unseat its author from his university position. Trouble issued not simply from the interviews themselves but from the way Kinsey and his team located their subjects, and even how they paid them. Indiana University received complaints from parents about Kinsey taking histories in the female dormitories, and one high school teacher was fired for helping the scientist obtain interviews, despite the fact that the individuals he recruited came from outside his own school. The president of Hunter College wrote to his counterpart at Indiana University in 1943 to complain that a young woman on campus was lining up her fellow students to meet with Kinsey, the "procuress" receiving a dollar per interviewee. He worried, probably correctly, about a public relations disaster should the story get out. The investigators also had to work out a special arrangement with Indiana University's auditors to explain research expenses such as "paying prostitutes for histories" or "setting up twenty people in a bar and paying the tab."[13]

The Lynds had referred briefly and euphemistically to "the sex function" in their studies of Middletown, and Gallup had counted it a scientific victory in the 1930s to be able to poll citizens on the funding and treatment of venereal disease without their taking offense. "Not many years ago it would probably have been considered impossible for students of public opinion to ask typical Americans what they were willing to do about the care of syphilis," he boasted in 1940. No previous survey, however, had come close to approaching the explicitness of the Reports' questions. The gathering of sexual histories through detailed one-on-one interviews, Kinsey's main technique, was therefore a subject of both controversy and titillation. "Imagine a total stranger trying to question you about the most intimate details of your sex history. Imagine him actually prying these details out of many thousands of run-of-the-mill Americans, ranging through the whole gamut of our social life, from the underworld to the blue-blooded 400," wrote one reporter with an evident desire to shock. Given the media's temptation to fasten upon the seamier side of sex research, Kinsey and his team worked diligently to separate the salacious from the scientific.[14]

Yet the border separating Kinsey's social scientific queries from less savory pursuits was always in danger of being disrupted. There was, to begin with, the wave of impostors: men posing as sex researchers who grasped the opportunity to interview women over the telephone or in person on the heels of the best-selling *Sexual Behavior in the Human Male.* Tales of Kinsey impostors cropped up all over the country in the late 1940s and early 1950s, the years when the female survey was in production. Radcliffe College students were just one of the groups who reported being asked "distasteful questions" by a purported interviewer for the "Kinsey Foundation." Similar incidents were reported in New York, Chicago, Los Angeles, San Diego, Palo Alto, Pasadena, Detroit, Cleveland, Tacoma, Houston, Louisville, Milwaukee, Kansas City, Rochester, Staten Island, Philadelphia, Indianapolis, and Silver Spring, Maryland. The NRC, attempting to protect both its own credibility and Kinsey's, put out a public warning about such impostors, informing the nation that the real scholars "do not use the telephone in their research and all carry credentials."[15]

Some women were deceived nonetheless. Several wrote to Kinsey in distress, hoping against hope that the "interview" they had just submitted to was legitimate. One, having received a phone call from a man who described himself as a Kinsey interviewer, cooperated with his questions because she was "in strong[?] sympathy with such reports." But after talking to friends and family, she was fairly sure she had been duped. "You can realize the embarrassing situation in which this now places me," she wrote. Another woman had an even more troubling tale to tell about a male acquaintance who claimed to be working for Kinsey, "compiling data for your next book." The impostor quizzed her about her sex life, explaining that he required a total of four or five sessions, including a physical examination; in return, she would receive a free copy of the study. The woman became increasingly suspicious upon hearing the supposed researcher's "vague and slipshod" questions, upon his request that she not tell his wife about the research—and ultimately, upon discovering her husband's wallet missing after the "interview." In response, Kinsey assured the woman that the man was an impostor. "All of us on our own staff are identifiable from the numerous magazine photographs which you must have seen," he rather presumptuously noted. He went on to encourage her to prosecute, writing, "We are distressed by these impostors who have made unwarranted contact with the public" and that he hoped to "make an example of this individual." Kinsey thereby affirmed the special right of the scientific sex investigator to pry into individuals' personal lives. But clearly, the invasiveness that his research required—asking intimate questions of a stranger—lent itself to intrusions of another kind.[16]

Only the mantle of science separated the respectable researcher from the "pervert," the credentialed from the criminal. And only if sexual secrets were plumbed with an eye to a legitimate contribution to social knowledge were such queries not deemed obscene or illegal. Most of the Kinsey impostors eluded the law, but one Minnesota man was arrested for "posing as a solicitor" for the Kinsey Report, and a California accounting student was sent to jail on a lewd conduct charge for interviewing housewives by telephone about their sex habits. Although the accountant-in-training reportedly "neatly tabulated the intimate replies in a notebook," this was not enough to make him a sanctioned questioner on sexual habits. As the apt headline of an Arkansas newspaper put it, "Poor Man's Dr. Kinsey Discovers Sex Survey Often Leads to Jail." Similarly, a Baltimore man's "obscene" movies of scantily clad women were seized by the Maryland courts in 1952—and then promptly turned over to Kinsey to study. The movie producer received a two-year suspended sentence. Kinsey, on the other hand, was allowed to examine the films as "highly valuable" material "for his scrutiny of American sexual habits." But the boundaries of what counted as valid sexual investigation were not always so easily patrolled. Kinsey's collection of erotic materials was seized by U.S. Customs when shipped through the mail, and movie regulators in 1948 "ruled that reference to Dr. Kinsey or his report cannot be used on the screen."[17]

The challenges posed by suppression and proliferation—the censorship of Kinsey's materials, on the one hand, and the emergence of imitators, on the other—meant that the *Sexual Behavior* team needed continually to shore up the scientific scaffolding of their research. From the vantage point of 1953, already the post-Kinsey era, the Committee for Research in Problems of Sex found it necessary to point out the courage of early sex investigators like Kinsey who had overcome numerous social taboos in order to make their science reputable. Before human sexual behavior could be put under the social scientific microscope, the Committee noted, it had first to be recognized as a "natural phenomenon suitable to be studied with the same detachment as digestion, muscular activity or nerve function." Supporters of the *Sexual Behavior* research were fashioned into heroic explorers, battling ignorance, superstition, and hypocrisy in an age not quite ready for its modern perspective on sex.[18]

Like other midcentury surveyors, Kinsey promoted his project as empirical, objective, and shorn of moralizing and prescription. As he wrote quite forcefully in the opening pages of the male volume, his goal was "to accumulate an objectively determined body of fact about sex which strictly avoids social or moral interpretations of the fact." He further explained in the female Report that while his findings might eventually prove useful in thinking about social problems, the research was undertaken purely to advance scientific truth. The look of the Reports certainly corroborated Kinsey's words. Packed with charts, graphs, and columns of figures, many of which took a good deal of work to decipher, the format of the studies was excellent evidence that they contained "science" rather than material appealing to prurient interests. As with the Lynds, Kinsey's "dispassionate objectivity"—his unbending refusal to interpret his own findings or come to any conclusions—was fervently praised by commentators. According to the majority of reviewers, the 1948 Report carried "the unmistakable ring of authority," underwritten by its "careful exposition of . . . statistical details," "numerous graphs," "thousands of files, curves, charts," and "carefully authenticated data." The tone of the survey, in other words, aided and abetted its contents. The "cold factuality of [its] presentation" assured the reader of its status as a "sober, scientific study," which as one reviewer approvingly observed, would "prove unsatisfactory to the seeker after literary titillation." Commentators frequently remarked, again favorably, that the Reports made dry and difficult reading and thus were "calculated to disappoint that portion of the public interest which is directed to other than sober study."[19]

Responding to controversy over the first volume and advance criticism of the second, Kinsey made even more vigorous claims for his inquiry in the 1953 introduction to *Sexual Behavior in the Human Female*. He sharply disagreed with those who believed it was not the scientist's place to investigate human sexuality, comparing them to the misguided critics of Copernicus and Galileo. "There is an honesty in science which refuses to accept the idea that there are aspects of the material universe that are better not investigated," he wrote. By invoking the "material universe" and comparing himself to the great observers of the physical world, Kinsey traded upon his status as a biologically trained, "real" scientist rather than a mere social scientist. His written statements consistently underplayed the sexual in favor of the "biological" and "behavioral," and he took every opportunity to compare the object of his current research to his earlier, distinctly non-racy, work in entomology. Kinsey's readers picked up on these cues, noting that the sex researcher's perspective on his subjects resembled that of the "zoologist who measures the physical data of an arthropod or the botanist who describes the color, size and growth of a flower." Kinsey's stance of detachment, his refrain that as a scientist he could only record, not judge, what he observed in American sexual behavior, and his constant comparison of survey research to natural science well expressed dominant trends in the social sciences more generally.[20]

In actuality, Kinsey called in additional reinforcements, enlisting his research in the cause of scientific progress, to be sure, but also of marital stability and democratic knowledge. Promoting the social good of marriage was a secondary line of defense, an older justification for intimate investigation that the scientist occasionally drew upon. This was a path already well trod by marriage advice manuals, the emerging field of marriage counseling, and college courses on the family such as the one Kinsey had taught at Indiana—all routes by which sexual knowledge had been removed from the realm of the indecent and domesticated across the earlier decades of the century. Kinsey argued in the Reports and in other public statements that facts such as his were vital to solving the problem of "sexual adjustment" in marriage. More candid information about sexual habits and desires, he asserted, would only strengthen the institution and, therefore, social stability.[21]

There was still another rationale at Kinsey's disposal. Like George Gallup and Elmo Roper, the author of the *Sexual Behavior* studies described his as a democratic science. He too praised his respondents and the public they stood in for. In a prefatory section titled "The Individual's Right to Know" in the female Report, Kinsey linked public availability of sexual statistics to time-honored principles such as the freedom of speech. Scientists had not only the right, but the obligation, to make findings such as his accessible to the maximum number because there was a vast popular demand for such knowledge. "It is for this reason, we believe, that some thousands of average American citizens have actively cooperated in the present research," he declared. It was on account of this irrepressible demand, reasoned Kinsey—if somewhat disingenuously, since he had explicitly pursued a large audience to begin with—that a study described as "dry and dull" by the press "was taken out of the hands of those who claimed the exclusive right to knowledge in this area and made a part of the thinking of millions of persons." Making specialist knowledge publicly available, Kinsey rallied the American people to his side, even against other scientists, whom he accused of underestimating the citizenry's capacity for scientific knowledge. Kinsey mused that "however well established the data might be," some felt "it would be inexpedient to publish them, for society was not ready to face such facts." He was pleased to note that this was not true of the public at large, which was ready and eager for his findings, no matter how unpalatable they might be. There was abundant evidence to contradict Kinsey on this point, but he testified that the average American was grateful for his scientific labors. "We have developed a faith in the capacity of people to view a subject objectively, even though it be sex," he pronounced in a 1948 issue of *Newsweek*. Again, like the pollsters, Kinsey made it clear that it was not his statistics that were in question, but simply individuals' ability to come to terms with them.[22]

Behind the talk of science for its own sake, of marriage as a crucial social institution needing "facts" to bolster it, of the public's right to sexual knowledge and the surveyor's ability to deliver it objectively, however, was another story. What Kinsey's funders and readers did not know was that the researcher had more ideological motives, which included demonstrating that all forms of human behavior, no matter how uncommon or socially condemned, were "natural." One scholar writes that "the fundamental tenet of Kinsey's sexual ideology was tolerance," and another observes that for Kinsey, nothing that "was biologically possible was *in itself* intrinsically harmful." But there was more at stake for the scientist. Reality—actual, documented behavior—could in Kinsey's view unmask hypocritical social values. The author of *Sexual Behavior in the Human Male* contended in 1948 that "the real clinical problem is a discovery and treatment of the . . . conflicts which lead particular individuals to crack up whenever they depart from the averages or socially accepted customs, while millions of other persons embrace the very same behavior, and may have as high rates of activity, without personal or social disturbance." In his view, dominant conventions, rather than the breaking of them, were at the root of Americans' sexual predicament.[23]

Publicly proclaiming that he took no position on the customs and moral codes that regulated American sexuality, Kinsey was secretly scornful of both. Sociologist Janice Irvine observes that Kinsey was "critical of the church, educational institutions, and homes" for instilling inhibitions about sex, and that "[his] disdain for culture, which he saw as an inevitably restricting force on an otherwise robust sexual energy, was palpable." This predisposition occasionally broke through the constraints of the Reports' scientific language, as in Kinsey's impassioned critique of existing sex offender laws—which he claimed 95 percent of American men routinely violated—and in his dismissal of established mores as comforting rationalizations, "mystical concepts that . . . have substituted for reality." Here he resembled no one quite so much as the Lynds, who had hoped to expose American culture's irrationalities by laying them out "objectively" for all to see. Kinsey hammered home the point that law and social conventions were extremely "remote from the actual behavior . . . of the average citizen." Uncowed by the Reports' scientism, some contemporary observers picked up on Kinsey's implied "moral philosophy," which seemed to support, among other things, "hedonistic ethics and sexual promiscuity." It did not take too much reading between the lines to sense his enthusiasm for documenting the ubiquity of many taboo or illegal sexual practices, from masturbation to oral and anal intercourse.[24]

As is now well known, historians, and more recently filmmakers, have found in Kinsey's proselytizing not simply a scientific but a personal agenda, stemming from his strict Methodist upbringing, his guilt about his own "deviant" sexual desires, and his hope that data about the extent of sexual diversity would relieve others of the kind of anxieties he carried with him for much of his life. In a recent biography, James Jones maintains that Kinsey was driven to sex research by private masochistic sexual obsessions and shame over his homosexual impulses, that his own sexual experimentation was wide-ranging, and that he, not his students, maneuvered to establish the marriage course that led to the *Sexual Behavior* research. A second biographer, Jonathan Gathorne-Hardy, disagrees with some of Jones's claims, particularly his categorization of Kinsey as homosexual. But he too has found that Kinsey was invested in sex research much earlier, and more profoundly, than he let on in his public statements. He discloses that Kinsey's keen interest in sexuality began as early as the 1920s, that he had an intense though ambiguous romantic relationship with one of his male graduate students in the 1930s, that he and his wife supported nudists during the same time, that Kinsey had read Robert Latou Dickinson's *A Thousand Marriages* in 1931 when it came out, and that, at least partly on account of a repressive childhood, the scientist "became obsessed by sex" before the opportunity of the marriage course came along.[25]

Others have noted that the parameters of Kinsey's sexual history interview were well established before his official history-taking began. Even earlier scholars of the Reports, who had little access to the researcher's private life, came to the determination that "cloaked in the unbiased empiricism of the dispassionate scientist lay the emotional preferences of a moral crusader." Contrary to his carefully managed public biography, it seems, Kinsey leapt at the chance to metamorphose from a studier of gall wasps into an investigator of human sexual behavior.[26]

Human Subjects and Scientific Objects

Helen and Robert Lynd, a reporter had written in 1929, "studied their simple city as dispassionately as an entomologist would study a beetle impaled upon a pin." Kinsey, an actual entomologist, claimed to adopt precisely this removed perspective toward his own object of study: U.S. sexual behavior. The scientist found it rhetorically useful to compare this research to his earlier work on insects, declaring that the two kinds of scholarship were not much different. But it is also true that many of his assumptions about how to conduct a survey on human sexuality were forged in the taxonomic training he embarked upon as a graduate student in the 1910s. As a gall wasp expert Kinsey was a zealous researcher and an avid, even compulsive, collector of specimens. He traveled tens of thousands of miles to track down samples all over North America and, propelled by a fierce work ethic, often worked late into the evenings classifying them. These patterns would well describe his *Sexual Behavior* work. The amassing of a vast sample, the patient cataloguing of details, the straightforward behavioralist assumptions, and the starting principle of abundant variation within species—key aspects of his wasp research—would all carry over into his study of human beings.[27]

There was, of course, one crucial difference: Kinsey was unable to observe and pin down human behavior in the manner to which he was accustomed with insects. As he put it in 1948, "The gathering of the human data would involve the learning of new techniques in which human personalities would be the obstacles to overcome and human memories would be the instruments whose use we would have to master." Although not as extensively as would William Masters and Virginia Johnson in their 1966 *Human Sexual Response,* Kinsey did observe and film live sexual activity— that of his staff members, their wives, and selected outsiders. This, however, was a closely guarded secret, and Kinsey also kept quiet about some of his other methods, such as attending sex sessions of a New York homosexual group and timing sexual encounters in men's rooms in Grand Central Station. In public explanations of his research, Kinsey noted his dependence on clinical studies by gynecologists, mammalian studies, observations made by parents and "scientifi-cally trained persons," and "socio-sexual approaches" that his staff had observed in various communities. Generally, Kinsey lamented the fact that most knowledge about human sexual behavior could only be obtained secondhand.[28]

But beginning in 1938 the scientist claimed to have developed another tool for gathering information about humans that he believed to be nearly as precise as the entomologist's direct observation. This was the sexual history interview, a confidential one-on-one session with a subject conducted by either Kinsey himself or one of the three collaborators he entrusted with his method and coding system: Wardell Pomeroy, Clyde Martin, and later, Paul Gebhard. Kinsey's problem as a scientist was the common one of how to build systematic knowledge out of specific, incommensurable units of information. But the task of uncovering "normal" sexual behavior was made much more complicated by the nature of Kinsey's research material: the narratives offered up by infinitely various, potentially untrustworthy human beings. Many of his critics would seize upon just this problem, asking how facts about normal American sexual habits could be determined under the social scientist's inexact conditions. In a way that Roper and Gallup's detractors had not, they pointed to the possibility of research subjects lying, withholding, misremembering, or exaggerating. Kinsey attempted to solve this problem in two different ways. First, and most obvi-

The *Sexual Behavior* researchers conducted lengthy one-on-one interviews with approximately 18,000 male and female subjects; Kinsey himself recorded 7,985. (Alfred Kinsey conducting a mock interview with a staff member, photo by William Dellenback, reproduced by permission of the Kinsey Institute for Research in Sex, Gender, and Reproduction, Inc.)

ously, he allowed masses of data to render particular individuals and answers invisible, obscured by an impressive array of curves and charts. Second, he actively promulgated a science of interviewing.[29]

This second route entailed a delicate balancing act. Kinsey asserted that any investigator studying sex was required first and foremost to be impartial and nonjudgmental. Comparing his work, as he so often did, to that of the natural scientist, he continued, "That much is expected of the student measuring the lengths of insect wings, recording the chemical changes that occur in a test tube, or observing the colors of the stars. It is not too much to expect similar objectivity of the student of human behavior." However, he went on to say something much more risky. Acknowledging the difficulty of collecting sexual secrets, Kinsey noted that "one is not likely to win the sort of rapport which brings a full and frank confession from a human subject unless he can convince the subject that he is desperately anxious to comprehend what his experience has meant to him." He argued, in fact, that "something more than cold objectivity" was needed in investigating a topic like sex. As Kinsey saw it, the surveyor "who at least momentarily shares something of the satisfaction, pain, or bewilderment which was the subject's, who shares something of the subject's hope that things will, somehow, work out right, is more effective, though he may not be altogether neutral."[30]

Here Kinsey characterized the sexual history session less as an exercise in extracting information than as "a communion between two deeply human individuals, the subject and the interviewer." But even as he wrote rather passionately about sharing in the pain and longings of others' sexual experience, he always returned to the goal at hand, pressing subjectivity into the service of scientific truth. Empathy, he explained, was simply part of his method, creating a more "effective," that is, accurate, set of facts about a person. Kinsey explained that changes in the interviewer's facial expression or inflection as well as hesitancies and spontaneity in his language, even "the flick of an eye," all needed to be controlled in order to extract a "true" sexual history from a subject. "If his reactions add up right," the researcher proclaimed, "then the subject is willing to tell his story." Sympathy and reassurance could thus be said to factor deeply into Kinsey's method, a messier technique than that of the entomologist's lab, but one that the scientist purported was reliable nonetheless.[31]

Kinsey could be vehement in his defense of his subjects' veracity, explaining to *Cosmopolitan* magazine that although some had suspected that women would lie in their interviews, female subjects were giving him the facts and were "glad to do it." Kinsey frequently asserted that the primary reason subjects participated in his study was to advance science. As he wrote to one of his correspondents, "We have no reason to believe that there is more than an exceedingly rare individual who contributes to our study in any other spirit." But Kinsey also delighted in telling reporters that he knew when subjects were lying about or covering up their experiences. Two of his techniques were particularly important in this regard. First, he always placed the burden of denial on the interviewee, asking not "Have you ever engaged in masturbation?" but "When did you first masturbate?" This he believed garnered more accurate responses, since it was "too easy to say no." Second, Kinsey was resolute about the necessity of "forcing" dishonest subjects to give honest answers. He acknowledged that his interviewees were volunteers, but stated that "as soon as an individual agrees to contribute he assumes the responsibility of serving scientific accuracy." Therefore, if the researcher determined that a subject was lying, "he should denounce the subject with considerable severity" and "refuse to proceed with the interview." If falsification was discovered after the fact, Kinsey reserved his right to track down the subject and demand that he or she rectify the record. Taught to be suspicious, to look for gaps or inconsistencies in subjects' histories, interviewers could spend a good deal of time eliciting an "accurate" answer to a single question—by employing a sympathetic reminder of neutrality, an "incredulous tone," or a sterner response if necessary.[32]

The *Sexual Behavior* interviewers, then, were meant to possess a very particular set of skills. First, as Kinsey wrote to a potential staff member, researchers were preferably in their thirties or forties and had to be willing to travel extensively. Beyond those qualifications, the interviewer had to be able "to meet persons of all social levels and quickly win confidence and cooperation from utter strangers." If establishing cross-class trust had presented a problem for pollsters, it was a much more significant one for Kinsey, given the kind of data he was soliciting, and he expressed a preference for interviewers who had "clinical or institutional experience with the lower social level." Paul Gebhard's experience with the Works Projects Administration during the New Deal, which the scientist assumed had acquainted him with just that sort, was a plus. Kinsey also demanded open-mindedness toward all manner of sexual behavior. "In order to obtain a frank and complete record from our subjects," he wrote, "it is imperative that our interviewers be able to accept any type of human sexual act without passing judgments on its moral or social significance." In one of his favorite refrains, he urged, "We cannot use anyone who is afraid of sex." The *Sexual Behavior* interviewers were to be not just social scientists but socially adept, at ease with all kinds of people and practices.[33]

Joining Kinsey's interviewing team was a rigorous process that entailed (as it did for the clerical staff as well) first giving one's sexual history. After this step was completed, Paul Gebhard remembered going through "a real interrogation" for four days by Kinsey and his other future collaborators. The lead investigator also exerted a large degree of control over his co-workers once hired. They trained for a year in the interviewing technique and only gradually progressed from taking college students' histories to taking those of "special groups like prostitutes or homosexuals." Other stipulations, especially the expectation that they would spend approximately half their time on the road conducting interviews, could create personal strains for the researchers. Clyde Martin later recalled how strenuous the research trips were. "We might be carrying on five or more interviews with mature adults or as many as ten college students a day." The result was that "by the end of the day I would feel as though I had been pulled through the eye of a needle [after] interacting with so many persons in an intense fashion."[34]

Kinsey himself was a tireless worker and he expected the same of

214 · Surveying Normal Selves

his staff, who often complied by working evenings and weekends to keep up with the taxing pace of research. The interviewing team was under pressure to obtain sexual histories as quickly as possible to meet the total goal of one hundred thousand, and this could militate against Kinsey's equally strong interest in collecting full and unusual histories. Writing in 1954 from Los Angeles, where he was interviewing, Gebhard wrote to his boss, "As luck would have it, everyone I have seen thus far is either a juicy two-pager or a multiple-marriage man. One person was both. This has not facilitated my obtaining the maximum number of men in the minimal amount of time!" The intricacy of some individuals' experiences could extend the interview into well over the allotted two hours; in one famous instance, a session with a subject took seventeen hours to complete. The ongoing tension between quantity and complexity is evident in Gebhard's recollection that "when running behind schedule we would pray that the next individual would be young, inexperienced, and blessed with an excellent memory."[35]

Although he hoped to capture the rich diversity of American sexual habits, Kinsey did not extend the same principles to the composition of his research team, which was made up solely of white, Anglo-Saxon, Protestant men. The number of staff members employed at the Institute for Sex Research doubled after the publication of the first Report, five women joining its ranks. However, female staffers were confined to library and clerical work, even as the interviews for *Sexual Behavior in the Human Female* accelerated. For a radical sexual thinker, Kinsey subscribed to rather conventional social attitudes, explaining that women could not interview for him because they were unable to spend so much time away from home and remain happily married. He also ruled out interviewers with Jewish names, fearing that they would make subjects uncomfortable and thus skew the results. Wardell Pomeroy later noted that Kinsey believed "only WASPs . . . could interview everybody."[36]

All of the sexual history interviews—whether of women or men, blacks or whites—were thus conducted by "unmarked" individuals ostensibly capable of interviewing subjects about intimate matters without influencing in any way their answers. If he was aware of opinion pollsters' methodological literature on rapport, Kinsey did not learn anything from it. Most striking in this regard, given midcentury mores, was his assumption that male interviewers could unproblematically elicit accurate information from female subjects. One psychotherapist, pointing this out, called for women interviewers on Kinsey's staff. "It is inadequate to have interviewers of men and women carried on by men only," she charged. "Regardless of how scientific an attitude, the interviewer is a human being, and the material must be received, recorded and interpreted through the medium of that personality." Few other critics, however, noticed or objected to the makeup of the research team or contemplated how it might have affected their results.[37]

The sexual history interview, revised and expanded in the years following its first iteration in 1938, was composed of 350 to 521 questions, depending on the life experience of the particular subject. The roster of questions was memorized by the interviewers, asked over the course of (on average) two hours, and the answers recorded in numbers, symbols, and checkmarks on a single sheet in a special code so highly guarded that the key for it was never written down. Paul Gebhard recalled that "the numerous questions were laboriously committed to memory, a process requiring months of practice and simulated interviews . . . Ultimately one became so proficient that the questions came to one's lips almost without volition."[38]

The *Sexual Behavior* researchers not only had to carry hundreds of questions in their heads. They also had to abide by the formidable principles that Kinsey had devised to ensure that the interviews yielded scientifically valid results. The researchers were exhorted to, among other things, assure privacy and confidentiality, put the subject at ease, establish rapport, move from less to more sensitive topics, recognize "the subject's mental status," engage in "supplementary exploration" when necessary, adapt their vocabulary for those of different social levels, avoid bias in their spoken or body language, ask even the most personal queries without embarrassment, look individuals in the eye, ask questions as rapidly as possible, cross-check answers for accuracy, and, on top of all that, avoid "controversial" issues such as politics. One of Gebhard's recommenders wrote to Kinsey, "Your needs are very exacting." This was something of an understatement. Kinsey expected his interviewers to be almost superhuman in their interviewing skills. As he wrote in the female volume, explaining why the research was not progressing more rapidly, there were few persons "available and qualified to meet the demands placed upon an interviewer on this project."[39]

Indeed, it was likely for this reason that both Wardell Pomeroy and Clyde Martin were granted draft exemptions in the early 1940s as the U.S. mobilization for war overseas began. As Robert Yerkes of the NRC put it in his letter to the Selective Service Board, writing of the latter, "Mr. Martin is especially valuable . . . because of his training and experience in the work and the large measure of confidence and reliance which Professor Kinsey places in him." In agreeing, the draft board may have been persuaded by Yerkes' argument that Kinsey's facts would be "of quite exceptional value to persons responsible for the control of soldier and civilian personnel" and the NRC's plea for the "fundamental importance" of the *Sexual Behavior* research, "particularly in the present social situation." Kinsey's work may not have been as central to the effort as that of other social scientific experts like Roper and Gallup, but his findings about sexual relations could shed light on the morale, "activity," and health of the troops. The deferments of the Kinsey researchers attest to the perceived usefulness of all kinds of social scientific facts to federal agencies during wartime.[40]

A few commentators, including psychologist Lewis Terman, were dubious about what they termed Kinsey's "occult insight" into other human beings. But most critics, a good number of whom agreed to submit to sexual history interviews, were willing to accede to his claim to have obtained trustworthy human data. One of Kinsey's subjects testified to his method's effectiveness: "Instead of being embarrassed or inhibited, I answered each question as matter-of-factly as if it had concerned my name and address," she marveled. She continued, "I suppose that is the secret of the Kinsey technique. I was conscious that the extremely personal questions came with more rapid-fire impact, so that I didn't have time to stop and think whether or not I should be embarrassed or feel guilty, whether I should hedge or lie." Kinsey's elaborate system of validating interview data—retaking selected histories, comparing the interviews given by pairs of spouses or other sexual partners, cross-checking for internal consistency, and testing interviewers' reliability with each other—effectively persuaded most skeptics. In this fashion, Kinsey seemed to have solved the recurring problem of social science's reliance on human subjects.[41]

A Taxonomy of American Behavior

From the thousands of interviews the *Sexual Behavior* researchers conducted—approximately 5,300 male and 5,940 female histories for the first two reports—the Institute for Sex Research staff calculated the figures on sexual behavior that made their way to publication. Kinsey's statistics were radically compressed from thousands of interviews and millions of individual responses to hundreds of questions asked in varying ways by different interviewers. Paul Gebhard was disappointed to discover upon being hired that he was to be employed, not as a professional anthropologist as his training had prepared him, but as "an interviewer, Hollerith card puncher, calculation checker, index compiler . . . and general factotum." As his remark suggests, it took a vast amount of labor to transform long and detailed interviews, with questions like "What would you say was the main source of your early knowledge about sex?" and "Do you dream of giving or receiving pain, being forced to do something, or forcing someone to do something?" into serviceable charts and statistics. Using a Hollerith card sorter, even a straightforward table of results could take two days to produce. As Wardell Pomeroy remembered it, "We used to say that we were the highest paid clerical staff in the country." Because only the most highly aggregated figures allowed for comparison in "variable by case data matrix" form, the information Kinsey's team collected was increasingly stripped of social context—its relation to particular questions and full individual histories—as it was made into material useful for compiling mean frequencies. As individuals were converted into categories and personal experiences into statistics, the complicated interchanges between interviewers and subjects that constituted the basis for the *Sexual Behavior* studies were obscured.[42]

Kinsey has been called "extraordinarily atheoretical," and his survey hewed closely to overt sexual acts. Primarily interested in behavior, and in behavior that was easily measured and quantified, Kinsey designated "sexual outlet," or activity leading to orgasm, as his chief unit of analysis. His systematic design neatly broke down sexual practice into six separate types: masturbation, nocturnal emissions, heterosexual petting, heterosexual intercourse, homosexual outlet, and "animal contacts." Kinsey's team then correlated the frequency of these practices with twelve factors: sex, race, marital status, age, age at adolescence, educational level, occupational class of subject, occupational class of parent, rural–urban background, religion, religious adherence, and geographic origin.[43]

The choice of "outlet" as the measure of all sexual activity fulfilled certain objectives beyond the fact that it made for easy tabulation. One historian argues that Kinsey's schema "implied that all orgasms are equal" and thereby shifted heterosexual practice out of a position of prominence or normality. But it also neglected whole territories of expression, leaving out most sexual relations that did not result in orgasm—the main exception being petting, a practice Kinsey felt he could not ignore given its ubiquity in American society. Some activities even Kinsey judged to be "too marginal" or statistically minor to be worth counting in the Reports: swinging, group sex, sadism, masochism, transvestism, voyeurism, and exhibitionism. He minimized prostitution as a source of outlet and completely excluded public gay male sex. Peculiar assumptions run through Kinsey's interview schedule. A "bizarre dream" could include fetishism or "anything unusual" but not animals, for example. Men, but not women, were questioned about paying for sex, and there were more detailed questions about homosexual than heterosexual practices, allegedly because the latter were better known. From this rather quirky and uneven bundle of questions— "Do you prefer to have intercourse in the light or dark?" "Does seeing the nude buttocks of another (man, woman) arouse you sexually?" "Have you played strip poker with both males and females?"—was gleaned the portrait of American sexual behavior for which Kinsey would become famous.[44]

Some of Kinsey's statistics became as well known as the Reports themselves: the finding that 37 percent of American men had experienced homosexual contact, for example, and that nearly half of American women had engaged in premarital sex. But the dominant thrust of both volumes was the ubiquity of practices that contravened traditional mores and state laws. According to Kinsey, homosexual activity, animal contacts, masturbation, and premarital and extramarital sex together added up to a far larger share of "total outlet" than did sanctioned sexual behavior, namely, married heterosexual intercourse.

But there were other themes. One concerned the major cleavage of social class. Like the Lynds, Kinsey found this—in his survey of males, at any rate—to be the deepest division in his universe of subjects and the most important factor in his overall analysis. As Paul

Robinson writes, "The *Male* volume might almost be read as a sexual appendix to *Middletown*. Just as the Lynds established that differences in wealth and social background condemned Americans to radically divergent familial, educational, and cultural experiences, Kinsey showed that class distinctions found their way even into the bedroom, indeed into the most intimate details of erotic life." The differences between lower- and upper-class men were not ones of quantity but of type. Lower-class men (whom Kinsey clearly admired) engaged far more often in premarital intercourse, homosexual practices, and prostitution; upper-class men, in masturbation, petting, and foreplay. For men, age was also a critical factor in the frequency with which they engaged in sexual activity, while marriage, religion, and social change—three factors widely believed to determine sexual practices—were far less significant.[45]

By contrast, age and class were relatively unimportant in determining female behavior, a fact that Kinsey ascribed to women's lesser "conditionability," although this could not explain why religion and changing social mores were much more influential in structuring the frequency and nature, respectively, of their sexual experiences. However, Kinsey was less preoccupied in the female volume with understanding variability among women than he was with demonstrating that men and women's physical responses to sexual activity were identical. Anticipating Masters and Johnson, for example, he labeled the belief that women gained primary sexual satisfaction from vaginal intercourse a myth. Where men and women diverged, he asserted, was in men's greater responsiveness to psychological stimuli and women's lower rates of outlet across the board—the latter claim being the one finding of Kinsey's that affirmed popular beliefs about female sexuality. Kinsey aimed to challenge the conventional wisdom about men and women's differing sexualities. But as feminist critics have charged, his designation of the orgasm as the only gauge of sexual activity led him to construct his survey around a male model. Inclined toward an ethic of sexual abundance, Kinsey bewailed the fact that women were not adequately measuring up to men in sheer quantity of outlet. Like the marriage counselors of the day, his emphasis on the importance of heterosexual "sex adjustment" as a way of preserving the institution of marriage also demonstrates the confines of his own thinking and the cultural constraints within which his research operated.[46]

The sampling method that had produced this portrait of the population was rudimentary by the standards of the day. Most significantly, Kinsey rejected the probability sampling techniques reluctantly employed, and to some extent popularized, by opinion pollsters. Many have attributed this decision to the scientist's personality and expertise, noting that Kinsey was "an inveterate collector" whose early twentieth-century training as a naturalist left him both unschooled in and wary of sampling theory. Certainly, part of the explanation was Kinsey's lack of confidence in himself as a statistician and his taxonomic faith in large numbers. He clearly believed that only by gathering tens of thousands of subjects would he be certain to capture the full range of sexual practices; as he put it, "no statistical techniques can make a small sample represent any type of individual which was not present in the original body of data." But he was also certain that randomly chosen respondents would never cooperate with his unusual and detailed questions, rendering probability sampling useless. Kinsey rather defensively explained, "Human subjects cannot be regimented as easily as cards in a deck, and the investigator of human behavior faces sampling problems which are not sufficiently allowed for by pencil and paper statisticians." He argued that it was simply not feasible "to stand on a street corner, tap every tenth individual on the shoulder, and command him to contribute a full and frankly honest sex history." Statistical experts, notably a 1948 review team from the American Statistical Association (which included the lead author of the Social Science Research Council's assessment of the polls in the same year), nonetheless criticized Kinsey's decision not to employ probability sampling for even a small segment of his respondents so as to test his figures' generalizability.[47]

Kinsey's reply to such critics was a new technique he was developing in the 1940s, the hundred-percent sample. Initially, Kinsey took the history of just about any volunteer who came along, relied on "contact men," and used a snowball technique whereby he interviewed a particular subject and then as many of his or her acquaintances as could be persuaded to participate. Concerned about statistical challenges to his study, however, he increasingly turned down interviews with those he believed were already well represented in his sample. This led the scientist, usually eager for any sort of sexual data, to reject some of his volunteers. To a college student who in 1948 offered to give her history, for example, Kinsey explained his refusal by saying, "When we accept volunteers, we have no way of knowing how representative of the rest of the population such histories are."[48]

The hundred-percent method never accounted for more than a quarter of the histories included in the Reports, but the idea behind it was ingenious. Kinsey and his team would attempt to convince every member of a "social unit"—a particular sorority, a professional organization, a rooming house, a prison ward, or, most remarkably, hitchhikers in a given area—to contribute their histories. Often these campaigns of persuasion would begin with a lecture by Kinsey, who would waive his fees in exchange for the opportunity to collect sex histories. Once some in the group had given interviews, they worked on the others, cajoling them to do the same. The researchers were not above allowing peer pressure, and particularly the fear of being judged as "abnormal," to assist them in their data collection. "The holdouts were subject to considerable pressure," recalled Paul Gebhard, so that those who did not volunteer their histories "soon became aware that their reluctance was being attributed to some unknown but obviously serious, sexual problem." Comparing the results of the hundred-percent groups to the rest of his data set and finding few significant divergences, Kinsey believed he had trumped his statistically minded critics and produced a true picture of normal American sexual behavior.[49]

Reporting on the Normal

What appeared groundbreaking about Kinsey's research, as just about every commentator noted, was his vast number of subjects and his focus on "normal" sexuality. On the first count, Kinsey was confident that if his sample were large enough, its "generalizations should apply not only to the individuals which were actually measured, but to those which were never collected and which were never measured at all." Reviewers were awed by the scientist's plan to secure thousands of individual interviews, and from them, to distill the data points needed to mark out the American sexual terrain. On the second, Kinsey seemed to effect a revolution in sexual science by asking ordinary people, rather than those in the clutches of clinics or therapists, to detail their intimate habits. "Kinsey has one great advantage over the psychotherapist and the psychoanalyst," noted one observer. "His specimens are not neurotics, psychopaths, or psychotics in the meshes of emotional and social conflicts or legal entanglements, but average men, who are encountered daily on the street or the bus." Commentators were quick to praise the Reports' findings as "the greatest mass survey of normal sex activity in our society" and "the first work in all the mountain of writing on the subject which presents an authenticated picture of normal sexual behavior." No less an authority than George Gallup, aware of Kinsey's research in progress, noted in 1944 that "one of the most important studies ever undertaken in this country by a social scientist concerns the sexual behavior of normal individuals." The pollster was most impressed, he said, by Kinsey's skill at extracting opinions on private matters from ordinary Americans.[50]

Past sexual research, Kinsey claimed, was not applicable to the mainstream because it was clinic-based, drawn from miscellaneous sources, and therefore unable to speak to trends in the public at large. He emphasized the point in the opening chapter of *Sexual Behavior in the Human Male:* "None of the authors of the older studies," he wrote, "ever had any precise or even an approximate knowledge of what average people do sexually." Kinsey's mass survey was thus designed as "a first step in the accumulation of a body of scientific fact that may provide the bases for sounder generalizations about the sexual behavior of certain groups and, some day, even of our American population as a whole." Although his grandiose titles—referring to the universal "human male" and "human female"—suggested otherwise, the Reports were clearly intended and read as a compendium of American behaviors. Kinsey explicitly designated U.S. sexual behavior as unique, writing in the first Report that "Continental European patterns of sex behavior are so distinct from the American . . . that no additions of the European to the American data should ever be made."[51]

Kinsey trumpeted his approach as clearly superior to earlier trends in social research, in which, he chided, "observations on children, on senescent adults, on social groups, on gangs, or on whole towns are usually observations on *particular* groups, although they are presented as typical of life in all of America." Here Kinsey may have had *Middletown* in mind, but he had only acclaim for the national quantitative surveys pioneered by Gallup and Roper. It was, he wrote, "unfortunate that the products of academic studies are not more often put to the dollars and cents tests which have provided the incentives for increasingly better techniques in economic and public opinion surveying." Kinsey claimed, like the pollsters, to have sampled a cross-section of all populations, regions, and age groups in order to arrive at a scientific mirror of national sexual activity.[52]

Yet, if Kinsey's questions and therefore his findings reflected certain preoccupations, so did his methods of seeking out specimens for his study. In contrast to many contemporary researchers, his vision of the American public was expansive—indeed, in some cases more expansive than his funders would have liked. Robert Yerkes of the Committee for Research in Problems of Sex, worried about the ambition of the *Sexual Behavior* project and perhaps its fallout, had advised Kinsey in 1943 to limit his study to white men and women who belonged to "our U.S.A. culture." Yerkes urged him to leave aside "inquiry into human variants—racial, cultural, degree of typicalness, etc., etc." These he thought ought to be studied as "extensions or specialized inquiries" rather than as part of the primary investigation. Kinsey strongly resisted such pressure. Fashioning his sample from a presumed mainstream or typical would have violated his taxonomic principles and subverted his larger project of unsettling conventional understandings of what the "normal" was.[53]

Scholars have called the *Sexual Behavior* sample "unprecedented in its diversity." Although there were significant oversights in the Reports' claim to represent the nation, their multifaceted portrayal of the United States citizenry placed them squarely within post–World War II pluralistic currents. This can be seen in Kinsey's own emphasis on a comprehensive sample as well as his critics' reproaches for not paying proper attention to particular segments of the population. Even as Kinsey excluded certain groups, most notably African Americans, from his final analyses, he was well aware of the charges that this research design invited. *Middletown*'s exclusive focus on native whites had drawn virtually no notice; similarly, the Gallup Poll could depict national majorities and minorities as groups undifferentiated by race, gender, or class. But many reviewers registered that Kinsey referred to, and generalized about, data only from white men and women in his Reports. One neatly pared the scientist's claims down to size, recasting *Sexual Behavior in the Human Male* as "Sexual Behavior in the Human Male, White, U.S.A." Because of its sensational subject and its postwar publication, the acceptance of Kinsey's study in some sense hinged upon how well it could account for the vast diversity of American society. Careful analysts of the Reports' methods would challenge Kinsey's sample, arguing that it was more homogeneous and less representative than he made it out to be.[54]

The scientist's constructions, witting and unwitting, of normal sexual behavior were derived from his personal predilections as well as the exigencies of his research conditions. Although catholic in his search for sexual variation, Kinsey was in many ways a product of his time in determining whom and how many to include in his composite picture of human behavior. First and most striking, although several hundred African American subjects gave sexual histories, none of their data were used in computing the formal statistics in either of the Reports. Kinsey's justification for this omission fell back on his faith in large numbers: he believed he simply had not collected a sufficient quantity of sexual histories, especially from middle-class blacks, to make valid generalizations about that population. For this reason, he said, the results printed in the Reports were confined to American and Canadian whites. Although Kinsey noted in the first volume that "Negro groups" would be included in future publications, he did not remedy this problem in the second Report. In fact, the omission of African American data merits barely a mention in the female volume.[55]

Several historians have suggested that Kinsey consciously excised African Americans from his published sample for fear that contemporary myths about "Negro promiscuity" would undercut his statistics' legitimacy; if blacks were not counted, their data could not explain high rates of sexual misbehavior. In Miriam Reumann's reading, Kinsey's "shrewd assessment of American postwar racial ideologies" explains blacks' absence from the Reports, since findings about white men and women were less likely to be dismissed by his readers. Indeed, she has seen the exclusion of African American subjects as evidence of Kinsey's racial liberalism, his staunch belief that there were no sexual differences between those of different races. If the evidence is elusive on this point, Kinsey did note that "preliminary findings show that there are as many patterns of behavior among Negroes of different social levels as there are among whites," and that despite the small number of histories, "it is already clear that Negro and white patterns for comparable social levels are close if not identical." Yet it is also apparent that, like the Lynds, and to a great extent the pollsters, Kinsey was untroubled by the fact that what he described as a portrait of American sexual behavior (or even human sexual behavior) was in actuality a portrait of white America.[56]

On the other hand, Kinsey heavily oversampled college students, professionals, midwesterners, and gay men—those to whom he had easy access or, as in the latter case, a particular interest in tracking down. He also drew a significant portion of his sample from persons in prisons or other "total institutions." In fact, facing difficulties obtaining subjects from "the lower level," Kinsey obtained nearly all his working-class data from this group. Paul Gebhard later revealed that Kinsey believed prison populations were fairly representative of individuals with less than a high school education since "part of their culture was going to jail," an assumption both statistically problematic and quite revealing of his class prejudices. Facing pressure from his critics and analyses from his own staff showing the skewed nature of the penal data, Kinsey eventually omitted prisoners from the female volume, so that his sample of white nonprison females who had no education beyond grade school was tiny: only 181 cases out of the whole. This meant that the second Report had an even more pronounced middle-class bias than did the first.[57]

At the same time, Kinsey's understanding of "normal" sexuality was a striking departure from the Lynds' "typical" community or the pollsters' "average" American. Sexual differences, according to Kinsey, were ones of degree, not of kind, and could be charted along a single continuous curve. This kind of analysis culminated in his seven-point heterosexual–homosexual rating scale, which allowed an individual to occupy a position on a spectrum rather than a binary category of sexual identity. Furthermore, Kinsey "was able to exploit the confusion at the heart of normal," one of his key findings being that "nonnormative sexual activities are, in fact, the statistical norm." He fundamentally rejected the notion that any segment of the population could be marked off as "'normal,' 'modal,' 'typical,' or discretely different," writing that "normal and abnormal, one sometimes suspects, are terms which a particular author employs with reference to his own position on that curve." Extending this logic further, Kinsey questioned whether the terms *normal* and *abnormal* ought even to "belong in a scientific vocabulary."[58]

Indeed, Kinsey's uppermost agenda in the Reports was abolishing this dichotomy. Influenced by his taxonomic predilection for variety, the scientist began his research, he said, with "no preconception of what is rare or what is common, what is moral or socially significant, or what is normal and what is abnormal." He asserted: "This is first of all a report on what people do, which raises no question of what they should do, or what kinds of people do it." It was to this end that he had included in his survey "all kinds of persons and all aspects of human sexual behavior." Kinsey touted his study's diversity, the fact that "thieves and hold-up men," "bootleggers," and "ne'er-do-wells" were included in his statistics alongside "clergymen," "farmers," and "persons in the social register." Fascinated by the range of American sexual practices, Kinsey sought out the marginal, and this of course is one reason his research was so controversial.[59]

Nevertheless, the author of the Reports could not avoid characterizing his survey as documenting how "normal" people behaved sexually. Coupled with his statistical mode of presentation, this had the effect of, if not creating a single normal curve, then creating multiple ones, based on a given individual's age, sex, education, and class. In a telling passage, Kinsey explained how social scientists, generally concerned with aggregates, dealt with the problem of individuality: "It is, precisely, the function of a population analysis *to help in the understanding of particular individuals by showing their relation to the remainder of the group* . . . Without such a background, each individual becomes unique and unexplainable except through an elaborate investigation of him as an isolated entity. On the other hand, if there are adequate data on the group, a major portion of the work involved in understanding a particular individual is thereby eliminated." By characterizing mass statistics as the technology that allowed an external party to determine "the averageness or uniqueness of any particular person," Kinsey, so committed to dislodging concepts of the normal and abnormal, revealed how difficult it was to get away from the concept of the average. This was one of the paradoxes of his taxonomic project. By quantifying so intricately American sexual practices, Kinsey had hoped to avoid enshrining any single definition of the "normal." However, that same process of tabulation had the power, in others' hands, to make the category all the more legible.[60]

The Reports' authoritative-looking figures were something altogether different from what went on in the more private space of the interview, or in the other kinds of one-on-one exchanges that transpired between the *Sexual Behavior* researchers and their subjects. The sexual history interview, after all, required a certain amount of badgering. It also could lead to empathy, counseling, and ongoing contact. Some of those interviewed by the scientist kept in touch with Kinsey for years. And he on occasion took the initiative in recontacting former interviewees. "In connection with the history which you contributed sometime ago," Kinsey wrote to one such individual, "I wonder if you would care to stop in and see me again? I do not want you to feel obliged to come, but there have been some developments recently which make me feel that I can help you some more than I did when I first talked to you." He went on to say, rather emphatically, "You will understand that I am absolutely for you and will do anything I can to help you."[61]

A contemporary critic charged that "Kinsey has no interest in . . . [the interviewee] as person beyond what is needed to get the data." But even a cursory glance at Kinsey's correspondence with the general public, and with his subjects in particular, upends such a view. Letters asking for advice, following up on interviews, or simply responding to the *Sexual Behavior* research inundated Kinsey's offices at Indiana University. Kinsey once noted that he received seventy letters a day, "most of them so highly confidential that no one but myself can read or answer them—there are pleas, daily, that are piteous, humble, asking for a little information, a little understanding, that might salvage a life."[62]

Kinsey's compassion for those who wrote to him or whose histories he collected surfaced in numerous instances, most markedly in his correspondence with younger men struggling with their sexual identity. In one poignant such exchange, a mother whose son had returned from the Air Force and announced that he was a homosexual contacted Kinsey as a last resort. "We are so desperate we dare not pass up any opportunity to help our son," she wrote. Just three days later, Kinsey replied with specific recommendations for psychiatrists, as the woman had requested. But the supposedly impersonal scientist also included some very personal advice, urging tolerance and the possibilities open to one with homosexual leanings for navigating the social world: "It is a mistake for your son or anyone else to feel that the difficulties are insurmou[n]table, even though his history may be primarily or even entirely homosexual. The difficulties are primarily dependent upon society's reaction, and it is not impossible, even though it may present some difficulties, for an individual to learn to avoid social conflicts. It is very important that one learn to accept himself and to adjust his life in accordance."[63]

The correspondence continued, with the son this time sending

Kinsey at least two letters. The scientist intervened further, in heated language, telling the young man that his mother was "the inevitable product of the whole cultural attitude on the homosexual." He continued, "You are right in understanding that she cannot take the thing in the way she has and accomplish anything for you or anyone else." Kinsey included the previous letter he had sent to the mother as well as an article on homosexuality "which she may never have sent on to you." He closed by wishing his correspondent good luck and suggesting that he get in touch should he need additional help or want to give a sexual history. Kinsey, it appears, was quite willing to get in the middle of families and to involve himself personally in the lives of his subjects and readers. Clearly, the *Sexual Behavior* research was not the sum total of Kinsey's interest in sexuality. He did think himself capable of "salvaging a life" through his expertise in gathering social facts. Behind the Reports' claims, and the facts they put in circulation, then, stood intimate bonds between the surveyors and the surveyed. These relationships, however, were submerged so that the scientific story of the Kinsey Reports could come to the fore.[64]

Kinsey was dependent on his interviewees for raw material, but he relied just as much on those who helped to procure them. Gathering comprehensive data was an essential plank in the Reports' claim to representativeness. With no apparatus comparable to the hundreds of interviewers fanned out across the country working for the pollsters—rigorous training and confidentiality were simply too important—the surveyor nonetheless sought a national sample. To line up his research material, Kinsey counted upon individuals who had volunteered their histories and were sympathetic to his project. These individuals were especially valuable in gaining access to difficult-to-reach histories. Referring to the tactics that the *Sexual Behavior* team used to make contact with "underground groups," Wardell Pomeroy noted, "We had to be very specific and have lines out so that we could convince them that they weren't endangering their own lives by giving us histories . . . we began to build up a reputation among them, and the grapevine carried us." In this way, Kinsey created a web of recruiters, supporters, and subjects who acted as "suppliers" for his project.[65]

Kinsey was particularly intent on developing contacts with homosexual communities. Two women who were most likely a lesbian couple, "Sammy and Joan," carried on a correspondence with Kinsey for several years, helping him locate subjects in New York City who were willing to disclose their sex lives. "We have been spreading the Good Word and campaigning for you steadily since last Spring," they wrote in 1946, adding, "We have a very respectable list of victims for you by now." They noted that the potential subjects were "rather a motley crew . . . some of them are good friends of ours, and some mere acquaintances. But we have extracted promises to visit you from a goodly number." Some in the pool were getting restless for the researcher's visit, they noted, and they promised to try to hold on to the "lukewarm prospects."[66]

One of the women wrote again in early 1948 to update Kinsey on her efforts to line up female subjects for the second Report. She heartily congratulated him on the publication of *Sexual Behavior in the Human Male,* expressing how proud she was of her own contribution to "such an important undertaking." In the rest of the letter she revealed her emotional stake in the research. She knew "enthusiastic Kinseyites must not assume that the world will be different overnight" but hoped nevertheless that the world would "be different because of this study, eventually." As she saw it, Kinsey's research was in some sense hers as well. This woman's participation in the research project could hardly be called disinterested, and it is likely that most of Kinsey's recruiters had their own mix of agendas for the Reports, at the very least making sure that they and those like them were accounted for in the studies' pages.[67]

Whatever knowledge the Reports contained, it was born of these specific, highly personal interchanges between the researchers and their recruiters and subjects. Kinsey, as he himself admitted, had to employ warmth and compassion to get at deeply private data. As such, the sexual statistics of the Reports amounted to an amalgam of researcher and researched, scrutiny and sympathy. But in the face of public doubts—and in order to fashion certain kinds of facts— Kinsey had to cover over this particular, rather inconvenient fact of their creation. He was not always successful. Kinsey's subjects, and the broader population they were intended to represent, often argued with his sexual statistics and the way they were produced. And yet, despite the controversy, despite the fierce glare of public attention and vehement debate the Reports triggered, more and more Americans would find it possible to imagine themselves as Kinsey's subjects.

6

The Private Lives of the Public

When I heard the people all talking
I thought they were only mocking
I never knew what I could do
'Til I got all the facts from you.

— "Thank You, Mister Kinsey," popular song, 1948

This side of the atomic bomb, there has been no incident which has created more stir in the personal lives of people than has the Kinsey report.

— National Conference of Social Work, 1949

By the late 1940s, Americans had been probed, queried, and surveyed for several decades. In the postwar era, they for the most part regarded as unremarkable their status as potential research subjects. Alfred Kinsey's inflammatory research would change all that, at least temporarily. It would be too simple to say that the controversy over the Kinsey Reports had only to do with their subject, sexual behavior. Reactions to the surveys concerned the broader issue of social scientific cataloguing and explanation applied to a new domain. Sexual behavior had been dragged out into the light before by Progressive Era purity campaigns as well as vaudeville acts, films, and novels. But here was "normal," private, everyday sexuality quantified and charted, subjected to the techniques of the expert, just as cultural values and political attitudes had been in the work of the Lynds and the pollsters.[1] One historian writes that whereas citizens were "bombarded" with information about "the dangers of public sexuality" before World War II, in its aftermath "Americans were eager to learn about the secret world of America's private life." Many saw Kinsey as the manufacturer of this desire. He was commonly portrayed as invading and stripping away the mysteries of intimate experience as well as undermining older values and traditions that regulated sexual propriety. A reviewer's words captured this sense of relentless incursion by the social scientist. Kinsey and his co-researchers, he wrote, "do not hesitate to spend thousands of hours in penitentiaries, until they win the confidence of inmates. No den of prostitution is too low, no gilded palace too high for his patient survey. There is no level of society which he has not penetrated, no state of the union where he or his emissaries have not gathered knowledge." The *Sexual Behavior* volumes were unsettling in part because they revealed the seemingly unavoidable tentacles of social science in all aspects of modern life. As one columnist observed after the first Report appeared, "We have been so *statisticized* in the United States that nothing is sacred anymore."[2]

At the same time, Kinsey's studies were presented to a population thoroughly steeped in social scientific talk. In the two decades following the publication of *Middletown,* the general public had become more savvy about survey techniques and findings. This familiarity led some to doubt the scientific cast of the Reports, such as a woman who wrote to Kinsey regarding the female volume, "Even dignifying all of this stuff with elaborate sets of statistics and calling it science does not make it intelligent or reliable reading." In the same vein, a columnist wryly compared Kinsey to prior, less scientific, collectors of sexual exploits: "Boccaccio told much better stories and did not bother with statistics. But unless you have charts and graphs these days . . . such experiences are not news." These readers understood that quantification and social scientific terminology could impart legitimacy to potentially dubious content.[3] Despite robust challenges to Kinsey's methods and claims, the power of aggregate surveys to describe and explain was evident in the tremendous level of public engagement with his findings. There were those who believed that the Reports' brand of knowledge constituted progress and others who believed just the opposite. Some rejected Kinsey's facts and figures altogether. Still others were deeply suspicious about the effects of his statistics, even if they accepted the numbers themselves as valid. As such, the *Sexual Behavior* surveys stirred up a debate about the place and uses of social scientific facts in American life. Pitched battles over the Reports' representativeness, their accuracy, their potential impact on legal codes and morals, and their explanatory limits speak to the range of issues at stake in individuals' accommodation to expert knowledge about the sexual state of the nation. But perhaps what was most striking in the midst of these debates was the fact that Americans were more eager than ever before to become research subjects— ready to conceive of themselves as case histories in an aggregate bank of survey data. Many citizens were not only willing to trust and use Kinsey's statistics. They were also willing to become statistics themselves.

A Nation of the "Kinsey-Conscious"

A 1952 magazine article on the already famous (or infamous) Dr. Kinsey billed itself as "a frank report on that man who asks thousands of people all those outrageous questions about their private lives." The author hoped, in what must have seemed only fair turnabout, to "throw an intimate light" on the professor who had authored the best-selling study, *Sexual Behavior in the Human Male*. Kinsey, described as "probably the only entomologist who needs no introduction," was the subject of scores of human interest stories in the late 1940s and early 1950s. His celebrity status at first glance appears strange: his background in zoology, his brusque manner, and his scientific dispassion all would seem to weigh against it. But the public fascination with Kinsey's research eclipsed that for any prior study, and some of that fascination adhered to the scientist himself.[4]

A rather dry and technical 800-page volume, the 1948 *Sexual Behavior in the Human Male* was nevertheless a national blockbuster. Its publisher, W. B. Saunders, heeding what it thought to be "a sophisticated market survey," expected the book to sell approximately 10,000 copies. Instead, the Report spent twenty-seven to forty-four weeks on national best-sellers lists, with sales reaching nearly 250,000 copies. As late as mid-1949 the New York Public Library was refusing to take reservations for the Report, its waiting list having grown so long. Publishers knew a good thing when they saw it. Three books about the male survey, racing to capitalize on the prodigious interest in Kinsey's statistics, came out in quick succession in 1948, and a 25-cent condensation summarizing the findings sold three-quarters of a million copies. One reporter observed that "the unseemly effort to muscle in on the fantastic sales of the epochal Kinsey Report on sex has taken on a violently competitive turn."[5]

Sexual Behavior in the Human Male may have been widely read, but it was much more widely known, via Kinsey's own tireless lecturing schedule as well as unrelenting coverage in the media, from small-town newspapers to national magazines. The Report was even incorporated into the plots of radio programs such as NBC's *One Man's Family*. Indeed, one writer surmised in 1952 that "the majority of the public has gained its knowledge of Kinsey solely from popular articles, radio, television, bull sessions and back fence gossip." Perhaps *Life* magazine put it best, opining that "as a phenomenal source of talk and controversy," the Report "virtually has attained the status of a new American institution." It speculated that "everybody but a few favorably situated hermits must be painfully aware that the Kinsey Report has been a godsend to radio comedians, nightclub jokers, gin mill raconteurs and connoisseurs of the shady quip." To many commentators, Kinsey's research seemed to be a topic that "everybody" was talking about. If this was not strictly true, youth groups, congregations, and professional organizations all over the nation—from the Town Hall Lecture Series in Beaumont, Texas, to the Council of Jewish Women in Birmingham, Alabama, to the Alpha Omega Dental Fraternity in Detroit—were listening to lectures and symposia on the Kinsey Report and "what it means to you." A Gallup Poll taken a month before *Sexual Behavior in the Human Male* even hit the bookstores found that 20 percent of the people questioned had knowledge of the Report and, furthermore, that the majority deemed it a "good thing." Commenting on an advertising conference devoted to Kinsey's impact on marketing, a columnist asked, "There must be some place where the good doctor's findings aren't being discussed, but where?"[6]

The country, as a Catholic weekly put it, had certainly become "Kinsey-conscious." The surveyor's name recognition was nothing short of remarkable. He was singled out as a greater celebrity than "a flock of Hollywood starlets" by *Daily Variety,* and his Report was judged to be one of the "10 subjects most likely to be the butt for show-biz humor during 1950" along with flying saucers, the atom bomb, the Trumans, and cold cures. The scientist's fame made him the target of autograph collectors and the subject of an article written by Mae West. It also earned him a ranking in *Focus* magazine's "10 Sexiest Men in the World," which listed Kinsey, or "Mr. Sex himself," alongside Tyrone Power, Joe DiMaggio, and others. The scientist was recognizable enough to be included in a *Look* magazine "Photoquiz" and a *Quick* magazine "Quick Quiz." And *Billboard* magazine noted in October 1953 that "for the third consecutive week, a new record has been waxed which concerns the coauthor of the literary thesis 'Sexual Behavior of the Human Female.'"[7]

The Kinsey Reports themselves quickly became a stock phrase employed to denote any kind of extensive quantitative inquiry. A traffic report comparing male and female fatalities was called a "Kinsey-like statistic," and studies of all manner of entities, from labor mediators to lobsters, were dubbed "Kinsey Reports." In a typical formulation, *Charm* magazine stated: "No Kinsey report ever has been made on the vital, basic activity of eating." Philadelphia's Kinsey Distilling Corporation, in existence long before the Reports, was grateful to the scientist for "impress[ing] our brand name on the public consciousness," although it was unable to handle all the requests for the study it was receiving.[8]

Kinsey practically became a brand name himself, useful in selling pajamas and housewares, not to mention magazines. Media outlets that ignored the scientist did so at their peril, given the broad demand for commentary on his surveys—a sign some took to mean that journalistic standards were shifting. The editor of the *Cleveland News* lamented the fact that as a matter of "economic life or death" newspapers had "to compete for the favor and attention of millions who prefer soap opera to the Met brand; who will discuss the Kinsey Report more enthusiastically (and should I say more understandably?) than the mysteries of Formosa and Indonesia." Although a scientific study, Kinsey's research was, to the editor, a "pop" topic, the news equivalent of a soap opera. But it sold papers. This kind of news frenzy was itself noted as novel. A CBS radio broadcast about Kinsey mused, "Isn't the real point, perhaps, that no one would have thought of compiling such a book a couple of generations ago? Who would have published it? How many popular magazines would have given its contents a circulation running into the millions?" To such commentators, it was not solely the Reports' facts that were new. So was the unceasing public discussion about them. It was as if the nation's inhabitants were somehow united through mass-mediated gossip about Kinsey. There were precedents for this in the cult of celebrity, the avid appetite for news about movie stars that Robert and Helen Lynd had discovered in

Muncie. Interest in the Reports, as in the Middletown studies themselves, indicated a newer fascination with what the citizenry did but could not have known in the absence of widely available survey data.[9]

Kinsey's critics were well aware of how much publicity he commanded, and they found his ubiquity reprehensible. One woman who was perturbed by the effects of the surveyor's research on the youth of America was doubly so since, as she wrote to him, "you have a lot of weight as you're a nationally known person." Another chastised *Look* magazine and NBC for their role in disseminating the Reports' data indiscriminately, and particularly for the impact this would have on "thousands of young people" who would wind up with "mis-givings about their own parents['] pre-marital relationships." An angry letter-writer, evidently hoping to shame Kinsey, asked him: "Do you know for what your name stands now? . . . It is symbolic of every lewd joke ever told. I have yet to hear or read of it used in any other way." Neither Kinsey's fans nor his critics, it seems, could stop talking about him. Whether through jokes, media reports, conversation, or condemnations, news of Kinsey and his statistics made its way to an extremely broad audience. What chance, many wondered, did their own views or teachings about sexual morality stand against a social scientific celebrity's?[10]

The extent of the discussion surrounding the Reports similarly worried those who were convinced that nonspecialist audiences would buy Kinsey's conclusions lock, stock, and barrel, unable to sift through methodological flaws and media misrepresentations. Academic and popular reviewers evaluated the Report by different standards, and the former well understood the reach of the latter. Kinsey had presented his knowledge as democratic and even liberatory for ordinary Americans, but many would soon wish that the *Sexual Behavior* facts had remained in scientists' or physicians' hands. Noted a sociologist who authored a critique of the male volume, "The phenomenal sale of the Report is well known. It is highly regrettable that only a negligible fraction of its readers will recognize its limitations." It was not just scholars who felt this way. A writer for a Catholic journal asserted, for example, "The book is not intended, or suitable or recommended, for the technically untrained general reader. The recent pushing of the volume as a 'best seller' is to be deplored." Social scientific data like Kinsey's, many realized, quickly escaped the expert's grip and were not dependent on academic commentators or professional gatekeepers for their interpretation.[11]

Those in the business of attitude measurement, on the other hand, regarded the scientist's fame opportunistically. "From all this publicity," wrote two of them, "public opinion research reaps an unexpected reward, for the Kinsey book actually testifies, to a large public previously unaware of surveys, to the magic which is inherent in the research tools of sampling and interviewing." If the *Sexual Behavior* researchers had been able to extract valid data "of such a private nature" from thousands of Americans, and "provide in the process a wealth of new and important social data," their study was of great use in showcasing the potential of survey methods. Pollsters and other researchers, eager for both public acceptance and private information, hoped Kinsey's celebrity might lend more credence and even glamour to their labors. Provided the criticisms of the Reports were not too damning, the author's fame might work as a public relations tool for the whole field of survey research.[12]

Kinsey's relationship with marketers began more anxiously. Sleepwear manufacturers were reportedly alarmed about his finding in the second volume that fully half of married women slept in the nude, prompting them to conduct their own study that counteracted Kinsey's. But generally speaking, as they did with the facts produced by the Middletown studies and other surveys, business interests quickly sought avenues for profit in the Reports' charts and percentages. A 1953 conference was devoted to the topic "Will

Kinsey's New Report Revolutionize Marketing?" The question was whether "scientific sex" could and should be used to sell products, and specifically whether advertisers ought to target older women who were "at their sexual peak." From the editor of *Sales Management* to the vice president and director of research at the J. Walter Thompson Company, those responsible for selling urged attention to social research, singling out the Reports as particularly fruitful for their line of work.[13]

As Kinsey's facts traveled to diverse audiences, they took on special connotations that revealed much about citizens' concerns regarding information gathering during the early Cold War years. *Middletown*'s audiences—as opposed to its subjects—had been more intrigued than appalled by surveyors' queries. By contrast, a piece on opinion researcher Archibald Crossley, dubbing him the "Kinsey-of-Commerce," editorialized: "It's a goldfish life today for the average man. He doesn't have any secrets anymore. He's afraid to open his mouth for fear it'll be taken as a confession." Kinsey, in turn nicknamed "the Dr. Gallup of sex" by the *Los Angeles Times,* was synonymous with the intrusiveness of social research, his very name suggesting a modern lack of privacy. "The name 'Kinsey' is by now a byword which means to most people sexual revelations, a glimpse into the secret lives of our neighbors," noted *Adult* magazine. If the Reports quickly became shorthand for intimate prying, even more illuminating were those instances in which they were invoked apart from any specifically sexual associations. At the conclusion of an article about the monitoring of water consumption in Toledo, Ohio, "and all of its implications concerning activities in the American home becoming public information," a reporter made the leap to sex surveys: "We are beginning to wonder just what privacy there is left for the average citizen. We had thought Dr. Kinsey had reached the ultimate but this is just too much."[14]

Similarly, the newly extensive 1950 census, with its inquiries into the personal income of every fifth household, was frequently identified as a Kinsey-like development. A Republican congressman complained that "if the federal government continues to pry more and more deeply into private affairs, the 1960 or 1970 census questions may read like the Kinsey report." Likewise, a small-town California newspaper, winking at its readers, assured them that "it's only an idle rumor that the census department's next project is an expanded Kinsey Report." Remarking on the controversy, a columnist in Petersburg, Virginia, editorialized, "The hard fact is that we are a people inured to questionnaires about anything and everything." The writer predicted that census takers might "encounter a few tough nuts here and there," but more tellingly that "the average every fifth person, having been properly conditioned, will promptly and dutifully reveal his 1949 income. A people who have been answering all kinds of questions for Dr. Gallup, Professor Kinsey, et cetera, will not be greatly upset over the income item." Like the Lynds, Roper, and Gallup before him, Kinsey was shifting the terms of what could be asked, and what was beyond the bounds of legitimate inquiry. By 1950 many observers concurred that there was not much of a boundary left.[15]

In an era of vigilant anticommunism and state surveillance, Kinsey's survey stirred up anxieties about the extent of sanctioned investigation into individuals' personal lives. At the same time, his research was remaking public understandings of the private. The *Sexual Behavior* scholarship explicitly challenged censorship codes and sex crime laws; Kinsey was consulted by many lawyers and judges on these issues and testified in legal hearings. The Reports also made heretofore unmentionable sexual topics fodder for the news media. In 1948 the *New York Times* would not even accept advance advertising for the male volume, given its subject matter. But in a tremendously rapid turnaround in press reticence, once the floodgates opened, details of the first Kinsey Report swamped media channels. In fact, many newspapers and magazines did not even wait for the Reports to come out before speculating as to their findings. Rumors about the progress of both studies circulated in the national press from the mid-1940s to the early 1950s despite Kinsey's best efforts to control pre-releases of his data.[16]

A careful manager of the press and popularizer of his own work, Kinsey has been credited with creating an audience for the sex survey. Partly because of his influence, studies that had once been reading matter for experts "were increasingly directed straight to the public by way of the media." As John D'Emilio and Estelle Freedman write, Kinsey's studies "propelled sex into the public eye in a way unlike any previous book or event had done." In the twentieth century, they note, "the strongest assault on sexual reticence in the public realm emerged not from the pornographic fringe, nor from popular culture, but from the respectable domain of science." Or as one of Kinsey's correspondents put it, "Our nation is surely over[ly] sex conscious and fast being fed with the stuff of sensious [sic] movies, songs, stories and other derogatory materials and now you under the guise of DOCTOR add your extra bit to further push the self restraint aside."[17]

Facing Modern Facts

Kinsey's statistics gained much of their authority from a discourse that trafficked in "facts" and "reality." This was a potent vocabulary, and academic and popular commentators alike adopted it readily. Remarked one individual who was queried by the *Cincinnati Enquirer* in a man-in-the-street interview about the first Report, "I don't see how some people can say there's anything wrong in the book. It's all facts." Another observer simply stated: "These are a few of the facts of our sex lives which we will be learning in the year 1948." Many such readers treated Kinsey's figures as if they were inert and timeless truths waiting to be unearthed by the scientist. "By now it is trite to remark that . . . *Sexual Behavior in the Human Male* is undoubtedly the most important collection of sex facts ever printed," contended a reviewer for the *Journal of General Psychology*. It was, in the words of a reporter for the *Chicago Uptown News,* "one of the most far-reaching, modern, factual reports ever made." In commentaries on the female survey as well, Kinsey was portrayed as marshaling data that revealed brute reality. One fan, delighted by the uproar *Sexual Behavior in the Human Female* was causing, sent Kinsey an anonymous postcard. "Looks like most of them don't like the facts of life, they can't face the truth," the writer crowed.[18]

These commentators believed that Kinsey had in effect taken a snapshot of contemporary American behavior, and had come closer than had anyone else to describing social realities rather than cultural ideals. One admirer announced, "The 'facts' presented in Dr. Kinsey's reports are going to stand as the nearest approach to the 'truth of the matter' which will ever be available as a description of the sexual manners, modes, and mores of our generation of Americans." "There has resulted from the analysis of these 6,300 histories," claimed another reader, "more information about male sex behavior, more new facts, more new relationships made clear than ever existed before." This theme runs through countless discussions of Kinsey's research. In perhaps the most grandiose such account, a commentator termed the first Report "a scientific Book of Revelations," going on to say, "The work of Kinsey and his collaborators should be a powerful factor in freeing human society, from fantastic tribal taboos, from ecclesiastic prejudices, and from the savagery of medieval laws. This may indeed be known as the 'Alfred C. Kinsey age.'" The writer's equation of survey data with enlightened refutation of "taboos," "prejudices," and "savagery" expressed a common dichotomy—one Kinsey encouraged—between custom and science, tradition and modernity, ideals and reality. As a by-product, critics of the Reports were sometimes portrayed as simply backward, not fully in or of the modern age. One scholarly reviewer, for instance, compared Kinsey's critics to "primitives," arguing that their response to the disturbing news he delivered was "more suitable to skinclad savages than to civilized men." An observer noted, "It [was] as if any adverse criticism [of the Reports] would immediately brand one as Victorian."[19]

In many accounts, then, the Kinsey Reports were linked with a new way of knowing, one that was "modern" in its willing confrontation with stark, difficult realities. To one expert, the Reports were "a reflection of the public's new attitude toward a subject which at one time was treated as a mystery." To another, they revealed "our generation in a cold light, unrelieved by any sentiment." As a CBS radio broadcaster announced, "In this frank facing of disagreeable facts that our ancestors ducked; there is perhaps the real revolution in contemporary morals that Dr. Kinsey has hastened along." To some, the fact that Kinsey's findings were so distressing only confirmed their truth.[20]

Kinsey's data seemed particularly modern for another reason. They displayed sex in a novel way: in the technical language of social science, and specifically, quantification. Calling the Report an "epoch-making work," a reviewer proclaimed, "Here for the first time in history a sustained effort has been made to ascertain scientifically and to state statistically what is actually going on in the matter of sex behavior in our American culture." Whether these numbers were legitimate, however, was subject to debate. Scholarly criticisms of the Reports centered mainly on Kinsey's sampling technique (both his reliance on volunteers and the device of hundred-percent sampling), although some challenged his statistical methods (in particular, his small or unclear n, or number of subjects, for many of the questions asked), and his acceptance of individual recollections of long-past events. Few of these specific methodological critiques made their way into public discussions, and in any event they were different from laypeople's assessments of the

Reports' accuracy. The series of moves between asking intimate questions in lengthy interviews and then recording and tabulating the answers on a punch card machine—the real labor that went into crunching of data—was virtually invisible to readers. What they saw were statistics about who did what and how frequently.[21]

Reactions to this aggregate mode of representing intimate experience revealed deep-seated cultural tensions over numbers and what they could say about "normal" Americans. On the one hand, Kinsey's statistics fascinated people. His finding that 37 percent of American men experienced some kind of "homosexual contact," that 52 percent were sexually active by age sixteen, that more than half engaged in extramarital affairs, that nearly all masturbated, and that a sizable fraction participated in behaviors such as bestiality were quickly disseminated through the national media. "Survey data," sociologists recognize, "is perhaps the most manageable form of data, and this is one reason for its popularity . . . journalists as well as funding bodies tend to like this type of 'hard' data which can be easily summarized and quoted." This was certainly true of Kinsey's numbers, which easily became social facts, repeated again and again, and were nearly impossible to dislodge once in popular circulation.[22]

The figures Kinsey unleashed carried a great deal of weight *because* they were numbers: spare, clear, and direct. This was suggested by one observer who remarked, "The statistical tables and graphs speak for themselves." Quantification worked in the Reports' favor. Some reactions to the studies exhibited what can only be described as a fetish for numbers and the social scientific instruments that produced them. The reviewer for the *Annals of the American Academy* pronounced the first volume "powerful" and "one of the most important books of our time" because of the "herculean labor" that had been required to complete it. He went on to call the female *Report* an equally impressive statistical feat, the product of "fifteen years of labor" and "8,000 interviews":

Since each subject was asked between 300 and 500 questions, all together more than 3,000,000 answers were recorded. In addition, records were scanned including sexual calendars, diaries, correspondence, scrapbooks, 16,000 works of art, clinical studies, and many thousands of previously published studies. Hundreds of consultants gave advice on the project, and the results in the book are presented in 179 tables and 155 figures.[23]

Another commentator hypothesized that this "battery of statistics" was at the very heart of Kinsey's allure for Americans. Statistics' "very preciseness and absolutism make them all the more attractive to the literate public," he argued. "Not 'most' Americans, not 'nearly all,' but precisely 92.2 per cent have premarital intercourse. This is perhaps a prime ingredient of the *Report*'s popular appeal, and incredible sales." Numbers, he suggested, even if detached from the reality they were supposed to convey, could awe readers.[24]

On the other hand, the quantification of human behavior could be deeply threatening, as both the opinion pollster and the sex surveyor knew. Although he defended his strictly quantitative and behavioral approach, Kinsey acknowledged the popular perception of statistics as "cold" and unable to "measure human emotions." Indeed, if Gallup's and Roper's majority percentages were taken as proof of an ever more impersonal "mass" society, numbers like Kinsey's seemed a challenge to any knowledge or values that were not, or could not be, given the imprimatur of statistical science. Many religious thinkers, social critics, psychoanalysts, and psychiatrists worried about the ramifications of counting up sexual acts. "Whatever else sex may be, it is not, emotionally speaking, in the same class with the multiplication table," insisted one commentator, concerned about the impact of the first Report on the "human" qualities of sex and Christian ethical teachings. Religious critics in particular balked at the potential of social scientific findings to eclipse other standards of judgment, and they defended aspects of sexual experience that could not be encompassed by Kinsey's six varieties of "outlet."[25]

A multitude of social commentators challenged the first Report's austere scientific handling of intricate human questions. Anthropologist and psychoanalytically influenced critic Geoffry Gorer, referring to Kinsey's entomological past, cautioned that "an act which can consummate love and produce children cannot be measured with the calipers that determine the variation in the wingspan of wasps." He charged that "until Dr. Kinsey came along, sex had generally been viewed as one of the most complex of all human activities." Now, instead, "sex has been reduced to statistics." Gorer bemoaned but was resigned to the "atomization" of sex, seeing it as of a piece with contemporary developments that had fractured knowledge into "discrete and equal facts": intelligence tests, college exams, quiz shows, crossword puzzles, and public opinion polls. For all the persuasiveness of quantified facts, to label something "mere statistics"—a charge of numbers' inadequacy to express the whole truth—also minimized its significance. As Margaret Mead, a vocal critic of the Reports, dryly observed: "The major abstraction an anthropologist from Mars would get from reading the Kinsey report is that sex in this country is an important, meaningless physical act which men have to perform fairly often, but oftener if they have not gone to college." The idea of studying as fundamental a human activity as sex wholly abstracted from its social context seemed absurd and possibly dangerous to such critics. Even Mae West objected to "any interpretation of sex that looks upon it as a mere 'biological function.'" She asked, "Is man, then, to weigh all his emotions in test tubes and note down some kind of formula?"[26]

None, however, were more vehement in their disagreement with Kinsey than the professional psychiatric community, which was nearly unanimous in its assessment that his approach to sexuality was profoundly misguided. Conceding that it was "Kinsey's privilege to limit his research in a complex behavioral field to the extraction from it of whatever is countable," one psychiatrist sharply criticized the scientist's interpretations of what the data meant. He argued that people's sexual dilemmas did "not arise mostly, as Kinsey implies, from the individual's appreciation of his atypicality in relation to rigid legal and social scales," but instead emerged from multiple "other factors in a total life situation." This writer argued that "a suffering person is likely to view his designation as normal on grounds of taxonomic objectivity as somewhat beside the point."[27]

If professional psychiatrists and humanistic commentators cautioned that statistics could not tell a meaningful story of human sexuality, lay critics often focused on the fact that numbers told the wrong tale altogether: one drained of morality or even mystery. One columnist in 1949 jokingly urged women not to participate in Kinsey's study. "I can't help but feel that the women are making a mistake in being so obligingly co-operative," she wrote. "When it comes to love and sex, it has always been an advantage to women to be a little bit mysterious to men." If this caution was tongue-in-cheek, others worried more seriously about the effects of a stripped-down view of human intimacy. Quantification, some believed, led Kinsey to sidestep the most fundamental aspects of sexual relations. As one individual wrote to the scientist, "These men [in the male volume] have committed crimes . . . and you put it down complacently in statistics instead of in terms of human souls." The counting and registering of men's behavior without any attention to motivations or repercussions, this writer suggested, could not get at the truth of that behavior. The social scientist's emphasis on detachment—just reporting the "facts"—missed the point entirely, which was to judge some acts as good and others bad.[28]

Many associated the absence of moralizing in the Reports with the advance of scientific knowledge. A writer for the *Atlanta Constitution* pitied "poor informed modern youth," who were burdened with "choosing their mates scientifically." A *Baltimore Afro-*

American columnist similarly waxed nostalgic for an era when "each bride included a cook book [rather] than a Kinsey report in her trousseau, and when what sex life she had was adequate, or if it wasn't she never discovered it by experimenting." Both argued that, in some matters, ignorance was bliss. But whether or not readers endorsed Kinsey's tabulation of private life, to many it seemed an inevitable aspect of modern times. Wrote one college journalist critical of the quantitative trend, "America is developing a cult of statistics . . . And modern man is abandoning himself to a worship of statistics." Much like those who charged the Lynds with not seeing the heart of Muncie for the facts, these observers viewed Kinsey's passion for "that which can be measured" as symptomatic of an overly rational modernity.[29]

Significantly, by the time Kinsey's second volume arrived in 1953, the quantification of sexual behavior was not up for debate in the same way that it had been just five years earlier. Commentary on *Sexual Behavior in the Human Female,* by and large, did not fix on Kinsey's basic project of collecting intimate material and transforming it into statistics. Instead, critics seized upon the dangers of publicizing Kinsey's findings. This was partly because the public release of sexual facts about women promised to be more disruptive to social norms than the release of the male figures had been. But it was also because Americans in the brief time between 1948 and 1953 had become accustomed, no matter how grudgingly, to the social scientific takeover of intimate acts—that is, the right to think about sex in the language of numbers.[30]

Not everyone believed that Kinsey's facts—no matter how much scientific weight they mustered—ought to overturn established mores or could speak for the "normal." Indeed, the Reports would ignite a furious debate about what social statistics could say about America writ large. Many readers challenged the science of the *Sexual*

Behavior research. They contended that the studies were simply not accurate: that Kinsey's subjects could not possibly be representative of "good" Americans, that his sample was corrupted by reliance on the sexually deviant, that his interviews could not detect the wild exaggerations of his volunteers.

"Few, if any, researches depending on volunteer subjects have defined the scope of the universe to which their generalizations were to apply as ambitiously as the Kinsey project," pointed out one social scientist. If they did not articulate it in such technical language, many lay critics agreed with the sentiment: Kinsey had overreached in trying to speak on behalf of ordinary Americans. As one New Yorker complained to the scientist, Kinsey's questions might have been "answered correctly by the 5900 persons over 15 years but do not apply at all to the remainder of the 150,000,000 population of the country," adding, "Everyone knows this of course." The same challenge, reminiscent of Gallup's and Roper's struggles to promote scientific sampling, was implied in such headlines as "Sexual Behavior in 7,789 Women," the title of a skeptical review article. Once again, the question of representativeness would be at the crux of debates over survey research. Arguments sparked by Kinsey's tables and graphs exposed profound disagreements about how the national community could be known and what the implications of this knowing would be.[31]

To begin with, many readers of the Reports were not willing to allow a handful of Americans to stand in for them in matters of morality. "You have taken a few crackpots and held them up as the norm and yourself as God," complained one of Kinsey's angry correspondents. "Adultery and kindred offenses involving sex are neither tolerated nor secretly practiced by most people in New England," protested a *Boston Daily Record* editorial responding to Kinsey's statistic that 95 percent of American men could be hauled before the courts for their violations of sex laws. These writers, relying on their own imagined statistics about how Americans behaved, were not convinced by Kinsey's careful descriptions of his sample and statistical technique. To them, "normal" sexual behavior was closely tied to conventional morality, and no social scientific method, no matter how technically impressive, could untether the two concepts. In this understanding, the normal could never be merely statistical.[32]

Challenges to the Reports' representativeness were fueled by the suspicions many harbored about the particular Americans Kinsey had selected for his sample. The investigator, of course, had boasted about his survey reaching the "ne'er-do-well" as well as the "clergyman," and not discriminating between the sorts of sexual practices each favored. Scrutinizing the categories of subjects included in the Reports, some found outrageous the proposition that sexual or social "deviants" could be included in a study of normal sexual behavior. Apart from "prostitutes, prisons and psychiatric hospital interviewees," announced the acerbic Dorothy Thompson for the *Ladies' Home Journal,* "the Kinsey Report is a study of largely urban, predominantly college-educated, nonreligious and not overly reticent American males under thirty." Such critics were alert to those absent from the Reports, namely, well-behaved people like themselves. A certified public accountant from Detroit (and likely a Catholic) claimed to have made his own studies on the subject of sexual behavior that had resulted in less morally appalling conclusions than Kinsey's. He wrote to the scientist, "If more Catholics had been polled . . . your results would have been more correct." Similarly, the Catholic journal *America,* eager to exempt its readers from the activities Kinsey catalogued, called the first Report "a rich source of factual information concerning the status of sexual behavior in a small segment of the *American, white, non-Catholic, male population.*" These observers were unpersuaded of the survey's comprehensiveness as well as the capacity of aggregate results to reflect their own behavior. Importantly, however, their critiques implied that had Kinsey interviewed the right Americans, his statistics might be legitimate.[33]

Others were unwilling to make even that concession to the surveyor. Middletowners and large numbers of the unpolled had lodged scattered complaints about the particular sort of individuals surveyors had chosen to question. But this became a leading critique of Kinsey's Reports—and a more sweeping one. Challenges to sexual statistics were often at the same time a challenge to the "normality" of Kinsey's respondents. "No normal moral man or woman would submit to sex research questions," asserted one anonymous critic, casting aspersions on individuals for the very act of talking about their sexual histories with a surveyor. A reviewer of the female Report elaborated on this interpretation. "People who volunteer information about their sex life are not necessarily typical people," he charged. "One would like to know what kind of women these were who were willing to discuss the intimate details of their sex lives with a stranger and how truthful their answers were." By this logic, because only "abnormal" individuals were willing to be interviewed, the entire study was flawed. Some went still further in criticizing Kinsey's subjects and particularly those who populated *Sexual Behavior in the Human Female*. Given reigning conventions about female modesty, the idea of women submitting to interviews with the all-male research team was especially unsettling, and the women who participated in the study were vigorously criticized. Many concluded that Kinsey's female interviewees must have been prostitutes, or at the very least seriously maladjusted. Others dismissed women of any sort as especially unreliable subjects. Editorialized one popular magazine, "[We think] the professor may have bitten off more than he can chew in trying to compile the behavior of our talkative-silent, ignorant–too knowing, quibbling-forgetful, always unpredictable Women."[34]

In the end, some were simply unswayed by the claims of social science, preferring to trust their personal knowledge about mainstream sexual behavior and normal Americans over and above Kinsey's hard-won statistics. One of Kinsey's correspondents drew upon his own set of data—his marriage—to counter the *Sexual*

Behavior research. "I have lived with one woman for 46 years and I do not agree with your findings . . . when you show as one magazine reports that 62% of adult women practice masturbation—you're nuts." Although he signed his letter "One Man's Opinion," this writer clearly believed that Kinsey's survey of thousands did not outweigh his own singularly relevant facts. Another reader could not countenance the Reports' statistics for one simple reason: "In all my life; and I have been around some, I never, to my knowledge met a homosexual." Individual experience could still trump social scientific expertise, even if this was becoming more difficult in a culture infused by statistical knowledge.[35]

Purporting to fashion a "normal" out of prisoners, fringe characters, and many ethnic groups in addition to the "respectable," and claiming to have made a representative survey, Kinsey plainly hit a nerve. The Reports tapped into national ideals and self-image in a way that the Middletown surveys and Gallup Poll had as well. For this reason, those who protested Kinsey's findings could not simply disregard or dismiss them. They instead were compelled to defend their own understanding of representativeness, their own vision of the sexual public.

Calling the subjects of the female study "5,940 sex delinquents," for example, one woman argued that they couldn't possibly represent the mainstream, "the hundreds of thousands of women and mothers . . . who have never engaged in any pre-marital sex relationships." Pointing to Kinsey's finding that 50 percent of the women interviewed were not virgins when they wed, she insisted that the surveyor had utterly failed at "in any way portraying the womanhood of America as a whole" since "no adequate sampling of the women of America can be found among frequenters of 'bars, dance-halls and swimming pools' of the type that lend themselves to 'Socio-Sexual approaches.'" Similarly, one man, sure that wartime conditions had seriously skewed the *Sexual Behavior* data on marital fidelity, made a plea to Kinsey that he "please publish a statement to the effect that your figures in this phase of the sex study are not true of what a picture of the normal segment would be." In the process of arguing with sexual statistics, such critics betrayed both their allegiance to "the normal" and its objective determination through hard facts. Why else this emotionally vested interest in the representativeness of Kinsey's subjects, "the womanhood of America as a whole," or the "normal segment"? These responses to Kinsey's findings indicate widespread cognizance of social statistics' ability to define and categorize. They also suggest that many Americans' identification with an abstract and quantitatively conceived national community was strong indeed.[36]

Statistical Morality

The facts Kinsey's team issued in 1948, and then again in 1953, were, in an important sense, *new*. As a biologist at Johns Hopkins University saw it, "Once in a great while a book comes along which marks the commencement . . . of a scientific era. These are the books that virtually begin a new science, that blaze a trail into the unknown. Such a book is *Sexual Behavior in the Human Male*." For many, Kinsey's research was a "discovery" akin to Columbus's, revealing the terra incognita of normal American sexuality. By interviewing thousands of subjects, by synthesizing and categorizing their answers, and by thus constructing a publicly available compendium of sexual behavior, Kinsey had pried open a new world. Frequent comparisons of his sex research to the atomic bomb—the Reports themselves were sometimes referred to as the "K-bomb"— illuminate the impact of Kinsey's survey. Prior to the Reports' release, observed one commentator, Americans had a "collective ignorance of the ways of our fellows." His sense, that the Reports constituted a revolution in social knowledge, in the facts Americans knew about one other, was cause for celebration as well as condemnation. At the very least, Kinsey's sexual knowledge could not be ig-

The Private Lives of the Public · 257

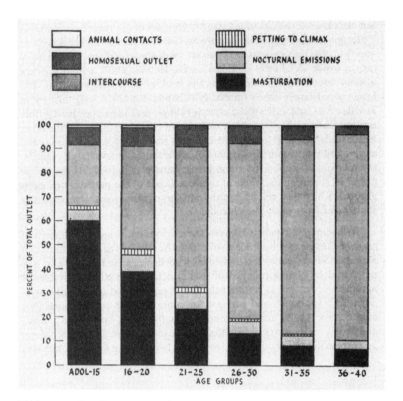

Tables on the frequency and types of sexual "outlet" took on new significance in the hands of a curious public, allowing individuals to measure their behavior against that of strangers. (Chart from *Sexual Behavior in the Human Male*, 1948, reproduced by permission of The Kinsey Institute for Research in Sex, Gender, and Reproduction, Inc.)

nored. As a minister put it, "It is not possible for Christians to return to a pre-Kinsey sexual era. Having facts about sex behavior, and consequent new insight into existing sex attitudes, there is no possible retreat into an ostrichlike position." He understood that such knowledge did not exist in the national consciousness in the same way before and after 1948. This is why, for all their hyperbole, those who talked of a radical break between a pre-Kinsey and a post-Kinsey era were correct.[37]

The Kinsey Reports, like the Gallup Poll, would upset many people's convictions that they knew something of the mores and morals of their neighbors. One observer, pointing to the wide array of practices uncovered in the Reports, perceived this when he wrote that Americans "are rather different from what any one American imagines, seeing the situation, as he must, from his own personal, group, or class viewpoint." This led many to wonder, as did one reviewer, what might be the "effect from the pouring of these masses of laboriously collected data into the stream of public thought." Most concluded that the wide publicity the Reports attracted could not help but impel social change, whether for good or ill. The Federal Council of the Churches of Christ in America declared, for instance, that the first Report, by dint of its scientific authority and its popular circulation, had "already become a social document" and was "bound to have an effect upon general attitudes in relation to sex." A journalist for a popular magazine agreed: "Gradually, inevitably, this study will find its way into the stream of literature, lecture, and conversation by which our sex behavior is guided and directed." Each of these commentators intuited that a collection of statistics— or, more precisely, public awareness of those statistics—could have dramatic consequences.[38]

Others suggested more concretely that Kinsey's facts were already serving to make traditional ways obsolete. *Reader's Digest* posed the question: "Have our conventions and moralities . . . been outmoded by the findings of modern science?" For those who accepted Kinsey's findings, the answer was obvious: Americans needed to face up to the sexual diversity in their midst. Some broadening of the permissible and "the normal" had to be effected. Sounding much like the Report's author, a writer for the *American Journal of Public Health* asserted, "Perhaps the most important conclusion from this whole study is that our conception of what is 'normal' sexual behavior must be radically revised." These partisans argued that greater tolerance and a revision of moral codes were the only logical outcomes flowing from new facts. They believed in a kind of social scientific realism: that Kinsey's statistics had turned up "the real," and that this discovery made lies of all the layers of custom and tradition that obscured it. Adopting this stance, one commentator proclaimed, "Obviously, to be of any value at all, a standard of sexual normality must be based on what we, the majority of Americans, *do,* rather than on what we say." The normal, such writers argued, could and even should be statistically determined.[39]

Those who called for a change in mindset and a smooth adjustment to Kinsey's findings were in the minority, however. Critics of all stripes disputed not the Reports' facts—although many, of course, did this—but instead their publication. As one angry reader charged, "These filthy books should only be in Dr.'s libraries *not* for the public." A group of letter writers put it more pithily: "Kinsey calls it realism, a SEWER is also realism but for obvious reasons we keep it COVERED." Kinsey's statistics were especially disruptive in the Cold War context, when national and sexual character were routinely conflated, whether in purges of homosexuals from the State Department or in political oratory that equated national weakness and moral decay.[40]

In this light, knowledge like Kinsey's was a threat not just to personal values and social norms but to the very health of the nation: its children, marriages, and moral fiber. One woman was inspired to write to Kinsey after hearing her minister mention that "the very first place Communism would attempt to strike in any country was at its moral foundation." She continued, "I wonder if you have not unwittingly lent yourself to this destructive design by your sensationally-publicized report on sex behavior (or misbehavior) in the human female." Many letters and editorials charged the professor with an almost criminal irresponsibility in unleashing data on the high rates of masturbation and extramarital activity among the impressionable. "Turning these sex reports loose upon the public is on a par with the Rosenberg crime in the atomic field," penned one irate reader. "Many young people who are already leading an uninhibited sex life will find their behavior rationalized in this book," charged another, decrying the male Report as "a regrettable influence on youngsters who are hovering on the brink." Yet another incensed reader complained to *Life* magazine that Kinsey was "certainly not helping to cut down divorce rates by telling 50% of the American wives their husbands are unfaithful!"[41]

Apprehension about the norms the Reports were establishing, and seeming to hold up for emulation, was widespread. If opinion polls' potential for creating a herd mentality was ominous to some, the idea that Kinsey's facts would usher in a new morality was downright alarming. Gallup and Roper had made the case that the majority will would be clearer and louder when conveyed quantitatively through their polls. Statistics of Kinsey's variety—the 50 percent of women who admitted to premarital sex, for example— carried a more worrisome potential, especially if the same equation between majorities and rightness held. A letter to a religious advice column in 1950 certainly confirmed such fears: the writer had been accused of a narrow-minded reaction to a shotgun wedding, and the accusers had "quoted the Kinsey report in defense." To many, a new definition of morality—"no worse than the next one"— seemed imminent in the post-Kinsey era.[42]

Critics of this bent were most agitated by what some termed "statistical morality," the notion that an action was socially acceptable simply because it was commonplace. Many claimed that Kinsey furthered the radical position that "ethics has only a statistical base." One of the researcher's correspondents, for instance, demanded whether "a wrong should be indulged because a pathetically large group do it." In one of the most gentle incarnations of this critique, a minister charged the first Report with an "unwitting value judgment affirming the existent as the 'real,' even implying at times that what *is* is what should be." Such reactions highlight rather strikingly the novel cultural context for social scientific information in the mid-twentieth century. Knowing what the numerical majority did seemed to be enough to encourage or alter behavior, and this was particularly threatening on sexual terrain. What is revealing about these worries is not so much that they predicted how Kinsey's data might operate, but the anxiety itself, which was joined to more general concerns about the imitative character of what commentators increasingly called a "mass society." Believing that family and religious bonds were weakening, many Americans feared that individuals would choose to be guided by statistics— and other people's actions—in the absence of traditional social anchors.[43]

Kinsey's decision to work with quantitative rather than qualitative data made this prospect much more plausible. Employing the all-purpose measure of outlet, the scientist's numerical charts invited measurements against the mean. To one *Cincinnati Enquirer* reporter writing of the male survey, "The 'clinical tables' at the end of the book" were "especially dangerous" since they made for easy comparisons and self-evaluation. Geoffrey Gorer, a sharp critic of Kinsey's "justification by numbers," complained that "'self-rating' has become so emotionally important for so many Americans that the greater number of popular papers have scoring cards by which one can rate oneself for knowledge or for the possession of certain qualities." He continued, "Now Dr. Kinsey has supplied a great number of tables by which one can rate oneself; and, in an appendix, has thoughtfully broken them down by age, education, marital status, etc. With a little trouble one can find out how one stacks up in frequency of 'outlet,' variety of 'outlet,' and even more intimate anatomical details, with one's peers." Gorer concluded that, in the Kinsey era, "'keeping up with the Joneses' acquires a new, and perhaps slightly ribald, significance." Sure enough, *Charm* magazine, in a year-end roundup that designated 1948 "the year of the Kinsey Report," reported that "an incredible lot of armchair lovers apparently found entertainment in scoring themselves off against the statistical sex behavior of their neighbors." Such breezy accounts surely only made for more worry among those wary of a culture in which moral standards were determined not by tradition but by sheer popularity.[44]

A fan of the Reports gleefully reported that "the latest saying along Broadway is: 'If it's all right with Kinsey, it's all right with me!'" A phalanx of psychologists and sociologists set out to test just this proposition on undergraduates at Princeton and UCLA, among other universities, their question being: Did mere familiarity with Kinsey's survey change students' sexual attitudes and activities? As these investigators well understood, social scientific data had a life and force of their own that extended far beyond the mere aggregation of facts. This knowledge could cause people to act in different ways, imagine their relationships in new lights, and reevaluate their beliefs. Margaret Mead was among those who believed in the potency of Kinsey's facts. "In our rapidly changing culture, we rely upon knowledge of what is 'done,' on what the majority of the people of our own age, sex, and class are doing," she explained. "Until the Kinsey report was published, people hadn't known whether they should have more sex or less. Now many are rushing to buy the book just to look themselves up." Indeed, at a 1948 forum on the male Report at Louisiana State University, an expert felt it necessary to offer what might have seemed an absurd piece of advice: that "no person should feel compelled to consult tables in the Kinsey report before deciding on his type of activity." In a society constantly seeking information about itself, in other words, statistical means could themselves become normative.[45]

Expectations about the permissive impact of the Reports were not mere fantasies of alarmists or traditionalists. Experts, pop and otherwise, described the cultural assimilation of sex research in similar but much more laudatory terms. Data, they agreed, could be therapeutic. A commentator for the *Nation* believed that this fact explained psychiatrists' strong criticisms of Kinsey. "One important and highly gratifying effect" of the male Report, he believed, was its "mass psychotherapeutic function . . . People work with touching eagerness through the appalling mass of boring charts and statistics in order to discover with relief that they are not outcasts, not psychopaths, not criminals." He argued, "If this relief from tension and guilt can be bought for $6.50, it is a most happy social accomplishment. But everybody in the guilt business is bound to feel at least a little angry." Others made a similar case regarding religious outcries against Kinsey's research, one writing that "the Report has been . . . bitterly assailed by authoritarian groups, particularly clerical ones, which have a vested interest in human insecurity and ignorance."[46]

The liberating effect of the Reports—their ability to free individuals from the "experts" (ironically enough) and the tyranny of hypocritical social codes—was their chief benefit according to this vein of analysis. Testifying to the sway of aggregates and employing majoritarian language, one commentator observed, "The trouble was that up to now nobody who belonged to this majority [who broke sexual taboos] could know that he did belong to a *majority;* hence people felt abnormal and guilty." This writer compared the silence around sexual behavior prior to the Reports to "a state of mind in the modern political dictatorship" where "the actual normal, average man is unaware of the fact that his neighbors, and ordinary men throughout the country, are equally discontented and critical." By putting a Cold War spin on Kinsey's research and praising the democratic potential of survey data, he was borrowing some of the scientist's own rhetoric. He was also countering those critics who believed that the *Sexual Behavior* statistics were a sign of American decline. Instead, the sexual knowledge of the Reports was proof of the freedom of thought in a liberal society.[47]

Kinsey's champions, no less than his detractors, swore by the power of numbers. "Whatever your weakness," explained a popular magazine to its female readership regarding the *Sexual Behavior* data, "you will find that you share it with countless American women." One expert, pleased about the rethinking of moral codes that Kinsey was causing, believed that "the Report has the psychological effect of lifting a large weight of guilt from the shoulders of the individual, divides the guilt, so to speak, among millions." Asserted another, "Good or bad, if you know that your sex life coincides with that of most of your fellow Americans, you will be freed of an oppressive sense of guilt." Being part of a statistical majority—even if the company one kept was in conventional terms misbehaving—was thought to convey great psychological rewards. A writer for the *New Yorker* reflected, "To be sure, people might still regret their actions, even after coming into possession of the Kinsey facts, but there is a substantial difference between remorse over having acted as a member of one per cent of the population and remorse over having acted as a member of ninety per cent." Implicit in commentators' analyses was the assumption that information about strangers' behaviors and national norms could have personal consequences. The statistical community and the individual's psychological well-being were thus tightly bound together.[48]

Indeed, there is much evidence to suggest that individuals *were* using Kinsey's data as a new, and more forgiving, standard by which to classify their own behavior. "The unexpected financial success of Dr. Kinsey's report," observed one writer, "has made evident the eager interest of a public starved for facts relative to the sexual conduct of its members." Access to such facts would help individuals determine whether and where they fit into an expanded category of the "normal." Again, the sexual accounting scheme of the Reports made this relatively easy. A West Point graduate who wrote to Kinsey, for example, found solace in the numbers the professor had compiled. "I know now that I'm not nor ever was a homo-sexual, but there were times when some of my actions as a small boy weighed heavily on my conscience," he acknowledged.

It seems so ridiculous now that I ever worried as a little logical reasoning then would have proven I couldn't be abnormal since I did no more than all the other boys in my group, in fact in many cases not so much . . . What interested me was your statements on the prevalence of homosexuality in young boys, and the fact that one poor fellow just as normal as any may be branded and ruined for life first because he was caught doing what thousands and thousands of others are doing and have done.[49]

For this writer, the *Sexual Behavior* data were a source of relief. Although he drew a different lesson from the facts and figures than did many of the outraged readers of the Reports, he too was suggesting that the researcher had created a standard of statistical morality that broke radically with the purportedly shared norms of the past. Kinsey applauded this reading of his data. Replying to a letter from a sixteen-year-old living in rural North Carolina who confessed his "abnormal" attraction for men and described himself as a *"lost boy,"* the scientist was sympathetic, with an evident desire to reassure. To do so, he invoked the comfort of numbers: "You must not worry about your problem. It is one that a great many people run into." He continued, "One of the worst things that can happen to a person is to have them feel that they are abnormal and different from other persons. You must not feel that for that probably is not true." Kinsey's interest in broadening the category of the normal comes through clearly in such statements. His columns and charts engendered the same hope in many individuals who came into contact with the Reports' findings.[50]

Within Kinsey's vast correspondence can be found thousands of individuals seeking and finding statistical reassurance. A man from New York, for example, inquired in 1944 as to how frequently married men typically masturbated, since he knew it was often seen as an adolescent activity. He noted, "I have suffered somewhat from the feeling that it meant I was to some extent abnormal." In another instance, a woman wrote to Kinsey regarding her and her partner's enjoyment of the "queer" practice of oral sex: "Please, in some way, let us know if this is right or if this is condoned . . . surely others are like this too. Are we to be condemned? Are we normal?" she begged to know. One African American woman who wrote up her interview experience with Kinsey for *Ebony* magazine, expressed her relief at hearing of the survey's findings:

> I learned quickly that as a social science researcher with a college degree, I had a sex life not unlike upper class women of any color. According to Dr. Kinsey, I and these women got more mental satisfaction and less physical gratification from sexual intercourse than persons with lower class standards . . . I was happy to learn that I am neither abnormal nor unusual since Dr. Kinsey's research for his next book about U.S. women found that a third are so-called 'cold' women.

Framing her own history against others like her—professional, upper-class, and well educated—this woman could easily find herself in Kinsey's masses of data on white females similarly situated, even if subjects like her would be eliminated from the Report's pages. Indeed, the format of the survey carefully structured her identification with these anonymous others. By lining up her sexual experience against Kinsey's categories, this woman could be satisfied that she was "normal." Her expectations about her own sexual fulfillment were, however, delimited by Kinsey's classificatory regime. "This does not mean that I am a 'nicer' woman," she wrote. "It does not mean that I am happier than women with other standards. As a matter of fact, I have less chance of sexual adjustment in marriage because I do hold these ideas which make it hard for me to relax when behaving sexually." As a certain kind of woman she inevitably encountered certain kinds of problems, and all of this was made transparent by the magic of social statistics. In this way, numbers about those one didn't know could become personally meaningful. In the responses of surveys' audiences, we can perceive a community, not of neighbors but of knowledge, taking shape. Indeed, Kinsey noted in the first Report that the most frequent queries interviewees had for the researchers involved "comparisons of the individual's activities with averages for the group to which he belongs" and the question "Am I normal?"[51]

Stand Up and Be Counted

Kinsey's success at securing the cooperation of thousands of strangers to answer his intimate questions was a tribute to his persuasive faculties. But it also revealed the peculiar attraction of social surveys for midcentury Americans. The pull of an emerging statistical community was most evident in the willingness and even enthusiasm with which individuals volunteered to be part of the *Sexual Behavior* research.

The popular media seized upon the fact that, following the publication of *Sexual Behavior in the Human Male,* individuals were volunteering in droves to take part in the survey. *Life* magazine observed, "It has become quite fashionable to be interviewed by Kinsey, and consequently there has been a waiting list." The 1949 Christmas shopping rush in Atlanta was said to outstrip even "the prospect of an interview with Kinsey," and the *Miami Daily News* reported that the scientist planned to "steer clear of the extroverts who clamor to be interviewed" while doing research in the city. "Such people have become so serious a problem," it related, "that Dr. Kinsey and his staff travel incognito and in groups of not more than three." Even accounting for media exaggeration, the amount of interest in participating in the *Sexual Behavior* research was extraordinary. And as the first Report attracted more and more publicity, requests for interviews increased. One Vermont newspaper let its readers know in 1952, "It's still not too late to sit down with the original Kinsey researchers and take one of the same kind of interviews that went into the book," but it noted that there was a good deal of competition for slots. The popular song "Oh! Dr. Kinsey (Why Don't You Question Me?)" hit close to the mark. A journalist for *Cosmopolitan* magazine interviewing Kinsey was able to "report at first-hand" that the telephone in the scientist's office rang regularly with calls from those hoping to volunteer.[52]

Hundreds of other individuals contacted Kinsey with the aim of serving as research subjects. These offers could be extended in a rather businesslike way. A fairly typical letter read: "Dr. Kinsey, Sir: I should like to volunteer to be interviewed for your records on the forthcoming sequel to SEXUAL BEHAVIOR IN THE HUMAN MALE. For classification purposes I will mention that I am an actress, married eight years, no children. Please notify me at the address below at any time I can be of service in your research." This woman's offer—and her attendant self-classification—were not at all unusual. Kinsey often acquiesced to such requests, especially if the individual fit a category for which he needed more histories. His courteous reply to this volunteer first thanked her for her interest. "It is very good of you to offer to help," he continued. "We should be glad to get your history. Your background is one which we need better represented in our study." In this fashion, Kinsey encouraged individuals to feel like active participants in his research.[53]

Revealing one's deepest secrets to a stranger, instead of causing shame or embarrassment, proved satisfying to some who gave their sexual histories. As did many who corresponded with Kinsey, individuals could find confirmations of their normality in a session with one of the *Sexual Behavior* team. One such man wanted Kinsey to know "that I found our visit enjoyable and helpful—most helpful, indeed. The confidence gained from your advice and experience has given me the assurance I was seeking." Similar testimonies from others help explain why Kinsey's research subjects were so loyal to the scientist. One woman responded to a perceived attack on his interview method in the pages of *Newsweek* by standing up for the "courageous Dr. Kinsey," as well as "the women who offered themselves so generously in the name of humanity as guinea pigs" for his study.[54]

What did it mean to become a guinea pig, one among thousands of other subjects and millions of accumulated facts? Accounts of those who revealed their role in Kinsey's research suggest that it was something of a thrill. A Canadian reporter who agreed to give her history disclosed that she had been "disturbed at the prospect of revealing the most intimate details of my life . . . But in very short order I was taking a completely objective view and finding the interview as clinical and impersonal as an examination by a doctor." She described her participation in the survey rather proudly: "I was an infinitesimal cog in one of the greatest fact-finding projects ever undertaken . . . Day by day, month by month, they [the interviews] add up to the first great mass of facts, and figures drawn from a cross-section of all social and educational groups, from which charts, curves and finally conclusions may be drawn." Kinsey's subjects who left public traces often commented both on their feelings of anonymity and their sense of importance in contributing survey data. Interviewees recalled this process in strikingly similar ways. One wrote for *Cosmopolitan* magazine, "Dr. Kinsey sits about six feet away, facing you. He marks checks, crosses and other symbols on a chart. It is no ordeal; you know that you are not making an impression—only a statistic." Another volunteer remarked, "My sex life now belongs to science . . . I am just a case number in the large collection in the files of the Kinsey research." Still another stated, "I have been Kinsey-ized. I have become a statistic, number umpity-ump in the record of 100,000 men and women that will make up Dr. A. C. Kinsey's study of human sex behavior." She went on to describe her transformation in some detail:

> When we were through, I looked at my sex history . . . My whole life was spread out in . . . dozens of little checks and crosses placed on the paper to tell a story to Dr. Kinsey, but meaningless to an outsider. And when I went out of that room, my identity would vanish as if a wave had washed over the sand. My anonymity would be complete. Later the sheet of paper would be run through a fabulous machine to break the answers down into their proper categories . . . No longer was I an individual; only a statistic to form a pattern along with thousands of other case histories. I felt about as significant in the scale of life as a star a million miles away.

This woman's words summarized not a complaint, but a fascination. Somehow, the merging of her life history with thousands of others through the "fabulous" technology of the Hollerith card puncher linked her to something almost cosmic in significance. As such, the Kinsey interview stood as a telling symbol of both the anonymity and the connectedness of the modern public.[55]

Just as finding one's place in a battery of statistics brought a welcome sense of comfort to many individuals, standing up and being counted had its own satisfactions, linking private, individual behaviors to a larger, if diffuse, community. The eagerness to take part in Kinsey's research was not restricted to those who underwent interviews. Many who never served as subjects sought to take part in the research and make their mark on the Reports. And plenty of information from volunteers arrived unbidden at Kinsey's Indiana University offices. One man who had read the male volume, but who had no prior contact with the surveyor, wrote: "I am making an offer to help out in the work. If it will be of any value to you, I am willing to give you a detailed history of my sex life; the inside story revealing my thoughts, aims, motives and mental picture, in regard to various phases of sex." A helpful, even eager, volunteer, he merely required from Kinsey the headings and topics he ought to structure his sexual history around. This man could give the scientist "typical instances and cases," as well as "particular cases (army experience) and instances." He added, "I am a touch typist and qualified to explain anything and everything for you." Attaching only a few conditions—that no one call on him in person, that his revelations be kept confidential, and that he be given a reasonable amount of time to write up the history ("I work on a night shift, am tired many times, must wait on myself" he wrote in explanation)—this correspondent believed his history would be "a valuable addition" to the *Sexual Behavior* research. Demonstrating a familiarity with the techniques of the social scientist for sifting experience into standardized categories, he noted, "You can punch out the facts and details on your card system or whatever you have."[56]

Others did much the same. One man sent his "frequency record" to Kinsey anonymously, with his annual number of dreams and climaxes recorded for the years 1942 to 1953. Another man, a Vermonter, kept records of his and his wife's sexual activity for years, sending regular installments to Bloomington. Both men may have taken a cue from Kinsey, who, in bold type in the 1948 Report, had urged "persons who have kept records or who are willing to begin keeping day by day calendars showing the frequencies and the sources of their sexual outlet . . . to place the accumulated data at our disposal." Although these particular individuals most likely never met Kinsey, they certainly exhibited an investment in his project. They also showed themselves to be thoroughly comfortable with a social scientific mode of reporting. On Kinsey's part, he never turned down offers from individuals to send in their sexual histories, but instead thanked them for adding valuable data to his files. He wrote to the Vermont man, for example, "This is excellent of you to keep such a record. It is out of this sort of specific material that we can get information which [is] not available in our interviews." These volunteered data often made their way into the narrative sections of the Reports, giving their authors a small role in structuring the knowledge contained therein.[57]

Embedded in these offers to help with the research was a subtle conversion of individual experiences into social scientific data. If volunteers were eager to share their stories, they were also fairly certain their histories were useful to science. Some who offered sexual data saw it as a practical transaction, where, in exchange for providing Kinsey valuable information, they could ask him for advice, counseling, or even money. In this vein, a woman from Roseburg, Oregon, wrote, "I would be willing to answer your questions, truthfully & to the best of my knowledge and it is true, I want something in return, I want you to tell me if you can, why my marriage has not worked out successfully." This woman wanted Kinsey's advice on her marriage, but "only after you had questioned me, so you would, perhaps, be better able to explain, for then you would know more about me." She thought the surveyor would be interested in her history in its own right. But she also expected that her own experiences might help "straighten out" other people's marriages. Individuals like these calculated their sex histories as commodities, believing they were worth the expert's attention and deserved repayment. Another writer, detailing her flagging interest in her marriage, asked for Kinsey's help, reasoning that "there must be others you have interviewed who have the same trouble as mine." She emphasized, "If at any time I can be a service to you I would appreciate it—it might help me at the same time, to live a happy & useful life—which I am not doing at the present time." In this woman's estimation, adding her life history to the survey might yield her some of its accumulated wisdom, and she saw this as a fair trade for her service to Kinsey. Similarly, a woman offered to be "interviewed for your new book as it might help me to understand my husband."[58]

Explicit bargaining over personal data was even more apparent in an Illinois woman's letter to Kinsey, which began, "I may be of help to you and you could help me out." Aware that the researcher was working on the female volume, she offered to share her experience "with the female side of sex," including her work as a "Madam" in several houses of prostitution in the West and her acquaintance with many lesbians. "You can see," she wrote, "I've known both sides of life in reality." Wearing her life history as a badge of authenticity, she offered to give Kinsey an interview, not as a way to gain expert knowledge, but as a means of getting out of debt. In a follow-up letter she reiterated her point, highlighting the advantages the scientist would gain from her own "expert" disclosures. "I do think I could give you some interesting data," she urged. "I am in dire need of money at present, so if you think it would be worthwhile and you could use information, such as I have, I would certainly like an interview." Traffic in knowledge moved in two directions. Individuals could barter their histories to get something out of social research, just as the social scientist employed individuals' experiences to compile aggregate data. The facts revealed in the *Sexual Behavior* volumes were thus very much a joint production.[59]

What stands out in all this offering up of sexual diaries, histories, and logs as "cases" for Kinsey's research is how readily many individuals were coming to understand their private lives through the social scientific categories he and others had made available. The Reports inspired record-keeping and a technical perspective on sex, readers and correspondents often adopting the surveyor's dry scientific language in writing of their own problems and questions. One of the men who regularly sent reports on his sexual activity to Kinsey, for example, pressed the scientist for more data on "the relationship of masturbation after marriage to orgasmic success in marital coitus." This was no social scientist, but an individual interested in improving sexual relations with his wife. He noted that he "would appreciate any rough data you could send me . . . I no doubt could use it to advantage in the calendars my wife and I are keeping."[60]

In the same vein, a California woman volunteered to send the professor her brother's notebooks containing his "early emotional history." Kinsey took her up on her offer, and after examining the notebooks remarked that he had "had a chance to go over them in detail and extract the material that was pertinent to our study of his case." Both Kinsey and this woman were able to understand her brother's emotional history as data. It was something extractable and separable from him—a "case history" to be analyzed against others—and this is what made it scientifically valuable. In a similar transmutation of intimate activities into raw data, one of Kinsey's recruiters wrote to ask him if male histories were still desired for the survey. The writer noted that the ex-husband of a former subject had expressed interest in an interview and wondered if "you might want him as a cross-check on Joan's history." For both Kinsey and this writer, the two histories could be considered discrete sets of information to be compared against each other to ensure scientific validity. More importantly, sexual data could be verified, corrected, or disproved—not by the subjects of that data but by the scientist.[61]

This is not to say that Kinsey's subjects and correspondents were not active participants in shaping their sexual narratives. Wrote a resident of a mental hospital who had interviewed with Kinsey, "It was a rare pleasure to be of some little assistance in your research work," work he believed would "push aside the cobweb of social ignorance." He was writing not simply to praise the scientist, however, but in order to elaborate on his record, "being denied—because of time—the chance to 'tell all.'" Many others fell into this category. A woman from Chicago wrote to Kinsey explaining that she and her husband "both certainly want to talk to you some more. I've thought of many things to add to my history." Divulged another interviewee, "Since you have gone there have been many things remembered that eluded me while in your room, forgotten details . . . Well, perhaps soon you will have more time and we shall sit again and they will come back." Many subjects were eager to share, to maintain their connection with Kinsey, and to remain involved in the research venture. Typical of this vein of correspondence was a New York man who contacted Kinsey to follow up on his interview. Recalling additional details about his childhood awareness of sexuality, he wrote: "You asked regarding situations that arouse sexual feeling. I forgot to mention reading about tortures & cruel acts, especially if in considerable detail. This may be a somewhat 'abnormal' response. However I have already made admissions which I have made to no other person so you may as well have it all."[62]

This urge to "tell all," to complete the record, and to contribute an accurate history, surfaces again and again in the letters subjects wrote to Kinsey. With a fastidious attention to detail, they contacted the scientist to correct and update their sexual narratives—an impulse at least as interesting as their histories themselves. Certainly, some of these individuals simply wanted to reflect further on what their interview had unleashed, responding to Kinsey or one of his colleagues as they would a therapist or confessor. But some subjects, it seems, also wanted to add to and expand upon their interview because it had become their "real" history as well as a trove of scientific data. A concern with correcting the record could thus indicate a profound acceptance of social scientific ways of thinking.

Playing the scientist with the aid of Kinsey's statistics, many aimed to classify their own sexual lives through a schema of typicality or normality. One such man contacted Kinsey after having read the female volume. "Of particular interest," he wrote, "was your indication that a new study of transvestism is being undertaken. I would like to stand up and be counted, if I'm not too late." In his desire to "stand up and be counted," this correspondent evinced something of the participatory desire that surveys stoked. Jeffrey Weeks has argued that "anonymous people whose sexual feelings were denied or defined out of existence were able to use sexological descriptions to achieve a sense of self, even of affirmation." This particular man, wanting to be counted as a transvestite, enclosed a thumbnail sketch of his sexual autobiography, adding, "You will find my case history somewhat typical." His hope for inclusion in the *Sexual Behavior* research carried with it the implicit agreement to take on its social scientific terminology and rules—so much so that he rendered his own, presumably highly individual, story as a "case history," classifiable by a scientist as "typical."[63]

Sexual statistics did not only affect understandings of how others behaved; they could also color how people conceived of their own experiences. Thus did individuals find it possible to objectify their sexual histories, as did the woman who wrote of Kinsey's "scientific approach" in the interview, "It seems, after awhile, like you're talking about someone else instead of yourself." Or another, who explained that her reaction to being interviewed "was not at all what I had expected." She wrote, "Never before had I realized that sex is the theme song that ties a life together." This equation of an individual's sexual history as recounted to Kinsey and that which "ties a life together" is a telling instance of the novel power of social scientific techniques to construct modern selves.[64]

Kinsey's subjects possessed a certain latitude to tell their stories as they wished, but their interviews, strained through surveyors' categories, were never pure exercises of self-creation. Through studies like the *Sexual Behavior* reports, citizens were learning to take the same "objective" stance toward their own lives that the Lynds had taken toward Middletown. Cultivating a distance from their own intimate histories, some Americans placed their experiences within a statistical framework and peered at those experiences like specimens, using the social scientist's words instead of their own to tell themselves who they were.

It is perhaps not surprising that Americans read so avidly about others' extramarital affairs and "homosexual contacts." But why did they so willingly donate to Kinsey their own sexual histories? Some claimed only to want to help science and humanity. For most, the motivations were undoubtedly more complex. One can imagine the multiple rewards for a volunteer: the possibility of gaining counseling and help, the ability to share secrets heretofore private, and the contribution of one's life experience to a grandiose research project. There was, however, a further benefit: membership in a community of potentially similar, although anonymous, others.

Soon after *Sexual Behavior in the Human Male* was published, literary critic Lionel Trilling commented on what he judged to be the significance of the study. Unlike many other observers, who emphasized Kinsey's shocking findings, Trilling delved into the root causes of the Report as a phenomenon, and specifically into what it revealed about contemporary American culture. He contended that the Kinsey Report was "an event of great importance in our culture," both "as symptom and as therapy": "The therapy lies in the large permissive effect the Report is likely to have, the long way it goes toward establishing the *community* of sexuality. The symptomatic significance lies in the fact that the Report was felt to be needed at all, that the community of sexuality requires now to be established in explicit quantitative terms." As Trilling saw it in 1948, sexual statistics were functioning as a form of solace and of community. Linking this trend to what he saw as the fragmentation of modern American society, he reflected, "We must assure ourselves by statistical science that the solitude is imaginary." By fastening upon *community*—and upon the forces propelling the Report to national prominence—Trilling was on to something that many of his contemporaries had overlooked in their fascination with the Report's contents. Not so sure of their old communities, some citizens sought in surveyors' statistics a new sort of companionship, a new way of belonging.[65]

What Trilling perceived was that, by the middle of the century, social scientific knowledge was fulfilling a peculiar function in the culture. It was not merely that Americans were being studied in a more intrusive fashion—in Kinsey's case, through detailed interviews about the most intimate aspects of their lives. It was that individuals were using the knowledge that accrued from such techniques in new ways: to place themselves in a spectrum of others, to evaluate themselves via social scientific categories, and even to discover a community in the numbers. If those who fell on the wrong side of the polls' flat percentages could find themselves newly in a minority, Kinsey's facts beckoned everyone in, from the "cold woman" to the transvestite. By reading the Report, one magazine claimed, "You are looking into the lives of your friends and acquaintances, your wives, your husbands, your own children. What's more important, you are learning much about yourself." Even Kinsey's most vociferous critics seemed to understand his survey's appeal. This was evident in their accusations that the scientist had crafted a statistical morality—and in their sense of inevitability that Kinsey's proliferating normal curves were the coming mode, perhaps the only mode, by which the nation's inhabitants could be known.[66]

The *Sexual Behavior* studies represented the fruition of several decades of social surveyors' attempts to speak for the nation, but they also signaled a departure. For Kinsey himself, but perhaps also for his readers, there was a certain strain simply in attempting to fit a singular container like "normal sexual behavior" around the statistical abundance of the Reports. Kinsey's research, after all, virtually exploded the idea of a national "average." No matter how often reporters and critics of the Reports talked in broad aggregates— "American womanhood" or the "normal man"—many readers wanted to know what the typical working-class Catholic man did in his bedroom, or what the average college-educated woman could expect from her marriage. In the end, Kinsey was able to loosen up the normal curve, making more room—and visibility—for those along its spectrum. As the sheer number of his correspondents discovering and declaring themselves "normal" made clear, though, they still sought expert assurances about where they fit in an expanded mainstream.

By exposing the range of sexual behavior, Kinsey and his team might have believed that they were liberating individuals from the tyranny of social codes. But their statistics, tirelessly repeated and argued over, encouraged a new understanding of what it meant to be normal. Out of thousands of personal, emotional conversations, the surveyors had manufactured an authoritative batch of medians and modes. The possibility of using these data to monitor or regulate was always just under the surface. The research it had sponsored, noted the Committee for Research in Problems of Sex, "offers the hope of greatly increasing our understanding of the typical and the aberrant types of human sex behavior and of factors which condition or control them." Similarly, referring to the charts supplied at the end of the male Report, a clinician noted that one could "easily determine how the sex history of a given subject compares with averages for others of the same age group, educational level, and religious or rural-urban background," and furthermore that "attempts to appraise, re-direct, or punish the behavior of individuals should be materially aided by the use of these tables."[67]

But the most important users of Kinsey's data were not social scientists or clinicians. They were the individuals whose own case histories mingled in the Reports. Subjects—actual or vicarious—of the *Sexual Behavior* research seized upon Kinsey's statistics, embracing new gauges by which they could judge themselves. In publishing the Reports, the taxonomist had meant to undermine the concept of normality, even to remove that category from the scientific vocabulary. Instead, a broad swath of Americans looked back at him, and his masses of data, to affirm that they belonged to it. Even, or perhaps especially, in the post-Kinsey era, citizens willingly positioned themselves along a sexual–behavioral spectrum, assessing themselves not against an average "total outlet" but against specific norms for their age, class, religion, or gender. The result was a more finely grained scale along which nearly everyone could at least aspire to be normal. Undoing this desire for a clear place among the whole was one revolution Alfred Kinsey was unable to effect.

Statistical Citizens

The reader may be puzzled at first glance by the fact that two seemingly independent lines of thought are developed in this book: the one an appraisal of the present characteristics of American culture . . . and the other a critique of current focus and methods in social science research. They are here included together because they so inescapably do belong together.

—Robert Lynd, *Knowledge for What?* 1939

The project of American social science has been America.

—Kenneth Prewitt, former director of the U.S. Census Bureau, 2002

A society saturated by facts about its members—"knowable" through the aggregated answers to surveys—was a curious one, and one first imaginable in the twentieth century. Modern surveys were built out of private information told to a stranger. Yet they permitted citizens to know what their metaphorical, if not their actual, neighbors were thinking and doing. More oddly still, they permitted some individuals a flicker of recognition or communion with statistics displayed in charts and graphs—even when they themselves had been excluded from the making of those numbers. The kind of public created by the dissemination of such knowledge about itself was at once highly intrusive and completely anonymous, self-scrutinizing and other-directed, familiar and impersonal. In a word, it was the backdrop for some of the peculiar tensions of life in a "mass" society: between being "oneself" and being known as a member of a group, between being an individual and being a statistic.

In the concrete techniques of the questionnaire and the interview, in public debates over survey findings, and in encounters between researchers and the researched, a new mode of knowing "ourselves" took shape in the twentieth-century United States. Robert Lynd understood in 1939 that "the characteristics of American culture" and the "current focus and methods in social science research" were intertwined. But we have not yet reckoned with the work polls and statistics performed in constituting that culture: Americans' sense of what their society is and how they belong to it. This book has argued that modern survey methods helped to forge a mass public. They also shaped the selves who would inhabit it, influencing everything from beliefs about morality and individuality to visions of democracy and the nation. Social scientific representations underwrote entities as abstract as "the typical American" and as intimate as an individual's self-understanding. Concepts as resonant as "mainstream culture," "public opinion," and "normal sexuality" were brought into being, at least in part, by surveyors and their toolkit of empirical techniques. That such constructs gained new social reality—for surveyors and laypeople alike—attests to the powerful effects of an aggregated America. They offer a partial explanation for the official, if not actual, cohesion of "the American public" in the middle decades of the century.[1]

As such, social scientific ways of ordering the world fed an anxious dialogue about mass society. The impersonal techniques of survey production privileged the national over the local, the aggregate over the individual, the average over the unique. Moreover, a sociologist's 1953 definition of the "mass"—it was heterogeneous, "composed of individuals who do not know each other," made up of "spatially separated" people, and without any organized leadership—described quite precisely the public created by midcentury social surveyors. Robert and Helen Lynd's subjects, after all, had been an actual community of neighbors before they were transformed into archetypical Americans. But George Gallup and Elmo Roper forged a purely statistical public from groups of randomly selected strangers. This shifting concept of community provoked worries about U.S. culture and society: over the bandwagon effect and "statistical morality." Such concerns about the "mass" are compelling proof of its recognition by, and visibility to, contemporaries.[2]

The questions surveyors posed—not the specific ones about cereal brands or sexual habits, but the underlying ones, such as Who can stand for America? Where is the majority? How do "we" behave?—were weighty. By asking them, community studiers as well as opinion pollsters helped to define who was part of the nation and the normal and who was relegated to the fringes or extremes. It is not coincidental, then, that the issues that most distressed the surveyors' critics—representation and influence—were political in nature. Americans who wrote to Gallup and Roper to complain about their lack of inclusion in the polls, or who deplored Alfred Kinsey's influence on mores, understood the cultural weight of social data. Facts that appeared to be merely empirical were always also freighted with the moral and the evaluative. What is clear in listening to the anger, skepticism, and relief of those ordinary citizens who wrestled with survey findings is that their understandings of themselves as members of a mass public flowed from such knowledge as well as from the techniques that produced it.

What surveyors aimed to do and what their facts *did* once they moved into radio broadcasts, newspaper reports, and common knowledge were not always or even usually congruent. Adopting the stance of the anthropologist to critique dominant trends in contemporary culture, Robert and Helen Lynd in fact fashioned a powerful marker of the "typical." George Gallup and Elmo Roper employed scientific sampling to better hear the voice of the "man in the street" but instead created an averaged-out and abstracted public opinion that severed attitudes from their source. Alfred Kinsey sought to uncover how ordinary Americans actually behaved in their sexual lives so as to liberate them from social conventions, but one of the key consequences of his *Sexual Behavior* studies, and the national discussion surrounding them, was the public shaping of "normal" private selves. Surveys may have transformed American culture; but Americans always also transformed the surveys.

There were plenty of citizens who refused to accept social scientific ways of knowing, of course, such as one of Kinsey's anonymous correspondents who mocked the scientific classification of human experience by signing his or her letter "Case #45697234 1/2, Age 23, no premarital sex, Catholic," as if the writer defied being summed up by these standard pieces of information. Or another who simply wrote, "I do not fit in any of you're catagories [sic] and pray to God I never will." But the distinctive characteristic of modern social surveying was the junction it created between knowledge and norms, permitting data points and percentages to penetrate individuals' lives in meaningful ways. Across the twentieth century, *Middletown*'s readers and even Muncie residents were learning to trust distant experts rather than their own perceptions of contemporary life, believing that "outside" assessments of the culture could best reveal it. Pollsters' multiple audiences were growing dependent, no matter how warily, on the kind of information opinion research proffered. All but Kinsey's fiercest critics ultimately accepted sex as a legitimate subject for surveyors, some importing his statistics into their very definitions of themselves. Americans, that is, were coming to objectify modern culture, to envision the public through the prism of majorities and minorities, and to find themselves in social scientific aggregates.[3]

Indeed, ordinary citizens' vigorous challenges to particular findings and the techniques used to reach them may have revealed their understanding of the power of the new surveys, or at least their sense that important questions would be determined by them. Individuals' bids for inclusion in the very statistics they distrusted and even condemned suggests that disagreement blended easily with accommodation to social surveying practices. The best evidence that the public was being remade by scientific surveys can be found in the sometimes reluctant, sometimes eager, embrace of their tools and vocabulary by a broad array of citizens. If many Middletowners resented being under the gaze of the Lynds in the mid-1920s, other Americans complained bitterly about being overlooked by Gallup and Roper in the following decades, and Kinsey had to turn away scores of volunteers who hoped to be interviewed for his Reports in the 1940s and 1950s. Becoming a statistic represented by midcentury a uniquely modern way of being.

Survey technologies never worked simply to normalize their subjects in the service of a consensus society, however. This would not account for their widespread appeal. Surveys could also encourage and give new weight, through numbers, to nonnormative habits, beliefs, and identities. Social statistics, highlighting both inclusion and exclusion, prompted some to imagine themselves into new collectives or to forge a minority consciousness. Kinsey's statistics, for example, would be a resource for the gay rights movement, preparing the ground for one form of modern "identity politics." The seemingly private and atomized act of divulging personal information to a suveyor, in other words, could have significant political effects. In such ways, social scientific data created novel possibilities for community and self-assertion even as they placed new constraints on self-fashioning. If this constituted a mass society, it was different from any we have known before, encouraging new links between strangers even as it eroded older bonds of family, religion, and locale.[4]

Social data, as we have seen, played a critical role in the cultural life of the midcentury United States. Surveyors' bold accounts of the "typical," "average," and "normal" ensured that statistics were at the very heart of major public controversies. But modern surveys were moving targets, much like the society they both reflected and defined. For all their homogenizing tendencies, they did permit challenge and revision. If the United States could be represented by a community of native-born whites in the late 1920s, it was also known through pollsters' aggregate majorities and minorities in the 1930s and 1940s and the Kinsey Reports' variegated normal in the postwar years.

The particular mass public of fifty years ago—characterized by an iconic Americanism, a majoritarian emphasis, and a fixation on the normal—does not exist in quite the same way today. Numbers can present conformity, but they can also project strife. Beginning in the mid-1960s, surveyors, influenced by new social movements, more emphatically called attention to the nation's fractures than had their predecessors. Just as a popular audience had developed for studies of "typical" American life several decades earlier, a new market composed of policy makers but also lay readers would emerge for inquiries such as Michael Harrington's *The Other America* of 1963, the Moynihan Report of 1965, and the Kerner Commission Report of 1968—studies that like their nineteenth-century predecessors emphasized class stratification and cultural and racial differences. The significant departure here was the later studies' pessimistic conclusions about the deep and perhaps unbridgeable divides among various groups of Americans. Social investigations into diversity and conflict had never waned since the height of the Chicago School, but general audiences for them had. The fact that in the 1960s volumes on race and poverty attracted more national attention than studies of the "mainstream" indicated that something substantial in the relationship between Americans and their surveyors was changing.

Indeed, after a decade that witnessed the "discovery" of poverty, major civil rights mobilizations, and then Black, Red, Gray, and

Gay Power, it would be difficult to speak credibly, either politically or scientifically, of a unitary America. Those taking the measure of nation in the 1960s and beyond sought to explain the United States less as a singular bundle of beliefs or an easily calculated center point than as a contending set of publics. Investigators wrote about "two societies, one black, one white." Pollsters recalibrated their strong majoritarian frame, detecting new significance in how men and women, young and old, Latinos and Asian Americans assessed presidents and purchases differently. Marketers, convinced that niches and "complexity" were becoming more relevant than the broad sweep, talked of "nine American lifestyles," inventing new psychographic categories of citizens such as "survivors," "belongers" and "emulators." Others mapped new "regional-culture" areas—"MexAmerica" in the Southwest and "Ecotopia" in the Pacific Northwest—onto the old singular nation.[5]

In the years following the Kinsey Reports, social scientific attention to diversity and variety would explode. The population, it seemed, could be fissured into ever smaller and more specific fragments for reasons of profit as well as politics. Market researchers were once again in the vanguard, discovering that their object was not anything so vague as "the public," but women between the ages of 18 and 49, or still more focused demographic groupings. Using methods of "narrowcasting" and "microtargeting," they searched as fervently for the niche as earlier surveyors had sought the mass. One of the "best business books of 1988," Michael Weiss's *The Clustering of America*, employed a technique called cluster analysis to distill forty distinct "neighborhood types" in the United States. What is more, he found this sort of national segmentation to be accelerating. When Weiss looked again at the purchasing habits as well as the "demographics, intellect, taste, and outlook" of different U.S. "consumption communities" in 2000, he no longer saw forty "lifestyle types" but sixty-two "modern tribes" (Rustic Elders, Young Literati, Greenbelt Families, and Grey Collars, to name a few)—a neatly summarized 55 percent increase in social differentiation in twelve short years. "For a nation that's always valued community," he intoned, "this breakup of the mass market into balkanized segments is as momentous as the collapse of Communism." Weiss surely overstated the case. Subdivision of this kind was the outgrowth of the ways minorities and majorities, but also more defined communities, were being stitched together statistically in the age of Gallup and Kinsey. In any case, it is worth asking: Had techniques like cluster analysis, enabled by powerful hard drives and updated marketing theories, turned up a newly diverse America? Or did they instead reveal a multiplicity that had always been there but was shielded from view by the assumptions and technological limitations of earlier surveyors? Or was there yet another explanation: that the confluence of new cultural currents and new social scientific techniques to elaborate them had *created* the new "tribes" and "lifestyles"?[6]

As surveyors' descriptions of new kinds of citizens—and a new sort of society—suggest, post-1960s developments may have made the search for the "typical American" and a singular public more problematic, but this did not mean that survey techniques lost their cultural force. On the contrary, the arrival of widespread focus group and personality testing allowed ever-more intricate methods of measuring citizens' preferences and selves to take root. Oddly enough, as with marketers' cluster analysis, this move away from a national "mass" returned surveyors to a world of face-to-face contacts and a form of data gathering that was more like the Lynds' than Gallup's, in their search for detailed, qualitative, and embedded knowledge about individuals. This move from the mass to the niche, in market and social research, underscored the flexibility of survey instruments, which both responded to and amplified the cultural sea change.

Significantly, new survey technologies, such as the popular Minnesota Multiphasic Personality Inventory, came with a more pronounced individualist rhetoric and psychological flavor. The Myers-Briggs Type Indicator, for example, developed in 1943 but not published until 1962 and not widely distributed until 1975, offered sixteen categories—through the matched pairs of Thinking-Feeling, Perceiving-Judging, Extraversion-Introversion, Sensation-Intuition—for Americans to slot themselves into. This was perhaps the logical path from the Kinsey Reports, which in one fell swoop did away with the normal curve *and* reassured individuals that they were normal. The Myers-Briggs, among the most frequently administered, and self-administered, tests today, was certainly a testament to the grip of popular psychology on Americans and their employers in the late twentieth century. But its appeal to consumers was also a reaction to the standardizing, indeed massifying, tendencies of modernist social science.[7]

Writing in 1979 and looking out upon a landscape pervaded by self-help literature running the gamut from "personal growth" to "creative divorce," two observers argued that the "applied behavioral and social sciences . . . have assumed an unprecedented role in what might be termed the 'consciousness industry,'" a broad constellation of professional and institutional entities devoted to "changing some aspects of the lives or identities of their clients." This of course had been true since the earliest days of surveyors' interventions in the lives of the poor, the criminal, and the sexually deviant. What was new was that consumers now paid for scientific expertise, not in the service of social knowledge but in the hope of individual, intimate transformation. In this sense, the late twentieth century saw the deepest penetration yet of social survey tools into everyday conversation and self-categorization. Corporate managers, popular experts, media figures, and ordinary citizens speak in a social scientific language that has become virtually indistinguishable from American culture at large.[8]

Survey techniques of the late twentieth century were certainly more personal, more individualized, and more intrusive than Middletowners could have imagined. This did not necessarily mean that they were less reductive. Political researchers, for example, following marketers' lead, hunted for the hidden link, whether the car model or the gardening habit, that could predict an individual's likelihood to vote Democratic or Republican. For this they depended on correlations pulled from vast databanks, themselves culled from "state voter-registration rolls, census reports, consumer data-mining companies and direct marketing vendors." This was a sort of aggregating that was also infinitely segmenting. In a parallel development, striving to solve once and for all Kinsey's problem of unreliable human subjects, market researchers invented techniques of "passive" rather than "active" measurement: innovations such as "portable people meters" that could record television watchers' viewing habits without having to depend on accurate reports from human beings about those same habits. Roper and Gallup had argued for the civic potential of their surveys on the ground of participation. But taking part in surveys is not what it used to be. Some investigators have begun to test the appeal of political platforms not by querying citizens about their opinions but by watching flashes of activity on subjects' MRI (magnetic resonance imaging) brain scans. The dawn of "neuromarketing"—whether of presidential candidates or soft drinks—to some seems, not (social) science fiction, but very close at hand.[9]

From the 1930s onward, Americans had not always liked being polled, but they did believe their own responses were critical to the project of a representative public. New developments in surveying the population suggest that in the future citizens might no longer be asked, at least not directly. Writes an expert on recent trends in commercial and security data-mining, the scope and depth of information gathering "took on dramatic new dimensions in the 1990s," as the Internet and high-powered computing were brought to bear on old questions about who was doing what, for the joint purposes of law enforcement and commercial gain. "Much of this," he notes, "took place out of the public's view, and largely without the public's direct consent."[10]

Faced with such profuse variety in the public—and in the instruments employed to take its pulse—the strand of midcentury social surveying that had gained traction from its claims to define the culture *in toto* found few toeholds. The few social scientists who continued to work in this vein, notably Robert Bellah in his *Habits of the Heart* and *The Good Society*, tended in fact to decry the lack of a coherent body of binding American values and habits. Others proclaimed that the public itself had vanished, subsumed by self-interest and private rather than civic engagements. Headline-grabbing studies of social trends convinced many that the nation had lost any sense of common commitment, that its inhabitants were isolated from one another and "bowling alone." As historian Wilfred McClay has noted, where social thinkers of the 1950s worried about the dangers of conformity, those of the 1970s and 1980s reversed course, their writings full of "concern for the nurturance of community and solidarity rather than individualism and autonomy."[11]

The mass public of the Gallup polls and the Kinsey Reports was born of a specific conjunction of cultural preoccupations and social scientific innovations. The same is true of the differentiated America found in survey research today. The recasting of "the public" into alternative publics, subcultures, and counterpublics is not unproblematic, however. Like older social scientific representations of the nation as a collection of typical whites or majority views, the new ways of picturing the population leave much out and congeal dynamic social processes. It remains difficult to find a public vocabulary that recognizes differences but also allows citizens to perceive the social or the whole in a complex fashion. Categorizations like "welfare queens," "angry white males," "soccer moms," and "security moms" demonstrate the allure of simplifications of the American public even as finer labels for subgroups are devised. These composites owe a debt to niche market thinking, but also to the inherently flattening tendencies of survey formats and terminology. The notion that the nation is fundamentally fractured into "red states" and "blue states" or that a clean 22 percent of the populace had turned to voting their "moral values"—as revealed by an exit poll—in the aftermath of the 2004 presidential election, are just the most obvious of these fictions. Misreadings of "the public" via the powerful conjunction of media narrative and quantified support seem just as likely in the twenty-first century as they had been in the twentieth.[12]

Amidst such talk of divisions and segments, some Americans began to look back nostalgically to the midcentury as a time of national unity and mass markets. In a series of works in the late 1990s and early 2000s, commentators bewailed not just the fraying of the citizenry, but the passing of the "greatest generation." Fantasies of a singular nation and culture—in part generated by older social surveys—continued to percolate, both in politicians' statements about "the American people" and in attempts to fashion icons representative of a multitudinous population. Publicizing the "new face of America" in 1993, *Time* magazine proposed that the future nation could be glimpsed in a computer-generated amalgam of the demographic average of the population, one slightly darker and less Anglo than the "typical" citizen of Middletown. Cultural theorist Lauren Berlant, noting that this image arrived on the heels of the widely reported finding that European Americans would soon be eclipsed as the statistical majority, wrote that it was "suffused with nostalgia for . . . a stable and dominant collective identity." A growing recognition of national disaggregation did not prevent, and could even promote, a desire for a unitary Americanness.[13]

The hunt for the "Average American" hobbled along. In a quixotic 2005 book by that name, the search for the "nation's most ordinary citizen" entailed locating a person who matched the U.S.

statistical majority in 140 discrete, and rather idiosyncratic, categories. The individual had to be of average height and weight, own an electric coffeemaker, go to sleep before midnight, regularly use a seatbelt, live within three miles of a McDonald's, own a suburban house valued between $100,000 and $300,000, and so on. But this was no return to Middletown. (In fact, reasoning that the "ordinary citizen" had to live in a statistically normal community, the author bypassed Muncie for its lower-than-average marriage rate, its submedian household income, and its dearth of Hispanic residents.) Unlike the Lynds' "Middletown Spirit," this checklist did not add up to a meaningful bundle of characteristics that aimed to describe a culture. In fact, the statistically "average" American was so elusive as to be an oddity, as peculiar as the "exotics" to whom the Lynds had compared Middletowners in 1929.[14]

Others searched more intently for an index to the whole, sometimes retracing the steps of earlier surveyors to do so. Middletown still lures marketers and pollsters, even if the seemingly atypical city of Las Vegas is now its competitor as a testing laboratory for consumer products and television shows. Ongoing political studies of Muncie, for example, contend that the community continues to predict the nation's vote. The city remains "typical," some claim, in its economic profile as well as its divorce, robbery, and book-borrowing rates. A recent survey, going by the name of Middletown Media Studies and inspired by the Lynds' work, sought, via telephone questionnaires, diary studies, and direct observation, "to determine how digital and other media were used on a daily basis in typical American homes." Other researchers returning to Middletown, and aware of the city's riches in longitudinal social data, are at long last trying to make the Lynds' study more demographically representative, including black Middletowners in their sights. A team of social scientists is currently attempting to retrieve baseline data on Muncie's African American community from 1924 to 1977.[15]

If "Middletown" was gradually becoming more representative,

many were coming to believe that Kinsey's Reports were less so. Kinsey's figures on sexual behavior, used not only by gay advocacy groups but also by the Centers for Disease Control to estimate and track the spread of the Human Immunodeficiency Virus (HIV) in 1986, were vigorously challenged in the closing decades of the twentieth century. New scholarship revealing Kinsey's less-than-neutral stance on the topic of homosexuality provided a ready avenue for casting doubt on the surveyor's entire research program—and perhaps sexual science itself. But Americans still could not stop talking about the scientist, as dramatized accounts of his career as a sex surveyor appeared in print, on stage, and on the big screen. Controversies over Kinsey's research—the "sex panic" unleashed by the female Report triggering a congressional inquiry in 1954 and costing Kinsey his Rockefeller funding, for example—never wholly subsided. They again became news in 2004, when a panel of conservative scholars and policy makers, voting on the thirty most "dangerous books" of the previous two centuries, ranked the Kinsey Reports fourth, just after works by Marx, Hitler, and Mao. A major follow-up study to the *Sexual Behavior* research in the 1990s by a man dubbed "the new Kinsey" faced some of the same foes as had the Reports of 1948 and 1953. Working with the National Opinion Research Center at the University of Chicago, Edward Laumann's sex survey—initially intended to gather information on HIV transmission—became the subject of yet another congressional debate, after which the administration of the first George Bush withdrew its funding. Private foundations took up the slack, and the first of three studies was published in 1994. Heralded as the first comprehensive and reputable scientific study since the *Sexual Behavior* reports, *The Social Organization of Sexuality* was said to prove that Americans enjoy happier marriages and are more faithful to their spouses than had previously been supposed. As Miriam Reumann writes, "The news media were quick to note that the 1990s survey, in contrast to Kinsey's, offered a portrait of American sexual practices that repudiated the apparent triumph of a major 'sexual revolution,'" an event that the scientist was often blamed for causing.¹⁶

Meanwhile, the production of political and market research intensified. By the mid-1960s, national opinion polling had spread throughout world. The Gallup Poll itself boasted thirty-two affiliates and conducted surveys in nearly fifty countries. A 1983 study found that 23 percent of U.S. respondents had been interviewed in the past year at least once and that twenty million citizens were polled annually. Questions continued to surface, however, about the capacity of polls to measure and inform public opinion. Political scientist James Fishkin, urging more deliberative and nuanced ways of researching attitudes, was just one who argued that the "people's voice" had been lost because of—not despite—the welter of public opinion polls. The paradoxes of the polling enterprise linger. Over half of Americans surveyed in 1985 did not trust the representativeness of random sampling, and the response rate to telephone surveys has steadily declined since 1952. The "golden age of the household survey," with in-person interviews and relatively cooperative subjects, has ended. Yet, Susan Herbst writes, "few candidates run for office, express their views on current issues, or change campaign strategy without consulting opinion polls." At the same time, many Americans demonstrate a persistent desire to voice their opinions in patently unscientific and unrepresentative Internet surveys and other so-called SLOPs (selected listener opinion polls). Whether for entertainment or strategic impact—as during the 2004 election, when political action committees urged the like-minded to use electronic surveys to spin the reportage on presidential debates—polls continued to offer at least the simulacrum of civic participation in a statistical public.¹⁷

At the turn of the twenty-first century, arguments about how we quantify and characterize ourselves as a national population are alive and well, even if the terms of those arguments have changed. The very linking of "representative" and "democratic" survey technologies to "the public" across the midcentury decades guaranteed that numerical skirmishes would continue to be waged in the years that followed.

One such statistical battle, perhaps appropriately, has taken place around the oldest official survey of the population, and the only one that claims to count every member of the nation. Census data have always triggered controversy. But the 1990 census provoked a major lawsuit, spearheaded by New York City, even before that year's questionnaires had been placed in the mail. At issue was the "differential undercount" of minorities and the poor in inner cities, a problem quite familiar to early pollsters. In this case, however, neglecting such groups incurred the loss of political representation as well as funding for major metropolitan areas. Ten years later, the national census sat at the center of yet another legal and congressional battle, this time over the legitimacy of representing those same uncounted Americans by scientific sampling instead of physical tabulation. Here it was evident that the techniques that had so troubled Gallup's and Roper's correspondents at midcentury remained fundamentally mysterious to some in the halls of government. In a lawsuit against the U.S. Department of Commerce it was charged that by "using statistical methods commonly referred to as sampling" the census would "include millions and millions of people who are simply deemed to exist based upon computations of statisticians."[18]

Debates over who counts and how to count have not been confined to official number crunching. Having promoted quantitative data as an avenue not just to political but also to cultural visibility, surveyors like Gallup and Roper paved the way for many groups—especially those who had been rendered invisible in earlier surveys—to embrace the statistical banner. Biracial and multiracial Americans who wanted to count in their own particular way on the

2000 census forms were one striking example. But there were many others. In 1977 the National Gay Task Force had used Kinsey's findings on the prevalence of homosexuality in the 1940s and 1950s United States to pronounce that 10 percent the population was homosexual. In subsequent decades, gay advocacy organizations gladly took up a numerical slogan. "One in Ten" became a rallying cry, a favorite name for support groups, youth organizations, and cultural festivals as well as the tag of the first commercial radio program, on Boston's WFNX station, devoted to gay and lesbian listeners. The 10 percent claim in turn triggered a virtual cottage industry devoted to debunking that purportedly inflated number. The two sides of this demographic dispute, one suspects, had little in common beyond a belief in the rhetorical sway of numbers about "ourselves." Those who sought to dislodge the figure, like those who hoped to cement it, suspected that it worked to persuade others—politicians, journalists, marketers, and maybe even the man in the street—to bestow civic and cultural legitimacy upon a sexual minority significant enough to register as a double-digit percentage of the population. An implied equation between numerical strength and citizenship was seldom challenged, as if fewer rights were deserved by a gay population just 5—or 3 or 1—percent of the whole.[19]

Struggles over what we might call "statistical citizenship" were often proxy wars for representation in other realms of U.S. society. The tabulating of protesters and ralliers raised this issue repeatedly. In the wake of the 1995 Million Man March in Washington, D.C., organized as a show of "protest and unity" of African American men, the Nation of Islam threatened to sue the National Park Service for deflating the number of marchers in its reports. The decision soon after by Congress to bar the Park Police from giving official crowd estimates indicated that some numbers were *too* political to calculate. Equally illuminating was the formation of a watchdog coalition calling itself "Don't Count Us Out" in 2004, aimed at remedying "the consistent undercounting of minorities" by the Nielsen Media Research corporation. Asserting that a new technology for measuring television viewing did not adequately capture the presence of Hispanic and African American audiences and therefore illegitimately dampened their market power and cultural clout, Don't Count Us Out called upon Congress to regulate the raters. "Join us," its Web site urged the potential underrepresented, "and make sure your voice is counted." This seamless alignment of the consumer and civic voice was of course foreshadowed by the merger of commercial and political opinion research in the 1940s. When it turned out that the coalition was not a grassroots protest group at all but an effort engineered by the News Corporation to preserve its viewership ratings, Nielsen set up its own defense under the banner "Everyone Counts." This contretemps revealed the high stakes involved in representing the U.S. population in an age when just about everyone understood the politics of numbers. In the strategic corporate use of minority underrepresentation, it also suggested just how complicated statistical citizenship had become.[20]

A number of scholars and journalists have recently contended that the rapid growth of entrepreneurial, ideological, think-tank, and corporate-sponsored data, not just in the United States but around the world, has made social research even more fragile and less trustworthy than it was previously. Yet how can we get along without these measures, incomplete and distorted though they may be? The fact that dependence on and distrust of surveyors' data continue to come fused together, in the era of the Middletown studies and the Kinsey Reports but even today, indicates that perhaps this too is a characteristic of a modern public. Not sure of the information we live by—where it comes from, how to verify or challenge it—we nonetheless do live by it. As one Frenchman relayed to a journalist during the outbreak of Muslim youth riots in Paris in late 2005, many of his compatriots believed that "surveying by race or religion is bad, it's dirty, it's something reserved for Americans and . . . we shouldn't do it here." He continued by musing, "But without statistics to look at, how can we measure the problem?" Although disavowing the impulses behind survey knowledge, this man acknowledged that numbers allow societies to track inequalities and gaps, to apprehend things they have no other easy way of knowing.[21]

Who are we? What do we believe? Where do we fit? Social surveys entered Americans' lives promising to answer these questions. The truth is that we still want to know. And so statistical struggles over how to aggregate and disaggregate the United States will remain with us. And we will continue to live in a world shaped by, and perceived through, survey data.

Notes

Abbreviations

ERP Elmo Roper Papers, Archives and Special Collections
   at the Thomas J. Dodd Research Center, University of
   Connecticut Libraries, Storrs

GGI George H. Gallup Papers, Series II Subject Files:
   "Crank Letters" (1953–1956), University of Iowa
   Libraries, Iowa City

GGP George H. Gallup Papers, The Gallup Organization,
   by special permission of George Gallup Jr., Princeton,
   New Jersey

HIT History of the Kinsey Institute for Sex Research
   Interview Transcripts, Indiana University Center for
   the Study of History and Memory, Bloomington

HSC History of the Small City Study, Middletown Studies
   Collection, originals at Rockefeller Foundation
   Archives

KCF Letters from the Crank File, Kinsey Institute Archives

KIA The Kinsey Institute for Research in Sex, Gender, and
   Reproduction, Archives, Bloomington, Indiana

KST Letters from Short-Term Correspondents, Kinsey
   Institute Archives

MSC Middletown Studies Collection, Archives and Special
   Collections Research Center, Ball State University,
   Muncie, Indiana

RHL   Robert S. and Helen Merrell Lynd Collection, Manuscript Division, Library of Congress, Washington, D.C.

Introduction

1. Lawrence C. Lockley, "Notes on the History of Marketing Research," *Journal of Marketing* 14 (1950): 734; William Stott, *Documentary Expression and Thirties America*, rev. ed. (1973; Chicago: University of Chicago Press, 1986), 71.

2. Cynthia Crossen, *Tainted Truth: The Manipulation of Fact in America* (New York: Simon and Schuster, 1994), 12; John Gregory, "Clinical Study of the American Male," *Philadelphia Sunday Bulletin*, 8 Feb. 1948; "'According to Statistics,'" *Philadelphia Boot and Shoe Recorder*, 1 May 1950.

3. On fiction, see Carol Nackenoff, *The Fictional Republic: Horatio Alger and American Political Discourse* (New York: Oxford University Press, 1994). On photography, see Wendy Kozol, *Life's America: Family and Nation in Postwar Photojournalism* (Philadelphia: Temple University Press, 1994). And on history, see Michael Kammen, *Mystic Chords of Memory: The Transformation of Tradition in American Culture* (New York: Vintage Books, 1991). Jean M. Converse, *Survey Research in the United States: Roots and Emergence, 1890–1960* (Berkeley: University of California Press, 1987), 1. I thank Dorothy Ross for helping me clarify the unique nature of survey knowledge.

4. Henry D. Hubbard, front matter, in Willard Cope Brinton, *Graphic Presentation* (New York: Brinton Assoc., 1939).

5. Few historians have probed deeply this connection between new modes of measurement and "mass society." For exceptions, see Olivier Zunz's description of "individuals as statistics" in his *Why the American Century?* (Chicago: University of Chicago Press, 1998), 48–57; and Daniel J. Boorstin's discussion of "statistical communities" in *The Americans: The Democratic Experience* (New York: Random House, 1973), 165–244.

6. Theodore M. Porter, *Trust in Numbers: The Pursuit of Objectivity in Science and Public Life* (Princeton: Princeton University Press, 1995); Mary Poovey, *A History of the Modern Fact: Problems of Knowledge*

in the Sciences of Wealth and Society (Chicago: University of Chicago Press, 1998); Alain Desrosières, The Politics of Large Numbers: A History of Statistical Reasoning (Cambridge, MA: Harvard University Press, 1998); James C. Scott, Seeing Like a State: How Certain Schemes to Improve the Human Condition Have Failed (New Haven: Yale University Press, 1998); Joshua Cole, The Power of Large Numbers: Population, Politics, and Gender in Nineteenth Century France (Ithaca, NY: Cornell University Press, 2000); Andrea Rusnock, Vital Accounts: Quantifying Health and Population in Eighteenth-Century England and France (New York: Cambridge University Press, 2002); Ian Hacking, "Biopower and the Avalanche of Printed Numbers," Humanities in Society 5 (1982): 279–295. Hacking dates the "avalanche" to the years between 1820 and 1840, although he notes that the "volcano" did not erupt in the United States until the 1880s. Michel Foucault, The History of Sexuality (New York: Vintage, 1990), 1:139. For useful histories of data collecting in the United States before the twentieth century, see Margo Anderson, The American Census: A Social History (New Haven: Yale University Press, 1988); Viviana A. Zelizer, Morals and Markets: The Development of Life Insurance in the United States (New York: Columbia University Press, 1979); and Patricia Cline Cohen, A Calculating People: The Spread of Numeracy in Early America (Chicago: University of Chicago Press, 1982). For an overview of state information-gathering projects, see Paul Starr, "The Sociology of Official Statistics," in The Politics of Numbers, ed. William Alonso and Paul Starr (New York: Russell Sage Foundation, 1987).

7. Zunz, Why the American Century? 49.
8. For a good overview of social scientific tools and methods in this period, see Converse, Survey Research; and Jennifer Platt, A History of Sociological Research Methods in America, 1920–1960 (Cambridge: Cambridge University Press, 1996). For precursors, see Stephen Stigler, The History of Statistics: The Measurement of Uncertainty before 1900 (Cambridge, MA: Harvard University Press, 1986); Theodore M. Porter, The Rise of Statistical Thinking, 1820–1900 (Princeton: Princeton University Press, 1988); and Ian Hacking, The Taming of Chance (Cambridge: Cambridge University Press, 1990). On the modern social scientific disciplines, see Mary O. Furner, Advocacy and Objectivity: A Crisis in the Professionalization of American Social Science, 1865–

1905 (Lexington: University Press of Kentucky, 1975); Thomas L. Haskell, *The Emergence of Professional Social Science: The American Social Science Association and the Nineteenth-Century Crisis of Authority* (Urbana: University of Illinois Press, 1977); Alexandra Oleson and John Voss, eds., *The Organization of Knowledge in Modern America, 1860–1920* (Baltimore: Johns Hopkins University Press, 1979); Robert C. Bannister, *Sociology and Scientism: The American Quest for Objectivity, 1880–1940* (Chapel Hill: University of North Carolina Press, 1987); Dorothy Ross, *The Origins of American Social Science* (Cambridge: Cambridge University Press, 1991); and Mark C. Smith, *Social Science in the Crucible: The American Debate over Objectivity and Purpose, 1918–1941* (Durham, NC: Duke University Press, 1994). On the rise of professionalism and professional societies more generally, see Thomas L. Haskell, ed., *The Authority of Experts: Studies in History and Theory* (Bloomington: Indiana University Press, 1984); Andrew Abbott, *The System of Professions: An Essay on the Division of Expert Labor* (Chicago: University of Chicago Press, 1988); and Paul Starr, *The Social Transformation of American Medicine* (New York: Basic Books, 1982).

9. Desrosières, *Politics of Large Numbers,* 199–209; Zunz, *Why the American Century?* 36–45; John Carson, "Army Alpha, Army Brass, and the Search for Army Intelligence," *Isis* 84 (1993): 278–309; Guy Alchon, *The Invisible Hand of Planning: Capitalism, Social Science, and the State in the 1920s* (Princeton: Princeton University Press, 1985); Ellen Herman, *The Romance of American Psychology: Political Culture in the Age of Experts* (Berkeley: University of California Press, 1995); Donald Fisher, *Fundamental Development of the Social Sciences: Rockefeller Philanthropy and the United States Social Science Research Council* (Ann Arbor: University of Michigan Press, 1993); Michael Lacy and Mary Furner, eds., *The State and Social Investigation in Britain and the United States* (New York: Cambridge University Press, 1993); Gene M. Lyons, *The Uneasy Partnership: Social Science and the Federal Government in the Twentieth Century* (New York: Russell Sage Foundation, 1969); Edward T. Silva and Sheila A. Slaughter, *Serving Power: The Making of the Academic Social Science Expert* (Westport, CT: Greenwood Press, 1984).

10. Lockley, "Notes"; Henry L. Minton, *Lewis M. Terman: Pioneer in Psychological Testing* (New York: New York University Press, 1988);

JoAnne Brown, *The Definition of a Profession: The Authority of Metaphor in the History of Intelligence Testing, 1890–1930* (Princeton: Princeton University Press, 1992); Leila Zenderland, *Measuring Minds: Henry Herbert Goddard and the Origins of American Intelligence Testing* (New York: Cambridge University Press, 1998); John Carson, *The Measure of Merit: Talents, Intelligence, and Inequality in the French and American Republics, 1750–1940* (Princeton: Princeton University Press, 2006); Nicholas Lemann, *The Big Test: The Secret History of the American Meritocracy* (New York: Farrar, Straus and Giroux, 1999); JoAnne Brown, "Mental Measurements and the Rhetorical Force of Numbers," in *The Estate of Social Knowledge,* ed. JoAnne Brown and David K. van Keuren (Baltimore: Johns Hopkins University Press, 1991), 143; Richard Gillespie, *Manufacturing Knowledge: A History of the Hawthorne Experiments* (New York: Cambridge University Press, 1991); Annie Murphy Paul, *The Cult of Personality: How Personality Tests Are Leading Us to Miseducate Our Children, Mismanage Our Companies, and Misunderstand Ourselves* (New York: Free Press, 2004); and Daniel J. Czitrom, *Media and the American Mind: From Morse to McLuhan* (Chapel Hill: University of North Carolina Press, 1982).

11. Robert Wiebe, *The Search for Order, 1877–1920* (New York: Hill and Wang, 1967), 40, 43. The discipline of sociology was predicated upon this transition from "community" to "society," articulated most famously by Ferdinand Tönnies as *Gemeinschaft* and *Gesellschaft* but also by other nineteenth-century social philosophers, such as Auguste Comte and Émile Durkheim, who explored how social relations were being transformed by industrialization and particularly the division of labor.

12. Ian Hacking notes the obsession with "the statistics of deviance" in the mid-nineteenth century in his "Making Up People," in *Reconstructing Individualism: Autonomy, Individuality, and the Self in Western Thought,* ed. Thomas C. Heller et al. (Stanford: Stanford University Press, 1986), 222. On the shift to studies of normality, see Émile Durkheim, "Rules for Distinguishing between the Normal and the Pathological," in *The Rules of Sociological Method,* ed. George E. G. Catlin, trans. Sarah A. Solovay and John H. Mueller (1895; New York: Free Press, 1964); Georges Canguilhem, *On the Normal and the Pathological,* trans. Carolyn R. Fawcett (Boston: Reidel, 1978); Michel

Foucault, *The Birth of the Clinic: An Archaeology of Medical Perception*, trans. A. M. Sheridan Smith (New York: Pantheon Books, 1973); and Elizabeth Lunbeck, *The Psychiatric Persuasion: Knowledge, Gender, and Power in Modern America* (Princeton: Princeton University Press, 1994).

13. Paul Starr, *The Creation of the Media: Political Origins of Modern Communications* (New York: Basic Books, 2004), 385; Diana C. Mutz, *Impersonal Influence: How Perceptions of Mass Collectives Affect Political Attitudes* (Cambridge: Cambridge University Press, 1998), xvi.

14. For an example of historians using survey data, see David P. Thelen, "The Public against the Historians: The Gallup Poll, 1935–1971," *Reviews in American History* 4 (1976): 614–618. For excellent studies of social investigation as it bears on public policy, see Michael B. Katz, *The Undeserving Poor: From the War on Poverty to the War on Welfare* (New York: Pantheon Books, 1989); Herman, *Romance of American Psychology;* Daryl Michael Scott, *Contempt and Pity: Social Policy and the Image of the Damaged Black Psyche, 1880–1996* (Chapel Hill: University of North Carolina Press, 1997); Daniel T. Rodgers, *Atlantic Crossings: Social Politics in a Progressive Age* (Cambridge, MA: Belknap Press of Harvard University Press, 1998); and Alice O'Connor, *Poverty Knowledge: Social Science, Social Policy and the Poor in Twentieth-Century U.S. History* (Princeton: Princeton University Press, 2001). Studies of elite uses of social science include Loren Baritz, *The Servants of Power: A History of the Use of Social Science in American Industry* (Middletown, CT: Wesleyan University Press, 1960); Christopher Simpson, ed., *Universities and Empire: Money and Politics in the Social Sciences during the Cold War* (New York: Free Press, 1998); Michael E. Latham, *Modernization as Ideology: American Social Science and "Nation-Building" in the Kennedy Era* (Chapel Hill: University of North Carolina Press, 2000); and John P. Jackson Jr., *Social Scientists for Social Justice: Making the Case against Segregation* (New York: New York University Press, 2001). Two recent books, although still trained on manipulation and control, examine the broader effects of social scientific (and especially psychological) studies: Lauren Slater, *Opening Skinner's Box: Great Psychological Experiments of the Twentieth Century* (New York: W. W. Norton, 2004); and Rebecca Lemov, *World as Laboratory: Experiments with Mice, Mazes, and Men* (New York: Hill and Wang, 2005).

15. Earlier (and regular) controversies over counting and describing the population centered on the U.S. census: how to count slaves, how to apportion political power, and how to devise immigration quotas. For a useful overview, see Anderson, *The American Census;* and Desrosières, *Politics of Large Numbers,* 188–194. The latter notes, "The United States is the country where statistics has displayed the most plentiful developments. But it is also the country where the apparatus of public statistics has never experienced the integration and legitimacy that its French, British, and German counterparts . . . have managed to acquire." For this reason, "more than in other countries, statistical references [in the U.S.] were linked to the process of argumentation rather than to some truth presumed to be superior to the diverse camps facing off"; quotations on 189 and 192.

16. Burkart Holzner and John H. Marx, *Knowledge Application: The Knowledge System in Society* (Boston: Allyn and Bacon, 1979), 320; Tom Harrisson and Charles Madge, *Britain by Mass-Observation* (1939; London: Cresset Library, 1986); Tony Kushner, *We Europeans? Mass-Observation, "Race," and British Identity in the Twentieth Century* (Burlington, VT: Ashgate, 2004); Liz Stanley, *Sex Surveyed, 1949–1994: From Mass-Observation's "Little Kinsey" to the National Survey and the Hite Reports* (London: Taylor and Francis, 1995); Sabine Frühstück, *Colonizing Sex: Sexology and Social Control in Modern Japan* (Berkeley: University of California Press, 2003); Robert M. Worcester, ed., *Political Opinion Polling: An International Review* (New York: St. Martin's Press, 1983); Laura DuMond Beers, "Whose Opinion? Changing Attitudes towards Opinion Polling in British Politics, 1937–1964," *Twentieth Century British History* 17 (2006): 177–205; Jon Cowans, "Fear and Loathing in Paris: The Reception of Opinion Polling in France, 1938–1977," *Social Science History* 26 (2002): 71–104. Differences between U.S. and European data collection persist. Commercial enterprises, for example, have much less access to personal data under European privacy laws than they do in the United States. See "Europe Zips Lips: U.S. Sells ZIPs," *New York Times,* 7 Aug. 2005.

17. E. C. White, "Is Muncie Really 'Middletown'?" *Muncie (IN) Evening Press,* 10 Oct. 1930.

18. Converse, *Survey Research,* 18.

19. On this point, see Theodor W. Adorno's 1957 argument in "Sociology and Empirical Research," as reprinted in *Critical Sociology: Selected*

Readings, ed. Paul Connerton (New York: Penguin Books, 1976), 237–257.

20. W. Lloyd Warner, ed., *Yankee City,* abridged ed. (New Haven: Yale University Press, 1963), 135–136, 166–167. See David Thelen's similar discussion of an "imaginary mass whole" in his *Becoming Citizens in the Age of Television: How Americans Challenged the Media and Seized Political Initiative during the Iran-Contra Debate* (Chicago: University of Chicago Press, 1996), 14. Social data resembled what historian Michele Hilmes describes as "the misleadingly realistic but always motivated and partial representations of our national media" (*Radio Voices: American Broadcasting, 1922–1952* [Minneapolis: University of Minnesota Press, 1997], 289).

21. Adolphe Quetelet, *A Treatise on Man and the Development of His Faculties,* English trans. (1835; Edinburgh: William and Robert Chambers, 1842), 8–9; "The American Majority Man: He Is a Reluctant Internationalist . . . Who Hopes for the Best in World Affairs but Expects the Worst," *Newsweek,* 4 Aug. 1947, 32–33. On the concept of the "mass subject," see Michael Warner, "The Mass Public and the Mass Subject," in *The Phantom Public Sphere,* ed. Bruce Robbins (Minneapolis: University of Minnesota Press, 1993); and Harold Mah, "Phantasies of the Public Sphere: Rethinking the Habermas of Historians," *Journal of Modern History* 72 (2000): 167.

22. This survey was part of sociologist Robert Lynd's Depression-era study of Montclair, New Jersey; RHL, R2:C3. Hacking, "Making Up People," 229. See also Michel Foucault, *Technologies of the Self: A Seminar with Michel Foucault,* ed. Luther H. Martin et al. (Amherst: University of Massachusetts Press, 1988); and Nikolas Rose, *Governing the Soul: The Shaping of the Private Self* (New York: Routledge, 1990), esp. 213–258.

23. Key works in the midcentury debate over mass society include Max Horkheimer and Theodor W. Adorno, "The Culture Industry: Enlightenment as Mass Deception," in *Dialectic of Enlightenment,* trans. John Cumming (1944; New York: Herder and Herder, 1972); Herbert Blumer, "The Mass, the Public, and Public Opinion," in *New Outline of the Principles of Sociology,* ed. Alfred McClung Lee (New York: Barnes and Noble, 1946), 185–193; Dwight Macdonald, "A Theory of Mass Culture," *Diogenes* 3 (1953): 1–17; Elihu Katz and Paul F. Lazarsfeld, *Personal Influence: The Part Played by People in the Flow*

of *Mass Communications* (Glencoe, IL: Free Press, 1955); Daniel Bell, "America as a Mass Society: A Critique," *Commentary* 22 (1956): 75–83; William Kornhauser, *The Politics of Mass Society* (Glencoe, IL: Free Press, 1959); Edward Shils, "The Theory of Mass Society," *Diogenes* 39 (1962): 45–66; and Harold L. Wilensky, "Mass Society and Mass Culture: Interdependence or Independence?" *American Sociological Review* 29 (1964): 173–197. For helpful overviews of the literature on mass society and mass culture, see Patrick Brantlinger, *Bread & Circuses: Theories of Mass Culture as Social Decay* (Ithaca, NY: Cornell University Press, 1983); and James R. Beniger, "Toward an Old New Paradigm: The Half-Century Flirtation with Mass Society," *Public Opinion Quarterly* 51, pt. 2, suppl. (1987): S46–S66.

24. Anderson noted the role of censuses in creating the imagined nation in his *Imagined Communities: Reflections on the Origin and Spread of Nationalism,* 2nd ed. (New York: Verso, 1991). Most scholars who have followed him have concentrated on the use of such techniques for nation building from above; see, for example, Scott, *Seeing Like a State.* In recent decades, analyses of "mass" behavior and belief have been more often the province of psychologists, political scientists, and communication theorists than historians. See, for example, Robert B. Cialdini, *Influence: The Psychology of Persuasion* (New York: Quill, 1993); Elisabeth Noelle-Neumann, *The Spiral of Silence: Public Opinion, Our Social Skin,* 2nd ed. (Chicago: University of Chicago Press, 1993); Mutz, *Impersonal Influence;* James W. Carey, *Communication as Culture: Essays on Media and Society* (Boston: Unwin Hyman, 1988); and the recent work of historian Alison Landsberg, *Prosthetic Memory: The Transformation of American Remembrance in the Age of Mass Culture* (New York: Columbia University Press, 2004).

1. Canvassing a "Typical" Community

1. Allan Nevins, "Fascinating Spectacle of an American Town under the Microscope," *New York World,* 17 Feb. 1929; C. Hartley Grattan, "A Typical American City," *New Republic,* 27 Feb. 1929, 48; H. L. Mencken, "A City in Moronia," *American Mercury,* Mar. 1929, 381; Stuart Chase, "Life in Middletown," *Nation,* 6 Feb. 1929, 64.

2. Robert S. Lynd and Helen Merrell Lynd, *Middletown: A Study in Contemporary Culture* (New York: Harcourt, Brace, 1929); the book's

subtitle was inconsistent in later editions, sometimes reading "A Study in Modern American Culture" and sometimes "A Study in American Culture." Raymond B. Fosdick as quoted in Charles E. Harvey, "Robert S. Lynd, John D. Rockefeller Jr., and *Middletown*," *Indiana Magazine of History* 79 (1983): 350. Fosdick added, "I do not know that this is legitimate criticism. It is just possible that this is a work of genius."

3. Allen Eaton and Shelby Harrison provide the figure for the number of surveys completed by the end of 1927 in *A Bibliography of Social Surveys: Reports of Fact-Finding Studies Made as a Basis for Social Action; Arranged by Subjects and Localities* (New York: Russell Sage Foundation, 1930), xxix; Whiting Williams, "Through the Looking Glass," *Saturday Review of Literature*, 30 Mar. 1929.

4. Hannah Arendt, *The Human Condition* (Chicago: University of Chicago Press, 1958); Mark Seltzer, *Bodies and Machines* (New York: Routledge, 1992), 100, 106. On the social survey tradition, see Martin Bulmer, Kevin Bales, and Kathryn Kish Sklar, eds., *The Social Survey in Historical Perspective, 1880–1940* (Cambridge: Cambridge University Press, 1991); and Jean M. Converse, *Survey Research in the United States: Roots and Emergence, 1890–1960* (Berkeley: University of California Press, 1987). On community studies specifically, see Maurice R. Stein, *The Eclipse of Community: An Interpretation of American Studies* (Princeton: Princeton University Press, 1960); Arthur Vidich, Joseph Bensman, and Maurice Stein, eds., *Reflections on Community Studies* (New York: Wiley, 1964); and Joyce E. Williams and Vicky M. Maclean, "The Legacy of Community Studies," in *Diverse Histories of American Sociology*, ed. Anthony J. Blasi (Boston: Brill, 2005), 370–404. For the crosscurrents in European and American reform projects in this period, see Daniel T. Rodgers, *Atlantic Crossings: Social Politics in a Progressive Age* (Cambridge, MA: Belknap Press of Harvard University Press, 1998).

5. Donald K. Gorrell, *The Age of Social Responsibility: The Social Gospel in the Progressive Era, 1900–1920* (Macon, GA: Mercer University Press, 1988); Thomas L. Haskell, *The Emergence of Professional Social Science: The American Social Science Association and the Nineteenth-Century Crisis of Authority* (Urbana: University of Illinois Press, 1977), 91–121, quotation on 102; Carroll D. Wright, *The Working Girls of Boston*, Fifteenth Annual Report of the Massachusetts Bu-

reau of Statistics of Labor (Boston: Wright and Potter, 1889), 3; Michael Katz, *In the Shadow of the Poorhouse: A Social History of Welfare* (New York: Basic Books, 1986); Maurine W. Greenwald and Margo Anderson, eds., *Pittsburgh Surveyed: Social Science and Social Reform in the Early Twentieth Century* (Pittsburgh: University of Pittsburgh Press, 1996).

6. On the gendered organization of social investigation at the turn of the century, see Ellen F. Fitzpatrick, *Endless Crusade: Women Social Scientists and Progressive Reform* (New York: Oxford University Press, 1990); Regina G. Kunzel, *Fallen Women, Problem Girls: Unmarried Mothers and the Professionalization of Social Work, 1890–1945* (New Haven: Yale University Press, 1993); Kathryn Kish Sklar, *Florence Kelley and the Nation's Work: The Rise of Women's Political Culture, 1830–1900* (New Haven: Yale University Press, 1995); and Helene Silverberg, ed., *Gender and American Social Science: The Formative Years* (Princeton: Princeton University Press, 1998). On foundations, see Barry Karl and Stanley N. Katz, "The American Private Philanthropic Foundation and the Public Sphere, 1890–1930," *Minerva* 19 (1981): 236–270; Donald Fisher, *Fundamental Development of the Social Sciences: Rockefeller Philanthropy and the United States Social Science Research Council* (Ann Arbor: University of Michigan Press, 1993); Ellen Condliffe Lagemann, *The Politics of Knowledge: The Carnegie Corporation, Philanthropy, and Public Policy* (Middletown, CT: Wesleyan University Press, 1989); and Judith Sealander, *Private Wealth and Public Life: Foundation Philanthropy and the Reshaping of American Social Policy from the Progressive Era to the New Deal* (Baltimore: Johns Hopkins University Press, 1997).

7. Dorothy Ross, *The Origins of American Social Science* (Cambridge: Cambridge University Press, 1991), provides the most comprehensive account of these developments. Vivien Palmer as quoted in Martin Bulmer, "The Decline of the Social Survey Movement and the Rise of American Empirical Sociology," in Bulmer, Bales, and Sklar, *The Social Survey*, 304; see also Martin Bulmer, *The Chicago School of Sociology: Institutionalization, Diversity, and the Rise of Sociological Research* (Chicago: University of Chicago Press, 1984). The shift in emphasis from normative to objective social science should not be overstated. Mark C. Smith, in *Social Science in the Crucible: The American Debate over Objectivity and Purpose, 1918–1941* (Durham, NC: Duke Uni-

versity Press, 1994), persuasively argues that "purposive" social science remained in tension with newer modes in the interwar years; Robert Lynd features prominently in his discussion of the former. Jennifer Platt, in *A History of Sociological Research Methods in America, 1920–1960* (Cambridge: Cambridge University Press, 1996), 67–105, has also argued that "scientism" neither actually nor rhetorically captured the range of social scientific practices at midcentury.

8. J. F. Steiner, review of *Middletown,* in *Social Service Review* 3 (1929): 506. Midcentury sociologist Warner Gettys classified pre-1914 studies as "presociological" because of their focus on social problems and public opinion or legislative action. Similarly, August Hollingshead in 1948 outlined three stages of community study: the "normative-meliorative" (1895–1915), the "analytical" (1915–1929), and the "scientific" (1929–1948); *Middletown* was the bridge to the last stage. See Williams and Maclean, "Legacy of Community Studies," 375–376.

9. Eaton and Harrison, *Bibliography of Social Surveys,* iii–viii. For the topics covered by the Chicago studies, see Bulmer, *Chicago School of Sociology;* Stow Persons, *Ethnic Studies at Chicago, 1905–45* (Urbana: University of Illinois Press, 1987); and Henry Yu, *Thinking Orientals: Migration, Contact, and Exoticism in Modern America* (New York: Oxford University Press, 2001).

10. Clark Wissler, foreword, in *Middletown,* v; Norman J. Ware, review of *Middletown,* in *American Economic Review* 19 (1929): 828. Stephen Turner argues, however, that claims of topical and methodological novelty in the Middletown studies "were quite false" because academic sociologists—many of them trained by Franklin H. Giddings at Columbia—had used many of the same techniques in their studies, including J. M. Williams's *An American Town* (1906), Warren Wilson's *Quaker Hill* (1907), and Newell Sims's *A Hoosier Village* (1911); see Turner's "The World of the Academic Quantifiers: The Columbia University Family and Its Connections," in Bulmer, Bales, and Sklar, *The Social Survey,* 283–284.

11. On Rockefeller Jr. and the ISRR, see Albert F. Schenkel, *The Rich Man and the Kingdom: John D. Rockefeller, Jr., and the Protestant Establishment* (Minneapolis: Fortress Press, 1995), 121–165; Harvey, "Robert S. Lynd"; and Martin Bulmer and Joan Bulmer, "Philanthropy and Social Science in the 1920s: Beardsley Ruml and the Laura Spelman Rockefeller Memorial," *Minerva* 19 (1981): 347–407. Galen Fisher to

Rev. John McDowell, 4 Dec. 1922, and William Bailey, "Purpose of Study Defined," 15 Mar. 1923; both in HSC, 1, 7.

12. R. Lynd to Brown University president H. P. Faunce, 14 Feb. 1929, RHL, R4:C7; Dwight W. Hoover, *Middletown Revisited* (Muncie, IN: Ball State University, 1990), 1. Other accounts of *Middletown*'s evolution can be found in Richard Wightman Fox, "Epitaph for Middletown: Robert S. Lynd and the Analysis of Consumer Culture," in *The Culture of Consumption: Critical Essays in American History, 1880–1980*, ed. Richard Wightman Fox and T. J. Jackson Lears (New York: Pantheon Books, 1983), 101–141; and *Journal of the History of Sociology* 2, no. 1 (1979–1980), which is devoted to Robert Lynd's life and work.

13. The Lynds replaced William Bailey, a sociologist at Northwestern and the first director of the survey. Galen Fisher's summary of the fifth conference on the Small City Study, 29 June 1923, HSC, 12–13; "Memorandum regarding Small City Study to the Members of the Institute," 16 Apr. 1924, copy from the Rockefeller Foundation Archives, MSC. Robert Lynd was frequently treated as the sole author of *Middletown* by the sponsoring institute (and by commentators since), despite the fact that Helen Lynd was hired to work on the project half-time and would become the co-author. Robert Lynd was careful to correct this misperception. He wrote to the author of *Middletown*'s foreword: "Mrs. Lynd and I have worked on Muncie jointly from the outset and shall publish it as a joint report. I should be glad, therefore, to have you change the word 'author' wherever it appears to 'authors'" (R. Lynd to Clark Wissler, 19 Mar. 1928, MSC, Box 8). *Middletown,* once excised of Helen Lynd's contributions, was accepted as Robert Lynd's doctorate, although Helen noted that this "was a fake process" (Helen Merrell Lynd, with the collaboration of Staughton Lynd, *Possibilities* [Youngstown, OH: Ink Well Press, 1983], 38). For Robert Lynd and Helen Merrell's meeting and other biographical details, see Hoover, *Middletown Revisited,* 3–4.

14. R. Lynd's autobiographical notes from 1963, RHL, R1:C1; see also his notes (1922) in Middletown Research Files, RHL, R4:C7. Robert Lynd's anonymous article "But Why Preach?" *Harper's,* June 1921, 82–83, demonstrates in greater detail his grappling with religious ideas and practice. His intellectual influences are traced in Smith, *Social Science in the Crucible,* 120–158, and Fox, "Epitaph for Middletown."

See Helen Lynd's discussions of religion in *Possibilities*, 26, 51. R. Lynd memos, 17 May and 28–29 June 1923, HSC, 15, 16. Fox ("Epitaph for Middletown," 118) describes the "masterfully diplomatic" way in which the Lynds walked the line between the Institute's interests and their own.

15. Lynd retrospectively called his experiences at Elk Basin his "awakening to facts of life." He claimed that his two articles on Standard Oil were "responsible for my getting the chance to do the 'Small City Study' . . . on my own terms (tho that took some struggle to do)," but he did not explain this irony in any depth; autobiographical notes in RHL, R1:C1. The Lynds' son has speculated that this was a case of "the boss . . . dealing with an outspoken shop-floor militant by making the man a foreman" (Staughton Lynd, *Living Inside Our Hope: A Steadfast Radical's Thoughts on Rebuilding the Movement* [Ithaca, NY: ILR Press, 1997], 24). That the minister Harry Emerson Fosdick—the brother of one of Rockefeller's lawyers, Raymond Fosdick—was a supporter of Lynd's also influenced the ISRR's decision (Hoover, *Middletown Revisited*, 4). See Robert S. Lynd, "Crude-Oil Religion," *Harper's*, Sept. 1922, 425–434, and "Done in Oil," *Survey*, 1 Nov. 1922, 137–146 (Rockefeller's response to the latter came in the same issue of *Survey*: "A Promise of Better Days," 147–148); and Staughton Lynd, "Robert S. Lynd: The Elk Basin Experience," *Journal of the History of Sociology* 2, no. 1 (1979–1980): 14–22. Lynd's exposé led Rockefeller to take a public stance against the twelve-hour day. See "A Rockefeller Hits Labor Abuses," *Literary Digest*, 11 Nov. 1922, 9–10.

16. Notes from 16 Nov. 1926 conference, with a 30 Nov. addendum, on (what was now called) "The Study of a Small Industrial City," RHL, R4:C7 (the reviewers, respectively, were Gardner Murphy and Arthur L. Swift); "Minutes of Staff Conference held on Jan. 11, 1926," MSC. Galen Fisher to R. Lynd, 23 Apr. 1927; "General Comments by S. Went on Section I of Small City Study," 5 May 1927; memorandum from Trevor Bowen to R. Lynd on "Home Section of the Small City Study—Chapters X to XV inclusive," 27 May 1927; all in RHL, R4:C7. For the ongoing discussion regarding the Lynds' objectivity, see HSC as well as the running correspondence between Galen Fisher and Robert Lynd in RHL, R4:C7.

17. H. Lynd, *Possibilities*, 34, 38; R. Lynd, "Problem of Being Objective in Studying Our Own Culture," lecture outline for talk at Princeton University, 9 Dec. 1938, RHL, R2:C2. The evidence regarding the final

publication history of *Middletown* is somewhat unclear. Some scholars claim that the Institute disavowed it altogether, while others contend that it supported Harcourt's publishing of the book. See F. L. van Holthoon's discussion of the evidence in "Robert Lynd's Disenchantment: A Study of Robert Lynd's Cultural Criticism," in *The Small Town in America*, ed. Hans Bertens and Theo D'haen (Amsterdam: VU University Press, 1995), 35–36.

18. This first description was the study's title when it was turned over to the Lynds. See Galen Fisher to R. Lynd, Summer 1923, HSC, 17.

19. See *Middletown*'s "Note on Method," 507–512. The research assistants were Faith Williams, Dorothea Davis, and Frances Flournoy. I use "Middletown" rather than "Muncie" to refer to the Lynds' research site because it better expresses the fact that the community, as described in the Middletown studies, was as much their social scientific creation as it was a real place.

20. R. Lynd, "Problem of Being Objective"; H. Lynd, *Possibilities*, 35, 37.

21. Memorandum from R. Lynd regarding Small City Study, 28 Mar. 1924, and R. Lynd to Raymond Fosdick, 16 June 1926; copies from the Rockefeller Foundation Archives, MSC. Robert Lynd was never a naïve empiricist, always recognizing that social scientists had a "selective point of view" and were unable to escape their own value judgments. This early refrain of objectivity in connection with the Middletown project can be read as a sign of his professional insecurity as well as the power of a new social scientific imperative. See his *Knowledge for What? The Place of Social Science in American Culture* (Princeton: Princeton University Press, 1939).

22. R. Lynd, "Problem of Being Objective"; George W. Stocking Jr., "The Ethnographic Sensibility of the 1920s and the Dualism of the Anthropological Tradition," in *Romantic Motives: Essays on Anthropological Sensibility*, ed. George W. Stocking Jr. (Madison: University of Wisconsin Press, 1989), 208–275.

23. *Middletown*, 4; R. Lynd, "Re—Social Studies," memorandum for the Commonwealth Fund, 6 May 1926, 4–5, RHL, R4:C7. Richard Fox calls *Middletown* "one of the first, if not the very first, functionalist works in American sociology" (Fox, "Epitaph for Middletown," 122). For a fuller discussion of the Lynds' methods, see John Madge, *The Origins of Scientific Sociology* (New York: Free Press of Glencoe, 1962), 133–141.

24. *Middletown*, 5; memo from Faith Williams (giving comments on the

manuscript), undated, RHL, R4:C7. Richard Fox has posited that for Robert Lynd, anthropology "offered an attractive compromise, one that was midway between religion and scientific sociology" because it allowed "questions of value" to be raised. See Fox, "Epitaph for Middletown," 121.

25. R. Lynd to Institute staff, Oct.–Nov. 1923, HSC, 18. See the materials in "Research Files," RHL, R4:C7, and "Interview Schedules," RHL, R5:C9; quotation is from the latter, in the document "'True'–'False' Questionnaire on Muncie Attitudes."

26. *Middletown*, 24. Brian W. Dippie, *The Vanishing American: White Attitudes and U.S. Indian Policy* (Middletown, CT: Wesleyan University Press, 1981), 228–236. On the search for authenticity at the turn of the century, see T. J. Jackson Lears, *No Place of Grace: Antimodernism and the Transformation of American Culture, 1880–1920* (New York: Pantheon Books, 1981).

27. *Middletown*, 80, 53–72.

28. Ibid., 495, 498. William Ogburn, *Social Change with Respect to Culture and Original Nature* (New York: Huebsch, 1922).

29. *Middletown*, 477, 218, 294, 426 n. 13, 269.

30. Ibid., 1; R. Lynd, lecture notes for talk to Rotary, 1935, RHL, R8:C13; John Lewellen, "Lynd Finds Muncie Now a 'Small City,'" *Muncie Evening Press*, 28 June 1935; R. Lynd, "Miscellaneous Items about Robert S Lynd," 9 Mar. 1954, RHL, R2:C2; H. Lynd, *Possibilities*, 35–36.

31. H. Lynd, *Possibilities*, 36; Rosa Burmaster to R. Lynd, 1926 or 1927, RHL, R4:C7; Frederic Heimberger to R. Lynd, 23 June 1937, RHL, R1:C1. Leslie Kitselman to R. Lynd, 13 Feb. 1937, 8 May 1937 (also to H. Lynd), and 4 June 1937; the first and third of these letters are in RHL, R1:C1; the second is in RHL, R8:C13. George Dale to R. Lynd, 1 Jan. 1936, RHL, R1:C1. For other examples, see R. H. Myers, Vice President of the Merchants National Bank, to R. Lynd 29 Apr. 1937; Max Mathews to R. Lynd, 3 Aug. 1937; C. V. Sursa of Muncie Industrial Company to R. Lynd, 19 Oct. 1937; and Robert Myers of Ball State Teachers College to R. Lynd, 19 May 1960 (all in RHL, first two in R8:C13, last two in R1:C1). See also R. Lynd to Richard Greene, 24 Apr. 1960, MSC, which refers to a clipping Greene had sent about a restudy of Muncie.

32. *Middletown*, 120, 509; H. Lynd, *Possibilities*, 35–36.

33. C. A. Millspaugh, "'Middletown' Talks Back," from the "Beacon," unknown publication, RHL, R8:C13; E. C. White, "Is Muncie Really 'Middletown'?" *Muncie Evening Press,* 10 Oct. 1930; the cartoon is quoted in C. E. Ayres, "Who Owns Middletown?" *New Republic,* 21 Aug. 1929. For two attempts to discern how Middletowners felt about the Lynds, see Raymond G. Fuller, "Muncie Looks at Middletown," *New Republic,* 8 Sept. 1937, 127–128; and Anthony Edmonds, "Middletown: A Community Reacts to Social Science," *Proceedings of the Indiana Academy of the Social Sciences,* ser. 3, vol. 19 (1984): 87–93.

34. "Nearly Everybody Now Has Car Here," *Muncie Evening Press,* 29 Oct. 1924; June Mull, "Book Reveals Cross-Section of Muncie's Community Life," *Muncie Morning Star,* 11 Jan. 1929.

35. Robert Lynd was skeptical about locals' claims of having read the book. Mull, "Book Reveals Cross-Section"; "Much in Demand," *Muncie Sunday Star,* date unknown, RHL, R7:C12; J. D. Willard, confidential memorandum, 19 June 1929, RHL, R4:C7; Delaware County, Indiana, Community School of Religion, "Courses of Study," Jan.–Mar. 1930, RHL, R7:C12; "Activities of the Members of the Muncie Federated Club of Clubs," *Muncie Sunday Star,* 20 Jan. 1929; "Cornerstone," *Muncie Morning Star,* 9 Sept. 1929.

36. Robert S. Lynd and Helen Merrell Lynd, *Middletown in Transition: A Study in Cultural Conflicts* (New York: Harcourt, Brace, 1937), ix, xi. See Lynd's apology in his 1935 speech to Muncie's Rotary Club, as related in Lewellen, "Lynd Finds Muncie Now a 'Small City;'" R. Lynd, "Problem of Being Objective."

37. Unknown author to Lynn Perrigo, 15 Jan. 1935, Lynn Perrigo Collection, MSC; Clarendon Ross to R. and H. Lynd, 26 June 1929, RHL, R4:C7; Ray N. Towers to R. Lynd, 25 Nov. 1929, RHL, R4:C7; Wilber E. Sutton, "Comment," *Muncie Evening Press,* Oct. 1929, RHL, R7:C12.

38. "Last Meeting," Rotary Club report in local Muncie newspaper, RHL, R7:C12; see also, "Discusses Book about Muncie: Normal Dean Addresses Local Rotary Club," *Muncie Evening Press,* 7 May 1929, and the articles "Rotary in Middletown" and "Criticism True and False," *Rotarian,* May 1929, 15–16, 30–31. John Lewellen, "Muncie Schools Ready to Receive Criticisms," *Muncie Evening Press,* 1 Nov. 1929; White, "Is Muncie Really 'Middletown'?"

39. George B. Lockwood, "'Typical' Americans," *Muncie Evening Press*, 4 July 1931, and "Something Good Out of 'Middletown,'" *Muncie Evening Press*, 26 Aug. 1931; Elbert Scoggins to R. Lynd, 13 July 1930, RHL, R4:C7; unknown author to Lynn Perrigo, 28 Nov. 1934, Lynn Perrigo Collection, MSC. See also the correspondence between the Lynds and Muncie residents in RHL, R8:C12.

40. Editorial, *Muncie Morning Star,* 11 Jan. 1929; White, "Is Muncie Really 'Middletown'?"

41. White, "Is Muncie Really 'Middletown'?"; White here was referring to Lynd's comments in Henry James Forman, "What's Right with America? As Observed by Sinclair Lewis, Walter Lippmann, Will Durant and Robert S. Lynd," *McCall's,* Nov. 1929.

42. Lockwood, "Something Good Out of 'Middletown.'"

43. Unknown source quoting remarks of another individual to Lynn Perrigo, 19 Nov. 1934, Lynn Perrigo Collection, MSC; Robert Lynd summarized this vein of critique in his lecture notes for a talk to Rotarians, 1935, RHL, R8:C13; Rosa Burmaster to R. Lynd, 1926 or 1927, RHL, R4:C7; Sutton, "Comment."

44. Lola Goelet Yoakem to R. Lynd, 24 May 1937; C. A. (Clarence) Millspaugh to R. Lynd, 29 Apr. 1937; both in RHL, R8:C13.

45. White, "Is Muncie Really 'Middletown'?"; "Dr. Lynd Winding Up His Labors," unknown Muncie publication, 27 June 1935, RHL, R8:C12; Lockwood, "'Typical' Americans."

46. "Lynd's Accuracy Is Questioned by Muncie Pastor," unknown Muncie publication, 1937, RHL, R1:C1; Robert S. LaForte and Richard Himmel, eds., "'Middletown Looks at the Lynds': A Contemporary Critique by the Reverend Dr. Hillyer H. Straton of Muncie, Indiana, 1937," *Indiana Magazine of History* (1979): 248–264; "Pastor's Picture," *Time,* 5 July 1937, 5. See also Straton's editorials for the *Muncie Evening Press:* "Ex-New Yorker on 'Middletown,'" 29 Apr. 1937, and "Comment," 5 Aug. 1937.

47. Bray Hammond, "How Americans Live: Change and Bewilderment in Middletown," *New York Sun,* 19 Jan. 1929.

48. R. Lynd, *Knowledge for What?* 19, 50. On the development of twentieth-century anthropological understandings of culture, see George W. Stocking Jr., "Franz Boas and the Culture Concept in Historical Perspective," in *Race, Culture, and Evolution: Essays in the History of Anthropology* (Chicago: University of Chicago Press, 1968), 195–233;

and A. L. Kroeber and Clyde Kluckhohn, *Culture: A Critical Review of Concepts and Definitions* (New York: Vintage Books, 1952).

49. W. Lloyd Warner et al., *Democracy in Jonesville: A Study in Quality and Inequality* (New York: Harper and Row, 1949), ix.

50. William Bailey, "Factors Conditioning the Selection of a Small City Project," 2 Feb. 1923, HSC, 4. For the original plans for the study, see Galen Fisher's letters to William L. Bailey of 22 Jan. and 10 Feb. 1923, HSC, 3, 5.

51. Smith, *Social Science in the Crucible*, 133; R. Lynd memorandum, Oct. or Nov. 1923, HSC, 18; *Middletown*, 8.

52. *Middletown*, 8; Richard Jensen, "The Lynds Revisited," *Indiana Magazine of History* 75 (1979): 306; memorandum from R. Lynd regarding Small City Study, 28 Mar. 1924, copy from the Rockefeller Foundation Archives, MSC; *Middletown*, 511. On Muncie's atypical population, see Jensen, "The Lynds Revisited"; Jensen points out that Oshkosh, Wisconsin (47 percent native white), or Michigan City, Indiana (52 percent), would have been more "typical" cities of the urbanized Midwest. On Muncie's African American population, see Jack S. Blocker, "Black Migration to Muncie, 1860–1930," *Indiana Magazine of History* 92 (1996): 297–320. Staughton Lynd, noting that his parents both grew up in all-white Protestant communities, suggests that their choice to study a similar community can be understood as "what their life experience qualified them to do" (S. Lynd, "Making Middletown," *Indiana Magazine of History* 101 [2005]: 235). John Madge, in *Origins of Scientific Sociology*, 133–134, is one who described *Middletown* as developing a scientific approach to specifying sources and methods. It should be noted that even some later accounts praised the Lynds' "ingenuity" for targeting a homogeneous population and thereby "eliminating the effects of urbanization" on their study of industrialization. See Stein, *Eclipse of Community*, 49.

53. *Middletown*, 9; Jensen, "The Lynds Revisited," 308.

54. Fox, "Epitaph for Middletown," 119; Richard Lingeman, *Small Town America: A Narrative History, 1620–Present* (New York: Putnam, 1980), 258–320.

55. *Middletown*, 332 n. 1, 480, 482–485. On the Klan in the 1920s in Muncie and in Indiana, where it had the largest membership in the nation, see E. Bruce Geelhoed, "The Enduring Legacy of Muncie as Middletown," in *The Other Side of Middletown: Exploring Muncie's*

African American Community, ed. Luke Eric Lassiter, Hurley Goodall, Elizabeth Campbell, and Michelle Natasya Johnson (Walnut Creek, CA: Alta Mira Press, 2004), 36; and Leonard J. Moore, *Citizen Klansmen: The Ku Klux Klan in Indiana, 1921–1928* (Chapel Hill: University of North Carolina Press, 1991).

56. *Middletown,* 485. This is not to discount the importance to the town of Muncie's Central High basketball team, depicted in the 1986 film *Hoosiers* (dir. David Anspaugh). *Middletown's* superficial treatment of power relations has been the most persistent retrospective criticism of the study, although contemporary reviewers did not single this out for comment.

57. Robert Lynd and a team of graduate students performed the fieldwork for the restudy, which was originally intended only as an appendix to a revised edition of *Middletown;* see Hoover, *Middletown Revisited,* 11. Robert S. Lynd, with the assistance of Alice C. Hanson, "The People as Consumers," in *Recent Social Trends in the United States,* ed. Research Committee on Social Trends (New York: McGraw-Hill, 1933), 2:857–911. On planning in the 1930s, see Richard S. Kirkendall, *Social Scientists and Farm Politics in the Age of Roosevelt* (Columbia: University of Missouri Press, 1966); and Patrick D. Reagan, *Designing a New America: The Origins of New Deal Planning, 1890–1943* (Amherst: University of Massachusetts Press, 1999). Richard Fox, in "Epitaph for Middletown," argues that between the two Middletown studies Robert Lynd had given up on change from below and espoused a top-down vision of technical social scientific expertise as the only solution to unhealthy cultural developments. *Middletown in Transition,* xiv.

58. *Middletown in Transition,* 205 n. 1, 293, 233. This ability to compare conditions persuaded some commentators to view *Middletown in Transition* as the more scientific of the two studies; see Curtiss Schafer, "Middletown Again Viewed by Lynds," *Minneapolis Journal,* 16 May 1937.

59. *Middletown in Transition,* 22.

60. Ibid., 74–101; unknown author to Lynn Perrigo, 28 Nov. 1934, Lynn Perrigo Collection, MSC; Frederic Heimberger to R. Lynd, 16 June 1937, RHL, R1:C1. The Lynds were criticized from several different quarters for neglecting the X family in the first study. One important source was Lynn I. Perrigo, a graduate student at the University of

Colorado who had lived in Muncie for a decade. Perrigo criticized *Middletown* and its neglect of the X family in his essay "Muncie and *Middletown,* 1924 to 1934," and he passed the essay along to Robert Lynd (Hoover, *Middletown Revisited,* 11; Rita Caccamo, *Back to Middletown: Three Generations of Sociological Reflections* [Stanford: Stanford University Press, 2000], 81–100). On the Lynds' reading of Marx, see Madge, *Origins of Scientific Sociology,* 130; Stein, *Eclipse of Community,* 58; and Henry Etzkowitz, "The Americanization of Marx: *Middletown* and *Middletown in Transition,*" *Journal of the History of Sociology* 2, no. 1 (1979–1980): 41–54.

61. Milton M. Gordon, *Social Class in American Sociology* (New York: McGraw-Hill, 1963), 64; *Middletown in Transition,* 402.

62. *Middletown in Transition,* 489, 490, 403–418, 509; Van Holthoon, "Robert Lynd's Disenchantment."

63. R. Lynd to Robert T. Crane (of the Social Science Research Council), 9 Mar. 1932, and R. Lynd to J. Steele Gow, Executive Director of The Maurice and Laura Falk Foundation, 4 Dec. 1930; both in RHL, R2:C2. R. Lynd, "Memorandum on the Study of Changing Family Patterns in the Depression," RHL, R2:C3. The turn to the "normal" was evident across many fields. See, for example, Julia Grant, "Constructing the Normal Child: The Rockefeller Philanthropies and the Science of Child Development, 1918–1940," in *Philanthropic Foundations: New Scholarship, New Possibilities,* ed. Ellen Condliffe Lagemann (Bloomington: Indiana University Press, 1999), 131–150.

64. R. Lynd, "Problem of Being Objective."

65. Quotes from Dr. Shriver and William Bailey, "Purpose of Study Defined," and Galen Fisher, summary of fifth conference on the Small City Study, 11 May 1923; both in HSC, 7, 12. *Middletown in Transition,* xiv. One of the few instances of *Middletown* being used as the Lynds hoped it would be was a University of Wisconsin summer school for industrial workers, where students surveyed their own communities, using the study as a model. See "Workers Try New Plan of Study at U.," *Madison (WI) Capital Times,* 6 July 1931.

66. For a very few, *Middletown*'s lack of prescriptions was also its downfall. One reviewer complained that the Lynds' survey suggested major problems and "deep changes that are going on in the whole structure of our civilization," but that "it does not tell us what we want to

322 · Notes to Pages 69–70

know": which is, what to do about them (Ayres, "Who Owns Middletown?").

2. Middletown Becomes Everytown

1. Helen Merrell Lynd, with the collaboration of Staughton Lynd, *Possibilities* (Youngstown, OH: Ink Well Press, 1978), 40; Ernest R. Groves, review of *Middletown*, in *The Family*, Oct. 1929, 188; Alfred Harcourt to Robert Lynd, 2 Mar. 1929, RHL, R4:C7. Harcourt wrote additionally, "I am fully aware of the favorable and important situation in regard to MIDDLETOWN . . . The book is going to justify all our expectations."

2. For sales figures, see Richard Wightman Fox, "Epitaph for Middletown: Robert S. Lynd and the Analysis of Consumer Culture," in *The Culture of Consumption: Critical Essays in American History, 1880–1980*, ed. Richard Wightman Fox and T. J. Jackson Lears (New York: Pantheon, 1983), 122. "Middletown: Adoptions and Reorders, 1929–1930," Harcourt, Brace and Co. memorandum, undated, RHL, R7:C12; A. D. Sheffield, "Recent Books of Special Interest," *Wellesley Alumnae Magazine*, undated, 306, RHL, R7:C11; *New York Times*, 27 Apr. 1929.

3. *Fort Myers (FL) Church News*, 8 June 1929; *Dayton Herald*, 18 Nov. 1930; *American Teacher* 14, no. 3 (1929); *New York Medical Week* 8, no. 36 (1929). R. Clyde White to R. Lynd, 28 Feb. 1929; RHL, R4:C7; Lon Ray Call, "What We Would Change in Middletown," sermon delivered at the First Unitarian Church, Louisville, KY, 22 Sept. 1929 (reprinted in the *Louisville Unitarian*); "'Middletown,' Book, Reviewed by Pastors at Luncheon Meeting," *Riverside (CA) Press*, 11 Feb. 1931; "Books to Get Acquainted With," *Social Work Publicity Council Bulletin*, Mar.–Apr. 1929; Raymond B. Fosdick, "A Summons to the Adventurous Life" (commencement speech at Smith College), *New York Times*, 23 June 1929; Harcourt, Brace and Co. advertisement in the *New York Times Book Review*, 13 Jan. 1929, 15. For generic references to Middletown, see the *Springfield (MA) Evening Union*, 3 Sept. 1930; "Mexico's Middletown," *Saturday Review of Literature*, 19 July 1930, 1; A. L. Kroeber, review of *Tepoztlán*, in *American Anthropologist* 33 (1931): 236–238; and "A Larger 'Middletown'?" *Boston Herald*, 22 Dec. 1929. See also Leo C. Rosten,

"A 'Middletown' Study of Hollywood," *Public Opinion Quarterly* 3 (1939): 314–320.

4. *American Historical Review* advertisement section, undated, 1929, RHL, R7:C12.

5. Raymond B. Fosdick as quoted in Charles E. Harvey, "Robert S. Lynd, John D. Rockefeller Jr., and *Middletown*," *Indiana Magazine of History* 79 (1983): 350.

6. Whiting Williams, "Through the Looking Glass," *Saturday Review of Literature*, 30 Mar. 1929, 824; "Some Rattling Good Stories," *Good Housekeeping*, June 1929, 204; Lynn Dumenil, *The Modern Temper: American Culture and Society in the 1920s* (New York: Hill and Wang, 1995), 9; Frederick Lewis Allen, *Only Yesterday: An Informal History of the Nineteen-Twenties* (New York: Harper and Bros., 1931). See also, from this period, Harold E. Stearns, ed., *Civilization in the United States: An Inquiry by Thirty Americans* (New York: Harcourt, Brace, 1922).

7. John S. Gilkeson Jr., "The Domestication of 'Culture' in Interwar America, 1919–1941," in *The Estate of Social Knowledge*, ed. JoAnne Brown and David K. van Keuren (Baltimore: Johns Hopkins University Press, 1991), 153–174; Warren I. Susman, "The Culture of the Thirties," in *Culture as History: The Transformation of American Society in the Twentieth Century* (New York: Pantheon Books, 1984), 154, 156. Susan Hegeman argues that an emphasis on culture seemed to answer "a particular descriptive need in the modernist moment, when older conceptions of history and temporality had begun to seem, for various reasons, no longer adequate to explaining the specific experiences of alienation and difference Americans felt from others in their communities, their nation, the world" (Hegeman, *Patterns for America: Modernism and the Concept of Culture* [Princeton: Princeton University Press, 1999], 4). "Gossip: Of People and Things," *Survey* (London), 15 Dec. 1929, 361; "The Problems of the U.S.A.," *Saturday Review* (London), 29 June 1929, 866.

8. R. L. Duffus, "Getting at the Truth about an Average American Town," *New York Times Book Review,* 20 Jan. 1929, 3.

9. For analyses of the cultural production of Americanism in the 1930s, see William Stott, *Documentary Expression and Thirties America*, rev. ed. (1973; Chicago: University of Chicago Press, 1986); David P. Peeler, *Hope among Us Yet: Social Criticism and Social Solace in Depression*

America (Athens: University of Georgia Press, 1987); Michael Denning, *The Cultural Front: The Laboring of American Culture in the Twentieth Century* (New York: Verso, 1997); and Jason Loviglio, *Radio's Intimate Public: Network Broadcasting and Mass-Mediated Democracy* (Minneapolis: University of Minnesota Press, 2005). "Sociology and Economics," *Review of Reviews,* Feb. 1929, 29–30; Elsie McCormick, "A Piece of Her Mind," *New York World,* 4 Mar. 1929. Comparisons to Lewis are too numerous to list, but see Willoughby G. Walling, "Here's Biography of Small Town as Guide to Novelists," *Chicago Daily Tribune,* undated, RHL, R7:C12; Gilbert Seldes, "The Road to Athens," *Bookman,* Oct. 1928; and Maxwell A. Lerner, "Middletown Has an Air of Mr. Babbitt's Zenith, Ohio: Objective Study of City Smacks of the Literary," *New York Evening Post,* 9 Feb. 1929. Expressing a contrary view, Henry Hazlitt of the *New York Sun* commented that while *Middletown* "was, ostensibly, a 'detached' sociological study," it was clear that the Lynds "were incapable of seeing this town except through Mr. Lewis's eyes" (review of *Dodsworth,* undated, RHL, R7:C12).

10. Gretchen Mount, "A Fascinating Document," publication and date unknown; "Books of Inquiry Interest," *Inquiry,* undated, 66; both in RHL, R7:C12. Even relatively recent academic commentary has singled out *Middletown* for its scientific stance. In 1979, for example, Richard Jensen credited *Middletown* with moving "sociology away from the reform-oriented community survey toward a scientific study of culture" (Jensen, "The Lynds Revisited," *Indiana Magazine of History* 75 [1979]: 318).

11. Sheffield, "Recent Books of Special Interest."

12. Christopher Shannon, *Conspicuous Criticism: Tradition, the Individual, and Culture in American Social Thought, from Veblen to Mills* (Baltimore: Johns Hopkins University Press, 1996), 28; Duffus, "Getting at the Truth," 3; review of *Middletown* in *Book-of-the-Month Club,* Feb. 1929, RHL, R7:C12; "The Average American City under a Ruthless Microscope," *Boston Herald,* 18 May 1929; Williams, "Through the Looking Glass," 824; review of *Middletown* in *Information Service* 8, no. 19 (11 May 1929); Henry M. Busch, "Main Street under a Microscope," *Survey,* 15 Mar. 1929, 775; "Average American City under a Ruthless Microscope"; Stuart Chase, "The Bewildered Western World," *New York Herald Tribune,* 3 Feb. 1929, books column, sec. 11.

13. Clark Wissler, foreword, in Robert S. Lynd and Helen Merrell Lynd, *Middletown: A Study in Contemporary Culture* (New York: Harcourt, Brace, 1929), vi. Wissler, it should be noted, was a "eugenics-conscious writer" who in 1923 had championed Nordics as "the hope of the immediate future" and believed "it would be criminal not to give the best thought of the time to the conservation of whatever virtues this stock possesses" (Eric B. Ross, "The 'Deceptively Simple' Racism of Clark Wissler," *American Anthropologist* 87 [1985]: 390–393). Advertisement for *Middletown,* in *New Republic,* 6 Mar. 1929, RHL, R7:C12; "A Larger 'Middletown'?" "Scientists Study a Typical City of the Midwest," publication and date unknown, RHL, R7:C12.

14. "The Truth about Ourselves," *Literary Digest,* 15 June 1929; Howard Vincent O'Brien, "Two Books about Ourselves: How We Live and What We Think About," *Chicago Daily News,* 27 Feb. 1929; H. L. Mencken, "A Treatise on the Americano," *Baltimore Evening Sun,* 14 Jan. 1929; "Scientists Study a Typical City of the Midwest"; Lerner, "Middletown Has an Air." Mencken's words were used in Harcourt's marketing of *Middletown,* only to be removed after protests by Robert Lynd, who wrote: "I shall be very glad if and when your advertising department drops out those three or four words in the Mencken review in which he compares 'Middletown' to a 'dirty novel.' Such publicity does not help me professionally and I do not believe this sort of emphasis helps the book. The culminating emphasis of the reviews is that 'nobody interested in American life can afford to miss this book.' Wouldn't some such appeal as this chop as much wood as the 'dirty novel' appeal?" (R. Lynd to Harcourt, Brace, RHL, R4:C7).

15. Harvey W. Zorbaugh, review of *Middletown,* in *Journal of Education Sociology* 2 (1929): 549. Anthropologist A. L. Kroeber similarly noted the newfound ability of Western society to analyze itself, to "lay itself on the dissecting table alongside a foreign or dead culture" (Kroeber as quoted in Gilkeson Jr., "Domestication of 'Culture,'" 160).

16. "An American Town," *Times Literary Supplement* (London), 28 Feb. 1929, 155; "Contemporary American Culture," *Congregationalist,* 23 May 1929, 696.

17. "Some Statistics on Main Street," Walla Walla, WA, newspaper, publication and date unknown, RHL, R7:C12; Norman J. Ware, review of *Middletown,* in *American Economic Review* 19 (1929): 329; Donald

R. Murphy, "Americans at Home and Abroad: A Typical Town," unknown Des Moines, IA, publication, 21 Apr. 1929, RHL, R8:C12.

18. "A Larger 'Middletown'?"

19. Margo J. Anderson, *The American Census: A Social History* (New Haven: Yale University Press, 1988), 133–134; Mae M. Ngai, *Impossible Subjects: Illegal Aliens and the Making of Modern America* (Princeton: Princeton University Press, 2004), 21. Gary Gerstle charts the fates of what he calls "civic nationalism" and "racial nationalism" in *American Crucible: Race and Nation in the Twentieth Century* (Princeton: Princeton University Press, 2001). See also Matthew Frye Jacobson, *Whiteness of a Different Color: European Immigrants and the Alchemy of Race* (Cambridge, MA: Harvard University Press, 1998), 39–90.

20. "Nearly Everybody Now Has Car Here," *Muncie Evening Press,* 29 Oct. 1924, 2; Williams, "Through the Looking Glass"; Douglas L. Hunt, review of *Middletown,* in *Annals of the American Academy of Political and Social Science* 146 (1929): 271.

21. Margaret Mead, *Coming of Age in Samoa: A Psychological Study of Primitive Youth for Western Civilization* (New York: W. Morrow and Co., 1928); Robert Redfield, *Tepoztlán, a Mexican Village: A Study of Folk Life* (Chicago: University of Chicago Press, 1930); William Soskin, "Books on Our Table," *New York Evening Post,* undated, RHL, R7:C12; Isabel Paterson, "Books and Other Things," *New York Herald Tribune,* 29 Jan. 1929; Sheffield, "Recent Books of Special Interest"; John Dewey, "The House Divided against Itself," *New Republic,* 24 Apr. 1929. Dewey was apparently a major fan of the Middletown study. Wrote Henry Busch to Robert Lynd, "I understand John Dewey has been quoting 'Middletown' on every possible occasion" (15 Mar. 1929, RHL, R4:C7).

22. "A Genuine Document in Sociology," *Constable's Monthly List* (UK), June 1929, 5; *Middletown,* 9; Lerner, "Middletown Has an Air."

23. Call, "What We Would Change in Middletown."

24. R. Clyde White to R. Lynd, 28 Feb. 1929, RHL, R4:C7; Winfred Ernest Garrison, "An American Cross-Section," *Christian Century,* 21 Feb. 1929, 265; J. F. Steiner, review of *Middletown,* in *Social Service Review* 3 (1929): 508. Steiner argued that by "arbitrarily ruling 2,000 Negroes out of the picture, the task was simplified but at the expense of distorting the situation," and that the same was true for the "700 for-

eign-born persons whose role in the life of the city and progress in adjustment to American urban conditions" had been neglected. Steiner was just one of many critiquing the Lynds' lack of attention to Prohibition.

25. Chase, "Bewildered Western World"; Allan Nevins, "Fascinating Spectacle of an American Town under the Microscope," *New York World*, 17 Feb. 1929; H. L. Mencken, "A City in Moronia," *American Mercury*, Mar. 1929, 379; Lois and Gardner Murphy, "The Social Sciences Humanized," *Journal of Adult Education* (undated): 293, RHL, R7:C12.

26. John Dollard, *Caste and Class in a Southern Town* (New Haven: Yale University Press, 1937); N. B. Cousins, "The World in Books," *Current History*, June 1937, 4. Similarly, the reception that greeted *Middletown* presents a telling contrast to the reception of Gunnar Myrdal's major social scientific study on race relations, the 1944 *An American Dilemma*. Robert Lynd called it "the most penetrating and important book on our contemporary American civilization that has been written." But, notes Walter A. Jackson, the study was published "without great fanfare" and "did not create an immediate sensation." Indeed, the editor at Harper and Brothers "doubted that such a long, scholarly treatise would sell and insisted that [its backer] the Carnegie Corporation agree to cover any losses that Harper's might incur." See Jackson, *Gunnar Myrdal and America's Conscience: Social Engineering and Racial Liberalism, 1938–1987* (Chapel Hill: University of North Carolina Press, 1990), 241–242.

27. Advertisement in *New York Times Book Review*, 13 Jan. 1929, 15; advertisement in *Tide*, May 1929; advertisement in *Printers' Ink*, 16 May 1929, 173. This last advertisement quoted reviews in *Advertising and Selling* ("My thought, when I had finished it, was that the Lynds had lifted the roof off every house in town and made an inventory of everything and everybody in it") and *Sales Management* ("Of great interest to all who sell and advertise").

28. "Muncie Not as Book Suggests," *Muncie Evening Press*, 26 Mar. 1930. *Business Week* ran a three-part series titled "Middletown—Ten Years After," on 26 May, 2 June, and 9 June, 1934; the text quoted is from the first of these articles, 15.

29. For example, Maury Maverick, a congressman from Texas, found the study useful for its conclusions about attitudes of ordinary Americans

328 · Notes to Pages 88–90

toward the Home Owners' Loan Corporation and the New Deal more generally (*Congressional Record*, 75th Congress, First Session, 23 June 1937, 8158–59). Carl Van Doren, "What Are the Deep Changes in Progress in the Small [American City?]: Important Survey Results Bared in Lynds' New Book," *Boston Herald*, 24 Apr. 1937; "The Lynds Again Examine 'Middletown'; Find Great Changes in 10 Chaotic Years," *Harcourt, Brace News*, 15 Apr. 1937, RHL, R8:13; James S. Tyler, "The American People Survive a Decade," *Advertising and Selling*, 22 Apr. 1937, 64–65; review of *Middletown in Transition* in *Tide*, 1 May 1937, 14.

30. As quoted in "New 'Middletown in Transition' Stresses Cultural Patterns," *Harcourt, Brace News*, 15 Apr. 1937, RHL, R8:C13; "Sales Management's Public Relations Index to 90 Large Corporations," *Sales Management*, 1 May 1938, 18; "'Typical' American City Puts Clamp on Advertising, Trade-ins," *Electrical Merchandising*, Dec. 1938, RHL, R7:C11; "'Middletown' Goes to School" (Chicago: Nation's Schools, 1941), MSC; *Living on "McCall Street" in "Middletown"* (New York: McCall Corp., 1937).

31. "Muncie, Ind. Is the Great U.S. 'Middletown': And This Is the First Picture Essay of What It Looks Like," *Life*, 10 May 1937, 15–25; letters to the editors on "Middletown-Muncie," *Life*, 24 May 1937; F. B., "American Way of Life Viewed in Sharp Relief," *Chicago Daily Tribune*, 15 May 1937. As E. Bruce Geelhoed has observed, "With a circulation in the hundreds of thousands, *Life* may have done more to popularize 'Muncie as Middletown' in the public imagination than the Lynd studies" (Geelhoed, "The Enduring Legacy of Muncie as Middletown," in *The Other Side of Middletown: Exploring Muncie's African American Community*, ed. Luke Eric Lassiter et al. [Walnut Creek, CA: AltaMira Press, 2004], 30). See also Vicki Goldberg, *Margaret Bourke-White: A Biography* (New York: Harper and Row, 1986), 188–190; and Wendy Kozol, *Life's America: Family and Nation in Postwar Photojournalism* (Philadelphia: Temple University Press, 1994).

32. See esp. Susman, "Culture of the Thirties."

33. B. L. C., review of *Middletown*, in *Catholic World*, Aug. 1929, 635; Mencken, "A City in Moronia," 379.

34. *Middletown in Transition* remained on best-sellers lists for at least seven weeks. See the *New York Herald Tribune* books column for 16

May–4 July 1937, RHL, R8:C13. Van Doren, "What Are the Deep Changes"; Lee Berry, "This World of Books," *Toledo Blade,* 6 May 1937; John Chamberlain, "Books," *Scribner's Magazine,* July 1937, 62.

35. "Mirror of America," *Christian Century,* 5 May 1937, 575; Herschel Brickell, "The Literary Landscape," *Review of Reviews,* May 1937, 58; F. B., "American Way of Life Viewed in Sharp Relief"; Charles Hanson Towne, "Transition of Middletown," *Chicago Herald-Examiner,* 23 Apr. 1937.

36. "Topics of the Times," *New York Times,* 29 Mar. 1938; *Middletown in Transition,* 403–417.

37. L. S. Ayres and Co., "An Announcement to the Residents of Muncie," 17 Apr. 1937, RHL, R8:C13; Max Mathews to R. Lynd, 3 Aug. 1937, RHL, R1:C1; letter from "wife of newspaper man on the Star" to Leslie Kitselman, 11 May 1937, RHL, R1:C1; "Catholic Priest Comments on Findings of Dr. Lynd: Many Mistakes in Study of Muncie Claimed," *Muncie Evening Press,* 22 May 1937, 8; John B. L. to R. Lynd, 26 May 1937, RHL, R8:C13; "Muncie Unlikely to Agree with Findings of Dr. Lynd," *Muncie Evening Press,* 13 Apr. 1937.

38. Newspaper clipping from either the *Muncie Morning Star* or *Muncie Evening Press,* 1937, sent to the Lynds by Leslie Kitselman, RHL, R1:C1; C. A. Millspaugh, "'Middletown' Talks Back," from the "Beacon," unknown publication, 8 Jan. 1938, RHL, R8:C13; Paul Kelso, "'Middletown' Authors Leaving Today after Two Weeks' Visit," *Muncie Star,* 26 June 1935; H. L. Carr to R. Lynd, 5 Jan. 1941, RHL, R8:C13. See also "Street in Housing Project Is Named for Robert Lynds," *Muncie Evening Press,* 4 Jan. 1941; and Wilbur E. Sutton, "Muncie Always Marches," in *Indiana Today: A Work for Newspaper and Library Reference,* ed. C. Walter McCarty et al. (Indianapolis: Indiana Editors' Association, 1942), 466.

39. John B. L. to R. Lynd, 26 May 1937, RHL, R8:C13; Robert H. Myers to R. Lynd, 6 June 1937, RHL, R1:C1. For local reports on Bourke-White's visit to Muncie, see John Lewellen, "Margaret Bourke-White in the City for Week," and "Country's Ace Photographer to Take Picture Series Here," *Muncie Evening Press,* 5 Apr. 1937; Paul Kelso, "City Council Goes on Parade before Famed Camera Artist," *Muncie Morning Star,* 6 Apr. 1937; "Muncie Is Honored," *Muncie Morning Star,* 7 Apr. 1937; "Photographer Club's Speaker," *Muncie Morning*

Star, 13 Apr. 1937; "Famous Photographer Ends Camera Study of Muncie," *Muncie Evening Press*, 20 Apr. 1937.

40. Leslie Kiselman to R. and H. Lynd, 8 May 1937, RHL, R8:C13; letters to the editor on "Middletown-Muncie," *Life*, 24 May 1937; letter from widow in the Y family to Leslie Kitselman, quoted by the latter in a letter to R. and H. Lynd, 4 June 1937, RHL, R1:C1.

41. Robert H. Myers to R. Lynd, 6 June 1937, RHL, R1:C1; John Lewellen, "Typical Muncie's Typical Family," pictures to the editors, *Life*, 5 July 1937, 74. Lewellen was later asked by *Life* to "photograph New York as it looks to a Midwesterner" and turned the tables by having several humorous photos published.

42. "Muncie Is Honored." Another protracted controversy over the representation of Middletown followed the Public Broadcasting System's *Middletown* film series in 1982, particularly one segment on high school students entitled "Seventeen." Meg McLagan traces the debates in "Constructing America: Middletown, Seventeen and the Politics of Representation" (M.A. thesis, New York University, 1989). Even Robert Lynd's *New York Times* obituary of 1970 would draw critique in Muncie for claiming that although the Middletown books were required reading at many universities, they were not taught at Muncie's Ball State University (in fact, the book was then being used in three courses). "Reply to 'Times' Obituary: Ball State Says 'Middletown' Is Used in Sociology Courses," *Muncie Star*, 6 Nov. 1970.

43. "Nearly Everybody Now Has Car Here," 2; Muncie Chamber of Commerce, "Facts to Remember about Muncie, Indiana," RHL, R8:C12; Rosa Burmaster relayed the information about the Main Street sign in a letter to R. Lynd in 1926 or 1927, RHL, R4:C7.

44. "Muncie Not as Book Suggests"; "Just Here and There," *Muncie Star*, undated, RHL, R7:C12. The "bicycle author" was Robert Lynd, who, to the amusement of some in town, continued to ride a bicycle even when automobiles were available.

45. John B. L. to R. Lynd, 26 May 1937, RHL, R8:C13; John Lewellen, "Meet the 'Typical Family' of America's 'Typical City'; They're Now in Chicago on an Expense-Free, Two-Day Outing," *Muncie Evening Press*, 5 June 1937. Also on the typical family contest, see "Typical Family to Make Trip by Airplane," *Muncie Evening Press*, 22 May 1937; "'Typical' Family Awed by Acclaim," *New York Times*, 18 Oct. 1938; "Our Family Sizes," *New York Times*, 19 Oct. 1938.

46. Mayor Rollin H. Bunch, as quoted in "Middletown: 'Typical American City,' Muncie, Indiana Has Changed Little in Decade," *Literary Digest,* 24 Apr. 1937, 32–33; "America Needs Churches, Says Bishop Fisher," Indiana newspaper, date unknown, RHL, R7:C12; John B. L. to R. Lynd, 26 May 1937, RHL, R8:C13; Sutton, "Muncie Always Marches," 466.

47. R. Lynd to Richard Greene, 24 Apr. 1960, MSC. In *Knowledge for What?* (Princeton: Princeton University Press, 1939), Robert Lynd qualified his description of Middletown even though he reiterated its ability to speak for the nation: "With allowances for the heavily native-born, Protestant, small-city, Middle Western character of Middletown's population, most of the assumptions there set down would probably apply widely throughout the country" (62 n. 10). Helen Lynd wrote in 1978, "We certainly never made any claim that it was a specifically typical city" (H. Lynd, *Possibilities,* 34). Interestingly, sociologist Paul Lazarsfeld claimed to have discovered in a Depression-era study on national magazine circulation that the city that "came closest to [the] average profile" was Muncie, Indiana. See his "In Memoriam: Robert Staughton Lynd, 1892–1970," *American Sociologist* 6 (1971): 266.

48. C. Warren Vander Hill, "Middletown: The Most Studied Community in America," *Indiana Social Studies Quarterly* 33 (Autumn 1980): 47–57; Bill Spurgeon, "'Middletown' Goes Under the Microscope—for Happiness," *Muncie Star,* 1 July 1978; Bob Barnet, "All Together Now: Let's Be Typical!" *Muncie Star,* 18 Apr. 1982. The major follow-up studies to *Middletown* and *Middletown in Transition* were the "Middletown Man" community study project of 1974, funded by the Indiana Committee on the Humanities; the longitudinal study ("Middletown III") funded by the National Science Foundation and headed by University of Virginia sociologist Theodore Caplow, begun in 1976; Peter Davis's six-part documentary film series, *Middletown,* funded in part by the National Endowment for the Humanities and aired in 1982; and a collaborative ethnography of Muncie's African American community, Lassiter et al., *Other Side of Middletown.* On Middletown III, see Theodore Caplow et al., *Middletown Families: Fifty Years of Change and Continuity* (Minneapolis: University of Minnesota Press, 1982); Theodore Caplow et al., *All Faithful People: Change and Continuity in Middletown's Religion* (Minneapolis: University of Minnesota Press, 1983); Dwight W. Hoover's discussion in "Changing Views of Community Studies: Middletown as a Case Study," *Journal of the His-*

tory of the Behavioral Sciences 25 (1989): 111–123; and Mark C. Smith's "From *Middletown* to Middletown III: A Critical Review," *Qualitative Sociology* 7, no. 4 (1984): 327–336. On the film series, see Dwight Hoover, *Middletown: The Making of a Documentary Film Series* (Philadelphia: Harwood Academic, 1992). A restudy and book under the direction of Caplow were subjects of a Public Broadcasting System documentary aired in 2001, *The First Measured Century: The Other Way of Looking at American History* (BJW, Inc., in association with New River Media, 2000). Rita Caccamo gives an account of most of these studies in her *Back to Middletown: Three Generations of Sociological Reflections* (Stanford: Stanford University Press, 2000). The Center for Middletown Studies, established in 1984 at Ball State University in Muncie, now keeps track of further research on the community.

49. Caplow has noted the "systematic neglect of African Americans in the vast literature of Muncie as Middletown" as well as his own part in continuing that pattern in his replication of the original Middletown study in 1977–1978, using the exact same questions as the Lynds had in the mid-1920s (Caplow, afterword, in *The Other Side of Middletown,* 270). An attempt to correct for the omission of African American data in one of the Lynds' surveys can be found in Theodore Caplow, Howard M. Bahr, and Vaughn R. A. Call, "The Middletown Replications: 75 Years of Change in Adolescent Attitudes, 1924–1999," *Public Opinion Quarterly* 68 (2004): 287–313.

50. R. Lynd, "Problem of Being Objective in Studying Our Own Culture," lecture outline for talk at Princeton University, 9 Dec. 1938, RHL, R2:C2; here, Lynd also noted his discomfort with the commercialization of the study—the fact that his having surveyed Middletown meant that "*Esquire* tries to seduce you into writing a brochure & an adv[ertisin]g agency to make a market study. And so on." On a later occasion, Lynd related to a Muncie friend: "This is the price one pays for having written a pair of books viewed now as 'classics'" (R. Lynd to Richard Greene, 24 Apr. 1960, MSC).

51. Ellsworth Faris, "Journalism—Not Sociology," *Journal of Higher Education* 9 (1938): 229–230; George A. Lundberg, review of *Middletown in Transition*, in *Journal of the American Statistical Association* 32 (1937): 813; Ernest W. Burgess, review of *Middletown in Transition*, in *American Journal of Sociology* 43 (1937): 487.

3. Polling the Average Populace

1. George Gallup and Saul Forbes Rae, *The Pulse of Democracy: The Public-Opinion Poll and How It Works* (New York: Simon and Schuster, 1940), v. On the rivalry between the *Literary Digest* and the "scientific pollsters," see Maurice C. Bryson, "The *Literary Digest* Poll: Making of a Statistical Myth," *American Statistician* 30, no. 4 (1976): 184–185; David W. Moore, *The Superpollsters: How They Measure and Manipulate Public Opinion in America* (New York: Four Walls Eight Windows, 1992), 31–55; and Michael Wheeler, *Lies, Damn Lies, and Statistics: The Manipulation of Public Opinion in America* (New York: Liveright, 1976), 67–70.

2. Gallup and Rae, *Pulse of Democracy*, 118; Mildred Parten, *Surveys, Polls, and Samples: Practical Procedures* (New York: Harper and Bros., 1950), 2.

3. George Gallup, "Polling Public Opinion," *Current History*, Feb. 1940, 23.

4. For a broad overview of the shifting definitions and measurements of "public opinion," see W. Phillips Davison, "Public Opinion," in *International Encyclopedia of the Social Sciences*, ed. David L. Sills (New York: Macmillan, 1968), 13:188–197.

5. Charles Tilly addresses the broad "repertoire of collective action" for expressing public sentiment in his "Speaking Your Mind without Elections, Surveys, or Social Movements," *Public Opinion Quarterly* 47 (1983): 461–478, as does Susan Herbst in her *Numbered Voices: How Opinion Polling Has Shaped American Politics* (Chicago: University of Chicago Press, 1993). For the best extended analyses of straw poll techniques, see Claude E. Robinson, *Straw Votes: A Study of Political Prediction* (New York: Columbia University Press, 1932); and Herbst, *Numbered Voices*, 69–87. On magazine polls, see Parten, *Surveys, Polls, and Samples*, 37.

6. W. I. Thomas and Florian Znaniecki, *The Polish Peasant in Europe and America* (Boston: D. Badger, 1918); Charles E. Merriam and Harold F. Gosnell, *Non-Voting: Causes and Methods of Control* (Chicago: University of Chicago Press, 1924); Henry Yu, *Thinking Orientals: Migration, Contact, and Exoticism in Modern America* (New York: Oxford University Press, 2001), 15–92. Jean Converse provides a useful summary of academic attitude research in the 1920s and 1930s in her

Survey Research in the United States: Roots and Emergence, 1890–1960 (Berkeley: University of California Press, 1987), 54–86, as does Jennifer Platt in *A History of Sociological Research Methods in America, 1920–1960* (Cambridge: Cambridge University Press, 1996). Richard Gillespie, *Manufacturing Knowledge: A History of the Hawthorne Experiments* (New York: Cambridge University Press, 1991). James R. Beniger, *The Control Revolution: Technological and Economic Origins of the Information Society* (Cambridge, MA: Harvard University Press, 1986), 376.

7. George Creel, *How We Advertised America* (New York: Harper and Bros., 1920), 3–4. See also Harold D. Lasswell, *Propaganda Technique in the World War* (New York: Alfred A. Knopf, 1927).

8. Edward L. Bernays, *Propaganda* (New York: H. Liveright, 1928) and *Crystallizing Public Opinion* (New York: Boni and Liveright, 1929). Walter Lippmann, *Public Opinion* (New York: Harcourt, Brace, 1922) and *The Phantom Public* (New York: Harcourt, Brace, 1925); John Dewey, *The Public and Its Problems* (New York: Holt, 1927). On Lippmann's involvement in propaganda work, see Christopher Simpson, *Science of Coercion: Communication Research and Psychological Warfare, 1945–1960* (New York: Oxford University Press, 1994), 16–17. On the effects of dictatorships on American social thought, see Edward A. Purcell, *The Crisis of Democratic Theory: Scientific Naturalism and the Problem of Value* (Lexington: University Press of Kentucky, 1973), 95–138; and Benjamin L. Alpers, *Dictators, Democracy, and American Public Culture: Envisioning the Totalitarian Enemy, 1920s–1950s* (Chapel Hill: University of North Carolina Press, 2003). For social scientific work on persuasion, see Kurt Lewin, *The Conceptual Representation and the Measurement of Psychological Forces* (Durham, NC: Duke University Press, 1938); Kurt Lewin, "Group Decision and Social Change," in *Readings in Social Psychology,* ed. T. M. Newcomb and E. L. Hartley (New York: Holt, 1947), 330–344; Solomon Asch, "Group Forces in the Modification and Distortion of Judgments," *Social Psychology* (New York: Prentice-Hall, 1952); Solomon Asch, "Studies of Independence and Conformity: A Minority of One against a Unanimous Majority," *Psychological Monograph* 70 (1956): whole no. 416; and Elihu Katz and Paul F. Lazarsfeld, *Personal Influence: The Part Played by People in the Flow of Mass Communications* (Glencoe, IL: Free Press, 1955).

9. Roper and Crossley's third partner in this venture was Arthur Dougall of Stewart, Dougall and Associates, a market research firm. See Archibald Crossley to Arthur Dougall, 30 June 1949; "For Release," 4 Feb. 1950; and memorandum from Arthur Dougall to the President and Board of Directors of Middletowns, Inc., 24 Mar. 1950; all in ERP. Interestingly, their list of characteristics for selecting these test cities did not differ markedly from the Lynds' criteria for the Middletown study.

10. Richard Ohmann, *Selling Culture: Magazines, Markets, and Class at the Turn of the Century* (New York: Verso, 1996), 62–117, quotation on 110. Conference on Unemployment, *Recent Economic Changes in the United States* (New York: McGraw-Hill, 1929), xviii, xxi. For broad changes in marketing and advertising in the twentieth century, see Stephen Fox, *The Mirror Makers: A History of American Advertising and Its Creators* (New York: Random House, 1984); Roland Marchand, *Advertising the American Dream: Making Way for Modernity, 1920–1940* (Berkeley: University of California Press, 1985); William R. Leach, *Land of Desire: Merchants, Power and the Rise of a New American Culture* (New York: Pantheon, 1993); Jackson Lears, *Fables of Abundance: A Cultural History of Advertising in America* (New York: Basic Books, 1994); and Walter Friedman, *Birth of a Salesman: The Transformation of Selling in America* (Cambridge, MA: Harvard University Press, 2004).

11. Lawrence C. Lockley, "Notes on the History of Marketing Research," *Journal of Marketing* 14 (1950): 734. See also Beniger, *The Control Revolution*, 376–398. Most histories of market research credit Charles Coolidge Parlin, the Curtis Publishing Company's director of research, for building the field in the 1910s and inspiring research departments at other firms, such as U.S. Rubber and Swift & Company.

12. Richard S. Tedlow, *New and Improved: The Story of Mass Marketing in America* (New York: Basic Books, 1990), 344; Susan Strasser, *Satisfaction Guaranteed: The Making of the American Mass Market* (New York: Pantheon, 1989); J. George Frederick, *Business Research and Statistics* (New York: Appleton, 1920), 68–69, 75.

13. C. S. Duncan, *Commercial Research: An Outline of Working Principles* (New York: Macmillan, 1919), 35, 30; Frederick, *Business Research and Statistics*, 5, vii.

14. Strasser, *Satisfaction Guaranteed*, 150–153; Duncan, *Commercial Research*, 168–183, quotation on 186; Parten, *Surveys, Polls, and Sam-*

ples, 39–40; Paul F. Lazarsfeld and Marjorie Fiske, "The 'Panel' as a New Tool for Measuring Opinion," *Public Opinion Quarterly* 2 (1938): 596–612; Converse, *Survey Research,* 91–92.

15. Parten, *Surveys, Polls, and Samples,* 43. For contemporary radio studies, see Hadley Cantril and Gordon W. Allport, *The Psychology of Radio* (New York: Harper and Bros., 1935); Paul F. Lazarsfeld and Frank N. Stanton, eds., *Radio Research* (New York: Duell, Sloan, and Pearce, 1941); and Paul F. Lazarsfeld and Harry Field, *The People Look at Radio* (Chapel Hill: University of North Carolina Press, 1946). For a history of radio's "audience intellectuals," see Kathy Newman, *Radio Active: Advertising and Consumer Activism, 1935–1947* (Berkeley: University of California Press, 2004), 17–51.

16. Roper, Speech to the Sales Executive Club, 19 Mar. 1940, ERP. On the ties between polling and commercial research, see Converse, *Survey Research,* esp. 87–127, and Daniel J. Robinson, *The Measure of Democracy: Polling, Market Research, and Public Life, 1930–1945* (Toronto: University of Toronto Press, 1999). Robinson, who primarily examines polling in Canada, argues that "opinion polling developed conceptually and methodologically largely as an adjunct of consumer surveying" (6).

17. John Broadus Watson, foreword, in Henry C. Link, *The New Psychology of Selling and Advertising* (New York: Macmillan, 1932), vii; Gallup, "Tomorrow's Customers: Where Are They Coming From?" date and place of speech unknown, GGP; Roper, Speech to the Sales Executive Club. Gallup won Advertising and Selling's annual advertising award in 1935, the Advertising Gold Medal Award in 1965, the Parlin Award of the American Marketing Association in 1965, the Christopher Columbus International Prize for Outstanding Achievement in the Field of Communications in 1966, and the Distinguished Achievement Award of the New Jersey chapter of the American Marketing Association in 1975. See "The Contributions of George Gallup to Advertising," GGP.

18. Archibald Crossley, interview with Rena Bartos, undated, 1–2, and interview with Dick Baxter, 7 Apr. 1977, 5–6, ERP; Karen S. Buzzard, *Chains of Gold: Marketing the Rating and Rating the Markets* (Metuchen, NJ: Scarecrow Press, 1990), esp. 10–27; Converse, *Survey Research,* 112.

19. For biographical material in this and the next paragraph, see Roper, in-

terview with Robert O. Carlson, 14 Aug. 1968, 1–4, 9–12, 14, 31–42, as well as Roper's curriculum vitae (circa 1949), ERP.

20. A great deal of social scientific work during the war focused on opinion and morale, with Samuel Stouffer's extensive *American Soldier* survey being the most prominent example. For accounts of wartime public opinion work, see Ellen Herman, *The Romance of American Psychology: Political Culture in the Age of Experts* (Berkeley: University of California Press, 1994), 48–81; and Converse, *Survey Research,* 162–185.

21. J. J. O'Malley, "Black Beans and White Beans," *New Yorker,* 2 Mar. 1940, 20, 24. For Gallup's career path, see Becky Wilson Hawbaker, "Taking 'the Pulse of Democracy': George Gallup, Iowa, and the Origin of the Gallup Poll," *Palimpsest* 74 (1993): 98–113; Robinson, *Measure of Democracy,* 39–63; and George Gallup, "Looking Back over 41 Years of Polling," essay submitted to the *Saturday Review,* Aug. 1976, GGP. Gallup, interview with Frank Rounds, 9 Oct. 1962, Columbia University Oral History Collection, Columbia University, New York, 40–41; Gallup, interview with Rena Bartos, undated, 2, ERP. See also "The Contributions of George Gallup to Advertising," GGP; and George Gallup, "My Y & R Years," *The Link: Young & Rubicam,* Fall 1982. On the "Gallup Method," see Gallup, "History and Development of the Impact Method of Advertising Research," 14 Nov. 1949, 11–12, GGP; George Gallup, "Guesswork Eliminated in New Method for Determining Reader Interest," *Editor & Publisher,* 8 Feb. 1930, 1, 55; and George A. Brandenburg, "Telephone Surveys Puncture Radio Claims to Intensive Coverage," *Editor & Publisher,* 30 Jan. 1932, 6–7.

22. Robinson, *Straw Votes,* 147–162; Gallup, interview with Frank Rounds, 119–120; "Gallup's (ARI's) Experience in the Motion Picture Industry," GGP; Susan Ohmer, "Measuring Desire: George Gallup and Audience Research in Hollywood," *Journal of Film and Video* 45 (1991): 3–28; "Gallup Poll News Release Schedule, 1935–1991," GGP; O'Malley, "Black Beans and White Beans," 20; "Poll: Dr. Gallup to Take the National Pulse and Temperature," *News-Week,* 26 Oct. 1935, 23.

23. Frederick, *Business Research and Statistics,* 25; Gallup and Rae, *Pulse of Democracy,* 106–107; Roper, *Where the People Stand* (CBS broadcast), 2 Jan. 1949, ERP.

24. Gallup, "Guesswork Eliminated"; Gallup and Rae, *Pulse of Democracy*, 127. All of the pollsters, for example, jumped to correct an unflattering media characterization of Crossley's radio research in 1946. The offending article was "Exit Crossley," *Time*, 30 Sept. 1946, 96, 98 (Gallup to editors, *Time*, 15 Oct. 1946; Roper to editors, *Time*, 18 Oct. 1946; both in ERP). Roper and Gallup complimented each other's work, participated in conferences together, sent each other relevant articles, and generally supported each other when brickbats were being thrown at polling's "research fraternity," as the latter described it (Gallup to Roper, 29 Sept. 1942, ERP; see also their running correspondence in ERP).

25. George Gallup, "I Don't Take Sides," *Nation*, 30 Dec. 1944, 795–796; Gallup and Rae, *Pulse of Democracy*, 93, 106; Roper, *Where the People Stand* (CBS broadcast), 26 Dec. 1948, ERP. Roper was overtly critical of McCarthyism and active in the National Urban League, the Fund for the Republic, the Atlantic Union Committee, the National Conference of Christians and Jews, and the Connecticut Commission on Civil Rights. For his work on behalf of Democrats, see Roper to Paul M. Butler, 18 Feb. 1955; Roper to Hubert Humphrey, 2 June 1955; and Estes Kefauver to Roper, 14 Dec. 1955; all in ERP.

26. Roper, "Who Is Complacent?" (CBS broadcast), 3 May 1942, ERP; Gallup and Rae, *Pulse of Democracy*, 144, 4; Elmo Roper, "What People Are Thinking," *New York Herald Tribune*, 30 Nov. 1944.

27. Gallup and Rae, *Pulse of Democracy*, 6–11; the only hint that Americans, too, might be susceptible to demagoguery came in Gallup's discussions of political machines, and particularly the Long regime in Louisiana (153–166).

28. Elmo Roper and Julian L. Woodward, "Democracy's Auxiliary Ballot Box," *New York Herald Tribune*, 4 Apr. 1948; Gallup, "We, the People, Are Like This—A Report on How and What We Think," *New York Times Magazine*, 8 June 1941, 3; Leo P. Crespi, "The Interview Effect in Polling," *Public Opinion Quarterly* 12 (1948): 99–111; Pearl London, "Ringing Doorbells with a Gallup Reporter," *New York Times Magazine*, 1 Sept. 1940, 9.

29. Gallup, "The Problems and Values of Opinion Measurement," speech at the Boston University Founders' Day Institute, 13 Mar. 1948, GGP; George Gallup, "The People Are Ahead of Congress," *New York Times Magazine*, 29 Mar. 1942, 16, 35; Gallup, "The 'People's Platform,'" American Institute of Public Opinion, 1956, GGP; "Inter-

view with George Gallup: How 55 Million Vote," *U.S. News & World Report,* 23 May 1952, 63; Roper, WEAF radio program, "Youth Meets Government," 23 Apr. 1939, ERP; Roper, "Who Is Complacent?"

30. Gallup and Rae, *Pulse of Democracy,* 12–13. Gallup was deeply influenced by a 1919 article that argued for "bringing back into our national life the habit of common discussion of common problems" through the open forum, lyceum, and chautauqua: Glenn Frank, "The Parliament of the People," *Century Magazine,* July 1919, 401–415, quotation on 405. Bryce as quoted in Gallup and Rae, *Pulse of Democracy,* 125.

31. Gallup and Rae, *Pulse of Democracy,* 5, 117; Gallup, "The Future of Polls," speech at Iowa City Conference, Feb. 1949, GGP.

32. For his argument on "making the mass articulate," see George Gallup, "Government and the Sampling Referendum," *Journal of the American Statistical Association* 33 (1938): 131–142, and "Polling Public Opinion," 57. Elmo Roper, "Why Marketing Research?" speech to the Life Insurance Institute, 8 Dec. 1942, ERP.

33. George Gallup, "Putting Public Opinion to Work," *Scribner's Magazine,* Nov. 1936, 39. "The question which haunts me," Roper revealed to his radio audience in 1949, was whether his survey had helped produce the outcome of the previous election: "for once polls become a force influencing the outcome, rather than a technique merely measuring the voters' intentions, then polls are on dangerous ground" (Roper, *Where the People Stand* [CBS broadcast], 2 Jan. 1949, ERP). Studies of the bandwagon phenomenon appeared even in the pages of the journals to which pollsters subscribed. Donald T. Campbell, the author of one such article, observed that "the general principle that *groups tend toward consensus of opinion,* and that *the communication of the opinions of members affects such consensus* is one of the most recurrent and consistent findings of social psychology" (Campbell, "On the Possibility of Experimenting with the 'Bandwagon' Effect," *International Journal of Opinion and Attitude Research* 5 [1951]: 251–260, quotation on 251 [his emphasis]). He pointed out that Gallup had led the pollsters in denying this effect.

34. Roper, "Why Marketing Research?"; Richard W. Steele, "The Pulse of the People: Franklin D. Roosevelt and the Gauging of American Public Opinion," *Journal of Contemporary History* 9, no. 4 (1974): 207, 215. See also Steven Casey, *Cautious Crusade: Franklin D. Roose-*

velt, American Public Opinion, and the War against Germany (New York: Oxford University Press, 2001).

35. Key figures in the development of modern sample surveying in the United States were Rensis Likert, Samuel Stouffer, Paul Lazarsfeld, and Robert Merton. See Frederick F. Stephan, "History of the Uses of Modern Sampling Procedures," *Journal of the American Statistical Association* 43 (1948): 12–39; You Poh Seng, "History of the Development of Sampling Theories and Practice," *Journal of the Royal Statistical Society*, ser. A, vol. 114 (1951): 214–231; William Kruskal and Frederick Mosteller, "Representative Sampling, IV: The History of the Concept in Statistics, 1895–1939," *International Statistical Review* 48 (1980): 169–195; and Charles R. Turner and Elizabeth Martin, "The Development and Contemporary Use of Subjective Surveys" in *Surveying Subjective Phenomena*, ed. Charles F. Turner and Elizabeth Martin (New York: Russell Sage Foundation, 1984), 25–59.

36. Martin R. Frankel and Lester R. Frankel, "Fifty Years of Survey Sampling in the United States," *Public Opinion Quarterly* 51, pt. 2 (1987): S127–S138; James Wechsler, "Polling America," *Nation*, 20 Jan. 1940, 65, 66–67. On measuring the intensity of opinion, see Gallup, "The Quintamensional Plan of Question Design," *Public Opinion Quarterly* 11 (1947): 385–393. Michael Hogan discusses the aims and flaws of this technique in "George Gallup and the Rhetoric of Scientific Democracy," *Communication Monographs* 64 (1997): 169–170.

37. Leonora de Lima Andrews, "That Dreadful Interviewer Problem Again," *International Journal of Opinion and Attitude Research* 3 (1949–1950): 587. Frederick Mosteller et al., *The Pre-election Polls of 1948: Report to the Committee on Analysis of Pre-election Polls and Forecasts*, Bulletin 60 (New York: Social Science Research Council, 1949), 145; Donald Rugg, "'Trained' vs. 'Untrained' Interviewers," in *Gauging Public Opinion*, ed. Hadley Cantril and Associates (Princeton: Princeton University Press, 1944), 83. On the interviewer problem in general, see Douglas Williams, "Basic Instructions for Interviewers," *Public Opinion Quarterly* 6 (1942): 634–641; Selden Menefee, "Recruiting an Opinion Field Staff," *Public Opinion Quarterly* 8 (1944): 262–269; Paul B. Sheatsley, "Some Uses of Interviewer-Report Forms," *Public Opinion Quarterly* 11 (1947–1948): 601–611; Herbert G. Heneman Jr. and Donald G. Paterson, "Refusal Rates and Interviewer Quality," and Edith Witt, "The San Francisco Program for Improving

Standards," both in *International Journal of Opinion and Attitude Research* 3 (1949): 392–398, 435–446.

38. Paul B. Sheatsley, "An Analysis of Interviewer Characteristics and Their Relationship to Performance," pts. 1 and 2, *International Journal of Opinion and Attitude Research* 4 (1950–1951): 473–498, and 5 (1951): 79–94; George Gallup Jr., "The Trials and Tribulations of a Pollster," Aug. 1969, 17, GGP.

39. Eleanor P. Clarkson, "The Problem of Honesty," *International Journal of Opinion and Attitude Research* 4 (1950): 84; Robert N. King, "How to Lick the Problem of Interview Cheating," *Advertising and Selling*, Oct. 1942; Roper to Robert King, 16 Oct. 1942, ERP. For a discussion of "cheater traps," see Mosteller et al., *Pre-election Polls of 1948*, 141–142.

40. George Gallup, "Polls and Prophets," *Current History and Forum*, 7 Nov. 1940, 14; Paul B. Sheatsley, as quoted in Converse, *Survey Research*, 126.

41. "Interview with George Gallup: How 55 Million Vote," 64; Jerome H. Spingarn, "These Public-Opinion Polls: How They Work and What They Signify," *Harper's Magazine*, Dec. 1938, 101; Donald Rugg, "How Representative Are 'Representative Samples'?" in Cantril et al., *Gauging Public Opinion*, 145. Contemporary studies documented interviewers' tendency to overreport the categories "average" and "poor" quite significantly, and to underreport all other class gradations as compared to respondents' self-ratings. See Frederick Mosteller, "The Reliability of Interviewers' Ratings," in Cantril et al., *Gauging Public Opinion*, 98–106, esp. table 32 on p. 104.

42. Donald Rugg, "How Representative Are 'Representative Samples'?" 146; William Turnbull, "Secret vs. Nonsecret Ballots," in Cantril et al., *Gauging Public Opinion*, 77; Harold F. Gosnell and Sebastian de Grazia, "A Critique of Polling Methods," *Public Opinion Quarterly* 6 (1942): 378–390; Daniel Katz, "Do Interviewers Bias Poll Results?" *Public Opinion Quarterly* 6 (1942): 248–268; Cantril et al., *Gauging Public Opinion*, 113.

43. Mosteller et al., *Pre-election Polls of 1948*, 134–135; Robinson, *Measure of Democracy*, 56; Cantril et al., *Gauging Public Opinion*, 118.

44. See memorandum from Roper to his staff, "Probability Sample," 19 July 1949, and Sol to Roper, "Report on Status of Probability Sample," 21 Nov. 1949; both in ERP.

342 · Notes to Pages 132–136

45. Report from Elizabeth Wagner, "Probability Sample Experiences in New York City," 1949, ERP.
46. Report from Mary M. Crawford, "Probability Sample Experiences in New York City," 1949, ERP.
47. Crawford, "Probability Sample Experiences," ERP; Roper, "Probability Sample."
48. Gallup, "Polling Experiences, 1936–1948," speech at World Association of Public Opinion Research meeting, Paris, France, 7 Sept. 1949, GGP. Wrote Roper in 1951, "[I] have been raising questions in public print since 1944 as to whether or not election polls didn't do very much more harm than good" (Roper to F. T. Sutpen, 27 Sept. 1951, ERP). Ohmer, "Measuring Desire," 4. Roper sent the same 1952 letter to all of his clients. For the substance of it, see Roper to Ben Donaldson, Ford Motor Company, 12 Nov. 1952, ERP.

Election forecasts were always a precarious enterprise. Because market and political research so overlapped in personnel and methodology, pollsters knew that faulty projections could mean the loss of valuable accounts. A study of eleven hundred leading American business executives following pollsters' misfire in 1948 found that most were "shocked by the failure of the polls to predict correctly the election" (Harold Whitehead & Partners, LTD., "Market Research and the Election Polls Appraised by American Business Leaders," 3 Jan. 1949, ERP). The president of the A. C. Nielsen Company and the publisher of *Good Housekeeping*, one of Roper's clients, both worried about the impact of incorrect projections on market research (Art Nielsen to Roper, 5 Nov. 1948, ERP; J. R. Buckley to Roper, 10 Dec. 1952, ERP). Susan Ohmer notes that the 1948 election resulted in the cancellation of Gallup's ongoing contract with RKO and Disney; the latter hired the pollster on a case-by-case basis afterward (Ohmer, "Measuring Desire," 22).
49. Wheeler, *Lies, Damn Lies, and Statistics*, 28; Hogan, "Rhetoric of Scientific Democracy," 167–168.
50. Gallup noted that Roper's Fortune Survey regularly sampled the entire adult population, whereas the AIPO polls, with certain exceptions, included only the voting population (Gallup, *A Guide to Public Opinion Polls* [Princeton: Princeton University Press, 1944], 101). Robinson, *Measure of Democracy*, 51, 54, 56–57.
51. Liette Gidlow, *The Big Vote: Gender, Consumer Culture, and the Poli-*

tics of Exclusion, 1890s–1920s (Baltimore: Johns Hopkins University Press, 2004), 31, 3. See also Michael E. McGerr, *The Decline of Popular Politics: The American North, 1865–1928* (New York: Oxford University Press, 1986); and Alexander Keyssar, *The Right to Vote: The Contested History of Democracy in the United States* (New York: Basic Books, 2000). For a contemporary study on voting patterns in the 1920s, see Merriam and Gosnell, *Non-Voting.*

52. "Interview with George Gallup: How 55 Million Vote," 56; London, "Ringing Doorbells," 15; Roper, *Where the People Stand* (CBS broadcast), 11 June 1950, ERP. Elihu Katz and Paul Lazarsfeld expressed the commonsense social scientific knowledge of the 1940s and 1950s about women and politics: "Without endangering their self-respect or the respect of others, women can, to a greater extent than men, get through life without participating in, or having opinions about, public affairs" (*Personal Influence,* 271).

53. Roper, *Where the People Stand* (CBS broadcast), 2 Jan. 1949, ERP; Mosteller et al., *Pre-election Polls of 1948,* 81, 90, 162; Robinson, *Measure of Democracy,* 54.

54. Roper, *Where the People Stand* (CBS broadcast), 2 Jan. 1949; Gallup, "A Second Look at the 1948 Election," speech at the Iowa Conference, undated, 1949, GGP.

55. See the first Gallup Poll, "Relief and Recovery," 20 October 1935, in *The Gallup Poll: Public Opinion 1935–1971,* vol. 1, ed. George H. Gallup (New York: Random House, 1972), 1; and *The Gallup Poll,* vol. 1, pp. 3, 23, 53, 260, 209, 129, 717, 272, 357–358, and 307. Elmo Roper, "Fortune Survey," supplement to *Fortune,* July 1940, 1; Elmo Roper, "Fortune Quarterly Survey IV," *Fortune,* April 1936, 104–105, 208, 216.

56. Gallup, "We, the People, Are Like This," 3; Roper, *Where the People Stand* (NBC broadcast), 17 Feb. 1952, ERP; Roper, *Where the People Stand* (CBS broadcast), 22 Feb. 1948, ERP.

57. George Gallup (with H. G. Wells), "The Shape of Things to Come—1939," *Cosmopolitan,* Feb. 1939, 27; announcer, *Where the People Stand* (CBS broadcast), 15 Feb. 1948, ERP; Gallup, "Public Opinion, 1941," *Current History and Forum,* 23 Jan. 1941, 12; Michael Warner, "The Mass Public and the Mass Subject," in *The Phantom Public Sphere,* ed. Bruce Robbins (Minneapolis: University of Minnesota Press, 1993).

58. Henry Cassirer to Roper, 27 Feb. 1949, ERP.
59. Mosteller et al., *Pre-election Polls of 1948*, 53; Roper, interview with Robert O. Carlson, 25; O'Malley, "Black Beans and White Beans," 23; Williston Rich, "The Human Yardstick," *Saturday Evening Post*, 21 Jan. 1939, 70. A member of the AIPO office, itself a for-profit venture, noted in the late 1930s that only market research dollars allowed Gallup to "keep the thing alive financially" (John Maloney as quoted in Robinson, *Measure of Democracy*, 48).
60. Roper, "Fortune Quarterly Survey IV," 104; editor's note, "Fortune Quarterly Survey II," *Fortune*, October 1935, 56; Elmo Roper, "Fortune Quarterly Survey III," *Fortune*, January 1936, 46. Roper to Saville R. Davis, 15 Oct. 1952; Roper to Henry Link, 29 Sept. 1941; Roper to Albert Furth, 2 Jan. 1946; all in ERP.
61. Robert C. Dille to Roper, 14 Sept. 1956; Morrie Brickman to Eric Hodgins, 25 Sept. 1958; both in ERP. Readership services based on the "Gallup Method" had been created by Percival White of the Market Research Corporation of America and then Daniel Starch; they were quickly adopted by newspaper firms to guide editorial and advertising material beginning in the 1930s.
62. Memorandum from Eric to Roper, Bud and Carol, 19 Aug. 1957; Roper to Louis Cowan, 11 May 1948; Roper to the editor, *Pittsburgh Post-Gazette*, 24 Nov. 1948; both in ERP.
63. L. A. Kamins to Roper, 30 July 1946 and Roper's reply, 9 August 1946, ERP. See Elmo Roper, "The Public Looks at Business," *Harvard Business Review* 27 (1949): 165–174. Arthur Kornhauser, "Are Public Opinion Polls Fair to Organized Labor?" *Public Opinion Quarterly* 10 (1946–1947): 484–500, quotation on 485. Kornhauser's study examined 155 questions from 1940–1945, but his findings were particularly true of the AIPO. He found heavy bias both in the way questions were worded (of 155 questions, only 4 had a pro-labor bias, 80 to 90 were slanted against labor, and the remainder were balanced) and in the ways results were interpreted. See the replies to Kornhauser by Henry C. Link and Albert D. Freiberg, John H. Platten Jr., and Kenneth E. Clark in "Is Dr. Kornhauser Fair to Organized Pollers?" *Public Opinion Quarterly* 11 (1947): 198–212. Robert Lynd to Roper, 5 Apr. 1941; see also R. Lynd to Roper, 24 Jan. 1950; both in ERP.
64. Robinson, *Measure of Democracy*, 54. For an example of a poll on anti-minority sentiment, see Roper, "What People Are Thinking: Suspi-

cion of Minorities in U.S. Shown in Survey," *New York Herald Tribune,* 30 Oct. 1947. Roper ran other poll results on anti-Semitism and minority issues in his columns for 25 Jan., 8 Feb., 15 Feb., and 22 Nov. 1945; 7 Feb. and 16 May 1946; and 7 Oct. 1948. Roper to Geoffrey Parsons, *New York Herald Tribune,* 19 Jan. 1945. Mark Ethridge, *Louisville Times,* to Roper, 7 Mar. 1945; Roper replied on 14 Mar., saying that he was puzzled by this response, since at the *Herald Tribune* his "four articles on anti-minority sentiment brought a deluge of mail." All three letters in ERP.

65. Roper to Joseph McConnell, the president of NBC, 13 Dec. 1951, ERP. See also Roper to George Cornish, *New York Herald Tribune,* 2 Feb. 1945; Roper to Mark Ethridge, 14 Mar. 1945; Roper to Gardner Cowles, *Des Moines Register-Tribune,* 23 May 1945; Roper to Frank Stanton, CBS, 9 Aug. 1949; all in ERP. Newman, *Radio Active,* 109. "Elmo Roper: Public Opinion Is Big News in an Election Year," An NBC Packaged Program, ERP.

66. Roper to Donald Hobart, 18 May 1942, ERP; Ohmer, "Measuring Desire," 4–5; Newman, *Radio Active,* 29.

67. Memorandum from Roper to Bud Roper, Lou Harris, and Carol Crusius, 3 May 1955, ERP. On the shift from mass to niche marketing, see Buzzard, *Chains of Gold;* Joseph Turow, *Breaking Up America: Advertisers and the New Media World* (Chicago: University of Chicago Press, 1997); and Lizabeth Cohen, *A Consumers' Republic: The Politics of Mass Consumption in Postwar America* (New York: Alfred A. Knopf, 2003), 292–344. On segmentation in political campaigns, see Brian Balogh, "'Mirrors of Desires': Interest Groups, Elections, and the Targeted Style in Twentieth-Century America," in *The Democratic Experiment: New Directions in American Political History,* ed. Meg Jacobs, William Novak, and Julian Zelizer (Princeton: Princeton University Press, 2003), 222–249.

4. The Majority Talks Back

1. Roper, "Fortune Survey," *Fortune,* Apr. 1947, 6; ERP; Louis Moss, "Social Science and the Gallup Poll," *International Journal of Opinion and Attitude Research* 3 (1949): 23–25; Robert K. Merton and Paul K. Hatt, "Election Polling Forecasts and Public Images of Social Science: A Case Study in the Shaping of Opinion among a Strategic Public,"

Public Opinion Quarterly 13 (1949): 185–222. See also Don Cahalan, "Implications to the Social Sciences of the 1948 Mispredictions," *International Journal of Opinion and Attitude Research* 3 (1949): 157–168. An extended symposium entitled "The Opinion Polls and the 1948 U.S. Presidential Election" appears in the Spring, Summer, and Fall 1949 issues of *International Journal of Opinion and Attitude Research.*

2. Frederick Mosteller et al., *The Pre-election Polls of 1948: Report to the Committee on Analysis of Pre-election Polls and Forecasts,* Bulletin 60 (New York: Social Science Research Council, 1949), vii–viii, 1, 291. The SSRC's "long-established concern with the search for new knowledge" gave it "an active interest in developments relating to opinion and attitude research," and in 1945 it had established, with the National Research Council, a joint Committee on Measurement of Opinion, Attitudes and Consumer Wants. Another analysis of the 1948 polls would be launched just after the SSRC investigation; see Norman C. Meier and Harold W. Saunders, eds., *The Polls and Public Opinion* (New York: Henry Holt, 1949).

3. "An American Mother" to Roper, undated, 1950, ERP; anonymous (Santa Clara, CA) to Gallup, 20 Oct. 1952, GGP; John Libko (New York City) to Roper, 29 June 1952, ERP; I. Dudley Morris (New York City) to Roper, 9 Feb. 1953, ERP.

4. Gallup, "We, the People, Are Like This—A Report on How and What We Think," *New York Times Magazine,* 8 June 1941, 3; George Gallup and Saul Forbes Rae, *The Pulse of Democracy: The Public-Opinion Poll and How It Works* (New York: Simon and Schuster, 1940), 232, 158. Gallup portrayed Louisiana as a "banana republic" and as a "major blot on the nation's reputation for open and honest elections" (154).

5. John Harding, "Refusals as a Source of Bias," and Donald Rugg, "'Trained' vs. 'Untrained' Interviewers," in Hadley Cantril and Associates, *Gauging Public Opinion* (Princeton: Princeton University Press, 1944), 119, 90–91; Alfred Politz, "Validity and Reliability of Marketing Studies," speech to the Chicago chapter of the American Marketing Association in January 1948, in *The Politz Papers: Science and Truth in Marketing Research,* ed. Hugh S. Hardy (Chicago: American Marketing Association, 1990), 54; Mosteller et al., *Pre-election Polls of 1948,* 287.

6. Charles A. H. Thomson, "Public Relations of the 1940 Census," *Pub-*

lic Opinion Quarterly 4 (1940): 311–318; Pearl London, "Ringing Doorbells with a Gallup Reporter," *New York Times Magazine,* 1 Sept. 1940, 9.

7. See George Gallup, "Can We Trust the Common People?" *Good Housekeeping,* Oct. 1940, 21; and idem, "Putting Public Opinion to Work," *Scribner's Magazine,* Nov. 1936, 36. Roper to Rabbi Elmer Berger, 22 Apr. 1952; CBS promotional packet for Roper's broadcast series *Where the People Stand,* Mar. 1948; "Station Acceptance List," 8 July 1952; Joan V. Wilkens, NBC, to Mildred Strachan, 8 May 1953 and enclosure listing all stations carrying Roper's program; Elmo Roper, "A Pollster Can Never Be Right," *New York Herald Tribune,* July 1948, no date; Roper to Joseph McConnell, NBC, 13 Dec. 1951; Roper to Frank Stanton, CBS, 9 Aug. 1949; all in ERP. On one occasion Roper estimated that a third of this correspondence came from critics (Roper to Vermont Royster, 11 June 1952, ERP).

8. Patricia Esther Filbert (Orlando, FL) to Gallup, 14 Apr. 1956, GGI; anonymous woman (Carlisle, PA) to Gallup, 5 Apr. 1954, GGI; Mrs. W. G. Rouse (Dillon, MT) to Roper, 18 June 1951, ERP.

9. Elizabeth A. Stein (New York City) to Roper, 1 Aug. (year unknown), ERP.

10. Alice W. Baker (Redlands, CA) to Roper, 3 June 1951, ERP; Contented Ford Employee (Dearborn, MI) to Roper, 19 Sept. 1947, ERP; Charles E. Moore to Gallup, 7 May 1956, GGI; R. F. Holmes, 24 Oct. (1955 or 1956) to Gallup, GGI; anonymous to Gallup, undated, GGI.

11. Roper quoted this letter in his CBS broadcast *Where the People Stand,* 2 Jan. 1949; Roper, interview with Robert O. Carlson, 14 Aug. 1968, 52; both in ERP.

12. Unsigned to Gallup, undated, GGI; Reverend Joseph D. Mitchell (Signal Mountain, TN) to Roper, 25 Apr. 1949, ERP. An example of the last category of writer is Byron T. Gloor (New York City) to Roper, 30 Dec. 1952, ERP.

13. E. Dayton to Gallup, 21 Nov. 1954, GGI.

14. London, "Ringing Doorbells," 9.

15. For the charge of "guesswork," see Daniel Plaro (New York City) to Roper, 18 May 1952, ERP. The Taft committee chairman was quoted by Gallup in "Public Opinion and Depth Materials," speech to the American Association of Public Opinion Research, 15 June 1952, GGP.

16. Elinor Nevins (Nashville, TN) to Gallup, undated, GGP; Harry

Baruchin (New York City) to Roper, 8 May 1950, ERP; anonymous to Gallup (1956?), GGI.

17. Mrs. Robert W. Poindexter (Aspen, CO) to Gallup, 11 Nov. 1955, GGI; Robert Robusto (Baltimore) to Gallup, 29 July 1964, GGP.

18. D. J. Stoner (Pittsburgh) to Roper, 12 Sept. 1952, ERP; George Gallup, "Polling Public Opinion," *Current History*, Feb. 1940, 24. Gallup attributed the tailing off of this particular complaint in his last two decades of polling to growing public familiarity with scientific sampling. See Gallup, interview with Don Winslow, 29 Nov. 1979, pt. 2, 31, GGP.

19. R. D. Keim (New York) to Roper, 25 June 1946, ERP.

20. Roper to R. D. Keim, 19 July 1946, ERP. On another such occasion, Roper's secretary appended the note: "We wish that we could put you in touch with some of the other people who say to our interviewers something to the effect that 'This is the third time I have been interviewed by one organization or another in the last month!'" (Mildred Strachan to D. J. Stoner, 12 Sept. 1952, ERP). Gallup had a similar standard reply, drawn from his *Guide to Public Opinion Polls* (Princeton: Princeton University Press, 1948): "Since the average life expectancy of a person reaching the age of twenty-one is about fifty years, this means that the average person would have less than one chance in ten of ever being interviewed in his lifetime, with samples based upon an average of 3,000 per week." See Constance Wright, secretary to Gallup, to Mrs. Robert W. Poindexter (Aspen, CO), 30 Dec. 1955, GGI.

21. Gallup "Putting Public Opinion to Work," 39.

22. Susan Herbst, *Numbered Voices: How Opinion Polling Has Shaped American Politics* (Chicago: University of Chicago Press, 1993), 89–111, quotation on 107. John K. Jessup to Roper, 5 Jan. 1955, and Roper's reply of 25 Jan. 1955, both in ERP. The editor is quoted in Merton and Hatt, "Election Polling Forecasts," 207.

23. Roper, *Where the People Stand* (CBS broadcast), 13 Jan. 1952, ERP (Roper moved to NBC in 1952). See the running critique of the polls in one publication alone: Jerome H. Spingarn, "These Public-Opinion Polls," *Harper's*, Dec. 1938, 97–104; Paul Studenski, "How Polls Can Mislead," *Harper's*, Dec. 1939, 80–83; Lindsay Rogers, "Do the Gallup Polls Measure Opinion?" *Harper's*, Nov. 1941, 623–632; and Ernest Borneman, "The Public Opinion Myth," *Harper's*, July 1947, 30–

40. This vein of criticism has not abated. Key works include Pierre Bourdieu, "Public Opinion Does Not Exist," in *Communication and Class Struggle,* ed. Armand Mattelart and Seth Siegelaub (New York: International General, 1979); Benjamin Ginsberg, *The Captive Public: How Mass Opinion Promotes State Power* (New York: Basic Books, 1986); Christopher Hitchens, "Voting in the Passive Voice: What Polling Has Done to American Democracy," *Harper's,* Apr. 1992, 45–52; Lawrence R. Jacobs and Robert Y. Shapiro, *Politicians Don't Pander: Political Manipulation and the Loss of Democratic Responsiveness* (Chicago: University of Chicago Press, 2000); Adam J. Berinsky, *Silent Voices: Public Opinion and Political Participation in America* (Princeton: Princeton University Press, 2004); and George F. Bishop, *The Illusion of Public Opinion: Fact and Artifact in American Opinion Polls* (Lanham, MD: Rowman and Littlefield, 2005).

24. George Gallup, "Statement on the Karabian Bills Submitted to the California Legislature," Oct. 1973, GGP; Gallup, Testimony before the Committee to Investigate Campaign Expenditures, House of Representatives, 78th Congress, second session, pt. 12, Dec. 28, 1944; "Lee Knous Hits the Target," *Lafayette (IN) Leader,* 4 Dec. 1948. See also George Gallup, "On the Regulation of Polling," *Public Opinion Quarterly* 12 (1948–1949): 733–735; and Benjamin Ginzburg, "Dr. Gallup on the Mat," *Nation,* 16 Dec. 1944, 737–739. The House of Representatives' Special Committee to Investigate Tax Exempt Foundations also inquired into a 1954 poll conducted by Roper on opinions about the United Nations; the Committee wished to know if the poll had been supported by tax-exempt funds as well as "more about its history, sponsorship of the study and bias of the consultants and commentators" (Norman Dodd to Roper, 18 Mar. 1954, and Roper's reply of 24 Mar. 1954, both in ERP).

25. Roper to Margaret Hull (Woodside, NY), 3 July 1951, ERP; the 1948 letters were quoted by Roper in "Pollster Can Never Be Right."

26. Elinor Nevins (Nashville, TN) to Gallup, undated, GGP; anonymous (Pomona, CA) to Gallup, 23 Oct. 1954, GGI. Michael Schudson argues that journalists did not grapple with the problems of bias and objectivity in a serious way until after World War I; see his *Discovering the News: A Social History of American Newspapers* (New York: Basic Books, 1978), 121–159.

27. Harry Baruchin (New York City) to Roper, 8 May 1950, ERP; Moss,

"Social Science and the Gallup Poll," 23–25. See also Arthur Kornhauser, "Are Public Opinion Polls Fair to Organized Labor?" *Public Opinion Quarterly* 10 (1946–1947): 484–500.

28. Harry Baruchin (New York City) to Roper, 8 May 1950, ERP.
29. Advertisement, Citizens Committee for Eisenhower, *Chicago Daily News*, 10 July 1952; Ann Scott (New York City) to Roper, 14 Sept. 1950; H. Schuyler Foster, Department of State, to Rose Voce, Roper's secretary at Rockefeller Plaza, 2 Aug. and 14 Aug. 1950; H. Roth Newpher, International Broadcasting Division, Department of State, to Roper, 24 Oct. 1947; Monthly Opinion Report #1, Feb. 1952, Democratic National Committee, Research Division; Chester Bowles to Roper, 21 Oct. 1946, and Roper's reply, 24 Oct. 1946; Paul M. Nutt[?] (illegible), Office of the Administrator, FSA, to Roper, 3 Apr. 1942. All in ERP.
30. See Emil St. Sauer (Utica, MI) to Gallup, undated (1955?) and Richard Dovey (Houston, TX) to Gallup, 24 Mar. 1957; both in GGI. Stewart M. Ogilvy to Roper, 12 Oct. 1950, ERP; W. B. Chilton (Springfield, TN), undated (1955 or 1956), GGI; "Anti Loaded Dice" to Gallup, undated, GGI.
31. Douglas Denton Ward (Fontana, CA) to Gallup, 13 Apr. 1956, GGI; James A. Webb (Athens, GA) to Gallup, 23 June 1961, GGP; Frank Stanton, CBS, to Roper, 29 Mar. 1946, ERP.
32. Spingarn, "These Public-Opinion Polls," 102; E. B. Mann, *Guns Magazine,* to E. H. Ruby of the AIPO, 1 Sept. 1959. See also F. T. Hopkins, Solano Shooters, Inc., to Gallup, 11 Sept. 1959; Mel Hovland (Hollandale, MN) to Gallup, 2 Sept. 1959; and Gallup to John Berryman (Brooklyn, NY), 16 Mar. 1960. The NRA went on to campaign for an investigation of Gallup by the ethics committee of the American Psychological Association; see George Gallup to Chairman, Committee on Ethical Standards, American Psychological Association, 19 Nov. 1959. All in GGP.
33. Ina F. Hazen (Youngstown, OH) to Gallup, 17 Jan. 1955, GGI.
34. Eleanor Holmes (Ansonia, CT) to Roper, 6 June 1951, ERP; W. C. Hollingworth (Long Beach, CA) to Roper, 3 June 1951, ERP.
35. Joseph E. Glenn (Houston, TX) to Gallup, 23 Nov. 1954; "Not-Your-Dirty-Biased Lies" to Gallup, undated; J. M. Mottey to Gallup, Jan. (1955?); Anonymous to Gallup, undated, 1956; Alfred Petrash (Houston, TX) to Gallup, 15 Feb. 1956; all in GGI.

36. Margaret Jamison (Dallas, TX) to Roper, 12 Nov. 1957, ERP.

37. Roper, "A Pollster Can Never Be Right."

38. Byron T. Gloor (New York City) to Roper, 30 Dec. 1952, ERP; Theodore F. Baer (Laguna Beach, CA) to Roper, 26 Oct. 1950, ERP; Richard G. Hubler, "George Horace Gallup: Oracle in Tweed," *Forum and Century*, Feb. 1941, 95; Rogers, "Do the Gallup Polls Measure Opinion?" 623.

39. Roper, *Where the People Stand* (CBS broadcast), 28 May 1950, ERP; "Galloping Off!" *Chicago Tribune*, 5 Nov. 1942, ERP.

40. Edward Murrow, "Edward R. Murrow with the News," CBS broadcast, 5 Nov. 1952. For Roper's chagrined response, see his letter to Murrow, 27 Jan. 1953. Both in ERP.

41. Memorandum from Henry Luce to Mssrs. Paine, Furth, Davenport, Jessup, and Roper, 9 Apr. 1949; Roper to George Engelhard, 16 Mar. 1949; Mrs. Frances Rasmussen (Alameda, CA) to Roper, undated. All in ERP.

42. Don Wharton, "Man of Straws," *Today*, 12 Sept. 1936; Roper, *Where the People Stand* (CBS broadcast), 7 Nov. 1948, ERP.

43. Roper, *Where the People Stand* (CBS broadcast), 15 Feb. 1948, ERP; ibid., 2 Jan. 1949, ERP; Gallup and Rae, *Pulse of Democracy*, 13; Elmo Roper, "Problems and Possibilities in the Sampling Technique," *Journalism Quarterly* 18 (1941): 1.

44. Roper, *Where the People Stand* (CBS broadcast), 22 Feb. 1948; CBS-TV program with Elmo Roper, 27 Sept. 1951; both in ERP.

45. See, for example, Morrie Brickman, National Newspaper Syndicate, to Eric Hodgins, 25 Sept. 1958, ERP. He wanted Roper to make his column warmer and more personal, suggesting that he add more of the "human element" to flesh out the reporting of statistical percentages. "Elmo Roper: Public Opinion Is Big News in an Election Year," An NBC Packaged Program, 1952, ERP; Roper, *Where the People Stand* (CBS broadcast), 28 Mar. 1948, ERP; Gallup and Rae, *Pulse of Democracy*, 3. On the "personal touch" in advertising, see Roland Marchand, *Advertising the American Dream: Making Way for Modernity, 1920–1940* (Berkeley: University of California Press, 1985), 13–16.

46. Gallup and Rae, *Pulse of Democracy*, 4; George Gallup, "Polls and Prophets," *Current History and Forum*, 7 Nov. 1940, 14; Gallup, "We, the People, Are Like This," 3.

47. Gallup and Rae, *Pulse of Democracy*, 117.
48. For one survey on the polls, see Paul B. Sheatsley, "The Public Relations of the Polls," *International Journal of Opinion and Attitude Research* 2 (1948–1949): 453–468. For an earlier assessment of public opinion on polls, see Eric F. Goldman, "Polls on the Polls," *Public Opinion Quarterly* 8 (1944): 461–467. The editor is quoted in Merton and Hatt, "Election Polling Forecasts," 205–206.
49. Mildred Parten, *Surveys, Polls, and Samples: Practical Procedures* (New York: Harper and Bros., 1950), 3; Roper to George Engelhard, 16 Mar. 1949, ERP; Roper to Leslie Moore, 16 Nov. 1956, ERP.
50. Cantril et al., *Gauging Public Opinion*, vii.
51. Warren C. Price, "What Daily News Executives Think of Public Opinion Polls," *Journalism Quarterly* 30 (1953): 287–299, quotation on 287; Merton and Hatt, "Election Polling Forecasts," 214.
52. Gallup, "The Future of Polls," speech to Iowa City Conference, Feb. 1949; Gallup, "Polling Experiences, 1936–1948," speech at World Association of Public Opinion Research meeting, Paris, France, 7 Sept. 1949. Both in GGP.
53. Robert A. Baker (San Francisco, CA) to Roper, 15 Dec. 1952, ERP.
54. Mosteller et al., *Pre-election Polls of 1948*, 290, 80.
55. George Gallup, "The Case for the Public Opinion Polls," *New York Times Magazine*, 27 Feb. 1949, 11; "The Black & White Beans," *Time*, 3 May 1948.
56. John J. FitzGibbons (Goulds, FL) to Gallup, undated, GGI. Richard W. Steele has found that FDR, for example, trusted polls more than other public opinion measures such as the mail, personal contacts, and reports from inside governmental departments (Steele, "The Pulse of the People: Franklin D. Roosevelt and the Gauging of American Public Opinion," *Journal of Contemporary History* 9 [1974]: 195–216). On this point, see Susan Herbst, *Numbered Voices*, 89–111.

5. Surveying Normal Selves

1. Lee Cameron, "Is the Kinsey Report a Hoax?" *Life Today*, Aug. 1950, 3; "Kinsey Survey 'Differs' from Vote Polls," *Bloomington (IN) Daily Herald*, 4 Nov. 1948; "Editorial Points," *Boston Globe*, 18 Feb. 1949; "Kinsey Sex Book Blasted by Cardinal," *Indianapolis News*, 29 Dec. 1948. The *Baltimore Sun* reported that critics of Kinsey's

sampling process "increased in number after the error made by the public opinion polls in predicting the outcome of the last presidential election" ("Outline Given By Dr. Kinsey," *Baltimore Sun*, 24 Nov. 1948).

2. Alfred C. Kinsey, Wardell B. Pomeroy, and Clyde E. Martin, *Sexual Behavior in the Human Male* (Philadelphia: W. B. Saunders, 1948), 7. Here and throughout I refer to Kinsey, the lead investigator, as the author of the *Sexual Behavior* volumes. Contemporaries tended to identify him as the chief author of the Reports, and Clyde Martin noted that "all the written text was by Kinsey" (interview of Clyde Martin by James Jones, 8 Apr. 1971, HIT, #71-10, p. 6). Two more volumes were eventually published from the data after Kinsey's death in 1956.

3. John Gregory, "Clinical Study of the American Male," *Philadelphia Sunday Bulletin*, 8 Feb. 1948.

4. Harry Oosterhuis, *Stepchildren of Nature: Krafft-Ebing, Psychiatry, and the Making of Sexual Identity* (Chicago: University of Chicago Press, 2000); Sabine Frühstück, *Colonizing Sex: Sexology and Social Control in Modern Japan* (Berkeley: University of California Press, 2003), 83–115; Margaret Mead, *Coming of Age in Samoa: A Psychological Study of Primitive Youth for Western Civilisation* (New York: W. Morrow, 1928); Nathan G. Hale Jr., *The Rise and Crisis of Psychoanalysis in the United States: Freud and the Americans, 1917–1985* (New York: Oxford University Press, 1995); Katherine B. Davis, *Factors in the Sex Life of Twenty-Two Hundred Women* (New York: Harper and Bros., 1929); Robert Latou Dickinson and Lura Beam, *A Thousand Marriages: A Medical Study of Sex Adjustment* (Baltimore: Williams and Wilkins, 1931); Lewis M. Terman et al., *Psychological Factors in Marital Happiness* (New York: McGraw-Hill, 1938). For a review of early sexological research, including nineteenth-century European efforts, see Paul Robinson, *The Modernization of Sex: Havelock Ellis, Alfred Kinsey, William Masters, and Virginia Johnson* (New York: Harper and Row, 1976). See also Vern L. Bullough, *Science in the Bedroom: A History of Sex Research* (New York: Basic Books, 1994); and Julia A. Ericksen with Sally A. Steffen, *Kiss and Tell: Surveying Sex in the Twentieth Century* (Cambridge, MA: Harvard University Press, 1999). The latter estimate that 750 sex surveys were completed during the twentieth century (viii). On British sex surveys in the same period, including the "Little Kinsey" survey, see Liz Stanley,

*Sex Surveyed, 1949–1994: From Mass-Observation's "Little Kinsey"
to the National Survey and the Hite Reports* (London: Taylor and
Francis, 1995).

5. *Sexual Behavior in the Human Male,* 19–20. As Jeffrey Weeks writes,
Kinsey "was never over-generous in his assessment of the contribution
of either his contemporaries or his precursors" (Weeks, *Sexuality and
Its Discontents: Meanings, Myths and Modern Sexualities* [London:
Routledge and Kegan Paul, 1985], 69.

6. Kinsey's previous published work included *Introduction to Biology*
(1926), *The Gall Wasp Genus Cynips: A Study in the Origins of the
Species* (1930), and *The Origins of Higher Categories in Cynips*
(1936). The marriage course was a noncredit class for male and female
seniors and graduate students dealing with "the legal, economic, sociological, psychological, and biological aspects of marriage." Details on
the controversy it provoked at Indiana can be found in Thomas D.
Clark, "Professor Kinsey at Indiana," in *Indiana History: A Book of
Readings,* ed. Ralph D. Gray (Bloomington: Indiana University Press,
1994), 313–323, or in any biography of Kinsey.

7. Cornelia V. Christenson, *Kinsey: A Biography* (Bloomington: Indiana
University Press, 1971); Wardell B. Pomeroy, *Dr. Kinsey and the Institute for Sex Research* (New York: Harper and Row, 1972). The same
capsule story is related in Bullough, *Science in the Bedroom.* Bullough
writes, for example, that Kinsey "ended up" as coordinator of the marriage course and started taking students' histories "to add to his own
knowledge" (168).

8. Janice M. Irvine, *Disorders of Desire: Sex and Gender in Modern
American Sexology* (Philadelphia: Temple University Press, 1990), 35.
For detailed accounts of the research agendas of the Bureau of Social
Hygiene and the Committee for Research on Problems of Sex, see
James H. Jones, *Alfred C. Kinsey: A Public/Private Life* (New York:
W. W. Norton, 1997), 417–441; and Sophie D. Aberle and George W.
Corner, *Twenty-five Years of Sex Research: History of the National Re-
search Council Committee for Research in Problems of Sex, 1922–
1947* (Philadelphia: W. B. Saunders, 1953), 45–46.

9. Bullough, *Science in the Bedroom,* 169–171; Aberle and Corner,
Twenty-five Years of Sex Research, 48.

10. Albert Deutsch, "Daring Pioneer Conducts First Mass Study of Human Sex Habits," *PM,* 7 Jan. 1947; Herbert Ratner to Alan Gregg, as
quoted in David Allyn, "Private Acts/Public Policy: Alfred Kinsey, the

American Law Institute and the Privatization of American Sexual Morality," *Journal of American Studies* 30 (1996): 421 n. 59; Pomeroy, *Dr. Kinsey,* 262. Kinsey himself, according to his collaborator Paul Gebhard, "felt we should have the most reputable and conservative publishing house we could find" (interview of Paul Gebhard by James Jones, 29 Oct. 1971, HIT, #71-55, p. 51).

11. Weeks, *Sexuality and Its Discontents,* 79. On the obstacles facing the emerging field of sexology in the late nineteenth and twentieth century, see ibid., 61–95; see also Lynn Gorchov, "Sexual Science and Sexual Politics: American Sex Research, 1920–1956" (Ph.D. diss., Johns Hopkins University, 2003). Henry L. Minton, *Departing from Deviance: A History of Homosexual Rights and Emancipatory Science in America* (Chicago: University of Chicago Press, 2001), 176–195; interview of Clyde Martin, HIT, 42–43; interview of Glenn Ramsey by James Jones, 15 Mar. 1972, HIT, #72-1, pp. 20–21.

12. See Geoffrey Gorer, "Justification by Numbers: A Commentary on the Kinsey Report," *American Scholar,* Summer 1948, 280.

13. *Sexual Behavior in the Human Male,* 11–13; interview of Wardell Pomeroy by James Jones, 19 July 1971, HIT, #71-21, pp. 12, 14–15; Clark, "Professor Kinsey at Indiana," 318. The Reports were preceded by at least one uproar over sexual surveying, involving the distribution of sex questionnaires at the University of Missouri in 1929. See Lawrence J. Nelson, *Rumors of Indiscretion: The University of Missouri "Sex Questionnaire" Scandal in the Jazz Age* (Columbia: University of Missouri Press, 2003).

14. George Gallup and Saul Forbes Rae, *The Pulse of Democracy: The Public-Opinion Poll and How It Works* (New York: Simon and Schuster, 1940), 180. Two of Gallup's questions read: "Would you favor a government bureau that would distribute information concerning venereal diseases?" (Dec. 1936) and "In strict confidence and at no expense to you, would you like to be given by your physician a blood test for syphilis?" (Aug. 1937). Deutsch, "Daring Pioneer."

15. "Fake Kinsey Quiz Irks Radcliffe Girls," *Pawtucket (RI) Times,* 25 May 1951; "Women Given Warning Sex Queries Hoax," *Cumberland (MD) Times,* 5 Sept. 1951. For other instances, see "Citizens Warned of Man Questioning about Married Life," *Galveston (TX) Tribune,* 6 July 1951; "Button Your Lip, Josephine, If 'Kinsey' Man Phones You," *Rochester (NY) Sun,* 5 Jan. 1950; and clippings files, KIA.

16. Mrs. E. E. K. S. (woman, Silver Spring, MD) to Kinsey, 9 Mar. 1951,

KST; B. S. (woman, Bronx, NY) to Kinsey, 30 Dec. 1948, KST; Kinsey to B. S., 4 Jan. 1949, KST. In accordance with the guidelines of the Kinsey Institute for Research in Sex, Gender, and Reproduction, I have used the initials rather than the full names of Kinsey's correspondents.

17. "Kinsey Imposter Caught," *St. Paul Dispatch*, 25 Apr. 1950; "Jailed for Private 'Kinsey' Survey," *Chicago Sun-Times*, 6 June 1951; "Poor Man's Dr. Kinsey Discovers Sex Survey Often Leads to Jail," *Blytheville (AR) Courier-News*, 6 June 1951; "Producer of Obscene Movies Convicted, Kinsey Gets Films," *Baltimore Sun*, 13 Dec. 1952 (this article indicated that the police watched the films carefully, finding them "frail of plot and weak in suspense"). In 1950, U.S. Customs confiscated a collection of sexually explicit materials Kinsey had collected overseas; in 1957 the New York Federal District Court finally ruled in favor of the Institute for Sex Research in the ensuing lawsuit (Bullough, *Science in the Bedroom*, 184). "Overheard in Hollywood," *Motion Picture*, Oct. 1948.

18. Aberle and Corner, *Twenty-five Years of Sex Research*, 2. Carol Tavris argues that the low status of sexology is "one of the major reasons for the emphasis in modern sex research on physiology" (Tavris, *The Mismeasure of Woman* [New York: Simon and Schuster, 1992], 222).

19. *Sexual Behavior in the Human Male*, 5; see Kinsey's discussion in "The Scientific Objective," in Alfred C. Kinsey, Wardell B. Pomeroy, Clyde E. Martin, and Paul H. Gebhard, *Sexual Behavior in the Human Female* (Philadelphia: W. B. Saunders, 1953), 7–8; Alan Gregg, preface, in *Sexual Behavior in the Human Male*, v; Lotta Dempsey, "Dr. Kinsey Talks about Women," *Chatelaine*, Aug. 1949, 11; James R. Miller, "Sex Behavior of the American Male," *'47: The Magazine of the Year*, Dec. 1947, 14; E. Parker Johnson, "Books," *Bowdoin Alumnus*, Feb. 1948; Frank Groom Kirtz, "Books for Lawyers," *American Bar Association Journal* 35 (1949): 836.

20. *Sexual Behavior in the Human Female*, 8–9; Hans Lehfeldt, review of *Sexual Behavior in the Human Male*, in *Journal of Sex Education* (Dec. 1948): 113.

21. Beth Bailey, *From Front Porch to Back Seat: Courtship in Twentieth Century America* (Baltimore: Johns Hopkins University Press, 1989). See Ernest R. Groves, *Social Problems of the Family* (Philadelphia: Lippincott, 1927); Gilbert Hamilton, *A Research in Marriage* (New York: A. C. Boni, 1929); and Ernest W. Burgess and Leonard S. Cot-

trell, *Predicting Success and Failure in Marriage* (New York: Prentice-Hall, 1939).

22. *Sexual Behavior in the Human Female,* 10–12; Kinsey as quoted in "Kinsey Speaks Out," *Newsweek,* 12 Apr. 1948, 51.

23. For an extended commentary on the Reports' ideology, see Robinson, *Modernization of Sex,* 49–99, quotation on 50; Weeks, *Sexuality and Its Discontents,* 85; *Sexual Behavior in the Human Male,* 202. Janice Irvine explains Kinsey's philosophy this way: "that what is 'natural' is right, that sex is good and more is better" (*Disorders of Desire,* 37). Julia Ericksen and Sally Steffen write that Kinsey "proselytized in favor of tolerating all kinds of sexual tastes, a stance seemingly at odds with his insistence on scientific objectivity" (*Kiss and Tell,* 49).

24. Irvine, *Disorders of Desire,* 38, 51; *Sexual Behavior in the Human Female,* 13, 7–8; "Sexual Behavior in 7,789 Women," *Books on Trial,* Nov. 1953, 64.

25. Jones, *Alfred C. Kinsey*; Jonathan Gathorne-Hardy, *Alfred C. Kinsey: Sex the Measure of All Things* (London: Chatto and Windus, 1998), 82–91. Debate about Jones's biography has focused on his characterization of Kinsey as "homosexual" and his assessment of Kinsey's research as untrustworthy. Jones's critics charge first that Kinsey was happily married and sexually active with his wife (as well as other women) even as he formed sexual relationships with men; and that one point of his research was to destabilize categories such as "heterosexual" and "homosexual." Second, they note that extensive cleaning and rechecking of the Reports' data by Paul Gebhard in the 1970s confirmed most of Kinsey's statistical findings (Paul H. Gebhard and Alan B. Johnson, *The Kinsey Data: Marginal Tabulations of the 1938–1963 Interviews Conducted by the Institute for Sex Research* [Philadelphia: W. B. Saunders, 1979]). For reviews and critiques of Jones's biography, see Richard Rhodes, "Father of the Sexual Revolution," *New York Times,* 2 Nov. 1997; Martin Duberman, "Kinsey's Urethra (Jones: *Alfred C. Kinsey*)," *Nation,* 3 Nov. 1997; and Thomas Laqueur, "Sexual Behavior in the Social Scientist: Was Alfred Kinsey a Pioneer or a Pervert?" *Slate,* 4 Nov. 1997.

26. Ericksen and Steffen, *Kiss and Tell,* 57; interview of Glenn Ramsey, HIT, 7 (Ramsey, a participant in the marriage course, recalled that at the time when he gave his history, in 1938, "there was a fairly established set of questions"); Regina Markell Morantz, "The Scientist

as Sex Crusader: Alfred C. Kinsey and American Culture," *American Quarterly* 29 (1977): 566.

27. "The Average American City under a Ruthless Microscope," *Boston Herald*, 18 May 1929. James Jones notes that Kinsey's Harvard dissertation stood out in part for the size of the sample; indeed, Kinsey's critique of taxonomy as a field was similar to his critique of prior sex surveys: they both failed to collect enough samples. Jones additionally writes that after 1922 "the importance of varieties and individual variation became the defining features" of Kinsey's entomological work. See Jones, *Alfred C. Kinsey*, 201–230, quotation on 206. For further discussion of the continuities (and discontinuities) between Kinsey's insect and human research, see Stephen Jay Gould, "Of Wasps and WASPs," in his *The Flamingo's Smile: Reflections in Natural History* (New York: W. W. Norton, 1985); and Philip J. Pauly, *Biologists and the Promise of American Life: From Meriwether Lewis to Alfred Kinsey* (Princeton: Princeton University Press, 2000), 233–235.

28. *Sexual Behavior in the Human Male*, 9–10. On filming, see Jones, *Alfred C. Kinsey*, 605–614. For Masters and Johnson's techniques, see Irvine, *Disorders of Desire*, 78–86; and Robinson, *Modernization of Sex*, 120–190. Pomeroy, *Dr. Kinsey and the Institute for Sex Research*, 175–176, 232–233. Also see Paul Gebhard's account of Kinsey instructing him on the prevalence of homosexual activity in men's washrooms at Grand Central Station (interview of Paul Gebhard, HIT, 15–16). *Sexual Behavior in the Human Female*, 89–92.

29. To cite just one example of the suspicion aimed at survey subjects, see the discussion of whether Kinsey was getting "nice girls" or "exhibitionists" to agree to his interviews (Dempsey, "Dr. Kinsey Talks about Women").

30. *Sexual Behavior in the Human Male*, 41–42.

31. Ibid., 42; for Kinsey's account of drawing out a wary subject, see his description on p. 43.

32. Robert Van Gelder, "Interview with a Best-Selling Author: Alfred C. Kinsey," *Cosmopolitan*, May 1948, 118; Kinsey to J. M. (woman, Roseburg, OR), 18 Mar. 1952, KST; *Sexual Behavior in the Human Male*, 47–59; Gebhard and Johnson, *The Kinsey Data*, 20–22.

33. Kinsey to Dr. B. M. (man, Washington, DC), 25 June 1946, KST; interview of Paul Gebhard, HIT, 21. Anthropologist Clyde Kluckhohn's letter recommending Paul Gebhard for a research position with Kinsey

read: "Mr. Gebhard is not afraid of sex and has certainly learned to accept any type of human behavior without judgement in terms of our own culture" (Kluckhohn to Kinsey, 20 May 1946, correspondence between Kinsey and Gebhard, Martin, and Pomeroy, KIA).

34. An Institute secretary, for example, gave her sexual history as a condition of employment (interview of Eleanor Roehr by James Jones, 3 Sept. 1971, HIT, #71-40, p. 5). Interview of Paul Gebhard, HIT, 17, 23, 27; interview of Clyde Martin, HIT, 27.

35. In the end, more than 17,000 histories were recorded between 1938 and Kinsey's death in 1956. Another thousand or so were collected between 1956 and 1963; Kinsey himself recorded 7,985 in all. Paul Gebhard to Kinsey, 10 June 1954, correspondence between Kinsey and Gebhard, Martin, and Pomeroy, KIA; Bullough, *Science in the Bedroom,* 175; Gebhard and Johnson, *The Kinsey Data,* 12–13 (they note that "the original interview, in which forty-five minutes sufficed for a college student, had grown inexorably so that to adequately cover a moderately complex life several hours were required").

36. Pomeroy, *Dr. Kinsey,* 102–103.

37. Sophia J. Kleegman, "The Kinsey Report: Book Review and Roundup of Opinion," *American Journal of Psychotherapy* (July 1948): 414.

38. Gebhard and Johnson, *The Kinsey Data,* 16.

39. *Sexual Behavior in the Human Male,* 47–59; Clyde Kluckhohn to Kinsey, 20 May 1946, correspondence between Kinsey and Gebhard, Martin, and Pomeroy, KIA; *Sexual Behavior in the Human Female,* 37.

40. Robert M. Yerkes to the Chairman, Selective Service Board No. 1, 18 May 1942; Alan Gregg to Selective Service Board No. 1, 21 Oct. 1943; both in correspondence between Kinsey and Gebhard, Martin, and Pomeroy, KIA.

41. Lewis S. Terman, "Kinsey's 'Sexual Behavior in the Human Male': Some Comments and Criticism," *Psychological Bulletin* 45 (1948): 452; Anonymous, "I Was Interviewed by Dr. Kinsey," *Everybody's Digest,* Mar. 1950, 110; *Sexual Behavior in the Human Male,* 121–147. Pomeroy stated that the interviewers "could record within about ninety-eight percent of each other" (interview of Wardell Pomeroy, HIT, 23). Julia O'Connell Davidson and Derek Layder note that "even recent commentators comment favorably upon [Kinsey's] interviewing methods" (*Methods, Sex and Madness* [London: Routledge, 1994], 128).

42. Paul H. Gebhard, "The Evolution of a Sex Researcher," in *"How I*

Got into Sex," ed. Bonnie Bullough et al. (Amherst, NY: Prometheus, 1997), 167; Gebhard and Johnson, *The Kinsey Data,* 149–151, 238, 9; interview of Wardell Pomeroy, HIT, 15. On this form of survey tabulation, see Davidson and Layder, *Methods, Sex and Madness,* 83–86. More histories than noted here were collected, but for a variety of reasons not all of them would be used in compilation of the Reports.

43. Gebhard and Johnson, *The Kinsey Data,* 11.

44. Robinson, *Modernization of Sex,* 59, 116; Bullough, *Science in the Bedroom,* 180; Allyn, "Private Acts/Public Policy," 413–417 (Allyn argues that the absence of prostitution and public sex from Kinsey's numbers may have been motivated by Kinsey's interest in privatizing sexual activity and thus placing it outside the purview of legal regulation); Gebhard and Johnson, *The Kinsey Data,* tables 256, 424, and 44, on pp. 305, 473, and 91.

45. Robinson, *Modernization of Sex,* 93.

46. Jane Gerhard, *Desiring Revolution: Second-Wave Feminism and the Rewriting of American Sexual Thought, 1920 to 1982* (New York: Columbia University Press, 2001), 53–64. See also John P. De Cecco, "Sex and More Sex: A Critique of the Kinsey Conception of Human Sexuality," in *Homosexuality/Heterosexuality: Concepts of Sexual Orientation,* ed. David P. McWhirter, Stephanie A. Sanders, and June M. Reinisch (New York: Oxford University Press, 1990), 367–386; Davidson and Layder, *Methods, Sex and Madness,* 13–17; and Irvine, *Disorders of Desire,* 62.

47. Gebhard and Johnson, *The Kinsey Data,* 25; *Sexual Behavior in the Human Male,* 20, 93; William G. Cochran, *Statistical Problems of the Kinsey Report on Sexual Behavior in the Human Male* (Washington, DC: American Statistical Association, 1954). Ericksen and Steffen write that Kinsey ignored the advice of the ASA "and in fact never understood it" (*Kiss and Tell,* 58).

48. *Sexual Behavior in the Human Male,* 102–104; Kinsey to L. M. (woman, Stanford, CA), 5 Aug. 1948, KST.

49. *Sexual Behavior in the Human Male,* 93–102. For Kinsey's rationale for rejecting probability sampling in favor of the hundred-percent method, see *Sexual Behavior in the Human Female,* 23–31. Gebhard and Johnson, *The Kinsey Data,* 30.

50. *Sexual Behavior in the Human Male,* 18; Harry Benjamin, "The Kinsey Report: Book Review and Roundup of Opinion," *American Journal of*

Psychotherapy (July 1948): 400; Dempsey, "Dr. Kinsey Talks about Women," 10; James H. Lade, review of *Sexual Behavior in the Human Male,* in *Health News,* Apr. 1948, 16; George Gallup, *A Guide to Public Opinion Polls* (Princeton: Princeton University Press, 1944), 78.

51. *Sexual Behavior in the Human Male,* 34. It is unclear how Kinsey made this determination without obtaining a European sample.
52. Ibid., 17.
53. Yerkes is quoted in Jones, *Alfred C. Kinsey,* 440.
54. Irvine, *Disorders of Desire,* 43; Bentley Glass, "Sexual Behavior in the Human Male, White, U.S.A.," *Quarterly Review of Biology* 23 (1948): 39. On postwar pluralism, see Richard Polenberg, *One Nation Divisible: Class, Race, and Ethnicity in the United States since 1938* (New York: Penguin Books, 1980), 86–163; and Matthew Frye Jacobson, *Whiteness of a Different Color: European Immigrants and the Alchemy of Race* (Cambridge, MA: Harvard University Press, 1998), 246–273.
55. *Sexual Behavior in the Human Male,* 76; *Sexual Behavior in the Human Female,* 22.
56. Allyn, "Private Acts/Public Policy," 410 n. 18; Miriam Reumann, *American Sexual Character: Sex, Gender, and National Identity in the Kinsey Reports* (Berkeley: University of California Press, 2005), 235 n. 89; *Sexual Behavior in the Human Male,* 393.
57. Gebhard is quoted in Ericksen and Steffen, *Kiss and Tell,* 51; *Sexual Behavior in the Human Female,* 31.
58. This scale, still in use, is analyzed in McWhirter, Sanders, and Reinisch, *Homosexuality/Heterosexuality.* For an analysis of Kinsey's understanding of homosexuality and its impact, see Robinson, *Modernization of Sex,* 66–75; and Jennifer Terry, *An American Obsession: Science, Medicine, and Homosexuality in Modern Society* (Chicago: University of Chicago Press, 1999), 297–314. Michael Warner, *The Trouble with Normal: Sex, Politics, and the Ethics of Queer Life* (New York: Free Press, 1999), 55; *Sexual Behavior in the Human Male,* 199.
59. *Sexual Behavior in the Human Male,* 7, 39.
60. Ibid., 20 (his emphasis).
61. Kinsey to G. M. (man, Bloomington, IN), 22 May 1940, KST.
62. Seward Hiltner, *Sex Ethics and the Kinsey Reports* (New York: Association Press, 1953), 61; Van Gelder, "Interview with a Best-Selling Author," 118.

63. R. M. (woman, Terre Haute, IN) to Kinsey, 6 June 1951, and his reply, 9 June 1951, KST.
64. Kinsey to E. L. M. (man, Montauk, NY), 6 July 1951, KST.
65. Interview of Wardell Pomeroy, HIT, 2, 19.
66. E. S. S. and J. L. B. (women, New York City) to Kinsey, 12 Nov. 1946, KST.
67. E. S. S. (woman, New York City) to Kinsey, 26 Jan. 1948, KST.

6. The Private Lives of the Public

1. Paul Boyer, *Purity in Print: The Vice-Society Movement and Book Censorship in America* (New York: Scribner's, 1968); Allan M. Brandt, *No Magic Bullet: A Social History of Venereal Disease in the United States since 1880* (New York: Oxford University Press, 1985); Timothy J. Gilfoyle, *City of Eros: New York City, Prostitution, and the Commercialization of Sex, 1790–1920* (New York: W. W. Norton, 1992). On public images of sexuality, see Lary May, *Screening Out the Past: The Birth of Mass Culture and the Motion Picture Industry* (New York: Oxford University Press, 1980); Marybeth Hamilton, *"When I'm Bad, I'm Better": Mae West, Sex, and American Entertainment* (Berkeley: University of California Press, 1997); and Sharon R. Ullman, *Sex Seen: The Emergence of Modern Sexuality in America* (Berkeley: University of California Press, 1997).

2. David Allyn, "Private Acts/Public Policy: Alfred Kinsey, the American Law Institute and the Privatization of American Sexual Morality," *Journal of American Studies* 30 (1996): 417; Harry Benjamin, "The Kinsey Report: Book Review and Roundup of Opinion," *American Journal of Psychotherapy* (July 1948): 402; "'According to Statistics,'" *Philadelphia Boot and Shoe Recorder,* 1 May 1950.

3. Mrs. F. E. M. (Evanston, IL) to Kinsey, 6 Sept. 1953, KST; Malcolm W. Bingay, "News Values," *Tampa (FL) Times,* 17 Mar. 1949.

4. Nanette Kutner, "What I Know about Kinsey," *American Weekly,* 27 July 1952; "Here's Kinsey Again!" *Cleveland Press,* 5 Aug. 1952.

5. Thomas D. Clark, "Professor Kinsey at Indiana," in *Indiana History: A Book of Readings,* ed. Ralph D. Gray (Bloomington: Indiana University Press, 1994), 320; John D'Emilio and Estelle B. Freedman, *Intimate Matters: A History of Sexuality in America* (New York: Harper and Row, 1988), 285; Roger P. Bristol, "It Takes Courage to Stock 'Ta-

boos,'" *Library Journal*, 15 Feb. 1949, 261; Paul Denis, "New York Tall Tales," *New York Daily Compass*, 7 June 1949; Albert Deutsch, ed., *Sex Habits of American Men: A Symposium on the Kinsey Report* (New York: Prentice Hall, 1948); Morris L. Ernst and David Loth, *American Sexual Behavior and the Kinsey Report* (New York: Greystone Press, 1948); Donald Porter Geddes and Enid Curie, eds., *About the Kinsey Report: Observations by Eleven Experts on Sexual Behavior in the Human Male* (New York: American Library, 1948). Sales of the condensation are reported in Herbert H. Hyman and Paul B. Sheatsley, "The Kinsey Report and Survey Methodology," *International Journal of Opinion and Attitude Research* 2 (1948): 183. Sterling North, "North Reviews," *New York Post*, 23 May 1948. See also "Sex and the U.S. Publisher," *Newsweek*, 3 May 1948.

6. "Dr Kinsey Draws Overflow Audience to Wheeler Lecture," *Berkeley Daily Gazette*, 13 July 1948; "Kinsey Report on the Air," *Newsweek*, 8 Mar. 1948; Patty De Roulf, "Don't Blame It on Kinsey: The Strange Case of a Serious Scientific Report That Has Become a By-Word for Bad Behavior," *American Weekly*, 9 Mar. 1952, 6; Francis Sill Wickware, "Report on Kinsey," *Life*, 2 Aug. 1948; "Kinsey Report Is Dr. Banks' Topic," *Beaumont (TX) Enterprise*, 16 Oct. 1949; "Council Discusses the Kinsey Report," *Birmingham (AL) News*, 27 Jan. 1949; "Women Hear Talk on Kinsey Report," *Detroit News*, Oct. 1952, KIA; George Gallup, "The Gallup Poll: I.U. Man's Sex Study Wins Acclaim," *Indianapolis Star*, 21 Feb. 1948; "Rough Proofs," *Advertising Age*, 7 Sept. 1953.

7. "Making the Country Kinsey-Conscious," *America: The National Catholic Weekly Review*, 5 Sept. 1953, 531; Florence S. Lowe, "Washington Hullabaloo," *Hollywood Daily Variety*, 28 Oct. 1949; Alta Durant, "Just for Variety," *Hollywood Daily Variety*, 3 Jan. 1950; C. M. (man, Allston, MA) to Kinsey, 6 Sept. 1953, KST; Mae West, "An Open Letter to Dr. Kinsey from Mae West," *Cosmopolitan*, Mar. 1949, 42–43, 116; "10 Sexiest Men in the World (and Their Women)," *Focus* (Mar. 1952?), 28–35, KIA; "Look Photoquiz," *Look*, 17 July 1951; "Quick Quiz," *Quick*, 11 Feb. 1952; "Kinsey in the Alley: Tin Panners Give Sex Stuff a Whirl," *Billboard*, 17 Oct. 1953. The Kinsey musical recordings were "Kinsey's Book," "Hey, Dr. Kinsey," and "What's Her Whimsey, Dr. Kinsey?"

8. "Quick and the Dead," *Birmingham (AL) News*, 24 Dec. 1950; Phillip

Gelb, "BG Diet," *Charm,* Sept. 1949; "Confused," *New Yorker,* 18 Sept. 1948. See also the Kinsey Distilling Corporation's advertisement, printed in the *Chicago Tribune, Los Angeles Examiner,* and *New York Times* on 1 Sept. 1953, and reprinted in *Advertising Age,* 7 Sept. 1953. For other such references to the Reports, see the clippings files, KIA.

9. "Panel of Newspaper Editors 'Holds' City Club to the Last," *Cleveland Plain Dealer,* 29 Jan. 1950; Quincy Howe, "Frontiers of Science," CBS radio broadcast, 25 Nov. 1947, KIA. Before launching a commentary on Kinsey, the editor of *Harper's* wrote, "I must surrender a distinction my colleagues in public enlightenment have conferred on me, that of being the man who has editorial space at his disposal but has not discussed the Kinsey Report" (Bernard DeVoto, "The Easy Chair," *Harper's,* June 1948, 553). On the cult of celebrity, see Neal Gabler, *Winchell: Gossip, Power, and the Culture of Celebrity* (New York: Knopf, 1994).

10. E. F. (woman, Salisbury, NC) to Kinsey, 24 Aug. 1953, KCF; C. P. M. (woman, Long Beach, CA) to Kinsey, 29 Aug. 1953, KST; "J. J." to Kinsey, undated, KCF.

11. Paul Wallin, "An Appraisal of Some Methodological Aspects of the Kinsey Report," *American Sociological Review* 14 (1949): 210; Charles G. Wilber, "A Sampling of a Trend," *America: The National Catholic Weekly Review,* 21 Feb. 1948.

12. Hyman and Sheatsley, "Kinsey Report and Survey Methodology," 183–184.

13. "Client Can Relax: P.R. Agency Survey Contradicts Kinsey," *Advertising Age,* 5 Oct. 1953; "Kinsey's Findings Will Be Discussed at N.Y. Ad Forum," *Advertising Age,* 31 Aug. 1953; P. S. (man, New York City) to Kinsey, 1 Oct. 1948, KST; Arno H. Johnson, "Vacuums of Business Information Outlined at Marketers' Conference," *Advertising Age,* 2 Jan. 1950.

14. Hal Boyle, "Crossley Poll on American Male Makes Him a Goldfish, Boyle Says," *La Crosse (WI) Tribune & Leader-Press,* 31 Jan. 1949; "Dr. Kinsey Comes Here to Interrogate Women," *Los Angeles Times,* 3 Sept. 1949; Ethel Barron, "Kinsey: Can He Help You?" *Adult,* Jan.–Feb. 1954, 5; "The Ups and Downs of Water Consumption!" *Bloomington (IN) Herald-Telephone,* 2 Apr. 1953. On broad anxieties about privacy during this period, see Deborah Nelson, *Pursuing Privacy in Cold War America* (New York: Columbia University Press, 2002).

15. "Rep. Brown Opposes 'Prying' in Census," *Washington Record-Herald,* 16 Dec. 1949; "Dr. Kinsey Next!" *Greenfield (CA) News,* 13 Apr. 1950. See also "Uncle Snoopy: This Is the Year That Uncle Sam Conducts His Great Quiz Program," *Philadelphia Frankford Gazette Dispatch,* 31 Mar. 1950; and the *Cincinnati Enquirer* of 18 Dec. 1949 for associations among the census, Kinsey, and Gallup. "Note on a Dead Right," *Petersburg (VA) Progress-Index,* 14 Dec. 1949. Margo J. Anderson traces the decennial debates provoked by census taking in *The American Census: A Social History* (New Haven: Yale University Press, 1988).

16. See, for example, "Control of Sex Crimes May Be Aided by Famous Project," *Bloomington (IN) Star Courier,* 18 May 1951; and "State Sex Crime Committee Will Hear Dr. Kinsey," *Long Beach (CA) Press-Telegram,* 15 Dec. 1949. On the Kinsey Reports' effect on legal codes, see Allyn, "Private Acts/Public Policy"; and Vern L. Bullough, *Science in the Bedroom: A History of Sex Research* (New York: Basic Books, 1994), 183–185. Rochelle Gurstein argues that debates between what she calls the "party of exposure" and the "party of reticence" had already been raging for half a century by the time the Kinsey Reports arrived on the scene, although commentators often believed they were observing something new (Gurstein, *The Repeal of Reticence: A History of America's Cultural and Legal Struggles over Free Speech, Obscenity, Sexual Liberation, and Modern Art* [New York: Hill and Wang, 1996], esp. 252–260).

17. Paul Delbert Brinkman, "Dr. Alfred C. Kinsey and the Press: Historical Case Study of the Relationship of the Mass Media and a Pioneering Behavioral Scientist" (Ph.D. diss., Indiana University, 1971); Donald G. Hileman, "The Kinsey Report: A Study of Press Responsibility," *Journalism Quarterly* 30 (1953): 434–447; Julia Ericksen with Sally Steffen, *Kiss and Tell: Surveying Sex in the Twentieth Century* (Cambridge, MA: Harvard University Press, 1999), 59; D'Emilio and Freedman, *Intimate Matters,* 285; Mrs. E. H. M. (Princeton, IN) to Kinsey, 31 Aug. 1953, KST. Believing that the media had distorted some of his findings the first time around, Kinsey offered major newspapers prepublication access to the female Report in exchange for a promise not to print any articles before its release date in August 1953. See Kinsey to Milton Silverman of the *San Francisco Chronicle,* 3 June 1953, KST.

18. Mildred Miller, "The Enquirer's Questionnaire: Are You Planning to Read 'The Kinsey Report?'" *Cincinnati Enquirer,* 4 July 1948; James

R. Miller, "Sex Behavior of the American Male," '47: *The Magazine of the Year,* Dec. 1947, 3; Albert Ellis, review of *Sexual Behavior in the Human Male,* in *Journal of General Psychology* 39 (1948): 299; Ann Gerber, "Kinsey Report Blazes Trail to Sex Facts," *Chicago Uptown News,* 13 July 1948; anonymous (Waukegan, IL) to Kinsey, 26 Aug. 1953, KCF.

19. Review of *Sexual Behavior in the Human Female,* in *Bowdoin Alumnus,* undated, KIA; Carney Landis, "Book Reviews," *Diagnosis and Measurement of Intergroup Attitudes,* undated, 273, KIA; Benjamin, "Kinsey Report," 398; Hugh J. Parry, "Kinsey Revisited," *International Journal of Opinion and Attitude Research* 2, no. 2 (1948): 197; Herbert Ratner to Alan Gregg, as quoted in Allyn, "Private Acts/Public Policy," 421 n. 59.

20. Dr. Irving Sands as quoted in Ethel Barrow, "Kinsey: Can He Help You?" *Adult,* Jan.–Feb. 1954, 6; Emil A. Gutheil, "The Kinsey Report: Book Review and Roundup of Opinion," *American Journal of Psychotherapy* (July 1948): 415; Howe, "Frontiers of Science."

21. H. M. Parshley, review of *Sexual Behavior in the Human Male,* in *Human Fertility* 13 (1948): 23. There were many extended assessments of Kinsey's methods, most, on balance, favorable, including the American Statistical Association's review at the behest of the National Research Council in 1948. See W. Allen Wallis, "Statistics of the Kinsey Report," *Journal of the American Statistical Association* 44 (1949): 463–484; Wallin, "An Appraisal," 197–210; Hyman and Sheatsley, "Kinsey Report and Survey Methodology," 183–195; Jacob Goldstein and Nicholas Pastore, "Sexual Behavior of the American Male: A Special Review of the Kinsey Report," *Journal of Psychology* 26 (1948): 347–362; Clyde Kiser, "A Statistician Looks at the Kinsey Report," *Problems of Sexual Behavior* (New York: American Social Hygiene Association, 1948); Lawrence S. Kubie, "Psychiatric Implications of the Kinsey Report," *Psychosomatic Medicine* 10 (1948): 95–106; Lewis S. Terman, "Kinsey's 'Sexual Behavior in the Human Male': Some Comments and Criticism," *Psychological Bulletin* 45 (1948): 443–459; and William G. Cochran, Frederick Mosteller, and John W. Tukey, "Statistical Problems of the Kinsey Report," *Journal of the American Statistical Association* 48 (1953): 673–716.

22. Julia O'Connell Davidson and Derek Layder, *Methods, Sex and Madness* (London: Routledge, 1994), 86.

23. Parshley, review of *Sexual Behavior in the Human Male*, 25; M. F. Nimkoff, review of *Sexual Behavior in the Human Female*, in *Annals of the American Academy* 292 (1954): 178.

24. Parry, "Kinsey Revisited," 198.

25. Alfred C. Kinsey, Wardell B. Pomeroy, and Clyde E. Martin, *Sexual Behavior in the Human Male* (Philadelphia: W. B. Saunders, 1948), 20; Seward Hiltner, "The Kinsey Report," *Information Service* (Federal Council of the Churches of Christ in America), 10 Apr. 1948, 1. On Christian organizations' responses to the Reports, see Robert Cecil Johnson, "Kinsey, Christianity, and Sex: A Critical Study of Reaction in American Christianity to the Kinsey Reports on Human Sexual Behavior" (Ph.D. diss., University of Wisconsin–Madison, 1973).

26. Geoffrey Gorer, "Justification by Numbers: A Commentary on the Kinsey Report," *American Scholar* (Summer 1948): 282–283, 285–286; Margaret Mead as quoted in "Male Sex Habits Kinsey Didn't Disclose," *Magazine Digest,* July 1948, 51; West, "Open Letter to Dr. Kinsey," 116.

27. Jule Eisenbud, "The Kinsey Report: Book Review and Roundup of Opinion," *American Journal of Psychotherapy* (July 1948): 412–413.

28. Ruth Millett, "Will Survey of Sex Go Hard on Women?" *Denver Rocky Mountain News,* 11 July 1949; "J. J." to Kinsey, undated, KCF.

29. Doris Lockerman, "Marriage: Merger or Matrimony?" *Atlanta Constitution,* 22 Nov. 1949; Lula Jones Garrett, "Lipstick," *Baltimore Afro-American,* 5 Feb. 1949; James Ward Smith, "The Ethical Significance of the Kinsey Report," *Nassau Lit: A Princeton Review* 106, no. 4 (1948): 3–4.

30. Miriam Reumann notes, "Commentators took it as self-evident that the new volume would be more controversial than *Sexual Behavior in the Human Male*" (Reumann, *American Sexual Character: Sex, Gender, and National Identity in the Kinsey Reports* [Berkeley: University of California Press, 2005], 93).

31. Wallin, "An Appraisal," 198; anonymous (New York City) to Kinsey, 21 Sept. 1953, KCF; "Sexual Behavior in 7,789 Women," *Books on Trial,* Nov. 1953, 63.

32. "Case #45697234 1/2" to Kinsey, 2 Sept. 1953, KCF; "Dr. Kinsey's Shocking Sex Statistics," *Boston Daily Record,* 1 Sept. 1948.

33. *Sexual Behavior in the Human Male,* 39; Dorothy Thompson, "Some Observations on a Sensational Book," *Ladies' Home Journal,* May

1948, 12; S. W. M. (Detroit, MI) to Kinsey, 27 Aug. 1953, KST; Wilber, "A Sampling of a Trend" (his emphasis).

34. "A Friend to Mankind" (Daytona Beach, FL) to Kinsey, 21 Aug. 1953, KCF; "Sexual Behavior in 7,789 Women," 63; anonymous to Kinsey, undated, KCF; "Are the Women Kidding Kinsey? Sexual Behavior in Human Females May Have Professor K. Up a Tree," *Focus,* Mar. 1952, 63. Another journalist argued, "The sort of woman who would tell all to Dr. Kinsey is certainly not qualified to be taken as typical of anything, even though Dr. Kinsey is said to have found 10,000" (John Temple Graves, ". . . This Afternoon," *Rome [GA] News-Tribune,* 7 Oct. 1951). For a critique of this kind of reportage, see Virginia Roller Batdorff, "American Women vs. the Next Kinsey Report," *American Mercury,* Aug. 1953, 121–124. On the issue of women's veracity, see Reumann, *American Sexual Character,* 99–102.

35. Anonymous to Kinsey, undated, KCF; anonymous to Clara Kinsey, 28 Apr. 1949, KCF.

36. C. P. M. (Long Beach, CA) to Kinsey, 29 Aug. 1953, KST; anonymous (Amarillo, TX) to Kinsey, 26 Aug. 1953, KCF.

37. Bentley Glass, "Sexual Behavior in the Human Male, White, U.S.A.," *Quarterly Review of Biology* 23 (1948): 37. In one reviewer's words, "Kinsey's book is like an atom bomb to shake educators and parents out of their complacency" (Benjamin, "Kinsey Report," 406). Similarly, a 1947 CBS radio broadcast announced: "In January a book will appear which seems likely to have the same effect on some of our cherished beliefs as the atomic bomb had on the city of Hiroshima" (Howe, "Frontiers of Science"). E. Parker Johnson, "Books," *Bowdoin Alumnus,* Feb. 1948; Seward Hiltner, *Sex Ethics and the Kinsey Reports* (New York: Association Press, 1953), 209.

38. Johnson, "Books"; review of *Sexual Behavior in the Human Female,* in the *Bowdoin Alumnus,* undated, KIA; Hiltner, "The Kinsey Report," 1; Miller, "Sex Behavior of the American Male," 14.

39. *Reader's Digest,* as quoted in Justin Kase, "The Kinsey Frenzy," *Physical Culture,* Oct. 1948, 56; C.-E. A. Winslow, "Books and Reports," *American Journal of Public Health* 38 (1948): 573; Jules Archer, "Are You Sexually Normal?" *Eye,* Aug. 1950, 23. See also Leo Crespi, "The Moral Implications of Prevalence in the Kinsey Report," *International Journal of Opinion and Attitude Research* 3 (1949): 385–391.

40. Mrs. E. M. (Fort Lauderdale, FL) to Kinsey, 22 Aug. 1953, KST; "A Group of Enraged Women" to Kinsey, undated, KCF. On Cold War sexual and family anxieties, see Elaine Tyler May, *Homeward Bound: American Families in the Cold War Era* (New York: Basic Books, 1988); K. A. Cuordileone, "'Politics in an Age of Anxiety': Cold War Political Culture and the Crisis in American Masculinity, 1949–1960," *Journal of American History* 87 (2000): 515–545; David K. Johnson, *The Lavender Scare: The Cold War Persecution of Gays and Lesbians in the Federal Government* (Chicago: University of Chicago Press, 2004); and Reumann, *American Sexual Character.*

41. Mrs. F. E. M. (Evanston, IL) to Kinsey, 6 Sept. 1953, KST; "A Friend to Mankind" (Daytona Beach, FL) to Kinsey, 21 Aug. 1953, KCF; Mrs. Eugene Meyer, quoted in "Male Sex Habits Kinsey Didn't Disclose," *Magazine Digest,* July 1948, 50; Flora E. Weimerskirch, letter to the editors, *Life,* 23 Aug. 1948.

42. Letter to the "Personal Problem Clinic," *Philadelphia Lutheran,* 29 Mar. 1950, 30.

43. Hiltner, *Sex Ethics,* 237; "A Friend to Mankind" (Daytona Beach, FL) to Kinsey, 21 Aug. 1953, KCF; Hiltner, "The Kinsey Report," 2 (my emphasis). Even recent detractors of Kinsey and his reports have decried his "statistical base for a new morality" (Judith A. Reisman and Edward W. Eichel, *Kinsey, Sex and Fraud: The Indoctrination of a People* [Lafayette, LA: Lochnivar-Huntington House, 1990], 8).

44. Roy E. Dickerson, "Cincinnati Critic Takes Look at Controversial Kinsey Book," *Cincinnati Enquirer,* undated, KIA; Gorer, "Justification by Numbers," 283–284; James C. Fuller, "1948 Brought to Book: Some Clues as to What to Give Whom for Christmas," *Charm,* 1948, KIA.

45. E. S. S. (woman, New York City) to Kinsey, 26 Jan. 1948, KST. For the UCLA study, see F. Harold Giedt, "Changes in Sexual Behavior and Attitudes Following Class Study of the Kinsey Report," *Journal of Social Psychology* 33 (1951): 131–141. For the Princeton version, see "The Attitudes of College Students as Related to The Kinsey Report: A Socio-Psychological Inquiry from the Department of Psychology, Princeton University," KIA. Question 6 on the latter survey read: "Many of the sex practices described in the Kinsey Report were found to be more prevalent than formerly supposed. What do you feel are the implications of such a finding for the moral acceptability of the prac-

tices?" Question 7: "If you were undecided about engaging in and not engaging in a particular type of sexual activity, do you think the fact that a high percentage of the population engages in that activity would tend to influence you in favor of it?" (The general finding was that students' attitudes became more tolerant, but that their behavior was only moderately affected by knowledge of the Report.) For a review of the effects of the first Report, based on the Princeton study, see Leo P. Crespi and Edmund A. Stanley Jr., "Youth Looks at the Kinsey Report," *Public Opinion Quarterly* 12 (1948–1949): 687–696. Mead as quoted in "Male Sex Habits Kinsey Didn't Disclose," 51; Anne Weedman, "Kinsey Forum Draws Debates and Laughs," *LSU (Baton Rouge) Daily Reveille,* 3 Dec. 1948.

46. Martin Gumpert, "The Kinsey Report," *Nation,* 1 May 1948, 471; Parry, "Kinsey Revisited," 198.

47. Norbert Muhlen, "The Kinsey Report: The Private Life of the Public," *New Leader,* 21 Feb. 1948, 8.

48. "Will You Tell Kinsey That . . . ?" *Glance,* Apr. 1950, 10; Parry, "Kinsey Revisited," 198; Archer, "Are You Sexually Normal?" 23, 25; Bruce Bliven, "Books: The Kinsey Report," *New Yorker,* 3 Jan. 1948, 62.

49. Frank Groom Kirtz, "Books for Lawyers," *American Bar Association Journal* 35 (1949): 835, 836; Captain A. S. (man, Camp Hood, TX) to Kinsey, 8 Mar. 1948, KST.

50. K. D. M. (Nashville, NC) to Kinsey, Jan. 1948 (date unclear), and Kinsey's reply of 10 Jan., KST.

51. J. F. A. (man, New York City) to Kinsey, 31 Oct. 1944, KST; "Miss X" to Kinsey, undated, KCF; Mary X, "What I Told Kinsey about My Sex Life," *Ebony,* Dec. 1948, 45, 49. See Miriam Reumann's discussion of the black press and the female Report in *American Sexual Character,* 116–117. *Sexual Behavior in the Human Male,* 37.

52. Wickware, "Report on Kinsey," 90; Betsy Hopkins, "Christmas Shoppers Live by Brawny Law of Jungle," *Atlanta Constitution,* 18 Dec. 1949; Jack W. Roberts, "Dr. Kinsey in Miami, Studies Female Behavior," *Miami Daily News,* 21 Mar. 1949; "Kinsey's Work Far from Done," *Burlington (VT) Free Press,* 13 May 1952; "Oh! Dr. Kinsey (Why Don't You Question Me?)" lyrics and music by Neville Orane, 1948; Robert Van Gelder, "Interview with a Best-Selling Author: Alfred C. Kinsey," *Cosmopolitan,* May 1948, 118.

53. C. M. (woman, New York City) to Kinsey, 20 Mar. 1948, and Kinsey's reply, 25 Mar. 1948, KST.
54. D. M. (man, Chicago, IL) to Kinsey, 24 June 1940, KST; name withheld, "Letters," *Newsweek*, 23 Apr. 1951.
55. Lotta Dempsey, "Dr. Kinsey Talks about Women," *Chatelaine*, Aug. 1949, 10, 59; Van Gelder, "Interview with a Best-Selling Author," 18; Mary X, "What I Told Kinsey about My Sex Life," 45, 50; anonymous, "I Was Interviewed by Dr. Kinsey," *Everybody's Digest*, Mar. 1950, 109, 112. These accounts were scripted, to be sure. For others, see playwright Cornelia Otis Skinner's "Trial by Kinsey," *New Yorker*, 27 May 1950; and Alice G., "'I Told My Sex Secrets to Dr. Kinsey!'" *Bare*, Nov. 1953, 4–8. There were spoofs of these kinds of disclosure as well. One featured a woman's confession of lying to Kinsey. She called herself "a big, fat, lying statistic that keeps turning up over and over again" in the female volume (Elmira Zilch, "I Lied to Kinsey," *Ballyhoo*, 3 June 1954, 14).
56. L. M. M. (man, Tacoma, WA) to Kinsey, 5 Sept. 1948, KST.
57. Anonymous (Brooklyn, NY) to Kinsey, 29 Dec. 1953, KCF. See correspondence from R. P. M. (man, Enosburg Falls, VT) to Kinsey on 28 Oct. 1953 and 16 May 1954, and letters from Kinsey to R. P. M. on 4 June 1954, 30 Nov. 1954, and 9 Jan. 1956, KST. *Sexual Behavior in the Human Male*, 74. Kinsey noted that although individual interviews were the main source of data for his survey, "additional data have come from a considerable list of subjects with whom long-time social contacts have been maintained" as well as "persons [who] have turned in sexual calendars and diaries showing their day to day activities over some period of time . . . They admirably supplement the information routinely obtained on the standard histories."
58. J. M. (woman, Roseburg, OR) to Kinsey, 6 Mar. 1952; R. E. M. (woman, El Monte, CA) to Kinsey, 1 Nov. 1949; Mrs. N. S. (Portland, OR) to Kinsey, 29 June 1948; all in KST.
59. V. M. (woman, Waukegan, IL) to Kinsey, 2 Apr. and 7 Apr. 1949, KST.
60. R. P. M. (man, Enosburg Falls, VT) to Kinsey, 16 May 1954, KST.
61. Mrs. A. M. (Bellflower, CA) to Kinsey, Jan. 1955 (date unknown), and his reply, 14 Feb. 1955, KST; E. S. S. (woman, New York City) to Kinsey, 26 Jan. 1948, KST. See Kinsey's discussion of "comparison of spouses" as a check on the validity of interview data, in *Sexual Behavior in the Human Male*, 125–128.

62. L. L. (man, Long Beach, CA) to Kinsey, 25 June 1954; G. A. S. (woman, Chicago, IL) to Kinsey, 2 June 1955; F. S. (man, city unknown) to Kinsey, 21 June 1955; J. F. A. (man, New York City) to Kinsey, 31 Oct. 1944; all in KST.

63. R. D. G. (Seattle, WA) to Kinsey, 3 June 1955, KCF; Jeffrey Weeks, *Sexuality and Its Discontents: Meanings, Myths and Modern Sexualities* (London: Routledge and Kegan Paul, 1985), 94.

64. Interviewee quoted in R. B. Armstrong, "The Kinsey Report and Your Wife," *Action,* Oct. 1953, 15; anonymous, "I Was Interviewed by Dr. Kinsey," 110.

65. Lionel Trilling, "The Kinsey Report," in *The Liberal Imagination: Essays on Literature and Society* (Garden City, NY: Doubleday, 1950), 216 (his emphasis).

66. Miller, "Sex Behavior of the American Male," 4.

67. Sophie D. Aberle and George W. Corner, *Twenty-five Years of Sex Research: History of the National Research Council Committee for Research in Problems of Sex, 1922–1947* (Philadelphia: W. B. Saunders, 1953), 60; Parshley, review of *Sexual Behavior in the Human Male,* 27.

Epilogue

1. Robert Lynd, *Knowledge for What? The Place of Social Science in American Culture* (Princeton: Princeton University Press, 1939), ix.

2. Eliot Freidson, "Communications Research and the Concept of the Mass," *American Sociological Review* 18 (1953): 313. By the 1950s, prominent social commentators and cultural critics were also coming to recognize the shaping force of social surveys and market research on the culture at large. C. Wright Mills's *White Collar* (1951) and William F. Whyte's *Organization Man* (1956), for example, charged commercial research and personality tests with creating a population of bureaucratically minded individuals who were keenly aware of social norms and eager to adjust themselves to them.

3. "Case #45697234 1/2" to Kinsey, 2 Sept. 1953; anonymous (Champaign-Urbana, IL) to Kinsey, undated; both in KCF.

4. Jeffrey Escoffier, "Homosexuality and the Sociological Imagination: Hegemonic Discourses, the Circulation of Ideas, and the Process of Reading in the 1950s and 1960s," in his *American Homo: Community and Perversity* (Berkeley: University of California Press, 1998), 79–

98; John D'Emilio, *Sexual Politics, Sexual Communities: The Making of a Homosexual Minority in the United States, 1940–1970* (Chicago: University of Chicago Press, 1983).

5. United States Kerner Commission, *Report of the National Advisory Commission on Civil Disorders* (Washington, DC: U.S. Government Printing Office, 1968); Arlene Dávila, *Latinos, Inc.: The Marketing and the Making of a People* (Berkeley: University of California Press, 2001); Donald R. Kinder and Lynn M. Sanders, *Divided by Color: Racial Politics and Democratic Ideals* (Chicago: University of Chicago Press, 1996); Arnold Mitchell, *The Nine American Lifestyles: Who We Are and Where We're Going* (New York: Macmillan, 1983); Ronald D. Michman, Edward M. Mazze, and Alan J. Greco, *Lifestyle Marketing: Reaching the New American Consumer* (Westport, CT: Praeger, 2003); James Atlas, "Beyond Demographics," *Atlantic Monthly,* Oct. 1984, 49–50; Martha Farnsworth Riche, "Psychographics for the 1990s," *American Demographics* 11 (July 1989): 24–31, 53; Joel Garreau, *The Nine Nations of North America* (Boston: Houghton Mifflin, 1981).

6. Karen S. Buzzard, *Chains of Gold: Marketing the Ratings and Rating the Markets* (Metuchen, NJ: Scarecrow Press, 1990), 86–88. Michael J. Weiss, *The Clustering of America* (New York: Harper and Row, 1988) and *Clustered World: How We Live, What We Buy, and What It All Means about Who We Are* (Boston: Little, Brown, 2000), 10–11, 14. Ian Hacking has provided an accounting of how new categories create new people in "Making Up People," in *Reconstructing Individualism: Autonomy, Individuality, and the Self in Western Thought,* ed. Thomas C. Heller, Morton Sosna, and David E. Wellbery (Stanford: Stanford University Press, 1986), and "The Looping Effects of Human Kinds," in *Causal Cognition: A Multi-disciplinary Debate,* ed. Dan Sperber, David Premack, and Ann James Premack (New York: Oxford University Press, 1995).

7. Isabel Briggs Myers, *Manual: Myers-Briggs Type Indicator* (Palo Alto, CA: Consulting Psychologists Press, 1962). Self-help books based on the Myers-Briggs typology include David Keirsey and Marilyn Bates, *Please Understand Me: Character and Temperament Types* (Del Mar, CA: Prometheus Nemesis, 1978) and *Please Understand Me II: Temperament, Character, Intelligence* (Del Mar, CA: Prometheus Nemesis, 1998). For the history of the MMPI and Myers-Briggs instruments, see Annie Paul Murphy, *The Cult of Personality: How Personality*

Tests Are Leading Us to Miseducate Our Children, Mismanage Our Companies, and Misunderstand Ourselves (New York: Free Press, 2004), 45–73, 105–137. Murphy notes, in an intriguing parallel to *Middletown,* that the MMPI was based on an all-white, nearly all-Protestant group of Americans of largely Scandinavian descent.

8. Burkart Holzner and John H. Marx, *Knowledge Application: The Knowledge System in Society* (Boston: Allyn and Bacon, 1979), 320–321. Others have traced the therapeutic as a dominant theme of twentieth-century life, including Philip Rieff, *The Triumph of the Therapeutic: Uses of Faith after Freud* (London: Chatto and Windus, 1966); Christopher Lasch, *The Culture of Narcissism: American Life in an Age of Diminishing Expectations* (New York: Norton, 1978); T. J. Jackson Lears, *Fables of Abundance: A Cultural History of Advertising in America* (New York: Basic Books, 1994); and Ellen Herman, *The Romance of American Psychology: Political Culture in the Age of Experts* (Berkeley: University of California Press, 1995).

9. See, for example, Jon Gertner, "The Very, Very Personal Is the Political," *New York Times,* 15 Feb. 2004; and Jon Gertner, "The Mismeasure of TV," *New York Times,* 10 Apr. 2005. On MRI imaging, see John Tierney, "Using M.R.I's to See Politics on the Brain," *New York Times,* 20 Apr. 2004. In his *Strangers to Ourselves: Discovering the Adaptive Unconscious* (Cambridge, MA: Harvard University Press, 2002), Timothy D. Wilson gives a concise overview of developments in contemporary psychological research that have convinced some social scientists of the real limits on what human beings know about their own thoughts and perceptions.

10. Robert O'Harrow Jr., *No Place to Hide* (New York: Free Press, 2005), 4–5.

11. Robert N. Bellah et al., *Habits of the Heart: Individualism and Commitment in American Life* (Berkeley: University of California Press, 1985); Robert N. Bellah et al., *The Good Society* (New York: Knopf, 1991); Robert D. Putnam, *Bowling Alone: The Collapse and Revival of American Community* (New York: Simon and Schuster, 2000); Wilfred M. McClay, *The Masterless: Self and Society in Modern America* (Chapel Hill: University of North Carolina Press, 1994), 288. See also Robert Wuthnow's *Loose Connections: Joining Together in America's Fragmented Communities* (Cambridge, MA: Harvard University Press, 1998), itself a product of extensive survey research.

12. Morris P. Fiorina with Samuel J. Abrams and Jeremy C. Pope, *Culture War? The Myth of a Polarized America* (New York: Pearson Longman, 2005). Debates over the extent of political and cultural polarization in the contemporary United States are taken up in James Davison Hunter's *Culture Wars: The Struggle to Define America* (New York: Basic Books, 1991); Alan Wolfe's *One Nation, After All: What Americans Really Think about God, Country, Family, Racism, Welfare, Immigration, Homosexuality, Work, the Right, the Left and Each Other* (New York: Viking, 1998); and Thomas Frank, *What's the Matter with Kansas? How Conservatives Won the Heart of America* (New York: Henry Holt, 2004). For a critique of the "moral values" finding, see Larry M. Bartels, "What's the Matter with *What's the Matter with Kansas?*" working paper prepared for presentation at the annual meeting of the American Political Science Association, 1–5 Sept. 2005.

13. See, for example, Cass Sunstein, *Republic.com* (Princeton: Princeton University Press, 2001); Putnam, *Bowling Alone;* and Tom Brokaw, *The Greatest Generation* (New York: Random House, 1998). "The New Face of America," *Time,* 18 Nov. 1993; this was part of a special issue devoted to immigration and multiculturalism, including the implications for marketers of the "new ethnic consumer." For Berlant's incisive analysis, see her *The Queen of America Goes to Washington City: Essays on Sex and Citizenship* (Durham, NC: Duke University Press, 1997), 191–208, quotation on 203.

14. Kevin O'Keefe, *The Average American: The Extraordinary Search for the Nation's Most Ordinary Citizen* (New York: Public Affairs, 2005), 110.

15. "Leaving It in Las Vegas," *New York Times,* 7 June 2004; Graham Fraser, "Bellwether City Leans toward Clinton," *Toronto Globe and Mail,* 24 Sept. 1996. Ball State University sociologist Stephen Johnson has argued that Muncie's voting patterns are representative of the nation's. Editor's note, *International Digital Media and Arts Association Journal* 1, no. 1 (Spring 2004): 1; for the Middletown media study, see, in the same issue of that journal, Robert A. Papper, Michael E. Holmes, and Mark N. Popovich, "Middletown Media Studies," 5–55. Theodore Caplow, afterword, in Luke Eric Lassiter, Hurley Goodall, Elizabeth Campbell, and Michelle Natasya Johnson, eds., *The Other Side of Middletown* (Walnut Creek, CA: Alta Mira Press, 2004), 270. The marked absence of minority populations in the Lynds' work has in-

spired a number of corrective studies, including Hurley Goodall and J. Paul Mitchell, *A History of Negroes in Muncie* (Muncie, IN: Ball State University, 1976); Dwight W. Hoover, "To Be a Jew in Middletown: A Muncie Oral History Project," *Indiana Magazine of History* 81 (1985): 131–158; Dan Rottenberg, *Middletown Jews: The Tenuous Survival of an American Jewish Community* (Bloomington: Indiana University Press, 1997); and Lassiter et al., *Other Side of Middletown.*

16. Julia Ericksen and Sally Steffen, *Kiss and Tell: Surveying Sex in the Twentieth Century* (Cambridge, MA: Harvard University Press, 1999), 196–197. For recent Kinsey scholarship challenging the surveyor's neutrality, see James H. Jones, *Alfred C. Kinsey: A Public/Private Life* (New York: W. W. Norton, 1997); and Jonathan Gathorne-Hardy, *Alfred C. Kinsey: Sex the Measure of All Things* (London: Chatto and Windus, 1998). T. Coraghessan Boyle, *The Inner Circle* (New York: Viking, 2004); Sally Deering and Larry Bortniker, *Dr. Sex: A New Musical Comedy* (2005); Jason Zinoman, "That Sexual Researcher Again, This Time Played for Laughs," *New York Times,* 22 Sept. 2005; *Kinsey,* dir. Bill Condon (20th Century Fox, United Artist Films, 2004). PBS also made a documentary about Kinsey for its *American Experience* series (*Kinsey,* dir. Barak Goodman and John Maggio [Twin Cities Public Television/TPT and Ark Media, 2005]). Peter Gorner, "U. of C. Sex Study Sees Love, Loneliness," *Chicago Tribune,* 9 Jan. 2004. Edward O. Laumann et al., *The Social Organization of Sexuality: Sexual Practices in the United States* (Chicago: Chicago University Press, 1994). The other two books to come from the study are Edward O. Laumann and Robert T. Michael, eds., *Sex, Love and Health in America: Private Choices and Public Policies* (Chicago: University of Chicago Press, 2000), and Edward O. Laumann et al., *The Sexual Organization of the City* (Chicago: University of Chicago Press, 2004). Miriam Reumann, *American Sexual Character: Sex, Gender, and National Identity in the Kinsey Reports* (Berkeley: University of California Press, 2005), 209.

Kinsey has been a prime target for the Concerned Women of America and other conservative groups such as Phyllis Schlafly's Eagle Forum. For a sense of the conservative critique, see Judith A. Reisman and Edward W. Eichel, *Kinsey, Sex, and Fraud: The Indoctrination of a People* (Lafayette, LA: Huntington House, 1990), which charged (inaccurately) that information about children's sexual responses, obtained from adult pedophiles by Kinsey, and Kinsey's purported sexual experimentation with children, were the basis for modern sex education. In 1995 the Family Research Council similarly attacked Kinsey's data on preadolescent orgasm. This latter charge was taken up by Representative Steve Stockman of Galveston, Texas, who called for a congressional hearing. In 1997 the Concerned Women for America renewed the call for investigation. See News Bureau, "Bancroft Responds to Allegations from Family Research Council," 6 Sept. 1995, and "Statement by John W. Ryan, Chairman, the Kinsey Institute Board of Trustees, and Former President of Indiana University, 1971–1987," 7 Dec. 1997; both are University News Releases, Bloomington, Indiana. See also John Bancroft, letter to the editor, *Washington Post,* 28 Dec. 1995.

17. W. Phillips Davison, "Public Opinion," *International Encyclopedia of the Social Sciences,* ed. David L. Sills (New York: Macmillan, 1968), 13:189; James S. Fishkin, *The Voice of the People: Public Opinion and Democracy* (New Haven: Yale University Press, 1995), 80; Susan Herbst, *Numbered Voices: How Opinion Polling Has Shaped American Politics* (Chicago: University of Chicago Press, 1993), ix, 124, 127. On the "golden age," and on "pseudo-surveys" such as SLOPs and news television 900 polls, see Martin R. Frankel and Lester R. Frankel, "Fifty Years of Survey Sampling in the United States," *Public Opinion Quarterly* 51, pt. 2 (1987): S129, S135–S136.

18. On the 1990 and 2000 censuses and the conflicts leading up to them, see Margo J. Anderson and Stephen E. Fienberg, *Who Counts? The Politics of Census-Taking in Contemporary America* (New York: Russell Sage, 1999), esp. 1–10, 191–213, quotations on 5 and 200. Anderson and Fienberg note, however, that Congress has "long accepted the results from statistical sampling for population surveys other than the census, such as the employment rate that comes from the Current Population Survey" (200). Eric Schmitt, "Census Bureau against Use of Adjusted 2000 Count," *New York Times,* 1 Mar. 2001; Steven A. Holmes, "Los Angeles Will Challenge Bush on Census," *New York Times,* 21 Feb. 2001.

19. The 10 percent figure, argue Julia Ericksen and Sally Steffen, "transformed Kinsey's data on sexual behavior during three years of adult life into a measure of unchanging sexual identity" (*Kiss and Tell,* 160). For WFNX, see www.fnxradio.com, accessed Dec. 2005. Katherine Sender,

378 · Notes to Pages 298–299

Business, Not Politics: The Making of the Gay Market (New York: Columbia University Press, 2004), esp. 139–173.

20. Philip Kennicott, "500,000? 750,000? 1 Million?" *Washington Post,* 1 May 2004; Monte Reel, "Crowd Estimates: 30,000 to 500,000," *Washington Post,* 19 Jan. 2003. The Web site for Don't Count Us Out can be found at www.dontcountusout.com, and Nielsen's can be found at www.everyonecounts.tv; both accessed Dec. 2005. Raymond Hernandez and Stuart Elliott, "The Odd Couple vs. Nielsen," *New York Times,* 14 June 2004; Lorne Manly and Raymond Hernandez, "Nielsen, Long a Gauge of Popularity, Fights to Preserve Its Own," *New York Times,* 8 Aug. 2005. The charge of media underrepresentation of minority groups was not new; in fact, special collection and weighting techniques for African American and Hispanic broadcast stations were developed as a consequence of critiques in the mid-1960s (Buzzard, *Chains of Gold,* 158–159). On the merging of consumers and citizens more generally, see Lizabeth Cohen, *A Consumers' Republic: The Politics of Mass Consumption in Postwar America* (New York: Alfred A. Knopf, 2003).

21. See Lisa Anderson, *Pursuing Truth, Exercising Power: Social Science and Public Policy in the Twenty-first Century* (New York: Columbia University Press, 2003); Cynthia Crossen, *Tainted Truth: The Manipulation of Fact in America* (New York: Simon and Schuster, 1994); and Arjun Appadurai, "The Research Ethic and the Spirit of Internationalism," *Items: Social Science Research Council* 51 (1997): 55–60. Craig S. Smith, "What Makes Someone French?" *New York Times,* 11 Nov. 2005.

Acknowledgments

This study of studies has instilled in me a keen awareness of the myriad problems embedded in social research. At the same time, it has given me an immense appreciation for those who maintain the collections that made my own research possible. My thanks go first to the terrific staff of the Ball State University Archives in Muncie (that is, "Middletown"), Indiana. In Muncie, Bruce Geelhoed, then Director of the Center for Middletown Studies, offered abundant assistance, and Tony Edmonds went far beyond the call of duty in making my stay enjoyable. Working at the Kinsey Institute for Research in Sex, Gender, and Reproduction at Indiana University was also a pleasure. I am glad to be able to thank Kath Pennavaria for her Kinsey-related expertise, and Shawn Wilson and Catherine Johnson-Roehr for their guidance with permissions and images. Barbara Truesdell at Indiana's Oral History Research Center (now the Center for the Study of History and Memory) was similarly helpful in facilitating my visit. I am grateful to Betsy Pittman and Thomas Wilsted, at the University of Connecticut's Thomas J. Dodd Research Center, who tracked down relevant materials about Elmo Roper and the early days of polling. Sarah Van Allen of The Gallup Organization helped me locate images of the same. For graciously permitting me access to some of his father's papers before they were formally archived, I thank George Gallup Jr.; Sid Huttner at the University of Iowa Libraries also supplied generous help with George Gallup Sr.'s correspondence. Finally, I would like to thank the National Archives staff for their able assistance with the Robert and Helen Merrell Lynd papers.

The material infrastructure for this book came in the earliest stages from the Graduate School and History Department at Princeton University. For additional funding, office space, and interdisciplinary provocation, I am grateful to Princeton's University Center for Human Values and the Princeton Society of Fellows of the Woodrow Wilson Foundation. Other much-appreciated graduate support came from the Mellon and Whiting Foundations. As a faculty member at the University of Pennsylvania, I benefited from a Trustee's Council of Penn Women Summer Faculty Research Fellowship, and a year's leave from teaching supported by the Institute for Advanced Study in Princeton and the American Council of Learned Societies.

If archives furnish the bulk of a historical manuscript and funders allow it to come into being, sage counsel and sympathetic readers give it shape. On this score, I am indebted most of all to my dissertation adviser at Princeton, Daniel Rodgers, not just for his wisdom and intellect, which continue to awe me, but for his tremendous gifts as a mentor and teacher. Dan has been a rigorous and—far more rare—a compassionate and humane academic guide, and I count myself incredibly lucky to have worked with him. For his friendship and his example, not to mention his ongoing mentorship, I am supremely grateful. Also at Princeton, Liz Lunbeck was from the beginning a terrific supporter and ally whose research on psychiatry at the turn of the century opened new doors to me as a graduate student. Dirk Hartog gave freely of his time and wide-ranging knowledge, pushing me to fine-tune my thinking on many occasions.

I may investigate statistical communities in this book, but I have been fortunate in the writing of it to be surrounded by communities of a more immediate and gratifying kind: family, friends, colleagues, and students. Princeton's history department was one of these, and I thank its faculty and staff—past and present—for their help and encouragement at many stages of my graduate school career, particularly Steve Aron, Kathy Baima, Melanie Bremer, Laura Engelstein, Judy Hanson, John Murrin, Stan Katz, Audrey Mainzer, Nell Painter, Chris Stansell, and Sean Wilentz. Beyond the corridors of Dickinson Hall, Will Howarth, Paul Starr, and Viviana Zelizer were extremely helpful readers of portions of my dissertation. The graduate community is what made Princeton such a wonderful place, and I count my blessings for the many friends there who invigorated me as well as my work. Special thanks go to David Attis, Debbie Balfanz, Karen Caplan, Jamie Cohen-Cole, Adam Galinsky, Ignacio Gallup-Díaz, Nick Guyatt, Drew Levy, Ole Molvig, Benoît Monin, Lisa Purcell, Gary Rowe, Sam Roberts, Nicole Sackley, Amada Sandoval, Todd Stevens, Chuck Wooldridge, and the members of the Dissertation Writers' Group. Collectively, they made graduate school an almost unmitigated pleasure.

With little exaggeration, the same can be said for the Department of History at the University of Pennsylvania, which defies the odds by being both a scholarly powerhouse and a terrifically collegial place. For their welcoming spirit, and for making coming to work so interesting, I thank each and every one of my colleagues. In ways large and small Kathy Brown, Tom Childers, Ann Farnsworth-Alvear, Antonio Feros, Steve Hahn, Lynn Lees, Stephanie McCurry, Ben Nathans, David Ruderman, Kristen Stromberg Childers, and Beth Wenger lent me their support. For their camaraderie, I am most grateful to my fellow modern Americanists Michael Katz, Phoebe Kropp, Bruce Kuklick, Kathy Peiss, Barbara Savage, and Tom Sugrue. Conversations with each of them over the years made an imprint on this book, and I hope some of their combined intellectual firepower found its way between the covers. Three department chairs, Jonathan Steinberg, Sheldon Hackney, and Walter Licht, were tremendous advocates, helping me navigate the department, arrange leaves, and decipher university policies. And the department's extraordinary staff—Deborah Broadnax, Susan Miller, Joan Plonski, and Melissa Reilly Rihel—saved me on countless occasions; their many kindnesses are appreciated. I also wish to thank the graduate students in History and the History and Sociology of Science, and my undergraduates in cultural and intellectual history, who have made Penn such a bracing place to teach and to learn. Just a few miles north on Amtrak, Dan and Bettyann Kevles, Dodie McDow, and Alison Norris have also made Yale a stimulating haven.

I completed this book while a Member of the School of Social Science at the Institute for Advanced Study, in the most glorious scholarly setting imaginable. There, my gratitude goes especially to Joan Scott and Clifford Geertz for their suggestive reflections on my work, to the amazing Institute staff, and to the riotous lunchtime crowd for the debates and discussion that flowed all year long. For engaging with the ideas in this book and providing plenty of entertainment on the side, I am grateful to Caroline Arni, Patricia Clough, Paulla Ebron (my invaluable writing partner), Duana Fulwilley, John Meyer, John Mowitt, Kenda Mutongi, and Helen Tilley. John Mowitt has earned additional thanks not just for peppering me with relevant cites and movie references, but for coming up with this book's title.

Time and time again, I have been struck by the unique moral economy of academia, where individuals toil so freely and generously to improve each other's scholarship. I presented parts of this research at meetings of the American Historical Association, the Organization of American Historians, the American Studies Association, the History of Science Society, the Social Science History Association, the Policy History Conference, the Small Cities Conference, and Cheiron, and to seminars at Columbia University, Northwestern University, Yale University, the University of Delaware, and the University of New Hampshire. Each of these audiences helped me to ask new questions and see new things. Historians—but also sociologists, political scientists, communications scholars, and social psychologists—shared their own expertise and useful leads with me, including Ted Caplow, John Forrester, Susan Herbst, Elihu Katz, Miriam Reumann, Daniel Robinson, and Emily Thompson. I am indebted to others, many of whom I first met at Cheiron meetings, whose work in the history of the human and social sciences has taught me so much, especially John Carson, Ben Harris, Ellen Herman, and Jill Morawski.

When writing a book, I have learned, it is quite useful to have brilliant friends and colleagues. For taking precious time out of their own schedules to provide incisive criticisms of portions of this manuscript, I am deeply grateful to John Carson, Susan Herbst, Ben Nathans, Kathy Peiss, Barbara Savage, and Tom Sugrue. For reading the entire book in one incarnation or another—and improving it, in every case—I thank from the bottom of my heart Peter Agree, Howard Brick, the late Kenneth Cmiel, Daniel Horowitz, Michael Katz, Phoebe Kropp, Bruce Kuklick, Jackson Lears, Bryant Simon, and the anonymous readers for Harvard University Press. Peter Agree deserves special mention for his indispensable advice and counsel as I turned my dissertation into a book, as does Phoebe Kropp for her astute and generous reading. Several others were simply heroic for reading multiple drafts over the years, and even more so for remaining beloved friends. My happiest debts in this regard are owed to Ole Molvig, Dan Rodgers, and Nicole Sackley. For better or worse, they know this book nearly as intimately as I do.

This manuscript was lucky to land at Harvard University Press and in the hands of the incomparable Joyce Seltzer. She has my gratitude for her forthright opinions, her pitch-perfect sense of the book, and her early interest in and loyalty to this project. I thank as well Jennifer Banks and Donna Bouvier at the Press, and especially the fabulous manuscript editor Wendy Nelson for her skillful scrutiny of my every word. John Pollack at Penn's Van Pelt Library kindly helped me with several images, and Dan Amsterdam cheerfully tackled the index. Two journals allowed me to reprint parts of my articles that first appeared in their pages: "Where Main Street Meets Mainstream: *Middletown*, Muncie, and 'Typical America,'" *Indiana Magazine of History* 101, no. 3 (2005): 239–266, courtesy of the Trustees of Indiana University; and "'A Gold Mine and a Tool for Democracy': George Gallup, Elmo Roper, and the Business of Scientific Polling, 1936–1955," *Journal of the History of the Behavioral Sciences* 42, no. 2 (2006): 109–134, copyright © 2006 Wiley Periodicals, Inc. For editorial assistance with the former, my thanks go to Jim Connolly and Eric Sandweiss; for the latter, to Ray Fancher and Christopher Greene.

I cannot close without expressing my profound appreciation for many far-flung others, who even if they never read a word of the manuscript demonstrated their support for its author in manifold ways. Dear friends whom I first met in Piedmont, Cambridge, Andover, Princeton, and my current homes of Philadelphia and New Haven have regularly checked in, celebrated, and commiserated along the way. My four sisters and my brothers-in-law, Susan and Nigel Forman, Kate and Greg McClain, Becky and Matt Sniffen, and Jennifer Igo, have rooted for me unconditionally, and not once questioned the path I have taken—even as I wished that it brought me more regularly to California. Claire, Scott, and Charlotte, who all arrived during the final stages of book writing, are a sheer delight and already exerting the same pull. I thank as well my new family in Wisconsin, Dianne Molvig, Randy Korda, Ariel Molvig, and Anna Momont, who have welcomed me into their lives, homes, and marathon game-playing sessions.

My parents, John and Mittie Igo, have my gratitude for just about everything, but above all their unstinting stores of generosity, love, and confidence—not just during these years of researching and writing but for my whole life. They provided the sturdy foundation upon which everything else was built. As for my husband, Ole Molvig, what can I say in mere words? His steadfast support, his stunning intelligence, his sustaining sense of humor, his quest for the good life, his dissection of my work but also his many and lovely distractions from it have made my life better in every way. It is to my parents and to him that I dedicate this book.

Index

Addams, Jane, 25
Advertising. *See* Market research
African Americans, 18, 26, 29, 286,
  287, 297, 298, 378n20; and
  Middletown studies, 55–59, 67,
  77, 83–85, 90, 100, 293, 319n52,
  326n24, 331n48, 332n49; and
  polling, 131–134, 136, 137, 138,
  139, 140, 155; and Kinsey Re-
  ports, 225–227, 266, 370n51
Allen, Frederick Lewis, 71
Allyn, David, 360n44
American Association of Public
  Opinion Research, 118
American Commonwealth, The
  (Bryce), 123
American Dilemma, An (Myrdal),
  327n26
American Economic Association, 8
American Institute of Public Opinion
  (AIPO): founding of, 117–118; and
  "public-opinion glossary," 119.
  See also Gallup, George; Gallup
  Poll
American Negro, The (Johnson),
  70
American Social Science Association,
  26
American Sociological Society, 8

American Statistical Association,
  221–222, 360n47, 366n21
America Speaks! See Gallup Poll
Anderson, Benedict, 21, 309n24
Anthropology, 8, 14, 37, 38, 53–54,
  61, 72, 76. *See also under*
  Middletown studies
Anticommunism, 6; and Kinsey Re-
  ports, 243, 259–260
Anti-Semitism, 59, 144, 146, 214
Arendt, Hannah, 25
Asch, Solomon, 109
Association of National Advertisers,
  114
Audience Research, Inc., 117

Babbitt (Lewis), 58
Bailey, William, 313n13
Ball family, the, 62–63, 88, 94,
  320n60
"Bandwagon effect." *See under* Gal-
  lup, George; Polling; Roper, Elmo
Bellah, Robert, 291
Benedict, Ruth, 72
Beniger, James, 107
Berlant, Lauren, 292
Bernays, Edward, 108
Boas, Franz, 53–54
Booth, Charles, 25

Bourke-White, Margaret, 88, 93–95.
    See also *Life* (magazine)
Bowles, Chester, 173
Bryce, James, 123
Bureau of Labor Statistics (as labor
    statistics bureaus), 9
Bureau of Social Hygiene, 196

Caccamo, Rita, 320n60
Cantril, Hadley, 114, 126, 187
Caplow, Theodore, 100, 331n48,
    332n49
Carnegie Corporation, 9, 27, 153,
    327n26
Caste and Class in a Southern Town
    (Dollard), 84
Catholics: and Middletown studies,
    59–60, 67, 100; and Kinsey Re-
    ports, 253
CBS (Columbia Broadcasting Sys-
    tem): and Roper, 116, 141, 142;
    president contests survey results,
    174; and Murrow, 180
C. E. Hooper Co., 114. *See also*
    Hooper ratings
Censorship, 198, 201–202,
    243
Center for Middletown Studies,
    332n48
Centers for Disease Control, 294
Charities and the Commons (maga-
    zine), 37
Chase, Stuart, 23
Cherington, Paul, 115
Chicago School of sociology, 28, 29,
    30, 78, 286
Civil rights, 138, 146, 286
Class. *See* Social class
Cluster analysis, 287, 288
Clustering of America, The (Weiss),
    287
Cold War, 5, 242, 259, 263

College Humor poll, 106
Columbia Broadcasting System. *See*
    CBS
Committee on Public Information,
    108
Committee on Recent Economic
    Changes, 9, 72, 110
Committee for Research in Problems
    of Sex. *See under* National Re-
    search Council
Committee on Social Trends, 9, 61,
    70, 72
Commonwealth Fund, 61
Communism. *See* Anticommunism;
    Homosexuality: and anticommu-
    nism
Community studies, 4, 25, 54,
    312n8, 331n48
Comte, Auguste, 8, 305n11
Concerned Women of America,
    376n16
Congress of Industrial Organizations
    (CIO), 5, 170–171
Consumer Advisory Board, 61
Consumer surveys. *See* Market re-
    search
Converse, Jean, 17
Cooperative Analysis of Broadcast-
    ing, 114
Corner, George, 196
Cowles, Gardner, Jr., 116
Creel, George, 108
Crossley, Archibald, 103, 109, 113,
    131, 153, 172, 174, 242; chal-
    lenges *Literary Digest* straw poll,
    103–104; biography, 114–115. *See
    also* Crossley, Inc.; Crossley Radio
    Survey
Crossley, Inc., 114
Crossley Radio Survey, 114, 166,
    338n24
Cultural lag, 41, 49, 62

Databanks, 290
Data-mining, 290
Davis, Katherine B., 194
Davis, Peter, 331n48
D'Emilio, John, 244
Democratic National Committee, 173
Democratic Party. *See under* Roper, Elmo
Desrosières, Alain, 307n15
Dewey, John, 32, 81, 108, 109, 124, 326n21
Dewey, Thomas, 138, 152, 161, 181, 186, 188
Dickinson, Robert Latou, 194, 207
Division of Rural Attitudes and Opinion (U.S. Department of Agriculture), 107
Dollard, John, 84
"Don't Count Us Out," 297–298
Dougall, Arthur, 335n9
Du Bois, W. E. B., 25
Duncan, C. S., 111, 112
Durkheim, Emile, 305n11

Economics, 8, 28, 61, 86
Eisenhower, Dwight D., 163, 172, 180
Ellis, Havelock, 193
Engels, Frederick, 63
Ericksen, Julia, 357n23, 360n47, 377n19
Ethnic groups (ethnicity), 5, 14, 20, 55–56, 59, 77, 80, 83, 111, 133, 136, 287, 298, 375n13, 378n20. *See also* Immigrants
Ethnography, 9, 29, 40, 78

Factors in the Sex Life of Twenty-Two Hundred Women (Davis), 194
Farm Journal poll, 106
Farm Security Administration, 173

Fascism, 108, 121, 338n27
Fishkin, James, 295
Focus groups, 288
Fortune (magazine), 115–116, 144; "Consumer Outlook," 116
Fortune Survey (Quarterly Survey): founding of, 115–116; format of, 139–140, 143–144; funding for, 142–143, 144; Robert Lynd's critique of, 146; economic classifications used in, 147; sampling method, 166, 342n50; publisher of, 181. *See also* Roper, Elmo
Foucault, Michel, 7
Fox, Richard Wightman, 58, 313n14, 315nn23,24, 320n57
Frederick, J. George, 110–112, 118
Freedman, Estelle, 244
Freud, Sigmund, 193–194

Gallup, George, 13, 14, 113, 115; challenges *Literary Digest* straw poll, 103–104; and advertising, 114, 336n17; biography, 116–118; populism of, 121–123, 184–185, 339n30; aspirations for polling, 123; on "bandwagon effect," 125, 339n33; differences from Roper, 128, 136, 144–145, 146, 157; on election forecasting, 134, 342n38; in defense of polling, 151–152; on popular embrace of polling, 155, 188; celebrity of, 157–158; frustration over contested polls, 167; and Republican Party, 169; under congressional scrutiny, 169; compared to Kinsey, 192; on Kinsey's research, 223. *See also* American Institute of Public Opinion; "Gallup Method"; Gallup Poll; Polling. *See also under* Hollywood
"Gallup Method," 117, 144, 344n61

Gallup Poll, 104; founding of, 116–118; sampling method, 135–136, 140–141, 166, 342n50; biases of, 136–138, 344n63 (see also Polling: biases in); format of, 139; funded by corporations, 142–143, 146; cost of, 143, 344n59; compared to Kinsey Reports, 191–193; on venereal disease, 199, 355n14; on Kinsey Report, 238; international reach of, 295. See also American Institute of Public Opinion; Gallup, George

Gang, The (Thrasher), 29

Gathorne-Hardy, Jonathan, 207

Gay rights movement, 285, 287, 294, 297

Gebhard, Paul, 209, 213, 214, 215, 216, 217, 222, 227, 357n25, 358nn28,33

Geelhoed, E. Bruce, 328n31

General Foods, 112, 117

General Motors, 112

Gettys, Warner, 312n8

Goebbels, Joseph, 91

Gold Coast and the Slum, The (Zorbaugh), 29

Good Society, The (Bellah et al.), 291

Gorer, Geoffrey, 249, 261

Great Depression, 5, 9, 20, 61–63, 65, 86–87, 88–89, 98

Gurstein, Rochelle, 365n16

Habits of the Heart (Bellah et al.), 291

Hacking, Ian, 20, 302n6, 305n12, 373n6

Harcourt, Alfred, 35, 68, 322n1

Harcourt, Brace, and Co., 35, 60, 86, 325n14

Harrington, Michael, 286

Harvard Bureau of Business Research, 9, 110

Haskell, Thomas, 26

Hawthorne experiments, 10, 107

Hearst newspapers, 106, 114, 117

Hegeman, Susan, 323n7

Herbst, Susan, 106, 167, 295

Heterosexuality, and Kinsey Reports, 218, 219, 221, 228, 357n25

Hilmes, Michelle, 308n20

Hirschfeld, Magnus, 193

Hitler, Adolf, 91, 108

Hobo: The Sociology of the Homeless Man, The (Anderson), 29

Hollerith cards, 217, 218, 270

Hollingshead, August, 312n8

Hollywood, 2; and Gallup, 135

Home Owner's Loan Corporation, 327n29

Homosexuality: and Kinsey Reports, 192, 218, 219, 228, 247, 297; studied by European sexologists, 193; and Kinsey's subjects and informants, 197, 209, 213, 230–231, 232, 264–265; characterizations of Kinsey, 207, 294, 357n25; and anticommunism, 259. See also Gay rights movement

Hooper ratings, 145. See also C. E. Hooper Co.

Hoover, Dwight, 314n15, 320n60

Hoover, Herbert, 9, 61, 70, 72, 110

Hubbard, Henry D., 5

Hull-House Maps and Papers (Addams and Kelley), 25

Human Immunodeficiency Virus (HIV), 294

Human Sexual Response (Masters and Johnson), 209

Immigrants, 5, 10, 307n15, 375n13; as subjects of social surveys, 14, 18–19, 26, 29, 76–77, 107; as excluded from Middletown studies, 55–58, 67, 80, 82–85, 100, 326n24; and polling, 136, 147. *See also* Ethnic groups (ethnicity)

Indiana University: Association of Women Students, 194; and Kinsey, 194, 195, 196, 199

Indianola, Mississippi, 84

Institute for Sex Research, 195, 198, 214, 217. *See also* Kinsey, Alfred C.

Institute for Social and Religious Research (ISRR), 24, 30–31, 33, 58, 61, 70, 314n15; conflict with Lynds, 31, 33–35, 36–37, 38, 66, 74, 75–76, 314n17. See also *Middletown;* Rockefeller, John D., Jr.

Intelligence testing, 9–10, 14

Interchurch World Movement, 30

Irvine, Janice, 206, 357n23

Jackson, Walter A., 327n26

Jews: and Middletown studies, 59, 67, 100; excluded from Kinsey's research team, 214. *See also* Anti-Semitism

J. H. Cross Co., 114

Johnson, Charles S., 70

Johnson, Stephen, 375n15

Johnson, Virginia, 209, 220

Johnson-Reed Act, 80

Jones, James, 207, 358n27; controversy over biography of Kinsey, 357n25

J. Walter Thompson Co., 112, 115, 242

Katz, Daniel, 130

Katz, Elihu, 109, 343n52

Kelley, Florence, 25

Kellogg, Paul, 26–27

Kerner Commission, 286

Kinsey, Alfred C., 13; biography, 194–195, 207–208, 354n6, 357n25; taxonomic approach, 194, 208, 221, 225, 228, 229, 250, 358n27; impostors, 200–201; U.S. Customs confiscates collection of, 201–202, 356n17; personal agenda of, 205–208, 228, 357nn23,25, 360n44; religious bias of, 206; gender bias of, 214–215; on pollsters, 224; correspondence with interviewees and readers, 229–232; celebrity of, 236–242, 267–268. *See also* Kinsey Reports. *See also under* Marriage

Kinsey Reports, 13, 192; compared to Gallup polls, 191–193; precursors to, 193–194, 199, 355nn13,14; early history of, 194–198, 354n6, 355n10; claims of novelty, 194, 223–224, 256–258, 354n5, 368n37; funding of, 195–197, 355n10; requirements of research team, 197–198, 212–216; controversy over, 198–202, 234–236, 240–244, 246, 248–256, 258–262, 278, 353n1, 356n17, 365nn16,17, 366n21, 367n30, 368n34; justified as science, 202–204; as democratic, 204–205, 240, 263; methodology of, 208–217, 221–222, 228, 229, 231–232, 358n27, 359nn34,35,41, 360n47, 361n51, 366n21; sexual history interview, 209–212, 215–216, 219, 229–230; draft deferments for researchers, 216; "sexual outlet" as unit of analysis, 218–219, 220–221, 261; findings of, 219–221,

228, 247, 361n51; feminist critique of, 220–221; rejection of probability sampling, 221; hundred-percent sample, 222–223, 246; bias in, 225–227, 232–233; legacy of, 229, 236, 243–244, 251, 278–280, 297, 377n19; publicity surrounding, 237–243, 364n9; scholarly reception of, 240–241, 246; as "fact," 244–246, 247–248; as "modern," 245–246, 250–251; religious criticisms of, 248–249; psychiatrists' reception of, 249–250; criticized as unrepresentative, 251–256, 353n1, 368n34; impact on sexual mores, anticipated and real, 258–259, 260–262, 369n45; and "statistical morality," 260–261, 265, 278, 283, 369n43; as liberating, 262–267; desire to participate in, 267–268, 270–276, 277–278, 371nn55,57; reflections of interviewees, 269–270; recent debate over, 294–295, 376n16. *See also* Heterosexuality; "Little Kinsey" survey; *Sexual Behavior in the Human Female; Sexual Behavior in the Human Male. See also under* African Americans; Anticommunism; Catholics; Gallup Poll; Homosexuality; Market research; Marriage; Mass media; Mass society; Nation-building; Normality; Objectivity; Prostitution; Quantification; Social class
Kluckhohn, Clyde, 358n33
Knowledge for What? (R. Lynd), 114, 315n21, 331n47
Kornhauser, Arthur, 145, 344n63
Krafft-Ebing, Richard von, 193
Kroeber, Alfred L. (A. L.), 325n15
Ku Klux Klan, 59–60, 319n55

Labor unions, 5–6, 20, 33; in Middletown studies, 39, 62, 71, 88; as pressure group, 138; bias against in polling, 145–146, 147, 170–172, 344n63
Laissez-faire: and *Middletown,* 41, 42, 61; Robert Lynd biased against, 61; and *Middletown in Transition,* 63, 89, 90
Lambert, Gerard, 126
Landon, Alfred, 104
Laumann, Edward, 294
Laura Spelman Rockefeller Memorial Fund, 30
Lazarsfeld, Paul, 109, 331n47, 343n52
LePlay, Frederic, 25
Lever Brothers, 117
Lewin, Kurt, 109
Lewis, Sinclair, 58, 73, 324n9
Life (magazine), 88, 95, 97, 167, 328n31. *See also* Bourke-White, Margaret
Life and Labour of the People in London (Booth), 25
Link, Henry, 114
Lippmann, Walter, 108–109, 124
Listerine, 126
Literary Digest: straw poll, 103–104, 106, 117, 126; and Archibald Crossley, 114
"Little Kinsey" survey, 14
Long, Huey P., 155, 338n27
Louisiana, and resistance to polling, 155, 338n27, 346n4
Lubbell, Samuel, 144
Luce, Henry, 181
Ludlow massacre, 33
Lynd, Helen Merrell: biography, 31–32, 37; struggle to gain authorial recognition, 34, 313n13; on interviewing in Muncie, 44. *See also*

Lynd, Helen Merrell *(continued)*
Lynds, the (Robert S. and Helen Merrell)
Lynd, Robert S.: biography, 31–32, 36, 37, 61, 114, 314n15, 320n57; at Social Science Research Council, 61, 64–65; on Middletown studies, 100–101, 332n50; on polling, 146; on relationship between American culture and social science, 282; on Mencken's review of *Middletown*, 325n14; on Myrdal's *An American Dilemma*, 327n26. *See also* Lynds, the (Robert S. and Helen Merrell). *See also under* Fortune Survey; Laissez-faire; Marriage; Sociology
Lynd, Staughton, 314n15, 319n52
Lynds, the (Helen Merrell and Robert S.), 13, 14, 28; attempt to combine social science and social reform, 28, 64–67; as amateurs, 31, 36; relations with inhabitants of Muncie, 42–44, 46, 47–51; influence of Marx and Engels on, 63; statements about typicality of Middletown, 82, 331n47. *See also* Lynd, Helen Merrell; Lynd, Robert S.; *Middletown; Middletown in Transition;* Middletown studies

Magic Town (film), 1–2
Main Street (Lewis), 58
Malinowski, Bronislaw, 76
"Man in the street," 103, 105, 183, 284
Market research: early history, 9, 12, 102, 109–113, 335n11; and Middletown studies, 85–88, 96–97, 98, 99, 327n27, 332n50; and polling, 104–105, 113–118, 124, 125–126, 135, 143, 144–145, 147–149, 174, 186–187, 336n16,

342n48, 344n61; and Kinsey Reports, 237, 241–242; recent developments in, 287–288, 290, 295, 297–298, 372n2. *See also* Mass market; Niche marketing
Marriage: Robert Lynd and research into "normal," 65; Kinsey's course on, 194–195, 207, 354n6; and Kinsey Reports, 204, 205, 220, 221, 259; and *The Social Organization of Sexuality*, 294
Martin, Clyde, 191, 198, 209, 213, 216
Marx, Karl, 63
Massachusetts Labor Statistics bureau, 26
"Mass feedback technologies," 107
Mass market, 110, 113, 287–288, 292. *See also* Market research
Mass media, 12, 20, 108, 308n20; and Middletown studies, 45, 95; and polling, 142–148; and Kinsey Reports, 237–240, 243–244, 365n17
Mass public, 5, 18, 107, 282, 283, 285, 286; role of "average American" in shaping, 17, 19, 21; segmentation of, 291–292. *See also* Mass society; Nation-building
Mass society, 5–6, 10, 12, 20–21, 107–109, 282, 285, 302n5, 305n11, 309n24; and polling techniques, 123–124, 185–186; opinion surveys as counterweight to, 124; and Kinsey Reports, 261; defined, 282–283
"Mass subject," 19, 141
Masters, William, 209, 220
Maverick, Maury, 327n29
Mayo, Elton, 107
McClay, Wilfred, 291

Mead, Margaret, 72, 81, 193, 249, 262
Mencken, Henry Louis (H. L.), 23, 76, 84, 89, 325n14
Middletown, 2; widespread resonance of, 23–25, 68–85, 322n1; compared to previous social research, 24–30, 312n8; original motivations for, 24, 30, 32, 35, 55, 66; funding for, 24, 30, 33; novelty of, 29–30, 32–33, 36, 67, 312n10; as "typical" American city, 29, 51, 55–59, 64, 79–85, 85–86, 88, 95–99, 319n52, 326n24, 331n47 (see also under *Middletown in Transition*); methodology of, 35–39, 315n21, 319n52; conclusions of, 39–42, 59–60, 320n56; goals of, 39, 54, 66, 321n65; as social critique, 42, 66–67; populations excluded from, 54–60, 67, 76–77, 82–85, 90, 100, 326n24; PBS television series (1982), 330n42, 331n48. *See also* Institute for Social and Religious Research; Middletown studies. *See also under* Laissez-faire; Social class
Middletown in Transition, 43; debate in Muncie about, 51–52, 92–93; methods and findings of, 60–64; 320nn57,58; Middletown as "typical," 86–91, 93–95, 97–98; national reception of, 88–91, 327n29, 328n34. *See also* Middletown studies. *See also under* Laissez-faire; Social class
"Middletown Man," 331n48
Middletown Media Studies, 293
Middletowns, Inc., 109
Middletown studies, 13; reaction in Muncie to, 16, 42–53, 74, 91–98,

317n35, 330n42; as anthropology, 37–41, 46–47, 53–54, 55, 59–60, 65–66, 75–79, 81, 100, 102, 315n24, 325n15; legacy of, 66–67, 70, 98–102, 109, 324n10; and continued study of Muncie, 99–100, 293, 331n48, 375n15; as sociology, 100, 315n23, 324n10. *See also Middletown; Middletown in Transition. See also under* African Americans; Catholics; Immigrants; Labor unions; Market research; Mass media; Nation-building; Normality; Objectivity; Quantification; Sociology
Million Man March, 297
Mills, C. Wright, 372n2
Minnesota Multiphasic Personality Inventory, 288, 373n7
Mitchell, Wesley, 32
Moynihan Report, 286
MRI (magnetic resonance imaging), 290
Muncie, Indiana. See *Middletown; Middletown in Transition;* Middletown studies
Murphy, Annie Paul, 373n7
Murrow, Edward R., 180–181
Mussolini, Benito, 108
Mutz, Diana, 12
Myers-Brigg indicator, 289
Myrdal, Gunnar, 327n26

Nation-building: and surveys in general, 4, 5–6, 12, 18, 19, 20–21, 309n24; and Middletown studies, 72–73, 88–91, 98; and polling, 104–105, 121, 152; and Kinsey Reports, 239–240, 255, 256. *See also* Mass public
Nation poll, 106
National Broadcasting Co. *See* NBC

National Bureau of Economic Research, 27
National Bureau of Standards, 5
National Gay Task Force, 297
National Institute for Straight Thinking, 97
National Newspaper Syndicate, 144
National Opinion Research Center, 107, 294
National Research Council, 200, 216, 346n2, 366n21; Committee for Research in Problems of Sex, 195–197, 202, 225, 279
National Rifle Association, 174–175, 350n32
NBC (National Broadcasting Co.), 115, 116, 147, 183
Neuromarketing, 290
New Deal, 20, 61, 62, 213, 327n29
News Corporation, 298
Niche marketing, 148, 287–288, 292. See also Market research
Nielsen, Arthur Charles (A. C.), 114, 342n48
Nielsen Co., 112–113; as Nielsen Media Research, 298
Normality, 2, 11–12, 19, 285, 286, 289, 372n2; and Middletown studies, 29, 57–58, 66–67, 81–83; Robert Lynd's interest in, 64–65; and Kinsey Reports, 192, 193, 218, 223–225, 227–229, 251–256, 357n23; impact of Kinsey Reports on, 258–259, 264–267, 278–280

Objectivity: as social scientific value, 7, 9, 28, 33–34, 311n7; and Middletown studies, 28, 36–38, 47–49, 65–67, 74–75, 78–79, 89, 315n21; and polling, 118–119, 131, 170; and Kinsey Reports, 202–203, 210–211, 276

Office of Strategic Services, 116
Office of War Information, 116
Ogburn, William, 41
Ohmer, Susan, 342n48
Opinion Research Corporation, 117
Organization Man, The (Whyte), 372n2
Ouvriers Européens, Les (LePlay), 25

Paramount Pictures, 117
Park, Robert, 28
Parlin, Charles Coolidge, 335n11
Participant observation, 16, 37
Pathfinder poll, 106
Patterns of Culture (Benedict), 72
People meters, 290
Perrigo, Lynn, 320n60
Philadelphia Negro, The (Du Bois), 25, 30
Pierce, Walter M., 169
Pittsburgh Survey, 26–27, 28, 30
Polish Peasant in Europe and America, The (Thomas and Znaniecki), 30
Political machines, 121, 136, 138, 167, 338n27
Political science, 8, 28
Politz, Alfred, 156
Polling (public opinion), 102, 103, 105; early history of, 103, 106–118, 160, 174, 337n20, 340n35; and election of 1936, 103, 115, 126, 140, 168; and elections (general discussion), 103, 134–139, 342nn48,50; and history of "public opinion," 106; and democracy, 119, 121–123, 125–126, 138–139, 148–149, 339nn30,33; and propaganda, 124–126; and "bandwagon effect," 124–125, 169, 174–175, 182, 283, 339n33; methods, 126–134, 135–139, 182–183, 340n35, 341n41; "quintamensional plan of

question design," 127; "split-ballot technique," 127; challenges of interviewing, 127–134, 155–157, 341n41; and "cheaters," 128–129; and gender, 128, 130, 133, 136, 137, 138, 139, 156, 343n52; and "miniature electorate," 135–137, 141, 148; biases in, 135–139, 145, 344n63; and election of 1948, 137–138, 152–155, 161, 168, 180, 181, 186–189, 191, 339n33, 342n48, 352n56; and homogenization of public opinion, 139–149; corporate sponsorship of, 142–148, 344nn59,61,63; criticisms of, 142, 163–165, 168–172, 174–181, 348n18; of race relations, 146; struggle to legitimize, 151–157, 163–190, 348nn18,20, 349n24; popular interest in, 157–162, 178–179; findings challenged, 175–180; and election of 2004, 292, 295; recent trends in, 295; mutual support of members, 338n24. See also Crossley, Archibald; Gallup, George; Roper, Elmo. See also under African Americans; Immigrants; Labor unions; Market research; Mass media; Mass society; Nation-building; Objectivity; Poor, the; Quantification; Social class
Pomeroy, Wardell, 191, 209, 214, 216, 231
Poor, the, 14, 18–19, 26, 289; and polling, 126–127, 135, 155, 296, 341n41
Poverty, 7, 25, 95, 286
Princeton University, 100, 262, 369n45
Professionalization, of social investigation, 8, 27–28, 31, 61, 74, 101–102, 118, 119, 196, 338n24
Progressive Era. See Social reform

Prohibition, 83, 117, 174
Prostitution, 195; and Kinsey Reports, 199, 219, 254, 360n44
Psychiatry. See Kinsey Reports: psychiatrists' reception of
Psychological Corp., 112
Psychological Factors in Marital Happiness (Terman), 194
Psychology, 8, 28, 107, 109, 112, 262, 289
Public Opinion Quarterly, 118
Publishers Syndicate, 117

Quantification, 7, 9, 16, 25, 28, 285, 286, 296, 307n15; and Middletown studies, 34, 36–37; and polling, 107, 152, 172–175, 176, 183; and Kinsey Reports, 218, 224, 235–236, 239, 246–251, 261–262, 264–267
Quetelet, Adolphe, 19

Race. See African Americans; Polling: of race relations
Radcliffe-Brown, Alfred Reginald (A. R.), 38
Rae, Saul Forbes, 103
Recent Economic Changes. See Committee on Recent Economic Changes
Recent Social Trends. See Committee on Social Trends
Redfield, Robert, 70, 81
Republican Party, slant of polls toward, 130. See also under Gallup, George
Reumann, Miriam, 226, 294, 367n30, 370n51
Rivers, William Halse Rivers (W. H. R.), 38
Robinson, Daniel J., 136, 137, 336n16
Robinson, Paul, 219–220

Rockefeller, John D., Jr., 24, 30, 33, 34, 196, 314n15; and Ludlow massacre, 33. *See also* Institute for Social and Religious Research

Rockefeller Foundation, 27, 153, 195, 196, 197, 294

Roosevelt, Franklin Delano, 61, 62, 91, 104, 107, 140; use of polls, 125–126, 352n56

Roper, Elmo, 13; challenges *Literary Digest* straw poll, 103–104; and Middletowns, Inc., 109; on market research and public opinion polling, 113, 114; biography, 115–116; on potential of polling, 118, 124; and Democratic Party, 119, 169; populism of, 122–123, 180, 182; on "bandwagon effect," 125, 182, 339n33; differences from Gallup, 128, 136, 144–145, 146, 157; on "cheaters," 129; early experiments in probability sampling, 131–133, 155; on election forecasting, 134–135, 342n48; biases of, 136–137; on election of 1948, 138, 181, 182, 186–187, 339n33; and corporate sponsorship, 142–147, 342n48; objects to simplified polls, 144; on Hooper ratings, 145; interest in antiminority sentiment, 146, 344n64; on pollsters' emphasis on the majority, 148; on public faith in polls, 152; media commitments of, 157; on prejudice against pollsters, 167; on public commentary on his polls, 168, 169; critiques those who disputed polls, 178; "personal touch" of, 183–184; support for political causes, 338n25; congressional inquiry into polls of, 349n24. See also *Fortune* (magazine); Fortune Survey; Polling. *See also under* CBS

Ross, Dorothy, 28

Ross, Frank Alexander (F. A.), 30

Russell Sage Foundation, 27

Sampling methods, 16, 103, 123, 127, 340n35; estimating standard error, 126; quota, 127, 129, 131; probability, 131–134; public skepticism about, 163–168, 295, 296, 348nn18,20; pollsters' explanations of, 182–183; stratified, 187. *See also* Fortune Survey: sampling method; Gallup Poll: sampling method; Kinsey Reports: hundred-percent sample; Kinsey Reports: rejection of probability sampling; Roper, Elmo: early experiments in probability sampling

Schlafly, Phyllis, 376n16

School Attendance in 1920 (Ross), 30

Schudson, Michael, 349n26

Selective Service Board, 216

Selznick, David O., 117

Senji, Yamamoto, 193

Settlement houses, 26, 27

Sexual Behavior in the Human Female, 192; controversy surrounding, 251, 254, 367n30, 368n34. *See also* Kinsey Reports

Sexual Behavior in the Human Male, 191–192; as best-seller, 237–238. *See also* Kinsey Reports

"Sexual outlet." *See under* Kinsey Reports

SLOPs (selected listener opinion polls), 295

Small City Study. See *Middletown*

Smithsonian Institution, 9

Social class: in *Middletown,* 39, 42, 56, 59, 60, 67, 99; in *Middletown in Transition,* 62–63, 67; in Bourke-White photographs of

Middletown, 93–95; in polling,
126, 128, 129–131, 131–133,
136–137, 138, 139, 140, 145–146,
147, 155, 341n41; in Kinsey Reports, 213, 219–220, 227; in recent surveys, 286, 287–288
Social data. *See* Quantification; Survey research
Social Gospel, 26
Social Organization of Sexuality, The
(Laumann), 294
Social reform, 7, 13, 25–28, 30, 136,
195–196, 234
Social science: emergence of, 8, 25–
30; skepticism about, in Muncie,
49–53; and "national introspection," 72, 323n7; and election of
1948, 152–154, 189. *See also* Anthropology; Economics; Political
science; Professionalization, of
social investigation; Psychology;
Sociology; Survey research
Social Science Research Council, 27,
31, 61, 64, 142, 346n2; Committee on Analysis of Pre-election
Polls and Forecasts, 153–154, 156,
186, 189, 221–222
Social surveys. *See* Survey research
Sociology, 8, 28, 61, 109, 262, 282,
305n11, 312n10; impact of
Middletown studies on, 29–30, 78,
99, 100, 101–102, 315n23,
324n10; Robert Lynd as professor
of, 31, 61. *See also* Chicago School
of sociology
South Bend, Indiana, 32, 55
"Southerntown," 84
Spencer, Herbert, 8, 26
Standard error. *See under* Sampling
methods
Standard Oil, 33, 115, 314n15
Statistics. *See* Quantification
Steele, Richard W., 352n56

Steffen, Sally, 357n23, 360n47,
377n19
Stewart, James, 1
Stouffer, Samuel, 337n20
Straton, Hillyer H., 52–53
Straw polls, 103, 106, 118, 160, 174,
177
Sumner, William Graham, 8
Survey (magazine), 27
Survey research: impact of, 2, 4–6,
16, 18–21, 281–286, 372n2; and
knowledge about "ourselves," 2, 6,
20, 282; early history of, 3–4, 6–
10, 16, 24, 25–30, 311n7; American style of, 7–8, 14–15; transformations in, 7–8, 14, 27–30, 278–
280, 311n7, 312n8; bureaucratic
uses of, 9–10, 14; demand for, 10–
11, 12; and study of "marginal"
populations, 11, 25–26, 29; and
historians, 12–13; outside the U.S.,
14–15, 193, 295; conflict over, 15–
16; defined, 17; public embrace of,
17, 267, 284–285, 372n2; exclu-
sions of, 18–19; importance of
studying, as history, 21–22; type of
data produced by, 247; and forging
a minority consciousness, 285; after 1965, 286–299. *See also under*
Nation-building
Susman, Warren, 72

Taft, Robert, 163, 172
Tavris, Carol, 356n18
Taxi Dance Hall, The (Cressey), 29
Taylor, Frederick Winslow, 110
Tedlow, Richard, 110
Terman, Lewis, 194, 216
Theory of the Leisure Class, The
(Veblen), 32
Thomas, William I. (W. I.), 28, 30, 107
Thousand Marriages, A (Dickinson
and Beam), 194

Time (magazine), 167, 292
Tocqueville, Alexis de, 108
Tönnies, Ferdinand, 305n11
Trilling, Lionel, 277–278
Truman, Harry S., 138, 152, 161, 181, 186, 188
Turner, Stephen, 312n10

UCLA (University of California at Los Angeles), 262
Unions. *See* Labor unions
U.S. Census, 7, 9, 11, 13, 156, 307n15, 365n15; 1920 census, 80; 1950 census, 243; recent controversies over, 296–297, 377n18
U.S. Congress, 168, 169, 186, 294, 296, 297, 298, 349n24, 376n16
U.S. Customs. *See under* Kinsey, Alfred C.
U.S. Department of Agriculture, 107
U.S. Department of Commerce, 110, 296
U.S. Department of State, 173; Cold War purge of homosexuals, 259

Veblen, Thorstein, 32, 40

Walt Disney Co., 117, 342n48
Ward, Lester Frank, 8, 26
Warner, William Lloyd (W. Lloyd), 18, 54
War Production Board, 116
W. B. Saunders Co., 237
Weeks, Jeffrey, 276, 354n5
Weiss, Michael, 287–288

West, Mae, 238, 249
Western Electric Co., 107
Where the People Stand (radio show), 116, 141, 164
White Collar (Mills), 372n2
Whyte, William F., 372n2
Wiebe, Robert, 10
William the Conqueror, 6
Wissler, Clark, 75, 325n13
Woman's Home Companion, 112; poll, 106
Women: as marginalized social researchers, 27; in *Middletown*, 59. *See also* Kinsey, Alfred C.: gender bias of; Kinsey Reports: feminist critique of; Polling: and gender; *Sexual Behavior in the Human Female*
Women's National Republican Club, 172
Wood, Richardson, 115
Works Progress Administration / Works Projects Administration (WPA), 129, 213
World War I, 3, 9, 71, 107, 108
World War II, 5, 9, 15, 116, 225
Wright, Carroll, 26

"X family." *See* Ball family, the

Yerkes, Robert, 196, 216, 225
Young & Rubicam, 117

Znaniecki, Florian, 30, 107
Zorbaugh, Harvey, 78
Zunz, Olivier, 7